经管核心课程系列

国际金融（双语）
International Finance

姚迪克　编　著

复旦大学出版社

前　言

随着贸易金融壁垒的不断减少和互联网通信技术的飞速发展,金融市场全球化的大趋势已不可逆转。金融产品创新、国际银行业务持续改进不论从理论层面还是从实际操作层面都对从事这一行业的专业人员提出了新的挑战。无怪乎很多学者认为国际金融是经济金融学科中变化最大的一门课程。纵观我国的经济金融发展史,过去40年的成就尤其令人瞩目,在国际金融市场的地位和影响力也越来越重要。这对我们的人才培养,尤其是经济、金融专业以及管理专业的教学提出了更高的要求。经济或金融专业的学生如果缺乏一些国际金融知识的背景,也许很难完全理解目前国际金融市场发生的一切。

本书自2012年出版以来广受好评,许多院校选择本书作为其国际金融学课程的教材,且在实际使用中收到了良好的效果。不少院校的老师希望再版此书。许多教师和学生与我就书中某些理论概念的阐述做了大量积极的探讨与沟通,提出了许多非常有价值的意见与建议,对此我深受启发。由于经济金融的快速发展,原书中许多资料信息与内容已经无法真实地反映国际金融市场发展的现状,因此有必要对原书的一些信息与内容进行更新和修改。

除了在各个章节中更新了原书所有的数据之外,对第一章到第六章(尤其是第三章、第五章和第六章)都进行了大量修改,具体如下:

第一章国际金融导论。第二节修改了关于国际贸易和国际金融领域目前发展的现状,并且更新了相关资料与信息。第三节增加了相对优势理论在现实运用中存在局限性的论述,重新梳理了最后一节对全书结构部分的概述。

第二章国际收支。主要是对国际收支平衡与失衡以及各账户余额的解释进行了重新梳理。

第三章外汇市场。考虑到电子外汇交易已经是目前最重要的外汇交易方式,第一节增加了对电子外汇交易的描述;第二节增加了常用外汇的货币符号与代码,并对全书汇率表示方法做了统一的规定;第三节增加了远期外汇交易的起息日概念、外汇掉期概念与种类、掉期基点与远期汇率的关系及相关计算。

第四章国际货币体系。第三节增加了货币法定升值与贬值的概念以及有关特别提款权的论述,包括特别提款权的构成和发行等。第五节对现行各国汇率制度的安排进行了重新梳理和补充必要的内容。

第五章汇率决定与汇率预测。重新编写了第一节关于短期汇率决定的理论。第二节购买力平价理论中增加了货币内部购买力和外部购买力的概念，为推导购买力平价理论进行铺垫，运用汉堡包指数说明货币高估与低估的概念。第三节利率平价理论增加了货币市场对冲以避免汇率风险的方法，运用两个实例说明这种规避风险方法的具体步骤和实际意义。第四节远期平价与不抵补套利补充了息差交易的概念。在阐述汇率预测时重新梳理并增加了一些内容。

第六章货币风险管理的金融衍生品。重新编写了关于期货与远期合约的比较、货币期货的特点。增加了期货定价原理以及运用期货进行投机的特点。对货币期权的描述更加详细，包括如何解读期权报价、场外期权市场的发展、期权时间价值的决定因素等。

第七章国际金融市场。增加了关于伦敦同业银行拆借利率最新的发展动态及结果。在世界股票市场部分扩充了一部分内容，同时也简单介绍了中国股票市场的发展情况以及存在的问题。

第八章到第十一章基本延续原书的架构，内容也没有太大变化，主要是充实了一部分理论方面的内容并修正了之前版本的一些笔误。

在每章结尾按照每节的顺序进行了总结，同时将原来每章的概念题由15题增加至20题。概念题尽量覆盖每章的重点和难点，以及需要读者掌握的基本知识。

此次新版修订承蒙多位老师帮助，这里特别要感谢徐笑丁老师、曹雷老师和张晖老师，他们在整个修订过程中提出了许多有价值的建议并且在资料方面给予了很大的帮助。同时还要感谢复旦大学出版社对再版工作的大力支持。

由于水平有限，加之时间仓促，书中难免有疏漏、不当之处，恳请读者谅解，欢迎批评、指正。

姚迪克
2021年4月15日于上海

Contents

Chapter 1 INTRODUCTION TO INTERNATIONAL FINANCE 1

The Subject Matter of International Finance 2
The Environment of International Finance 3
The Theory of Comparative Advantage 13
The Benefits of Studying International Finance 16
The Structure of This Book 19
Summary 21
Key Concepts and Terms 22
Questions 23

Chapter 2 THE BALANCE OF PAYMENTS 25

Definition of the Balance of Payments 26
Balance of Payments Accounting 28
Accounts of the Balance of Payments 29
Surpluses and Deficits in the Balance of Payments Accounts 40
International Investment Position 44
The Current Account and the Macroeconomics 46
The Economic Relationship between Current Account and Financial Account 49
Summary 51
Key Concepts and Terms 53
Questions 54

Chapter 3 THE FOREIGN EXCHANGE MARKET 56

The Basics of Foreign Exchange Market 57
Spot Exchange Market, Exchange Rate Quotations, and Foreign Exchange Arbitrage 64
The Forward Foreign Exchange Market 76
Foreign Exchange Risk and Hedging Strategies 82
Other Types of Exchange Rates 88
Summary 93
Key Concepts and Terms 95
Questions 97

Chapter 4 INTERNATIONAL MONETARY SYSTEM 99

Definition of the International Monetary System 100
The Gold Standard (1876—1944) 101
Bretton Woods System (1944—1973) 106
Floating Exchange Rate System (1973—Now) 114
Exchange Rate Systems in Practice 118
Arguments for Fixed and Floating Exchange Rates 123
Summary 127
Key Concepts and Terms 130
Questions 131

Chapter 5 EXCHANGE RATE DETERMINATION AND FORECASTING EXCHANGE RATES 133

Exchange Rates Determination in the Short Run 134
Purchasing Power Parity (PPP) 140
Interest Rate Parity (IRP) 151
Real Interest Rates and Real Interest Parity 162
Exchange Rate Forecasting 165
Summary 168
Key Concepts and Terms 170
Questions 171

Chapter 6 FINANCIAL DERIVATIVES FOR CURRENCY RISK MANAGEMENT 173

Currency Futures 174
Currency Option 186
Currency Swaps and Interest Rate Swaps 199
Summary 207
Key Concepts and Terms 209
Questions 210

Chapter 7 INTERNATIONAL FINANCIAL MARKETS 212

Introduction to Financial Market 213
International Money Market 214
Eurocurrency Market 217
International Capital Market 224
Eurobond Markets 226
International Stock Market 229
Summary 235
Key Concepts and Terms 237
Questions 238

Chapter 8 THE BALANCE OF PAYMENTS ADJUSTMENT   240

Elasticity Approach (Relative Price Effects)   241
The Absorption Approach (Income Effects)   250
Summary   255
Key Concepts and Terms   257
Questions   258

Chapter 9 EQUILIBRIUM IN BALANCE OF PAYMENTS AND EXCHANGE RATE   260

The Monetary Approach   261
The Portfolio Balance Approach   269
Summary   275
Key Concepts and Terms   276
Questions   277

Chapter 10 MACROECONOMICS IN AN OPEN ECONOMY   279

The Aggregate Demand for the Aggregate Output   280
The IS, LM and BP Curves in an Open Economy   284
Summary   289
Key Concepts and Terms   290
Questions   291

Chapter 11 ECONOMIC POLICY UNDER FIXED AND FLOATING EXCHANGE RATE SYSTEM   293

Macroeconomic Goals in an Open Economy   294
Monetary Policy, Fiscal Policy and Capital Mobility   295
Economic Policy under Fixed Exchange Rate System   298
Economic Policy under Floating Exchange Rate System   303
Summary   307
Key Concepts and Terms   308
Questions   309

Chapter 1
INTRODUCTION TO INTERNATIONAL FINANCE

LEARNING OBJECTIVES

- Examine the subject matter of international finance.
- Understanding the environment of international finance, mainly the new development of world trade and financial markets.
- Consider the basic theory, comparative advantage, and its requirements for the explanation and justification for international trade and commerce.
- Discover the benefits of studying the course under the environment of integration and globalization.
- Describe the structure of the book.

Finance is an exciting word. Lots of students are interested in finance major, because they know (or their parents know) that people who work for financial institutions usually get higher pay. The word "international" is more fascinating. "International" is everywhere in our daily life. Today the international element in our lives is pervasive and virtually inescapable. If you look at your clothes closet, your kitchens, your living rooms, your dining rooms and your offices or even on the streets, you will find that many goods you use in your daily life are made in foreign countries or contain foreign components. Foreign goods and foreign countries still fascinate a lot of people here.

What does finance mean? It means the management of money (usually the public money) by governments, large firms or organizations, etc. Another meaning of the finance is provision of money when and where required. Since each country has its own currency, international finance is the management of money in an international environment.

This chapter discusses the subject matter of international finance. We'll introduce the environment of international finance, i.e., the fast development of world trade and investment and changes in trade patterns, and the globalization of financial markets. The gains from trade and the theory of comparative advantage will be discussed to show the need for international finance. The reasons to study international finance are also to be covered. Finally, we'll examine the structure of the book.

The Subject Matter of International Finance

International finance studies the monetary and macroeconomic relations among countries. International finance is a constantly evolving subject that deals greatly with real world issues such as balance of payments problems and policies, the causes of exchange rate movements and the implications of macroeconomic linkages between nations.

Many countries in the world are engaged in international business, such as exporting, importing, or direct and indirect foreign investment. The transactions arising from international business cause money flows from one country to another. The balance of payments is a measure of international money flows. The balance of payments is one of the most important economic indicators for the government policy-makers in an open economy. It influences a country's employment rate, interest rate, exchange rate and many other economic variables. Over the past 20 to 25 years, the U.S. has run huge trade deficits with the rest of the world, especially China. The U.S. government persistently accuses Chinese government of manipulating Renminbi (RMB, the Chinese currency) exchange rate. Why is the U.S. government concerned about its trade deficits? Why does it continuously complain that the RMB is undervalued? What are the impacts of the balance of payments problems on its domestic economy? What should a government do to correct its balance of payments disequilibrium? These and other questions are all we try to answer in this book.

Each country's currency is valued in terms of other currencies through the use of exchange rates. Currencies can then be exchanged to facilitate international transactions. Foreign exchange rate is the core subject matter in the field of international finance. The adoption of floating exchange rate system in 1973 provoked controversies over the pros and cons of the system itself. Many new theories have been developed to explain the causes of exchange rate movements. Those theories try to explain the phenomena which has never existed before in international finance. Chinese Renminbi has had much larger increase in its value against the U.S. dollar since 2005. And China has allowed a somewhat faster rate of increase in recent years. While the foreign pressure may have had some effects, the most important reason that Chinese government has allowed faster appreciation of the RMB is that conditions in Chinese economy have changed. With the higher economic growth rate the Chinese economy has also experienced an increasingly higher inflation rate in the past two decades. The appreciation of RMB can assist the government to tackle the overheating economy. We are going to introduce some basic theories about foreign exchange rate in details in this book.

One of the major developments in the past four decades has been the exponential growth in trading in derivative instruments such as currency futures, options and swaps. Financial derivatives provide valuable tools with the companies who face foreign exchange risk exposures. On the other hand, they are also used extensively by authorities, mutual funds, pension funds or even banks for speculations. Orange County of the state of California in U.S.A, Long-Term Capital Management, to just name a few, all suffered remarkable losses due to the derivatives speculations. Therefore, financial derivatives are also the major concerns for regulatory authorities. Some economists believe that they are the major causes for 2008 worldwide financial crises. In this book, we focus on the fundamentals of their use for hedging and speculative purposes.

The Environment of International Finance

International Economic Integration and Globalization

As the world becomes more integrated, countries become more interdependent. In today's world, no nation exists in economic isolation. All aspects of a nation's economy — its industries, service sectors, levels of income and employment, living standard — are linked to the economies of its trading partners. This linkage takes the form of so called international economic integration and globalization. Indeed, in a highly globalized and integrated world economy national economic policies cannot be formulated without evaluating their probable impacts on the economies of other countries.

Economic integration refers to trade unification between different states by the partial or full abolishing of customs tariffs on trade taking place within the borders of each state. Complete economic integration would imply free trade in all goods and services, perfect capital mobility, complete freedom of migration, complete freedom of establishment for businesses, and an unhindered flow of information and ideas. It would also imply the elimination of national differences in taxation, in the financing of social services, in the rules governing competition and monopoly, and in environmental regulation; and arguably a single currency. Complete economic integration is clearly a very distant prospect for the world as a whole, although some part of the way towards it has been covered in economic blocs such as the European Union (EU) and the North American Free Trade Agreement (NAFTA). Some further movement towards integration is widely considered desirable for countries with similar cultures; whether it is desirable at all is a matter of dispute, because there are wide differences in culture.

Globalization includes market integration, world governance, global society and mobility of peoples and information. For any **multinational corporation** (MNC) which is a firm with operations that extend beyond its domestic national borders, global business is the social science of managing people to organize, maintain, and grow the collective productivity toward accomplishing productive goals, typically to maximize profit and value for its owners and stakeholders.

The world is becoming more and more a borderless world for economic transactions as a result of World Trade Organization (WTO) negotiations to reduce trade restrictions, the continuing move by the EU toward a true United States of Europe with one currency, and trading arrangements such as the North American Free Trade Agreement uniting Canada, the United States, and Mexico into one large trading bloc. The trade pacts among the different countries have hastened the fall of international trade barriers. Here we briefly introduce the world's major trade pacts.

World Trade Organization (WTO) is an international organization to supervise and ensure that world trade flows as smoothly, predictably and freely as possible. It evolved from the "General Agreement on Tariffs and Trade" (GATT). There are 164 members in WTO now. China has been a member since December 11, 2001.

North American Free Trade Agreement (NAFTA) is an agreement reached in 1993 between Canada, Mexico and the United States making the three countries into a "free trade" zone.

European Union (EU) was originally formed with twelve members. The former of EU was European Community (EC). There are 27 members in EU now. It is a single Europe-wide market so that people, goods, and money can move around freely as if within one country. Nineteen members use the single currency — euro.

Association of South-East Asian Nations (ASEAN) is a political and economic group of the capitalist nations of South East Asia, formed in 1967 and comprising 10 countries: Brunei, Cambodia, Indonesia, Laos, Malaysia, Burma (Myanmar), the Philippines, Singapore, Thailand, and Vietnam. While the organization is committed to strengthening economic ties, progress has been limited. There has also been political cooperation. China joined the ASEAN in 2010, now known as **CHINA-ASIAN Free Trade Area (CAFTA)**. The free trade area came into effect on January 1, 2010, the ASEAN-China free trade area (ACFTA) was at the time the largest free trade area in terms of population and third largest in terms of nominal GDP.

Asia-Pacific Economic Cooperation (APEC) is a forum for 21 Pacific Rim countries to promote free trade and economic cooperation throughout the Asia-Pacific region. Australia, Canada, China, Japan, Korea, Russia and the United States are among the member countries.

Southern Common Market (Mercosur) is an economic and political agreement between Argentina, Brazil, Paraguay and Uruguay, Bolivia and Chile are associate members. Founded in 1991, Mercosur aims to promote free trade and the fluid movement of goods, people, and currency. It is now a full customs union.

Andean Community is a customs union comprising the South American countries of Bolivia, Colombia, Ecuador, Peru, Venezuela. In 1998, Andean Community and Mercosur signed an agreement for the creation of a free trade area. These countries are working with the United Nation Conference on Trade and Development (UNCTAD) to establish a Latin American common market.

Organization of Petroleum Exporting Countries (OPEC) is an inter-governmental organization of twelve developing countries — Algeria, Angola, Indonesia, Iran, Iraq, Kuwait, Libya, Nigeria, Qatar, Saudi Arabia, United Arab Emirates and Venezuela. One of the principal goals of OPEC is the determination of the best means for safeguarding the organization's interest, individually and collectively. It also pursues ways and means of ensuring the stabilization of prices in international oil markets.

Commonwealth of Independent States (CIS) is a regional organization whose participating countries are former Soviet Republics, formed during the breakup of the Soviet Union. Member states include: Armenia, Azerbaijan, Belarus, Georgia, Kazakhstan, Kyrgyz Republic, Republic of Moldova, Russia Federation, Tajikistan, Turkmenistan, Ukraine, and Uzbekistan. The purpose of the organization is to promote trade, finance cooperation in the region.

The Growth of World Trade and the Changes in Trade Patterns

The economic cooperation and trade pacts have made great contributions to the economic integration and globalization. The economic integration and globalization sped up the development of world trades and investments during the last several decades. Exports and imports as a share of national output have reached an unprecedented level for most industrial nations, while foreign investment and international lending have expanded more rapidly than world trade. As barriers to trade progressively fall, foreign markets are playing an increasingly important role in the viability of domestic industries. World trade of goods and services has expanded in a remarkable pace because of the reduction in trade barriers, lower transportation costs and advances in telecommunications, information technology and financial services. **Exhibit 1.1** lists the world merchandise exports by region and selected economy from 1948 to 2019. The total volume of merchandise exports increased from $59 billion in 1948 to $18,372 billion in 2019, a more than 310 times increase!

Exhibit 1.1   World Merchandise Exports by Region and Selected Economy

(billions of U.S. dollars and percentage)

	1948	1953	1963	1973	1983	1993	2003	2019
World	59	84	157	579	1,838	3,688	7,382	18,372
World	100	100	100	100	100	100	100	100
North America	28.1	24.8	19.9	17.3	16.8	17.9	15.8	13.9

(Continued)

	1948	1953	1963	1973	1983	1993	2003	2019
United States of America	21.6	14.6	14.3	12.2	11.2	12.6	9.8	9.0
Mexico	0.9	0.7	0.6	0.4	1.4	1.4	2.2	2.5
Canada	5.5	5.2	4.3	4.6	4.2	3.9	3.7	2.4
South and Central America and the Caribbean	11.3	9.7	6.4	4.3	4.5	3.0	3.1	3.2
Brazil	2.0	1.8	0.9	1.1	1.2	1.0	1.0	1.2
Chile	0.6	0.5	0.3	0.2	0.2	0.2	0.3	0.4
Europe	35.1	39.4	47.8	50.9	43.5	45.3	45.9	37.7
Germany①	1.4	5.3	9.3	11.7	9.2	10.3	10.2	8.1
Netherlands	2.0	3.0	3.6	4.7	3.5	3.8	4.0	3.9
France	3.4	4.8	5.2	6.3	5.2	6.0	5.3	3.1
United Kingdom	11.3	9.0	7.8	5.1	5.0	4.9	4.2	2.6
Commonwealth of Independent States (CIS), including associate and former member States②	—	—	—	—	—	1.7	2.6	3.4
Africa	7.3	6.5	5.7	4.8	4.5	2.5	2.4	2.5
South Africa③	2.0	1.6	1.5	1.0	1.0	0.7	0.5	0.5
Middle East	2.0	2.7	3.2	4.1	6.7	3.5	4.1	5.3
Asia	14.0	13.4	12.5	14.9	19.1	26.0	26.1	34.0
China	0.9	1.2	1.3	1.0	1.2	2.5	5.9	13.6
Japan	0.4	1.5	3.5	6.4	8.0	9.8	6.4	3.8
India	2.2	1.3	1.0	0.5	0.5	0.6	0.8	1.8
Australia and New Zealand	3.7	3.2	2.4	2.1	1.4	1.4	1.2	1.7
Six East Asian traders	3.4	3.0	2.5	3.6	5.8	9.6	9.6	9.6

Source: World Trade Statistical Review 2020, www.wto.org.
Note: Between 1973 and 1983 and between 1993 and 2003 export shares were significantly influenced by oil price developments.
① Figures refer to the Fed. Rep. of Germany from 1948 to 1983.
② Figures are significantly affected by including the mutual trade flows of the Baltic States and the CIS between 1993 to 2003.
③ Beginning with 1998, figures refer to South Africa only and no longer to the Southern African Customs Union.

As Exhibit 1.1 demonstrates, China has been the leading exporter in world merchandise trade. The volume of China's exports accounted for 13.6% of world merchandise exports in 2019. Another statistics shows that China's merchandise exports increased by an average of 4.8% during 2010 to 2019, and imports increased by 4.5% at the same time period. Those data reflects the major trade reforms China undertook during the 1980s and 1990s, including China's accession to the WTO in 2001. The accession, in turn, led to a steady decrease in tariffs on imports. Because of its large size and increased openness, China has become a major player in the world economy.

Figure 1.1 The Volume of World Export, Import and Real GDP Growth from 2012 to 2019
Source: WTO Secretariat for trade, consensus estimates for GDP.
Note: GDP growth is calculated with market exchange rate weights.

Figure 1.1 shows the volume of world export, import and the real GDP growth from 2012 to 2019. The volume of world merchandise trade declined in 2019 for the first time since the financial crisis of 2008–2009, weighed down by rising trade tensions and weakening economic growth. Merchandise trade volume declined by 0.1% in 2019, compared with 2.9% growth in 2018. World GDP growth slowed to 2.3 %, down from 2.9% the previous year. The U.S. dollar value of merchandise trade fell year-on-year, dropping 3% to U.S.$18.89 trillion in 2019. Trade declined more steeply in value terms than in volume terms due to falling export and import prices. Commercial services trade grew by 2% in 2019, down from 9% in 2018, as growth slowed and trade tensions escalated.

At the same time, the patterns of world trade have also experienced a profound change. Although traditional trade barriers such as tariffs have come down, and innovations in transportation and communications technology have shrunk the distance between nations, trade costs remain high in developing countries. High trade costs isolate developing countries form world markets, limiting their trade opportunities and impending growth. High trade costs also appear to disproportionately affect **small and medium-sized enterprises (SMEs)**, time-sensitive products and goods produced in **global value chains**.

The World Trade Organization **Trade Facilitation Agreement (TFA)** entered into force in February 2017 represents an important milestone by creating a multilateral framework for reducing trade costs. The TFA helps the movement of goods by simplifying international trade procedures including customs and border regulations, licensing and transit formalities, administrative processes, and documentation requirements. It also provides a global boost for jobs and growth. Full implementation of the TFA has the potential to reduce trade costs by an average of 14.3%. The computable general equilibrium (CGE) estimates see the TFA increasing global exports by between U.S.$750 billion and U.S.$1 trillion, depending on the speed and extent of implementation[1].

International trade has long been dominated by large companies, because they have the critical mass, organizational reach and relevant technologies needed to access and supply foreign markets. But owing to the introduction of internet and the rise of international production networks, many innovative and productive small firms now have the potential to become successful international traders as well. The opportunities to connect to world markets created by the information and communication technology revolution are particularly relevant for SMEs. E-commerce reduces the costs related to physical distance between sellers and consumers by providing information at a very low cost. Through online platforms, smaller businesses, including those in developing countries, can connect with distant customers. The rise of international production networks and of trade in global value chains, which has, to a large extent, been made possible by the information and communication technology revolution, also holds great potential to facilitate the internationalization of SMEs. While SMEs may find it difficult to compete along an entire line of activities, they can more readily integrate into global value chains by performing tasks in which they have a comparative advantage.

The digital technologies including the **Internet of Things, artificial intelligence, 3D printing** and **Blockchain** are likely to affect trade significantly in the years to come. One of the most significant effects of digital technologies is the extent to which they reduce various trade costs, such as transport and logistics costs, the cost of crossing borders, information and transaction costs, and the costs of cross-border payments. Transport and logistics costs combined account for more than half of the variation in trade costs in agriculture and manufacturing, and for more than 40% of the variation in trade costs in services[2]. Thus, the application of artificial intelligence, the Internet of Things and Blockchain to reduce transport and logistic costs are likely to have the largest effects on overall trade costs.

Over the last few decades, services have become the backbone of the global economy and the most dynamic component of international trade. The digital technologies affect the composition of trade in four ways. First, they increase the services component of

---

1 World Trade Report 2015.
2 World Trade Report 2018.

trade, because of the ease of supplying services digitally, because new services emerge and replace trade in goods, and because international production networks increase the services content of manufacturing goods. Second, digital technologies foster trade in certain type of goods (time-sensitive, certification-intensive and contract-intensive goods), while at the same time reducing trade in "digitizable" goods. In addition, the sharing economy business model may affect trade in certain consumer goods, such as housing and transport services. Third, digital technologies affect the complexity and length of global value chains, reducing the costs of coordinating geographically dispersed tasks, but at the same time providing increased incentives to locate or relocate production near large markets or near centers of innovation. Fourth, digital technologies change patterns of comparative advantage by increasing the importance of factors such as the quality of digital infrastructure and market size, as well as institutional and regulatory determinants of comparative advantage, including intellectual property protection.

These changes can open new opportunities. Trade in services creates meaningful welfare gains for society through a more efficient allocation of resources, a greater variety and quality in the services that consumers and producers can purchase, and by allowing the more productive services firms to expand. In sectors like healthcare, education and finance, in particular, these gains can directly improve development outcomes. A geographically diverse range of economies, including many developing economies, had benefited from the recent expansion of trade in services. The share of developing economies in global services trade has increased by more than 10% since 2005, and although the participation of least-developed countries is small, their share has also been rising significantly. A large number of jobs, both in developed and developing economies, is supported by services exports. The decline in service trade costs allows more services to be traded cross-border, which particularly benefits the developing economies and micro, small medium-sized enterprises, which rely predominantly on this mode of supply.

The Globalization of Financial Markets

The international trade and international investment have generated corresponding financial flows and it is now the rule rather than an exception that a firm must manage payments and receipts in currencies other than its own. Also we have witnessed a rapid integration of international financial markets in the last several decades. As a result, currency trading has recently undergone explosive growth. The **Bank for International Settlement (BIS)** has conducted triennial survey of foreign exchange and derivatives market activity every three years since April 1989. More than 1,200 financial institutions in 53 countries including China participated in 2019 survey. **Exhibit 1.2** is the foreign exchange market average daily turnover in April 2019. In the table, spot transactions, outright forwards and foreign exchange swaps were previously classified as part of the so-called "traditional foreign exchange market". The category "other products" covers highly leveraged transactions and other transactions whose notional amount is variable. Global foreign exchange market turnover was 241% higher in 2019 than in April 2004, with average daily turnover of more than $6.5 trillion compared with $1.9 trillion.

Exhibit 1.2 Global Foreign Exchange Market Turnover by Instrument

(Average daily turnover in April, billions of U.S. dollars)

Instrument	2004	2007	2010	2013	2016	2019
Foreign exchange instruments	1,934	3,324	3,973	5,357	5,066	6,595
Spot transactions	631	1,005	1,489	2,047	1,652	1,987
Outright forwards	209	362	475	679	700	999
Foreign exchange Swaps	954	1,714	1,759	2,240	2,378	3,203
Currency swaps	21	31	43	54	82	108
Options and other products	119	212	207	337	254	298
Memo: Turnover at April 2019 exchange rates	1,854	3,071	3,602	4,827	4,958	6,595
Exchange-traded derivatives	25	77	144	145	115	127

Source: BIS, *Triennial Central Bank Survey of Foreign Exchange and Derivatives Market Activity in April, 2019*. September 2019, www.bis.org.

Furthermore, as international barriers to free capital movement have significantly been reduced or in some places totally disappeared, firms have sought to exploit their comparative financial advantage and diversify their sources of funds by borrowing internationally rather than limiting themselves to their own domestic market. Cross-border financing becomes more and more popular for multinational corporations and other large firms. For reasons of market access and productivity, many firms have also embarked on programs of direct investment in foreign countries, with all the risks it entails.

International capital flows have grown significantly over the past several decades. Cross-border bank lending has been one of the most important channels for the expansion of such activity, especially before the 2008–2009 financial crisis. After the crisis, international debt securities issuance, especially in low-income and middle-income countries, has also picked up considerably in what has become known as the "second phase" of global liquidity. Global slowdown, market turbulence, and credit downgrades did not deter bond issuance by low-income and middle-income countries in 2019.

As **Exhibit 1.3** shows, new bond issuance by the 120 low-income and middle-income countries totaled $376 billion in 2019, 16% higher than the figure for 2018 but below the 2017 record high of $401 billion. Issuance in 2019 was characterized by a surge in bond issues by private sector entities; up 37% over the prior-year level to $129 billion. New issuance by sovereigns and other public sector entities increased at a more moderate pace, rising 7% to $247 billion.

Exhibit 1.3 Bond Issuance by Low-Income and Middle-Income Countries, 2018–2019

(billions of U.S. dollars)

	Public Issuers		Corporate Issuers		All Issuers	
	2018	2019	2018	2019	2018	2019
East Asia and Pacific	93.0	94.3	60.1	80.9	153.1	175.2
of which: China	63.7	60.7	50.4	71.6	114.1	132.3
Europe and Central Asia	25.3	50.2	10.4	15.7	35.6	65.8
Latin America and the Caribbean	73.7	59.0	20.9	22.9	94.6	82.0
Middle East and North Africa	12.7	13.3	0.3	0.0	13.0	13.3
South Asia	5.4	12.9	0.9	7.3	6.3	20.3
Sub-Saharan Africa	19.1	16.9	1.7	2.5	20.8	19.4
Low-income and middle-income countries	229.1	246.7	94.4	129.3	323.4	376.0

Source: World Bank Debtor Reporting System, www.worldbank.org.

China was the dominant player among low-income and middle-income countries. It issued $132 billion in international bonds in 2019, 16% higher than the previous year, and equivalent to 35% of the combined issuance by low-income and middle-income countries, the same percentage share as 2018. Bond issuance by private sector entities in China rose 42% in 2019 to $72 billion, in contrast to those by public sector entities, which fell 5% to $61 billion. Bond issues by other low-income and middle-income countries rose, on average, 5% in 2019 to $73 billion and were also characterized by a sharp jump in issuance by private entities, up 65%, and a contraction in issues by sovereigns and public sector entities, down 23%.

Cross-border links between banks and **non-bank financial institutions** (NBFIs) gained momentum in recent years. Banks cross-border claims on and liabilities to NBFIs have grown 63%, from $4.6 trillion in the first quarter of 2015 to $7.5 trillion in the first quarter of 2020[1]. Financial centers and large advanced economies play a prominent role, as hosts of the largest and most interconnected NBFIs such as central counterparties, hedge funds and investment funds. The size of banks' cross-border links to NBFIs in emerging market economies has also been on the rise.

Internationally active foreign banks are important providers of credit for borrowers in **emerging market economies** (EMEs). The foreign banks provide needed credit to EME borrowers and help boost financial capacity. But the reliance on foreign bank credit in EMEs has varied across countries, sectors and time. Foreign bank reliance refers to the

---

[1] 2021 BIS locational banking statistics, www.bis.org.

fraction of total credit to non-financial borrowers in a country (or a sector within a country, such as non-financial corporations) that is accounted for by the consolidated claims of foreign banks. This measure also includes bond financing and borrowing from non-bank creditors, which has increased and become a substantial source of credit for many EMEs. Some countries, for example, Mexico and Chile, heavily rely on foreign bank credit. Mexico's private sector is the most reliant, receiving nearly 50% of its credit directly from foreign banks (including foreign banks operating locally), and China's is the least.[1]

The characteristics of the nowadays financial markets can be summarized as the following:

- An increase in cross-border financing as MNCs raise capital in whichever market and in whatever currency offers the most attractive rates.
- Increasingly interdependent national financial markets.
- An increasing number of cross-border partnerships, including many international mergers, acquisitions, and joint ventures.
- An increasing number of cooperative linkages among securities exchanges.

The Creation of Financial Derivatives

The competition in the financial market spurs the creation of vast array of financial derivatives. **Derivatives** are financial contracts that are designed to create market price exposure to changes in an underlying commodity, asset or event. They were created to help manage the evolving risk-return profile. The 1980s have seen an explosion in the number of markets trading financial futures and options. Today the size of derivatives markets by some measures exceeds that for bank landing, securities and insurance. All these derivative products are being traded on a worldwide basis because the underlying instruments are being traded on a worldwide basis. They offer both definite opportunities and a distinct disadvantage to anyone involved in international trade or finance — exporters, importers, professional investors, company treasurers, bankers and portfolio managers — if he is not familiar with the products that are available and how they can be used.

In addition to risk management, derivatives markets play a very useful economic role in price discovery. **Price discovery** is the way in which a market establishes the price or prices for items traded in that market, and then disseminates those prices as information throughout the market and the economy as a whole. In this way market prices are important not only to those buying and selling but also to those producing and consuming in other markets and in other locations and all those affected by commodity and security price levels, exchange rates and interest rates. The price discovery process gives rise to the public interest concern, and historically it has been the motivation for the regulation of derivatives markets in the United States. Along with these economic benefits come costs or

---

1 BIS Quarterly Review, March 2019.

potential economic costs. Some firms, banks or even local governments have run up enormous losses either through a lack of understanding of the instruments or the taking of unduly risky positions. Long-Term Capital Management collapsed $1.4 trillion in derivatives on their books. In the process it froze up the U.S. dollar fixed income market. Barings bank was quickly brought to bankruptcy by over a billion dollars in losses from derivatives trading. Both the Mexican financial crisis in 1994 and the East Asian financial crisis of 1997 were exacerbated by the use of derivatives to take large positions involving the exchange rate.

The Theory of Comparative Advantage

Classical economist Adam Smith was a leading advocate of free trade on the grounds that the free trade promoted the international division of labor. According to Smith, mutually beneficial trade requires each nation to be the least-cost producer of at least one good that it can export to its trading partner. All countries benefit from free trade by specializing in the goods that they are best suited to produce because of natural or acquired advantages. In this case, if country A can produce cars more efficiently than country B while country B can produce wheat more efficiently than country A, country A will specialize in producing cars and country B will specialize in producing wheat. Then two countries can get what they want through trade. Total output of the two goods is higher than it would be if they both allocated resources to the less efficiently produced goods. This theory assumes that every country has at least one product with an absolute advantage that can be exported in exchange for the other goods it needs to import. But what if country A is more efficient than country B in the production of both wheat and cars?

The 19th-century British economist David Ricardo developed a theory called "comparative advantage" to show that economic well-being is enhanced even when one nation is absolutely more efficient in the production of all goods.

For an example of the benefits of free trade based on comparative advantage, we assume that U.K. is more efficient than France at producing both wheat and cars. With one unit of input (a mix of land, labor, capital, and technology, etc.), efficient U.K. can produce either 24 units of wheat or 12 units of cars. France can produce only 20 units of wheat or 4 units of cars with one unit of input. These production capabilities are as shown in **Exhibit 1.4**.

Exhibit 1.4　Production capability in U.K. and France

	Production Capability	
	Units of Wheat	Units of Cars
U.K.	24	12
France	20	4

If there is no trade between U.K. and France, each country divides its own inputs between wheat and cars. Assume both countries select to allocate 300 inputs to wheat and 700 inputs to cars, total output for each country is illustrated in **Exhibit 1.5**.

Exhibit 1.5   Production of U.K. and France before trade

	Wheat Production (unit)	Car Production (unit)
U.K.	300 × 24 = 7,200	700 × 12 = 8,400
France	300 × 20 = 6,000	700 × 4 = 2,800
Total output	13,200	11,200

According to Ricardo, U.K. has comparative advantage in producing cars (lower opportunity cost) than France's and France has comparative advantage in producing wheat. Therefore, U.K. produces only cars while France produces only wheat. Total output would be higher for both wheat and cars, as shown in **Exhibit 1.6**.

Exhibit 1.6   Specialization in U.K. and France

	Wheat Production (unit)	Car Production (unit)
U.K.	0	1,000 × 12 = 12,000
France	1,000 × 20 = 20,000	0
Total output	20,000	12,000

The combined output is 13,200 units of wheat and 11,200 units of cars. Without trade, each country can consume only what it produces.

One unit of input in U.K. has an absolute advantage over an input unit in France in both wheat and cars. Nevertheless, France has comparative advantage over U.K. in producing wheat. Note that in using units of production, France can "trade off" one unit of production needed to produce 20 units of wheat for 4 units of cars. Thus, a unit of car has an opportunity cost of 20/4 = 5 units of wheat, or a unit of wheat has an opportunity cost of 4/20 = 0.2 units of cars. Analogously, U.K. has an opportunity cost of 24/12 = 2 units of wheat per unit of car, or 12/24 = 0.5 units of cars per unit of wheat. That is to say, France's opportunity cost for producing wheat (0.2) is less than U.K.'s (0.5); while U.K.'s opportunity cost for producing cars (2) is less than France's (5). Thus, it is clear that U.K. is relatively more efficient in producing cars and France is relatively more efficient in producing wheat.

Both U.K. and France are now better off in terms of total output. The problem now is how to distribute those two goods between the two countries. Suppose the "exchange rate" is 4 units of wheat to 1 unit of car. Now Britain exports 3,200 cars to France for 12,800 units of wheat from France. In other words, U.K. now can consume 5,600 (12,800–7,200 = 5,600) units of wheat more than before, and France can consume more cars than before. **Exhibit 1.7** shows the situation.

Exhibit 1.7 Trade at a price of 4 units of wheat to 1 unit of car

	Wheat Production (unit)	Car Production (unit)
U.K.	12,800 (import)	12,000–3,200 = 8,800
France	20,000–12,800 = 7,200	3,200 (import)

This is an important result. Both countries have become richer because of trade even though one country had an absolute advantage in the production of both goods. Even though this is a simplified model, it shows a very important issue in international finance: How do we determine the trade ratio, i.e., the exchange rate of wheat versus the car? For example, if the ratio is not 4 units of wheat to 1 unit of car, instead it is 2 to 1. In this case, England must export 3,600 units of cars for 7,200 units of wheat. England's consumption is just as it was with no trade. U.K. will gain nothing from trade although it will lose nothing either. But France can consume more wheat and cars than before.

However, great changes have been taken place in today's international trade. Countries do not appear to specialize only in those products that could be most efficiently produced by that country's natural factors of production. Instead, governments interfere with comparative advantage for a variety of economic and political reasons, such as to achieve full employment, economic development, national self-sufficiency in defense-related industries, and protection of an agricultural sector's way of life. The best example is the U.S. trade protectionism prevailed under the Trump administration.

Modern factors of production are more complicated than that in this simple model. They include local and managerial skills, a dependable legal structure for settling contract disputes, research and development competence, educational levels of employees, energy resources, consumer differentials, supporting infrastructure (road, ports, and communication facilities), and possibly others.

Comparative advantage shifts over time as less developed countries become more developed and realize their latent opportunities. For example, the United Kingdom originally produced cotton textiles because of its comparative advantage, and shifted to U.S. later, and then shifted to Japan and to China. The classical model of comparative advantage also did not really address certain other issues such as the effect of uncertainty and information costs, the role of differentiated products in imperfectly competitive markets, and economies of scale.

The Benefits of Studying International Finance

Since we are living in a highly globalized and integrated world economy, it is clear that modern day financial management and investment is international in scope and requires the corresponding knowledge and expertise in order to be successful. The emergence of trans-national production networks is reshaping the relationship between foreign direct investment and international trade. The expansion of the MNC has reached unprecedented level since the late 1960's. **Exhibit 1.8** lists the top 30 of the largest 100 MNCs ranked by the size of foreign assets. The **United Nations Conference on Trade and Development (UNCTAD)** compiles the list every year in its *World Investment Report*. Oil giant Royal Dutch Shell topped the ranking followed by Toyota, Total and BP. Emerging market firms are mostly non-existent in this list with exception of COSCO (ranked 47th in the list), CNOOC (54th), Tencent (72nd), HNA Group (80th), of China. Many of the firms on the list are well-known MNCs with household names because of their presence in consumer product market. For example, General Electric, Royal Dutch Shell, Toyota, Honda, Siemens, Volkswagen and Microsoft are the names recognized by most people. Most of the top 100 multinational corporations are from developed countries such as U.S., U.K., Germany, Switzerland and Japan.

Exhibit 1.8 The World's Top 30 Non-Financial MNCs Based on Foreign Assets, 2017

(millions of U.S. dollars)

Ranking by Foreign Assets	Corporation	Country	Industry	Assets	Sales
1	Royal Dutch Shell Plc	U.K.	Mining, quarrying and petroleum	344,210	407,097
2	Toyota Motor Corporation	Japan	Motor vehicles	302,788	472,625
3	Total SA	France	Petroleum, refining and related industries	234,993	242,576
4	BP Plc	U.K.	Petroleum, refining and related industries	220,380	276,620
5	Volkswagen Group	Germany	Motor vehicles	219,917	506,348
6	Softbank Corporation	Japan	Telecommunications	214,863	292,928

(Continued)

Ranking by Foreign Assets	Corporation	Country	Industry	Assets	Sales
7	Exxon Mobil Corporation	U.S.	Petroleum, refining and related industries	203,626	348,691
8	British American Tobacco Plc	U.K.	Tobacco	189,214	190,643
9	General Electric Co.	U.S.	Industrial and commercial machinery	186,586	377,945
10	Chevron Corporation	U.S.	Petroleum, refining and related industries	183,643	253,806
11	Anheuser-Busch InBev NV	Belgium	Food and beverages	165,176	205,173
12	Vodafone Group Plc	U.K.	Telecommunications	160,139	179,412
13	Daimler AG	Germany	Motor vehicles	159,163	306,554
14	Apple Computer Inc	U.S.	Computer equipment	146,048	375,319
15	Honda Motor Co. Ltd	Japan	Motor vehicles	141,289	181,777
16	Siemens AG	Germany	Industrial and commercial machinery	133,842	160,698
17	BMW AG	Germany	Motor vehicles	130,265	232,050
18	Enel SpA	Italy	Electricity, gas and water	127,033	186,665
19	DowDuPont Inc	U.S.	Rubber and miscellaneous plastic products	126,935	192,164
20	Nissan Motor Co. Ltd	Japan	Motor vehicles	126,346	176,119
21	CK Hutchison Holdings Limited	China	Retail trade	125,804	140,795
22	Johnson & Johnson	U.S.	Pharmaceuticals	118,747	157,303
23	Glencore Plc	Switzerland	Mining, quarrying and petroleum	116,708	135,644
24	Deutsche Telekom AG	Germany	Telecommunications	112,734	169,506
25	Eni SpA	Italy	Petroleum, refining and related industries	111,723	137,836
26	Telefonica SA	Spain	Telecommunications	110,751	138,002
27	Iberdrola SA	Spain	Electricity, gas and water	110,592	132,752

(Continued)

Ranking by Foreign Assets	Corporation	Country	Industry	Assets	Sales
28	Microsoft Corporation	U.S.	Computer and data processing	108,325	250,312
29	Nestle SA	Switzerland	Food and beverages	106,790	133,627
30	Medtronic Plc	Ireland	Instruments and related products	95,902	99,816

Source: *World Investment Report 2018*, UNCTAD.

A financial manager of an MNC with operations in more than one country encounters new opportunities as well as new costs and risks. The primary goal of any firm is to maximize shareholder wealth. The challenge facing the multinational financial manager is to successfully develop and execute business and financial strategies in more than one culture or business environment.

Reaching that goal — maximizing profits — requires combining three critical elements. The first is that an MNC should have the ability to compete in an open marketplace in which labor, capital technology are moved freely without restrictions. The second is that the MNC should have high quality strategic management. To be able to recognize and develop investment opportunities in foreign markets, the multinational financial manager must understand the capabilities and limitations of traditional investment analysis, have a plan of attack for entry into and exit from foreign markets, and value the growth and abandonment options presented by foreign markets. The third is that the successful MNC should gain ready access to affordable capital. The access to the capital is so important that it allows the investment needed to obtain the technology, execute the strategy, and expand across global markets.

The financial opportunities of the MNCs are richer than those of the domestic corporations because of cross-border differences in investors' required returns and hence the corporations' cost of capital. Multinational financial management requires a thorough knowledge of the international markets in interest rates and foreign currency, as well as derivative markets in interest rate and currency futures, options, and swaps. In many ways, today's financial manager must be a jack-of-all-trades as well as master of one — finance.

Specifically, the knowledge of international finance can help a financial manager of a multinational corporation in the following two aspects:

- It helps the manager decide how international events will affect a firm and which steps can be taken to exploit positive developments and insulate the firm from harmful ones.
- It helps the manager to anticipate events and to make profitable decisions before the events occur.

Events include changes in exchange rate, interest rate, and inflation rate and asset values. We all know that high interest rate of a particular country comes with high inflation. High inflation also implies depreciation of the currency of that country. Some asset prices are positively affected by a depreciated currency, such as stock prices of export-oriented companies that are more profitable after depreciation. Some asset prices are negatively affected, such as stock prices of companies with foreign currency debt that lose when the company's home currency declines, because the company's debt is increased in terms of domestic currency. These connections between exchange rates, asset and liability values, and so on mean that foreign exchange is not simply a risk that is added to other business risks. Instead, the amount of risk depends crucially on the way exchange rates and other financial prices are connected. Jobs, bond and stock prices, food prices, government revenues and other important economic variables are all tied to exchange rates and other developments in the global financial environment. Only by studying international finance can a manager understand matters such as these.

All in all, an understanding of multinational financial management is crucial to success in today's marketplace, and equally essential in tomorrow's marketplace. This is unquestionably true for firms competing directly with foreign firms, such as a domestic auto industry in competition with international automakers. It is also true for domestic firms whose suppliers, customers, and competitors are increasingly likely to be from foreign countries. In today's business environment, the success of firms in service and manufacturing industries depends on their ability to recognize and exploit imperfections in national markets for both products and factors of production and work effectively within the political and economic constraints imposed by foreign governments.

The Structure of This Book

This book is designed for junior or senior level undergraduates majoring in finance. It can also be used by students and professionals lacking in up-to-date training in modern financial theory. This book is also useful for those who expect to obtain jobs created by international investment, international banking, and multinational business activity. Other readers may have a more scholarly concern with "rounding out" their economic education by studying the international relationship between financial markets and institutions. The basic principles, models, and techniques of finance and investment are explained and illustrated with examples as they arise. It is very important for students to understand the material presented in this textbook. So at the end of each chapter there are conceptual questions summarizing the key ideas discussed in that chapter. Since great changes have been taken place in the modern financial market and the market changes almost every day, we need to know these changes. Therefore, we hope students should often read financial papers and magazines or visit the relative websites to be kept informed. It is not an easy task to fully master the whole theories and practices of international finance by just reading this textbook.This book is organized into four parts.

Part I (Chapter 1, 2, 3, and 4) is the basics of the international finance. Chapter 1 discusses the subject matter of international finance and the environment of modern international finance. It introduces the new development of world trade and financial markets, the theory of comparative advantage and why do we need to study the international finance. Chapter 2 discusses the balance of payments which is one of the causes for the international finance. The balance of payments of a country is one of the economic forces that cause exchange rates to fluctuate. Exchange rates respond to demand and supply to trade currencies. These demands and supplies arise from international trade flows and international capital flows. The chapter includes detailed descriptions of balance of payments accounts, their implications for a country's national economy. Chapter 3 examines the basics of foreign exchange market and foreign exchange rate. It is a core subject matter of the international finance. The topics include the characteristics, functions of the foreign exchange market, types of exchange rates such as spot exchange rates and forward rates, exchange rate quotations, foreign exchange arbitrage, nominal and real exchange rate, and effective exchange rate. Chapter 4 studies exchange rate system prevailed in the history, such as international gold standard, Bretton Woods system, floating exchange rate system, and various other kinds of the system adopted by nations worldwide today.

Part II consists of three chapters (Chapter 5, 6, and 7). Chapter 5 studies several important exchange rate theories and international parity conditions, specifically, the theory of short-run exchange rate movements, the purchasing power parity which determines the long-run exchange rates, interest rate parity, Fisher Equation, forward parity, Fisher Open, real interest parity and so on. Chapter 6 analyzes the financial derivatives, mainly currency futures, options and swaps. Chapter 7 introduces the international financial markets including the Eurocurrency market and Eurobond market.

Part III (Chapter 8 and 9) investigates the relationship between the exchange rate and the balance of payments. This part will introduce four models that examine the impact of exchange rate changes on the current account balance of a country. Chapter 8 focuses on the adjustment of balance of payments disequilibrium. It presents two earlier models known as the elasticity approach (relative price effects) and the absorption approach (income effects). Chapter 9 studies two modern theories, the monetary approach and the portfolio balance approach, which explain the determinants of balance of payments and exchange rate movements.

Part IV (Chapter 10 and 11) explains the macroeconomics in an open economy, and government policy implications for economic activities. Chapter 10 reviews some basic concepts of the macroeconomics. Chapter 11 examines how both exchange rate changes and macroeconomic policies impact on an open economy. A fundamental difference between an open economy and a closed economy is that over time a country has to ensure that it achieves both internal and external balance. The need for policy-makers to pay attention to the implications of changes in monetary and fiscal policy on the balance of payments is an important additional dimension for consideration in the formulation of economy policy in an open economy.

Summary

1. International finance is the management of money in an international environment. It studies the monetary and macroeconomic relations between countries.
2. The subject matter of international finance includes mainly balance of payments problems and policies, the causes of exchange rate movements and the implications of macroeconomic linkages between nations.
3. The financial environment has undergone a profound change over the past four decades. Economic integration and globalization are the main stream in today's world economy.
4. Economic integration means a nation's economy is linked to the economies of its trading partners. In an integrated market, all asset prices are necessarily equal across every country.
5. Globalization includes market integration, world governance, global society and mobility of peoples and information.
6. World economic cooperation and free trade pacts have hastened the development of world trade and investments. WTO, NAFTA, EU, and CAFTA, to just name a few, have greatly changed our life and also changed the way people doing businesses and investments.
7. International trade grows considerably over the past several decades. Trade patterns have experienced significant changes. Service trade has become the backbone of the global economy and the most dynamic component of international trade.
8. The significant effect of digital technologies including the Internet of Things, artificial intelligence, 3D printing and Blockchain on international trade is the extent to which they reduce various trade costs such as transport and logistics costs, the cost of crossing borders, information and transaction costs, and the costs of cross-border payments.
9. International capital flows have grown considerably over the past several decades. Cross-border bank lending has been one of the most important channels for the expansion of such activity.
10. Cross-border links between banks and non-bank financial institutions (NBFIs) gained

momentum in recent years.
11. International active foreign banks are important providers of credit for borrowers in emerging market economies.
12. Financial derivatives are created to manage risks involved in international trade and investment. They also play an important economic role in price discovery.
13. Financial derivatives bring economic benefits as well as costs. Some firms, banks or even governments have run up huge losses either through a lack of understanding of the instruments or the taking of unduly risk positions.
14. Classical economists Adam Smith and David Ricardo presented a theory to show free trade benefitting both countries. The theory of comparative advantage indicates that mutually beneficial trade can occur even when one nation is absolutely more efficient in the production of all goods.
15. However, in modern times, countries do not appear to specialize only in those products that could be most efficiently produced by that country's natural factors of production. Instead, governments interfere with comparative advantage for a variety of economic and political reasons. Furthermore, modern factors of production are more complicated than in the simple model established by the classical economists.
16. Three conditions are the MUST for a successful MNC to maximize profits: open marketplace, strategic management, and access to capital.
17. The knowledge and expertise in international finance helps a financial manager of a multinational corporation decide how international events will affect a firm and which steps can be taken to exploit positive developments and insulate the firm from harmful ones. It also helps the manager to anticipate events and to make profitable decisions before the events occur.
18. Events include changes in exchange rates, interest rates, inflation, asset and liability values. They all have impacts on a company's profits, investment decisions and returns.
19. An understanding of multinational financial management is crucial to success in today's and tomorrow's marketplace.

Key Concepts and Terms

1. Absolute advantage — 绝对优势
2. Andean Community — 安第斯共同体
3. Artificial intelligence — 人工智能
4. Asia-Pacific Economic Cooperation (APEC) — 亚太经济合作组织
5. Blockchain — 区块链

6. Bank for International Settlement (BIS) 国际清算银行
7. China-Asian Free Trade Area (CAFTA) 中国-东盟自由贸易区
8. Commonwealth of Independent States (CIS) 独立国家联合体
9. Comparative advantage 比较优势
10. Economic integration 经济一体化
11. Emerging market economies (EMEs) 新兴市场经济体
12. European Union (EU) 欧盟
13. Financial derivatives 金融衍生产品
14. Global value chains 全球价值链
15. Globalization 全球化
16. International finance 国际金融
17. Internet of Things 物联网
18. Multinational Corporation (MNC) 跨国公司
19. Non-bank financial institutions (NBFIs) 非银行金融机构
20. North American Free Trade Agreement (NAFTA) 北美自由贸易协定
21. Organization of Petroleum Exporting Countries (OPEC) 石油输出国组织
22. Price discovery 价格发现
23. Sharing economy 共享经济
24. Small and medium-sized enterprises (SMEs) 中小企业
25. Southern Common Market (Mercosur) 南方共同市场
26. 3D printing 3D 打印
27. Trade Facilitation Agreement (TFA) 贸易便利化协定
28. United Nations Conference on Trade and Development (UNCTAD) 联合国贸易与发展会议
29. World Trade Organization (WTO) 世界贸易组织

Questions

1. What is international finance?
2. What is the subject matter of international finance?
3. What does economic integration and globalization mean? What are the differences between the two?
4. List the causes of rapid growth in international trade and international capital movements.
5. What is the trend of world trade?
6. Why is it important for implementation of Trade Facilitation Agreement (TFA)?
7. How does the digital technology affect international trade?

8. What are the significant changes in international trade in recent years?
9. What are the characteristics of nowadays financial markets?
10. Why is it important for MNCs to raise funds internationally?
11. Are financial derivatives necessary? Why?
12. What are the harmful aspects of the financial derivatives?
13. What is price discovery?
14. Use your own words to describe the theory of absolute advantage.
15. Define and explain the theory of comparative advantage.
16. What are the factors of production in modern society? Why is the general principle of comparative advantage still valid?
17. Why should we learn international finance?
18. What is the goal of financial management? How might the goal of financial management be different for the multinational corporation than for the domestic corporation?
19. In order to maximize shareholder wealth, what are basic conditions required for a multinational corporation?
20. How does the knowledge of international finance help the managers of multinational companies to manage their business activities?

Chapter 2
THE BALANCE OF PAYMENTS

LEARNING OBJECTIVES

- Learn how nations measure their economic transactions with the rest of world and how the international transactions creates the balance of payments.
- Identify each account and subaccounts in the balance of payments.
- Understand the principles guiding balance of payments structure, what transaction should be recorded as a credit entry or a debit entry, and how the double-entry-bookkeeping system works.
- Explain the implications of BOP surplus and deficit for the recording country.
- Discover the relationship between current account and macro economy.
- Examine the economic relationships underlying the two basic accounts of the balance of payments — the current account and capital and financial account balances.

One of the most important economic indicators for governments in an open economy is the balance of payments (BOP). The BOP statistics often captures the news headlines and can become the focus of attention. A country's BOP reveals the country's economic transactions with the rest of the world. Because cross-border economic and financial flows affect economic performance, such as output and employment, and financial variables, such as interest rates and exchange rates, it is important for financial decision making to understand how this process occurs. Currency traders eagerly await the release of new balance of payments statistics because they know exchange rates will move with the new information.

This chapter examines the monetary aspects of international trade by considering the nature and significance of a nation's balance of payments and what the BOP statistics mean to the policy-makers. We begin with a general presentation of the BOP and the major transactions to which it refers. We study the principles guiding its structure and the interpretation of each type of transaction that is included. Particular attention is paid to the fact that the BOP always balances, meaning that it always comes out to zero. We'll analyze what is meant by the notion of a BOP surplus or deficit. In the later chapters we consider the role of the monetary authorities and the different ways that this balance can be achieved. We will also look at the functional relationship between the balance of payments and the overall economy.

Definition of the Balance of Payments

A country uses the BOP statistics to track its cross-border flow of goods, services, and capital. The balance of payments is the record of the economic and financial flows that take place over a specified time period between residents and non-residents of a given country. The International Monetary Fund (IMF) compiles statistics on each country's cross-border transactions and publishes a monthly summary of BOP statistics, although it is a common practice for most countries to supply BOP data on an annual basis.

To precisely understand this definition, we first need to be able to identify who is a resident and who is a non-resident. **Resident** is defined to include all economic units domiciled in the reporting country. **Non-resident** is anyone who is not domiciled in the reporting country. It is important to note that citizenship and residency is not necessarily the same thing from the viewpoint of the BOP statistics.

The term residents of a country comprise the general government, individuals, private non-profit bodies serving individuals, and enterprises, all defined in terms of their residential relationship to the territory of that country. Usually, any individual or firm who work or live in a country for more than one year, no matter what nationality they are, would be regarded as the resident of that country. For the purposes of BOP statistics, the subsidiaries of a multinational corporation are treated as being a resident in the country in which they are located even if their shares are actually owned by domestic residents. A foreign student who studies in a domestic school is regarded as the domestic resident.

Some exceptions regarding the resident are international organizations such as the International Monetary Fund, the World Bank, United Nations and so forth. These institutions are treated as being non-residents even though they may actually be located in the reporting country. Foreign embassies and foreign military bases are also in this category. For example, although U.S. embassy in Beijing is located in Beijing, salaries paid by the embassy to the Chinese staffs are included in China's balance of payments because they are regarded as transactions with a non-resident. Tourists are regarded as being non-residents if they stay in the reporting country for less than a year.

The criterion for a transaction to be included in the BOP is that it must involve a transaction between a resident of the reporting country and a non-resident of that country. In other words, the transaction included in BOP should be an international transaction. Purchases and sales between residents from the same country are excluded because those transactions belong to domestic transactions.

Second, BOP reflects **economic and financial flows** which are the international transactions in goods, services and financial assets or liabilities. Each of the following examples is a typical international transaction that is counted and recorded in China's balance of payments.

- A Beijing car dealer imports 50 Porsche Panamera from a German automobile distributor.
- The Chinese subsidiary of a U.S. firm, Hewlett-Packard pays dividends back to its parent firm in California.
- A Chinese tourist purchases a Cannon camera in Tokyo, Japan.
- Chinese charities donate food and clothes to people in drought plagued Africa.
- China National Petroleum issues company stocks in New York Stock Exchange.
- People's Bank of China purchases U.S. Treasury bonds in U.S. capital market.

It should be noted that the BOP just tracks the continuing flows of purchases and payments between a country and the rest of the world, it does not add up the value of all assets and liabilities of a country on a specific date like a balance sheet does for an individual company. Thus, BOP reflects flows of a country's assets and liabilities. Later in this chapter, we will discuss the data that records a country's stock of assets and liabilities — the international investment position.

The balance of payments provides detailed information of the demand and supply of a country's currency. The balance of payments statistics also shows a country's performance in international economic competition. Therefore, the BOP is one of the most important statistical statements for any country. It reveals how many goods and services the country has been exporting and importing and whether the country has been borrowing from or lending money to the rest of the world. In addition, whether or not the central bank has added to or reduced its official reserves is reported in the statement. The BOP data influences and is influenced by other key macroeconomic variables such as gross domestic product, employment levels, price levels, exchange rates, and interest rates. Governments take the data into account at the national level when they are making monetary and fiscal policies. Business managers and investors need the BOP data to anticipate changes in economic policies that might be driven by BOP events. Later in this chapter we'll analyze the relationship between BOP and macroeconomic variables in details.

Balance of Payments Accounting

All trades conducted by both the private and public sectors are accounted for in the BOP in order to determine how many foreign currencies are going in and out of a country. If a country has received foreign currencies, this is known as a credit, and, if a country has paid or given foreign currencies, the transaction is counted as a debit. Theoretically, the BOP should be zero, meaning that assets (credits) and liabilities (debits) should balance. But in practice this is rarely the case and, thus, the BOP can tell the observer if a country has a deficit or a surplus and from which part of the economy the discrepancies are stemming.

In theory, a so-called double-entry bookkeeping system is employed to record all economic and financial flows. A **double-entry bookkeeping system** records both sides of any two-party transaction with two separate and offsetting entries: a debit entry and a credit entry. An international transaction that results in a credit entry would also generate an offsetting debit entry, and a transaction that results in a debit entry would also generate an offsetting credit entry. In other words, every credit (debit) is matched by a debit (credit) somewhere to conform to principle of double-entry bookkeeping system. The result is that the sum of all the debit entries, in absolute value, is equal to the sum of all the credit entries. That is, with everything in, the country' balance of payments always "balances".

A **debit entry** records a transaction that results in a domestic resident making a payment abroad. A debit entry has a negative value in the BOP statistics. A **credit entry** records a transaction that results in a domestic resident receiving a payment from abroad. A credit entry has a positive value in the BOP statistics. An alternative way to determine which items are credits or debits is assuming that all transactions between the residents and non-residents must be conducted with foreign currency, which flows through the foreign exchange market. Thus, a credit transaction on a country's balance of payments corresponds to an inflow, or source, of foreign currency, whereas a debit transaction constitutes an outflow, or use, of foreign currency.

Before considering some examples of how different types of economic transactions between residents and non-residents get recorded in the BOP, we need to consider the various accounts that make up the BOP. The BOP is divided into three main categories: the current account, the capital and financial account and the official reserves account. Each general account is then subdivided into categories such as exports, imports, direct investment, portfolio investment, etc. When necessary, even more detail is available. In *Balance of Payments Statistics*, for example, the IMF regularly publishes member countries' balance of payments data divided into 112 different categories.

Accounts of the Balance of Payments

Current Account

The current account is used to mark the inflow and outflow of goods and services into and out of a country. Earnings on investment such as stocks and bonds (in the form of dividends and interests), both public and private, are also put into the current account. The last component of the current account is unilateral transfers. These are credits that are mostly worker's remittances, which are salaries sent back into the home country of a national working abroad, as well as foreign aid that is directly received. On the other hand, the debit side records the payments made to foreign countries or regions. The current account consists of four subaccounts.

Goods Trade includes raw materials and manufactured goods that are bought, sold or given away (possible in the form of aid). It is also called merchandise trade which represents exports and imports of tangible goods. The value of goods exports is recorded in the credit side (plus sign) of the BOP, and the value of goods imports is recorded in the debit side (minus sign). Combining the exports and imports of goods gives the goods trade balance or **balance of trade** (BOT). The BOT is typically the biggest bulk of a country's BOP as it makes up total imports and exports. When this balance is negative, the result is BOT deficit, meaning the country imports more than exports merchandise. The BOT surplus, on the other hand, means that the country's exports exceed imports.

Services Trade refers to receipts from tourism, transportation (like the levy that must be paid in Egypt when a ship passes through the Suez Canal), engineering, business service fees (from lawyers or management consulting, for example), insurance premium on movable goods during the course of shipment between countries as well as on the carriers themselves and other types of insurance such as life insurance, property insurance, and royalties from patents and copyrights. The services trade is sometimes called invisible trade. The services exports are credit items (an inflow of funds) and services imports are debit items (an outflow of funds). For the major industrial countries, this subaccount has shown the fastest growth in the past three decades.

Investment Income reflects receipts and payments of interest, dividends and profits from investment. This category is called primary income in the United States. This subaccount is mostly composed of income earned by MNCs on their direct foreign investment (investment in fixed assets in foreign countries that can be used to conduct business operations), and also income earned from foreign portfolio investments such as bonds and equities, bank deposits. In addition, wages, salaries paid to employees who work overseas are recorded in this subaccount. Income receipts represent the rewards for foreign investments, while payments reflect the rewards to foreign residents for their investments in the domestic economy. Therefore, income receipts received by domestic residents are credits, whereas income payments made to foreign residents are debits.

Unilateral Transfers are receipts and payments for which there is no corresponding compensation except goodwill in return. This subaccount can be further divided into private and government unilateral transfers. Examples of unilateral transfers are migrant workers' remittances to their families back home as well as gifts, inheritances, and prizes, funds provided by the government to aid in the development of a less-developed country, the payment of pensions to non-residents, contributions to international organizations and so forth. In U.S. BOP statistics, unilateral transfers are called secondary income. Receipts are recorded in credit entry, while payments in debit entry.

This completes the components of the current account. For most countries the current account is dominated by the balance of trade, which is the balance of export and import of merchandise. The BOT is widely quoted in the business press in most countries. For developed countries, the BOT is somewhat misleading, in that service trade is not included.

The following five examples of the current account transactions will show you how BOP accounting works.

Transaction 1: goods export

Suppose a Chinese exporter sells 2,000 T-shirts to a Wal-Mart store in Newark, New Jersey. The price of the T-shirt is $20,000. China's BOP will show a credit or a source of $20,000 of exports.

We mentioned earlier that balance of payments accounting is based on a double-entry bookkeeping system. A credit or source of $20,000 implies a debit or use of an equal amount. Suppose the Wal-Mart store pays for the T-shirt through Citigroup in New York. Now the Chinese exporter has a short-term claim of $20,000 on the Citibank. Expressed in T-accounts China's BOP will look like this:

Goods export		Short-term claims	
Debit(−)	Credit(+)	Debit(−)	Credit(+)
	$20,000	$20,000	

If these transactions were listed without the credit and debit titles, the export of goods would receive a (+), and the capital outflow item would receive a (−). It looks like the following:

Goods export: $20,000
    Short-term claims: −$20,000

Transaction 2: goods import

A Shanghai retailer buys $300,000 worth of laptops from Sony in Japan. The merchandise is billed in U.S. dollars and the retailer pays for the merchandise with a check drawn on Bank of China, Shanghai Branch.

In this case, the computer import represents an increase in China's tangible assets and is a use of foreign exchange. The check drawn by the Chinese retailer on a Shanghai branch of Bank of China represents an increase of short-term liabilities owed by a Chinese resident to a non-resident and is a source of foreign exchange. For China's BOP expressed in T-accounts, this transaction will appear as follows:

Goods import		Short-term liabilities	
Debit(−)	Credit(+)	Debit(−)	Credit(+)
$300,000			$300,000

Or,

Goods import: − $300,000
      Short-term liabilities: $300,000

From Transactions 1 and 2 we can calculate China's trade balance for the period which is equal to:

$$\text{Balance of trade} = \text{Export} - \text{Import} = \$20,000 - \$300,000$$
$$= -\$280,000$$

Transaction 3: travelling expenses (service export)

Mr. Williams, an American, decides to go to China for his three-week vacation. He buys a round trip ticket on China Air Lines for $2,500. His expenses in China for hotels, food, transportation and souvenirs come to the equivalent of $15,000. He pays the ticket in cash with dollars and obtains the RMB equivalent of $15,000 that he spends in China by selling dollars to a Chinese bank.

The $2,500 that Mr. Williams pays China Air Lines will be credited to passenger services in the balance of payments and the $15,000 that he spends in China will be credited to travel for a total of $17,500 of export of services for Chinese economy. On the other hand, China Air Lines increased its cash dollar holdings by $2,500 while the Chinese bank increased its cash dollar holdings by $15,000 for a total increase of $17,500 for Chinese economy. In other words, the service export generates a source of $17,500 worth of foreign exchange. This is offset by an increase of $17,500 worth of cash dollar holdings in the account "short-term claims". For China's BOP expressed in T-accounts, this transaction will appear as follows:

	Service export		Short-term claims
Debit(−)	Credit(+)	Debit(−)	Credit(+)
	$17,500	$17,500	

Or,

    Service export: $17,500

    Short-term claims: − $17,500

Transaction 4: income

Hewlett-Packard in Shanghai, a wholly owned Chinese subsidiary of the HP in California, has after-tax profits of the equivalent of $100,000 and declares a dividend of $50,000. The California headquarter uses the dividend to purchase long-term bonds issued by the Shanghai municipal government.

	Investment income		Direct investment
Debit(−)	Credit(+)	Debit(−)	Credit(+)
$100,000			$50,000

	Portfolio investment
Debit(−)	Credit(+)
	$50,000

Or,

    Investment income: − $100,000

    Direct investment: $50,000

    Portfolio investment: $50,000

As a wholly owned subsidiary, HP Shanghai represents a direct investment for HP California. Therefore, total profits of $100,000 including retained earnings and the declared dividend is counted as investment payment for China's BOP and a use of foreign exchange. Since HP Shanghai declares only half of its profits as dividend, it implies that the company will retain another half. Therefore, the rest $50,000 will be used as reinvestment by HP Shanghai. The non-distributed profits or retained earnings of $50,000 increase HP's direct investment in China. HP California is a U.S. resident enterprise and, hence, Chinese residents' liabilities on non-residents have increased by $50,000. By the same token, the long-term government bonds purchased by HP California with the dividend represent a $50,000 increase in non-resident portfolio investment in China. In T-accounts for China's BOP, these transactions will be recorded as above T-accounts show.

Transaction 5: unilateral transfer

Mr. Wang, who is a Chinese citizen but has been a resident of the United States for several years, transfers $10,000 from his account at a New York branch of Citicorp to his mother's account at Bank of China, Shanghai branch. There is no commercial quid pro quo involved in the operation. Thus, the transaction falls under the heading "immigrant worker's remittance" and represents a unilateral transfer and a source of foreign exchange for Chinese economy. The offsetting use of foreign exchange is an increase in Bank of China's short-term claims to the Citibank. These transactions will be recorded in China's BOP as follows:

Private unilateral transfers		Short-term claims	
Debit(−)	Credit(+)	Debit(−)	Credit(+)
	$10,000	$10,000	

Or,

Unilateral transfers:	$10,000
Short-term claims:	− $10,000

Exhibit 2.1 presents all the information resulting from Transactions 1 through 5. Although we were considering transactions related to the current account, the double-entry system made it necessary to consider transactions related to the capital and financial account as well. As we can see, at the end of Transaction 5 China has a current account deficit of $352,500. This deficit was offset by a $352,500 surplus in the capital and financial account. In fact, because of the double-entry bookkeeping system, the balance of the current and capital and financial accounts will always be equal to zero. The importance of this fact will become clear when we analyze the effects of BOP transactions on other economic and financial variables. We can complete the presentation of BOP accounting by taking a close look at the capital and financial account.

Exhibit 2.1 China's balance of payments after transaction 5

(U.S. dollars)

Current account	
+ Export	20,000
− Import	−300,000
= Trade balance	**= −280,000**
+ Service export	17,500
− Service import	—
+ Investment income (credit)	—

		(Continued)
− Investment income (debit)		− 100,000
+(−) Private unilateral transfers		10,000
+(−) Official unilateral transfers		—
= Current account balance		**− 352,500**
Capital and financial account		
+(−) Direct investment		50,000
+(−) Portfolio investment		50,000
+(−) Other long-term capital		—
+(−) Other short-term capital		252,500
+(−) Net errors and omissions		—
+(−) Change in reserves		—
= Capital and financial account balance		**= 352,500**

Capital and Financial Account

The capital and financial account are where all international capital transfers are recorded. This account was traditionally called the capital account. According to the International Monetary Fund, the **capital account** now refers to the acquisition or disposal of financial and non-financial assets (for example, a physical asset such as land, building or machinery) and non-produced assets, which are needed for production but have not been produced, like a mine used for the extraction of diamonds. Other examples of non-financial assets are patents and trademarks. The sale of patent rights by a domestic firm to a foreign firm is recorded as a credit of the transaction. Conversely, a domestic firm purchases patent rights from a foreign firm is recorded as a debit to the country's capital account. This account has been introduced as a separate component in the IMF's balance of payments only recently.

The **financial account** records the net value of flows of financial assets and similar claims (excluding official reserves flows). The financial account is broken down into three subaccounts, direct investment, portfolio investment and other investment.

Direct investment includes inflows and outflows of direct investment capital such as equity capital, reinvested earnings, and intercompany transactions between affiliated enterprises. If a U.S. company builds a factory in China, this is a foreign direct investment in China. Since the capital flows into our country, the transaction enters the credit side of China's BOP. If a Chinese company purchases a company in another country, the capital flows out of the country, the transaction enters the BOP as a negative cash flow. When residents of one country acquire a controlling interest (stock ownership of 10% or more) in a foreign firm, it is a direct investment. Whenever 10% or more of the voting shares in a Chinese company are held by foreign investors, the company is classified as the Chinese affiliate of a foreign company, and as a foreign direct investment. Similarly, if Chinese investors hold 10% or more of the control in a company outside China, that company is considered the foreign affiliate of a Chinese company.

Portfolio investment is the capital invested in activities that are purely profit-motivated. It includes cross-border transactions associated with long-term debt and equity securities, money market instruments, and derivative instruments. As mentioned in the discussion of investment income, the difference between direct investment and portfolio investment revolves around whether or not the investor intends to take an active role in the management of the enterprise the assets of which are being acquired. In many cases there is no ambiguity. Bonds, debentures and the like are clearly portfolio investment insofar as they confer no management or voting rights on their owners.

Other investment groups all the capital transactions that have not been included in direct investment and portfolio investment. It consists of various short-term and long-term loans, foreign currency deposits, and trade credits. These investments are quite sensitive to both changes in relative interest rates between countries and the anticipated change in the exchange rates. If China's interest rate is higher than other countries' interest rates and the value of RMB is expected to be up, China will experience capital inflows, as investors would like to deposit or invest in China to have higher returns.

The credits and debits of the capital and financial account transactions are like export and import of goods and services. For example, if a non-resident buys a Chinese corporate bond, you can think of this as China "exporting" a Chinese asset (a bond). Thus, the transaction should have the same sign as an export of a regular good. This transaction is therefore a credit entry on the Chinese financial account because it represents an inflow, or source of foreign exchange. In other words, this transaction gives rise to an increase in the supply of foreign currency because the non-resident needs Renminbi to purchase Chinese corporate bond. On the other hand, if a Chinese resident purchases stocks from the New York Stock Exchange, China is importing foreign financial assets. The transaction is then viewed as a debit entry because it represents an outflow, or use, of foreign exchange. Or, put it another way, this transaction gives rise to an increase in the demand for foreign currency — the U.S. dollars in this case.

In Exhibit 2.1, we can see that although there was no net movement in the long-term capital account, there was a surplus of $252,500 in the short-term capital account. In transaction 1, the short-term claims increased when the Chinese exporter extended a $20,000 trade credit to the U.S. importer. In transaction 2, short-term liabilities increased when the Japanese exporter accepted the $300,000 check drawn on the Bank of China. In transaction 3, short-term claims increased when China Air Lines and the Chinese bank accepted a cash of $17,500. In transaction 4, HP Shanghai purchased Chinese financial assets with profits they had earned in Shanghai. This transaction represented a capital inflow and thus an increasing in liability to foreigners. In transaction 5, short-term claims increased when the Bank of China, Shanghai branch accepted the $10,000 sight deposit at the New York branch of Citicorp. The difference shows a surplus of $252,500 in the other short-term capital subaccount.

The following two transactions are examples of financial account transactions.

Transaction 6: direct investment

An affiliate of Volkswagen (VW) in China has net profit of $250,000. The VW headquarter decides to reinvest it.

The VW affiliate in China is a resident of China, but the VW headquarter is the non-resident. When VW does not take the profit and reinvest it, it makes the direct investment to China. This is the example of retained earnings which are regarded as a direct investment. The foreign direct investment in China should be recorded on the credit side of capital and financial account in China's balance of payments statistics. The offsetting use of foreign exchange reflects in the investment income subaccount of the current account which is the payment China should make to the VW headquarter in Germany. Thus, it is a debit entry.

Direct investment		Investment income	
Debit(−)	Credit(+)	Debit(−)	Credit(+)
	$250,000	$250,000	

Or,

    Direct investment: $250,000
    Investment income: − $250,000

Transaction 7: portfolio investment

A Chinese investor buys $50,000 Dell computer's stock. He pays for the stocks with his bank deposits in New York Bank. The Chinese investor thus imports foreign assets. The transaction represents the capital outflows out of China or use of foreign currency. This is a Chinese portfolio investment to the U.S. For China's BOP, it will be recorded as follows:

Portfolio investment		Short-term liabilities	
Debit(−)	Credit(+)	Debit(−)	Credit(+)
$50,000			$50,000

Or,

    Portfolio investment: − $50,000
    Short-term liabilities: $50,000

Official Reserves Account

A key element in international economic and financial analysis is the amount of international liquidity or "reserves" held by the central authority of individual countries. If a country's payments to the rest of the world exceed receipts from the rest of the world, the country's central bank should either run down its official reserve assets, or borrow reserve assets from some foreign countries. Thus, **official reserves** are financial assets that could be used to settle international debts and claims. It includes monetary gold, special drawing rights (SDRs), the reserve position in the Fund and foreign exchanges.

Monetary gold is gold held by the authorities as a financial asset. Monetary gold was the major official reserve asset, but it is now little used in official reserve transactions. **SDRs** are reserves created by the IMF as bookkeeping entries and credited to the accounts of IMF member countries according to their established IMF quotas. They may be used in the settlement of balance of payments imbalances among countries participating in the Special Drawing Account administered by the IMF. More will be said about SDRs and IMF when we introduce the international monetary system. The **reserve position in the Fund** is basically the difference between the member's quota plus other claims on the Fund less the Fund's holdings of that member's currency. **Foreign exchanges** are major currencies used in international trade and financial transactions, and by far the largest component of total international liquidity. It includes monetary authorities' claims on non-residents in the form of bank deposits, treasury bills, short-term and long-term government securities, and other claims usable in the event of balance of payments need, including non-marketable claims arising from inter-central bank inter-governmental arrangements, without regard to whether the claim is denominated in the currency of the debtors or the creditors.

This account differs from the other accounts in the balance of payments insofar as it is the only account that records transactions with residents as well as non-residents. It also should be noticed that the rules for determining credits and debits are identical to the rules that govern the private sector's capital and financial account. If the central bank acquires international reserves, a debit is entered on the official reserves account, just as it is recorded on the private capital account if private residents acquire foreign assets. Once again, this debit receives a (−) in a presentation of the BOP that just lists items even though the reserves of the central bank are increasing. If, on the other hand, the central bank draws down its international reserves, there is a credit on the official reserves account, just as there is on the private capital account if private residents sell their foreign assets. In this case, the transaction would be recorded with a (+) even though the central bank's reserves are declining.

Let's take two examples to show how official reserves transactions are recorded.

Transaction 8: reserves transaction

The People's Bank of China pays $1 million to buy U.S. Treasury bonds from the Federal Reserve Bank, U.S. central bank.

The People's Bank of China is the central bank so the transaction must be recorded in the official reserves account. The PBOC increases its claims on non-residents by $1 million through the reduction of its official reserves. The decrease in reserve assets is recorded in the credit side. It is worth taking some time to think about this operation because our experience has been that, based on intuition, the contrary would seem to be true. The corresponding use of foreign exchange reserves comes about through the possession of U.S. government bonds, which is China's portfolio investment in U.S. The following T-accounts record this transaction:

Change in reserves		Portfolio investment	
Debit(−)	Credit(+)	Debit(−)	Credit(+)
	$1,000,000	$1,000,000	

Or,

  Change in reserves: $1,000,000
    Portfolio investment: − $1,000,000

The following transaction involves the central bank with a domestic resident. The reason that this transaction should be recorded in BOP is because the result of this transaction changes the official reserves position of PBOC.

Transaction 9: reserves transaction with a resident

Bank of Communication sells $800,000 to the PBOC for RMB. In this transaction the PBOC acquires international reserves, so there is a debit on the official reserves account. The corresponding source of foreign exchange reserves comes about through the disposal of claims on non-residents by Bank of Communication. This transaction is recorded as follows:

Change in reserves		Short-term claims	
Debit(−)	Credit(+)	Debit(−)	Credit(+)
$800,000			$800,000

Or,

  Change in reserves: − $800,000
    Short-term claims: $800,000

Exhibit 2.2 summarized China's balance of payments after the conclusion of Transaction 9. The current account has not changed. It is still in deficit by $352,500. The capital and financial account has changed. The direct investment subaccount has increased by $250,000. The portfolio investment subaccount has moved from a surplus of $50,000 to a deficit of $1 million due to the purchase of U.S. government bonds by PBOC. The short-term capital subaccount balance now is $852,500. The official reserves account has gone from zero to a deficit of $200,000 due to the reduction in foreign exchange holdings. When it comes to analyzing a country's external position, it is important to look at the individual accounts to see how the balance between the current and the capital and financial accounts is achieved.

Exhibit 2.2 China's Balance of Payments after Transaction 9

(U.S. dollars)

Current account	
+ Export	20,000
− Import	−300,000
= *Trade balance*	−280,000
+ Service export	17,500
− Service import	—
+ Investment income (credit)	—
− Investment income (debit)	−100,000
+(−) Private unilateral transfers	10,000
+(−) Official unilateral transfers	—
= **Current account balance**	**−352,500**
Capital and financial account	
− Direct investment	—
+ Direct investment	300,000
+(−) Portfolio investment	−1,000,000
+(−) Other long-term capital	—
+(−) Other short-term capital	852,500
+(−) Net errors and omissions	—
= **Capital and financial account balance**	**152,500**
Official settlements account	
+(−) Change in reserves	+200,000
= **Official settlements balance**	**+200,000**

Net Errors and Omissions

The double-entry bookkeeping system is employed in theory, but not in practices. In reality, there is not a system available whereby officials can simultaneously record the credit side and debit side of each transaction. Government statisticians base their figures partly on information collected and estimates. Current and financial entries are collected and recorded separately. Thus, there will be serious discrepancies between debits and credits.

Officials collect information from multiple sources that vary in coverage and reliability. For example, merchandise trade figures are derived from customs records and freight charges from reports by shipping organizations. They are probably the most reliable information. Service transactions such as the consulting fees can easily escape detection. Capital and financial account information is derived from reports by financial institutions indicating changes in their liabilities and claims to foreigners; these data are not matched with specific current account transactions. Short-term capital movements are particularly difficult to track, especially when there is intent to evade exchange controls, taxes and other restrictions. Capital movements may also lead or lag the transactions they are meant to finance. For example, an export shipped in the month of November or December may not be paid for until January or February of the following year.

For those reasons, the balance of payments always presents a "balancing" debt or credit as net errors and omissions. The net errors and omissions account ensures that the BOP actually balances because it offsets the cumulated net difference in the other accounts.

This account usually appears after the capital and financial account statistics.

Surpluses and Deficits in the Balance of Payments Accounts

The Concept of Basic Balance

Exhibit 2.3 is a simplified version of U.S. balance of payments (The BEA named it U.S. International Transactions) in 2019. The Bureau of Economic Analysis (BEA) under the U.S. Department of Commerce reports the BOP statistics each quarter during the year. We selected major items from the BEA complete version when we compiled this simplified version. It should be pointed out that the present U.S. balance of payments includes just two main accounts: the current account and the capital and financial account. The official reserves account is just a subaccount of the financial account. In order to make it consistent with our introduction of the BOP accounts, we separate the official reserves account from the financial account.

If we add up all the account balances in Exhibit 2.3, we'll see the result is zero. That is: the sum of the current account balance of − $480,226 million + the capital and financial account balance of $393,963 million + statistical discrepancy of $90,921 million + official reserves balance of $4,659 million equals to zero. BOP always balances since each credit in the account has a corresponding debit elsewhere. So what does BOP deficit or surplus mean?

However, while the overall BOP always balances this does not mean that each of the individual accounts that make up the BOP is necessarily in balance. For instance, the current account of the 2019 U.S. balance of payments was in deficit of − $480,226 million; the capital and financial account had a surplus of $393,963 million. Since there were errors and omissions when the data was collected, we add this figure ($90,921 million) to the capital and financial account. We have total of $484,884 million (− $480,226 million + $393,963 million + $90,921 million) which is on the credit side. It means that the money inflows from the rest of the world were more than money outflows in the U.S. Therefore, we can conclude that the U.S. ran BOP surplus in 2019.

Exhibit 2.3   U.S. International Transactions, 2019

(millions of dollars)

Current account	
(1) Exports of goods and services	2,528,262
(1.1) Goods	1,652,437
(1.2) Services	875,825
(2) Imports of goods and services	−3,105,127
(2.1) Goods	−2,516,767
(2.2) Services	−588,359
(3) Primary income receipts	1,135,691
(3.1) Investment income	1,128,966
(3.2) Compensation of employees	6,725
(4) Primary income payments	−899,347
(4.1) Investment income	−880,562
(4.2) Compensation of employees	−18,785
(5) Secondary income (current transfer) receipts	141,984
(6) Secondary income (current transfer) payments	−281,689
Balance on Current account	**−480,226**
(1) + (2) + (3) + (4) + (5) + (6)	
Capital and financial account	
(7) Capital account transaction, net	−6,244
(8) Financial account	
(8.1) Direct investment assets	−188,469
(8.2) Direct investment liabilities	351,629
(8.3) Portfolio investment assets	−46,570
(8.4) Portfolio investment liabilities	179,980
(8.5) Other investment assets	−201,053
(8.6) Other investment liabilities	266,350
(8.7) Financial derivatives other than reserves, net	38,340
Balance on capital and financial account	**393,963**
(7) + (8)	
(9) Statistical discrepancy	90,921
Official reserves account	
(10) Reserve assets	−4,659
Balance on Official reserves account	**−4,659**
Basic balance	4,659
(1) + (2) + (3) + (4) + (5) + (6) + (7) + (8) + (9)	

Source: Bureau of Economic Analysis, U.S. Department of Commerce, "U.S. International Transactions, 2019 and 2020", news release, December 2020.

This particular example shows that there are two equivalent ways to judge the BOP deficit or surplus. The first is the so-called **"basic balance"** which is sum of the two accounts, the current account and the capital and financial account. In practice, since there are omissions and errors in collecting the data, the statistic discrepancy should be included in the basic balance.

If the basic balance equals zero, the BOP balances; if it is greater than zero, the BOP is in surplus; if it is less than zero, it is in deficit. That is:

Current account + Capital and financial account + discrepancy = 0 (BOP balances)
Current account + Capital and financial account + discrepancy > 0 (BOP surplus)
Current account + Capital and financial account + discrepancy < 0 (BOP deficit)

The basic balance of the BOP of U.S. in 2019 was $4,658 million (− $480,226 million + $393,963 million) plus statistical discrepancy of $90.921 billion. Therefore, U.S ran BOP surplus in 2019 because the basic balance shows a positive number.

The alternative way to judge the BOP deficit or surplus is to observe the changes in a country's official reserves. If a country increases its official reserves during the reporting period, the country runs the BOP surplus and vice versa. As can be seen from the above table, the official reserves account is a debit entry of $4,659 million showing the increase of official reserves which exactly matches the basic balance. Thus, U.S. had a BOP surplus in 2019. This way shows an important balance of payments identity:

Current account + Capital and financial account + Official reserves account= 0

BOP deficit implies that the country's receipts from the rest of the world are less than the payments made to the rest of the world. The country may reduce its official reserves or borrow from the rest of the world. On the other hand, **BOP surplus** indicates a country can earn more foreign currencies than spend them or the country's receipts from the rest of the world exceed its payments to the rest of the world. The surplus nation may either finance the rest of the world or increase its official reserves. Next, we are going to discuss some individual accounts in the balance of payments.

Balance of Several Key Subaccounts

Balance of trade

Balance of trade or **trade balance** measures a country's merchandise exports and imports. If a nation exports more than imports, the nation runs surplus in its trade balance; if a nation exports less than imports, the nation runs deficit in its trade balance. In 2019, U.S. exported $1,652,437 million of goods and imported $3,105,127 million of goods, we say the United States had a $1,452,690 million trade balance deficit in 2019.

Balance of current Account

A **current account surplus** means that the country as a whole is increasing its stock of claims on the rest of the world; while a **current account deficit** means that the country is reducing its net claims on the rest of the world. Exhibit 2.3 indicates that the 2019 U.S. current account balance was − $480,226 million, which is a current account deficit.

The trade balance and current account balance derive much of their importance because estimates are published on a monthly basis by most developed countries. Later in this book we will see the current account can readily be incorporated into economic analysis of an open economy. More generally, the current account is likely to quickly pick up changes in other economic variables such as changes in the real exchange rate, domestic and foreign economic growth and relative price inflation.

Balance of capital and financial account

A **capital and financial account surplus** implies that the country has net capital inflows. The 2019 U.S. capital and financial account was a surplus of $393,963 million. There are two reasons that a country may have capital inflows. One is that nation probably has current account deficit, it must borrow from abroad to finance its current consumption. However, the burden of repaying the borrowed funds may reduce the nation's future prosperity. Another reason is that foreign investors may think the country's economic environment is good for investment. That kind of capital inflows is good for the country. The United States has generally run a large current account deficit because of the deficit in trade balance. However, since the U.S. is considered as a safe haven economy, i.e., a nation with little political risk, large inflows of foreign investments create a surplus in the capital and financial account of the U.S. BOP.

A **capital and financial account deficit** means that the reporting country has a net capital outflows. In this case, the country may have current account surplus. It will increase its international investment position and accumulate its foreign assets. For example, Japan has generally had a large current account surplus because of large merchandise trade surplus. However, the trade surplus is used to invest in foreign countries in plant and equipment, real estate, and other investments. Thus, Japan's capital account may run a large deficit.

The errors and omissions

Exhibit 2.3 shows that in 2019, the value of the U.S. current account was − $480,226 million, and the value of capital and financial account was $393,963 million. Hence, the sum of the two accounts is − $86,263 million. However, we explained that because of the double-entry system, the sum of the current account and the capital and financial account should be zero because capital must flow into a country if it has a current account deficit. Why was there the statistical discrepancy in 2019? The fact is that the government misses some transactions, and it estimates other transactions.

The United Sates was missing $90,921 million of credits in 2019. These credits are probably capital account transactions such as unmeasured U.S. sales of foreign assets and unmeasured purchases of U.S. assets by foreign residents, although freer trade and the emergence of the Internet have increased the difficulty that governments face in accurately measuring international trade.

Balance of official reserves account

Balance of official reserves account measures changes in the official stock of international reserve assets. The **official reserves account deficit** indicates that official reserves increase. U.S. increased its official reserves by $4,659 million in 2019 as Exhibit 2.3 indicates. On the other hand, the **official reserves account surplus** means a country's official reserves declines.

This account plays a critical role if a country adopts fixed exchange rate system, which we'll discuss in detail in Chapter 4. To fix the exchange rate, the central bank must be prepared to buy and sell its domestic currency with its stock of international reserves. If the central bank depletes its stocks of official reserves, the central bank will not be able to maintain the fixed exchange rate, and the country will be forced to devalue its currency.

International Investment Position

The capital and financial account balance is sometimes confused with the balance of international investment position. At any particular moment, a country will have a fixed stock of assets and liabilities against the rest of the world. The statistics that summarize this situation is known as the balance of international investment position or sometimes refers to international indebtedness. **International investment position** records a country's foreign assets and foreign liabilities at a point in time (usually the end of an accounting year). The capital and financial account balance, on the other hand, reflects the flows of assets and liabilities of the reporting country with the rest of the world within a period of time. Flows change stocks, and so it is with the balance of payments and the international investment position.

If a country has a current account surplus for the year, the country increases its foreign assets (or decreases its foreign liabilities). The value of its international investment position at the end of that year will be more positive (or less negative) than it was at the beginning of the year.

If the stock of a country's foreign financial assets is more than the stock of foreign-owned domestic financial assets, the nation is called a **net creditor**; if a nation's foreign financial asset stocks are less than stocks of foreign-owned domestic financial assets, the nation is called a **net debtor**. Exhibit 2.4 and Exhibit 2.5 list the top ten net creditors and net debtors from 2015 to 2019 in the world.

Chapter 2   THE BALANCE OF PAYMENTS

Exhibit 2.4   Net International Investment Position (Surplus), Top Ten Economies

(billions of U.S. dollars)

	2015	2016	2017	2018	2019
Japan	2,715.2	2,879.2	2,916.6	3,080.4	3,339.3
Germany	1,535.1	1,696.8	2,205.8	2,435.5	2,777.0
China	1,672.8	1,950.4	2,100.7	2,146.4	2,124.0
Hong Kong	1,003.1	1,153.8	1,421.2	1,282.5	1,563.1
Norway	698.5	736.0	883.3	801.6	993.0
Singapore	647.1	754.1	867.2	769.9	896.0
Switzerland	650.4	813.3	866.9	889.4	838.7
Saudi Arabia	689.8	597.3	623.6	657.6	671.1
Canada	323.2	304.0	586.8	564.5	774.6
Netherlands	367.6	457.2	529.8	636.8	819.2

Source: International Monetary Fund, December, 2020, www.data.imf.org.

As shown in Exhibit 2.4, Japan has most foreign claims than any countries have in 2019. This implies that Japan may have a positive investment income account. It also means that Japan could have a trade balance deficit while still having a balanced current account. In other words, Japan could import more goods and services from abroad than it exports out of the country without incurring foreign debt or selling assets to foreigners because it has a surplus on its investment income account.

Exhibit 2.5   Net International Investment Position (Deficit), Top Ten Economies

(billions of U.S. dollars)

	2015	2016	2017	2018	2019
United States	−7,460.2	−8,129.3	−7,622.2	−9,674.4	−11,050.5
Spain	−1,043.1	−1,003.3	−1,182.6	−1,092.0	−1,033.7
Brazil	−374.7	−566.6	−645.2	−595.4	−731.2
Ireland	−573.2	−496.9	−596.0	−677.5	−696.3
Australia	−673.7	−702.2	−771.2	−724.9	−655.1
Mexico	−529.1	−486.1	−553.1	−583.8	−647.9

(Continued)

	2015	2016	2017	2018	2019
Euro Area	−1,463.4	−987.7	−1,052.2	−545.4	−633.1
France	−309.4	−306.3	−554.2	−509.1	−625.3
India	−368.4	−367.3	−426.7	−433.7	−430.2
Turkey	−383.2	−367.6	−461.8	−369.5	−345.6

Source: International Monetary Fund, December, 2020, www.data.imf.org.

The United States was a net creditor before 1986. After that, it turned out to be a net debtor because of the large current account deficits. As Exhibit 2.5 shows, the U.S. net debts at the end of 2019 were more than $11 trillion. The persistent deficits in current account required U.S. to finance by increasing international borrowing.

The term net creditor and net debtor in themselves are not particularly meaningful. We need additional information about the specific types of claims and liabilities involved. The balance of international investment position therefore looks at the short and long-term investment positions of both the private and government sectors of the economy.

Of what use is the balance of international investment position? Perhaps of greatest significance is that it breaks down international investment holdings into several categories so that policy implications can be drawn from each separate category about the liquidity status of the nation. For the short-term investment position, the strategic factor is the amount of short-term liabilities (bank deposits and government securities) held by foreigners. This is because these holdings potentially can be withdrawn at very short notice, resulting in a disruption of domestic financial markets. The balance of official monetary holdings is also significant. Assume that this balance is negative from the U.S. viewpoint. Should foreign monetary authorities decide to liquidate their holdings of U.S. government securities and have them converted into official reserve assets, the financial strength of the dollar would be reduced. As for a nation's long-term investment position, it is of less importance for the U.S. liquidity position because long-term investments generally respond to basic economic trends and are not subject to erratic withdrawals.

The Current Account and the Macroeconomics

A country's balance of payments affects and is effected by nearly all of its key macroeconomic variables. One of them is the gross domestic product (GDP). As we know, an economy's consumption and investment of resources cannot be greater than the resources that it produces plus the resources that it borrows. It therefore implies that the entire BOP of a single nation is and must be always balanced. If a country's BOP is in disequilibrium, it actually means the country's basic balance is imbalanced. Now we

Chapter 2   THE BALANCE OF PAYMENTS

explore how current account surpluses and deficits are linked to national income, the saving and spending patterns of a country, including its government.

The Current Account and the Net Foreign Investment

The main categories of the current account are exports and imports of goods and services plus the investment income. If a country can produce more than it spends, the country possibly has current account surplus. When a country has current account surplus, it earns extra assets or reduces liabilities in its dealings with the rest of the world. Since the BOP must balance, the surplus country can either increase its official reserves or finance the rest of the world. In other words, the surplus country increases its foreign investment in the rest of the world.

If a country runs current account deficit, the country may produce less than it spend. To finance the deficit, it must pay by giving up assets or increasing its liabilities. In this case, the country reduces foreign investment or the foreign countries increase their investments in the deficit country.

If we define the **net foreign investment** (I_f) as the difference between a country's owned foreign assets and foreign liabilities, the current account could be regarded as the net foreign investment. That is:

$$CA = I_f \qquad (2.1)$$

where

CA: a country's current account balance

I_f: a country's net foreign investment

If **Equation 2.1** is negative, it indicates that the reporting country's foreign liabilities exceed its assets abroad during the reporting period because of the current account deficit. If it is positive, the country's total investment abroad is greater than foreign investment in the reporting country because of the current account surplus.

The Current Account and the National Saving (Investment)

In macroeconomics, the investment is linked to national saving. Since the current account balance is related to the foreign investment, it is also related to the national saving. The national saving can be used for either domestic investment (I_d) or foreign investment (I_f). As we know, one of the equilibrium conditions for a nation's economy is that national saving equals investment. It is expressed algebraically as:

$$S = I_d + I_f, \text{ or equivalently,}$$
$$I_f = S - I_d \qquad (2.2)$$

Substitute **Equation 2.2** for Equation 2.1 in I_f,

$$CA = S - I_d \qquad (2.3)$$

where

S: national saving

I_d: domestic investment

In other words, the country's current account balance equals national saving that is not invested at home. The current account surplus means that the national saving exceeds domestic investment; the extra saving then looks for other places to invest. The current account deficit means that domestic saving is not enough for domestic investment; the domestic economic entity must borrow from the rest of the world to meet its investment need.

The Chinese economy has experienced tremendous growth since the early 1980's. The current account of China's BOP had accumulated huge surplus during the period. One of the reasons for the huge current account surplus was China's high savings rate relative to domestic real investment rate. The current account surplus is also the most important reason for China's astonishing increase in foreign exchange reserve which have already surpassed 3 trillion U.S. dollars.

On the other hand, the perennial U.S. current account deficit resulted from the low domestic saving and high domestic real investment. U.S. then relied on foreign funds to eliminate the deficit. Some countries including China have been running large trade surpluses with the United States but reinvesting these funds in U.S. securities so U.S. had equally large surplus in the capital and financial account.

The Current Account and the National Income

The current account is also linked to national income identity in macroeconomics. The equilibrium condition for a nation's economy is that its total income equals total output. The total output is distributed to the following groups:

$$Y = C + I_d + G + X - M \qquad (2.4)$$

Where

Y: total output of goods and services

C: domestic consumption

I_d: domestic investment

G: domestic government spending

X: export

M: import

Since the export and import of goods and services dominate the current account in most countries, (X − M) represents the current account (CA). Rearranging **Equation 2.4** we get:

$$CA = Y - (C + I_d + G) \tag{2.5}$$

Here, Y is the total output of goods and services; $(C + I_d + G)$ represents the country's total expenditure. Therefore, a country's current account balance is the difference between its domestic production of goods and services and its total expenditures on goods and services.

An important aspect of this identity is that the current account balance is a macroeconomic phenomenon. It reflects imbalances between the total output and total expenditure. BOP surplus means that a country's total output is greater than its total expenditure; while BOP deficit indicates that a country's total output is less than its total expenditure. The country thus needs to import from the rest of the world to satisfy its extra spending. It is obvious that deficit country has to cut its expenditure or increase its total output to overcome the BOP deficit. This is a very important theory of the BOP adjustment and exchange rate determination. We'll examine this theory in detail in Chapter 8.

From equation 2.1, 2.3 and 2.5 we can conclude our analysis as follows:

Current account balance (CA)
= Net foreign investment (I_f)
= The difference between national saving and domestic investment ($S - I_d$)
= The difference between domestic product and national expenditure ($Y - E$)

We can use those identities to explain why a nation runs current account deficit or surplus. Assume a country has surplus in its current account balance. First, the country has an excess of exports over imports, services, investment income, and unilateral transfers. The country's net foreign investment is positive which means the country is acting as a net creditor to or investor in the rest of the world. Second, the country is saving more than it is investing domestically. The country becomes a net supplier of funds to the rest of the world. Third, the country is producing more (and has more income from its production) than it is spending on goods and services. It is able to export more goods and services to the rest of the world.

The opposite is true for a country with a current account deficit: the deficit country is a net foreign borrower; its domestic saving less than domestic investment, and the country with BOP deficit is spending more than production (or income).

The Economic Relationship between Current Account and Financial Account

We have already known from the previous discussion that the current account transactions are usually linked to capital flows. The basic economic and accounting relationship of the BOP is the inverse relation between the current and financial accounts. This is because according to double-entry bookkeeping system, the current account and financial account should be offsetting. Countries with large current account deficit are "financed" through equally large surplus in the financial account, and vice versa. Now we reexamine the relationship of the current account balance and financial account balance from the perspective of national income identity.

National income has three possible uses; it can be spent on current consumption, it can be saved (private savings), and we pay taxes to the government.

$$Y = C + S + T \tag{2.6}$$

where

Y: national income

C: consumption

S: savings

T: taxes

From the previous discussion, national income equals to the total output, or GDP (**Equation 2.4**), therefore,

$$C + S + T = C + I_d + G + CA, \text{ or}$$
$$CA = S - I_d - (G - T) \tag{2.7}$$

Now let's examine the national savings (S) which can be used for different ways. First, national savings can be used to invest domestically (I_d). Individuals buy domestic securities such as company bonds, stocks and other financial or non-financial products. Firms purchase investment goods to produce consumption goods. Second, individuals or enterprises use their savings to purchase government bonds which represent the government debts ($G - T > 0$). Third, national savings can also be used to buy foreign securities and assets (I_f) which are categorized as foreign investment. Therefore,

$$S = I_d + (G - T) + I_f \tag{2.8}$$

where

I_d: domestic investment

(G − T): government debt is more than tax income (government debt)

I_f: the net foreign investment (domestic residents' purchases of foreign assets in excess of foreign residents' purchases of domestic assets).

Then, by rearrangement **Equation 2.8**, we get:

$$I_f = S - I_d - (G - T)$$

We know that the net foreign investment (I_f) equals current account balance (CA). So,

$$CA = I_f = S - I_d - (G - T) \tag{2.9}$$

In other words, national savings less domestic investment and less the fiscal balance (government debt) equals the current account balance, which also equals the net foreign investment.

Suppose a nation's private saving rate is 5.2 percent of its total output, its private investment rate is 7.3 percent, and its fiscal budget deficit is 3.3 percent, what is the nation's current account balance and what should the nation do to balance its current account?

Applying **Equation 2.9**, we get the current account balance

$$CA = I_f = 5.2\% - 7.3\% - 3.3\% = -5.4\%.$$

In words, this nation's residents must borrow from abroad ($I_f = -5.4$ % of its GDP) to finance their investment expenditures and government debts, resulting in a current account deficit in the amount of 5.4 percent of total output.

Summary

1. The balance of payments is the record of the economic and financial flows that take place over a specified time period between residents and non-residents of a given country.
2. A BOP transaction is an international transaction, that is, the transaction occurs between a resident and a non-resident. A resident is defined as an economic unit (individual, households, firms and the public authorities, etc.) domiciled in the reporting country. It is important to note that citizenship and residency are not necessarily the same thing from the viewpoint of the BOP statistics.
3. Balance of payments accounting is based on the double-entry bookkeeping system which records both sides of any two-party transaction with two separate and offsetting entries: a debit entry and a credit entry.
4. A debit entry records those transactions that result in a domestic resident making a (foreign currency) payment abroad. A credit entry, on the other hand, records the transactions that result in a domestic resident receiving a (foreign currency) payment from foreign residents.
5. Put it another way, determining which items are credits or debits is assuming that all transactions between the residents and non-residents must be conducted with foreign currency, which flows through the foreign exchange market. Thus, a credit transaction on a country's balance of payments corresponds to an inflow, or source, of foreign currency, whereas a debit transaction constitutes an outflow, or use, of foreign currency.
6. The main accounts in the balance of payments are current account, capital and financial account and official reserves account. The current account includes export

and import of goods and services, investment income and unilateral transfers. The capital and financial account includes capital account, direct investment, portfolio investment and other long-term and short-term capital movements. The official reserves account shows the changes in official reserves. The errors and omissions account captures the unreported or omitted transactions. This account ensures that the BOP always balances.

7. The basic balance measures whether a country's balance of payments has achieved balance or not. It is the sum of current account and capital and financial account. If it equals zero, the BOP balances; if it is negative, the BOP is in deficit; if it is positive, the BOP is in surplus. Keep in mind that the basic balance also includes the statistical discrepancy, because we assume that the discrepancy results from mismeasurement of private transactions.
8. The alternative measure is the official reserves account. If there are no changes in a country's official reserves within a period of time, the country's BOP balances in that period of time. If a country increases its official reserves, the country is said to have BOP surplus; or if a country decreases its official reserves, the country runs BOP deficit.
9. Increase in official reserves must be recorded as a debit entry and decrease in official reserves must be recorded as a credit entry.
10. The official reserves account is the only account that records transactions with residents as well as non-residents. Any transactions, whether it occurs between residents and non-residents, or residents and residents, will be recorded on official reserves account as long as the transaction changes the country's official reserves level.
11. If the sum of the credits on a particular account is greater than the sum of the debits on that account, the account is said to be in surplus. If the sum of the debits on a particular account is greater than credits on that account, the account is said to be in deficit.
12. Because many balance of payments entries are estimated, the sum of the current account and the capital and financial account does not always equal zero as it should in a double-entry system. If the sum of the current account and capital and financial account is not zero, statisticians add a balancing item equal to the sum of all the measured items with sign reversed. This term is called the errors and omissions or statistical discrepancy.
13. The balance of payments of a country changes the country's international investment position which refers to the stocks of a country's international assets and liabilities at a point in time. It is also called international indebtedness.
14. A country's international investment position is changed every year by the flows of private and official funds measured in the balance of payments.

15. If the stock of a country's foreign financial assets is more than the stock of foreign-owned domestic financial assets, the nation is called a net creditor; if a nation's foreign financial asset stocks are less than stocks of foreign-owned domestic financial assets, the nation is called a net debtor. The United States has switched from being the world's largest net creditor to being the largest net debtor since the middle of 1980s.
16. When a country has a current account surplus, it has positive net foreign investment (that is, the country is acting as a net lender to or investor in the rest of the world); or, it is saving more than it is investing domestically; or, it is producing more (and has more income from its production) than it is spending on goods and services.
17. If a country runs current account deficit, the country is a net foreign borrower; or its domestic saving is less than domestic investment; or it is spending more than production (income).
18. The current account transactions are usually linked to capital flows. The basic economic and accounting relationship of the BOP is the inverse relation between the current and financial accounts, meaning if the current account has surplus, the capital and financial account has deficit and vice versa.
19. A country's domestic saving is linked to the country's current account through the following identity: $CA = S - I_d - (G - T) = I_f$. It means that the current account has a surplus only if the domestic investment plus the government debt do not exceed the domestic saving. Otherwise, the current account will be in deficit.

Key Concepts and Terms

1. Balance of payments (BOP)   国际收支
2. Balance of payments deficit   国际收支逆差
3. Balance of payments surplus   国际收支顺差
4. Balance of trade (BOT)   贸易差额
5. Basic balance   基本差额
6. Capital and financial account   资本与金融账户
7. Capital and financial account deficit   资本与金融账户逆差
8. Capital and financial account surplus   资本与金融账户顺差
9. Credit entry   贷方
10. Current account   经常账户
11. Current account deficit   经常账户逆差
12. Current account surplus   经常账户顺差
13. Debit entry   借方

14. Double-entry bookkeeping system 复式记账法
15. Direct investment 直接投资
16. Economic and financial flows 经济与金融流量
17. Errors and omissions 错误与遗漏
18. Goods trade 商品贸易
19. International investment position 国际投资头寸
    (International indebtedness)
20. Investment income 投资收入
21. Net creditor 净债权人
22. Net debtor 净债务人
23. Net foreign investment 国外投资净值
24. Official reserves 官方储备
25. Official reserves account 官方储备账户
26. Official reserves account deficit 官方储备账户逆差
27. Official reserves account surplus 官方储备账户顺差
28. Portfolio investment 证券投资，间接投资
29. Reserve position in the Fund 普通提款权，指国际货币基金组织的成员国存放于该组织的储备头寸，用于临时性应付国际收支逆差
30. Residents and non-residents 居民与非居民
31. Service trade 劳务交易
32. Special drawing rights (SDRs) 特别提款权
33. Statistical discrepancy 统计误差
34. Unilateral transfer 单方转移

Questions

1. What is balance of payments and what is balance of trade?
2. Distinguish the resident and non-resident. Indicate its importance in terms of BOP.
3. Explain the economic and financial flows recorded in a country's BOP.
4. What are the two main types of economic activity measured by a country's BOP?
5. What are the main component accounts of the current account? Give one debit and one credit example for each component account for the European Union.
6. Which items on the balance of payments are recorded as credits, and which items are recorded as debits? Why?
7. What is the difference between a direct foreign investment and a portfolio foreign investment? Which type of investment is a multinational industrial company more

likely to make?
8. What financial assets are categorized as official reserves?
9. What is the meaning of an account labeled "errors and omissions"? If this account is a credit, what does it imply about the measurement of other items in the balance of payments?
10. Explain the meaning of BOP surplus and deficit.
11. How can you know that a country runs BOP deficit from its official reserves account?
12. If the domestic monetary authority purchases gold from a domestic financial institution, how should this transaction be recorded and why?
13. Why does the BOP always balance?
14. What are the effects of each of the following on China's international investment position?
    a. Foreign central banks increase their official holdings of Chinese government securities.
    b. Chinese residents increase their holdings of the stocks issued by British companies.
    c. A Japanese pension funds sells some of its holdings of the stocks of Chinese companies in order to buy Chinese corporate bonds.
15. What is international investment position? What is the difference between international investment position and BOP?
16. If a country is a net debtor, will its investment income subaccount of the current account have surplus or deficit? Why?
17. If a country's domestic saving exceeds domestic investment, will the country run BOP deficit or surplus?
18. What does the current account surplus mean to Chinese economy?
19. Why is the U.S. government concerned the U.S. current account deficit?
20. How is the current account linked to capital and financial account?

Chapter 3
THE FOREIGN EXCHANGE MARKET

LEARNING OBJECTIVES

- Understand the basics of foreign exchange market, including the organization and function of the market, its size, characteristics and structure, the participants of this market, and the electronic foreign exchange trading.
- Examine in detail the spot transaction and the spot market, the different forms of foreign exchange quotations.
- Analyze the cross exchange rates and the opportunities arising from interbank arbitrage, especially the triangular arbitrage.
- Introduce the terms used to discuss movements in exchange rates.
- Discuss the forward market, forward quotes, and the calculation of the forward premiums.
- Study the risk exposure in international trade and investment and the need for forward exchange market.
- Examine various exchange rate definitions and their economic significance, particularly the nominal, real and effective exchange rate.

Whether you are a Chinese exporter selling souvenirs to a U.S. supermarket for dollars or a U.S. mutual fund investing in Japanese stocks, you will need find a way to exchange foreign currency into your own currency and vice versa. The foreign exchange is described as the life blood of international trade and investment. Most international financial transactions sooner or later involve an exchange of one currency for another. This is why the exchange rate and exchange rate determination play such an important role in international financial theory. This chapter lays the foundation for much of the discussion throughout the remainder of the book. It is critical to understand the contents of this chapter clearly and thoroughly.

The foreign exchange market allows one currency to be exchanged for another. The spot foreign exchange market is a market for immediate exchange. The forward market is where buyers and sellers agree to exchange currencies at some specified date in the future. In this chapter we first examine how the foreign exchange market as a whole is organized, what are the main functions of the foreign exchange market, who are the main participants in this market and so on. We then study the spot exchange market, the exchange rate quotations, the cross exchange rates and the foreign exchange arbitrage. Arbitrage profits are earned when someone buys something at a low price and sells it at higher price without bearing any risk. We'll also discuss the forward exchange market and the use of forward market as a hedging strategy. Finally, we describe different exchange rates such as nominal exchange rate, real exchange rate and effective exchange rate.

The Basics of Foreign Exchange Market

Foreign Exchange, Exchange Rate and Market

Foreign exchange is simply another country's money. American dollar is foreign exchange to any other countries' people except for the American people. British pond is foreign exchange to all the residents living outside the Great Britain. Within China, any money denominated in any currency other than Renminbi (RMB) is, broadly speaking, "foreign exchange". Foreign exchange takes the forms of cash, funds available on credit cards or debit cards, traveler's checks, bank deposits, checks, and drafts or other short-term claims. But, in the foreign exchange market described in this book, foreign exchange transactions almost always take the form of an exchange of bank deposits of different national currency denominations. Actual bank notes like dollar or Renminbi bills are relatively unimportant insofar as they rarely physically cross international borders. In general, only tourism or illegal activities would lead to the international movement of bank notes. The foreign exchange can also be defined as the act of trading different countries' moneys.

The most important character of foreign exchange is its convertibility; that is, foreign exchange could be converted into any of the other currencies. The main convertible currencies in the world are U.S. dollar, British pond, Japanese yen, and Euro. Those currencies are widely used in international trade and financial transactions.

Foreign exchange rate is simply the price of one currency in terms of another. For example, $1 = SFr0.8911 is the price of one U.S. dollar in terms of Swiss franc. Equivalently, SFr1 = $1/0.8911 = $1.1222, that is the price of one Swiss franc in terms of U.S. dollar. The dollar exchange rate refers to the dollar price in terms of other currencies; the RMB exchange rate is the price of Chinese yuan expressed by other currencies such as

¥1 = $0.1542, that is the value of RMB expressed by U.S. dollar.

Foreign exchange market is where currencies are bought and sold. The market provides the physical and institutional structure through which foreign exchange transactions are physically completed. The foreign exchange market serves three main functions. The first function is to convert the currency of one country into the currency of another. Because international trade and capital transactions normally involve the different currencies, it is necessary for transferring purchasing power between countries. The second function of the foreign exchange market is to provide international liquidity for international trade and investment. Since the movement of goods takes time, inventory in transit must be financed. The foreign exchange market provides a source of credit. There are different specialized instruments available to finance international trade. The third function is to provide some insurance against foreign exchange risk, by which we mean the adverse consequences of unpredictable changes in exchange rates. Without the foreign exchange market, international trade and international investment on the scale that we see today would be impossible; companies would have to resort to barter. The foreign exchange market is the lubricant that enables companies based in countries that use different currencies to trade with each other.

Size, Characteristics and Structure of the Foreign Exchange Market

The foreign exchange market is by far the largest financial market in the world in terms of trading volume. It has been growing at a rapid pace, reflecting a general growth in the volume of cross-border trade and investment. In March 1986, the average total value of global foreign exchange trading was about $200 billion per day. By April 1995, it was more than $1,200 billion per day. By April 2004 it had grown to $1.85 trillion. As of 2019, more than $6.59 trillion are traded in this market on a daily basis. This is several times the level of turnover in the U.S. government securities market, the world's second largest financial market. **Figure 3.1** illustrates the Bank for International Settlement data for surveys between 1989 and 2019. The expansion in foreign exchange turnover reflects the continuing growth of international trade and prodigious expansion in global finance and investment during the past three decades. The rapid increase in internationalization of financial activity also contributed to the enormous expansion in foreign exchange turnover.

Maybe it is difficult to comprehend how large this number is. Now let's take some examples so that you can compare. The U.S. GDP is about $21 trillion[1] in 2019. According to the daily turnover of more than $6.5 trillion, about three and half days foreign exchange trading volume will surpass the total value of the U.S. goods and services produced in an entire year. China's foreign trade on goods and services in 2019 was about $5.1 trillion[2]. The U.S. total volume of foreign trade investment, such as equities, bonds and derivatives

---

[1] Bureau of Economic Analysis, 2021, www.bea.org.
[2] China State Administration of Foreign Exchange, 2020, www.safe.gov.cn.

amounts 1–2 trillion per year. Those numbers will be meaningless if you compare them with the daily foreign exchange turnover in the foreign exchange market. Yet the number of people employed as foreign exchange traders in this industry is several thousand for the world as a whole.

The foreign exchange market is an informal, over-the-counter, around-the-clock market that includes the major commercial banks, and some specialized brokers in the principal financial centers throughout the world. They are connected by electronic communications systems such as **Society for Worldwide Interbank Financial Telecommunications (SWIFT)**. Unlike stock or commodity exchanges, the foreign exchange market has no centralized meeting-place and no formal requirements for participation. Nor is the foreign exchange market limited to any one country. When companies wish to convert currencies, they typically go through their own banks rather than entering the market directly.

The foreign exchange market is a 24-hour market and never sleeps. Somewhere on the planet, financial centers are open for business, and banks and other institutions are trading the dollar, euro, pound and yen and other currencies, every hour of the day and night, aside from possible minor gaps on weekends. Tokyo, London, and New York are all shut for only 3 hours out of every 24. During these three hours, trading continues in a number of minor centers, particularly San Francisco and Sydney, Australia. These marketplaces overlap.

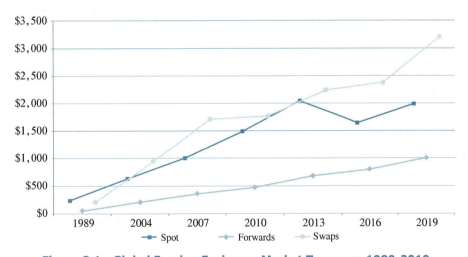

Figure 3.1 Global Foreign Exchange Market Turnover, 1989–2019

(daily averages in April, billions of U.S. dollars)

Source: Bank for International Settlements, "Triennial Central Bank Survey of Foreign Exchange and Derivatives Market Activity in April 2019", October 2019, www.bis.org.

In 2019, the U.S. dollar retained its dominant currency status, being on one side of 88% of all foreign exchange transactions, The share of trades with the euro on one side expanded somewhat, to 32%. By contrast, the share of trades involving the Japanese yen fell some 5%, although the Japanese yen remained the third most actively traded currency (on one side of 17% of all trades). The global share of emerging market economies (EMEs) rose about by 4% to 25% of total foreign exchange turnover in April, 2019, continuing the trend observed before. Turnover in the Chinese RMB, however, grew only slightly faster than the aggregate market, and the RMB did not climb further in the global rankings. It remained the eighth most traded currency, with a share of 4.3%, ranking just after the Swiss franc[1].

The widespread use of U.S. dollar reflects its substantial international role as: "investment currency" in many capital markets, "reserve currency" held by many central banks, "transaction currency" in many international commodity markets, and "intervention currency" employed by monetary authorities in market operations to influence their own exchange rate. In addition to those functions, U.S. dollar also serves as a "vehicle currency" which is a currency used to invoice international trade transactions. For most pair of currencies, the market practice is to trade each of the two currencies against a third common currency as a vehicle, rather than to trade the two currencies directly against each other. For example, a Chinese company wants to invest in Indian capital market. The company will probably sell RMB for U.S. dollar and then sell dollar for Indian rupee. Although this approach results in two transactions rather than one, it may be the preferred way, since the RMB/USD market and INR/USD market are much more active and liquid and have much better information than a bilateral market for the two currencies directly against each other. In this case, the use of the vehicle currency may be cheaper for the Chinese company than it directly sells RMB for Indian rupee.

Nowadays, the most important trading centers are the United Kingdom, the United States, Singapore, Hong Kong of China and Japan. The United Kingdom dominates the foreign exchange market with average daily volume of 43% of the whole volume. The next is U.S. whose accounts about 16.5% of activity, followed by Singapore, Hong Kong of China and Japan (7.5%, 7.5% and 6.5% of activity respectively). Major secondary trading centers include Zurich, Frankfurt, Paris, China and Sydney. China recorded a significant rise in trading activity, to $136 billion in 2019, or an 87% increase since 2016. China thus climbed several places in the global ranking to become the eighth largest foreign exchange trading center (up from 13th place three years previously)[2]. Because foreign exchange dealers are in constant telephone and computer contact, the market is very competitive; in effect, it functions no differently than if it were a centralized market.

Now we discuss the structure and the participants of the foreign exchange market. The structure of the foreign exchange market is shown in **Figure 3.2**. It also shows the different participants in this market.

---

1 All the statistics are from the Bank for International Settlements, 2021, www.bis.org.
2 All the statistics are from the Bank for International Settlements, 2020, www.bis.org.

Participants of the Foreign Exchange Market

Retail customers are made up of individuals, international investors, small businesses, speculators and the like who need foreign exchange for the purposes of operating their businesses or tourism. They are also called foreign exchange end-users. Normally, they do not directly purchase or sell foreign currencies themselves but operate by placing buy/sell orders with the local commercial banks. The foreign exchange needs of individuals are usually small and account for only a tiny fraction of all currency transactions. The retail customers are shown on the top and bottom of Figure 3.2.

Commercial banks (market dealers) and other financial institutions carry out buy/sell orders from their retail clients and buy/sell currencies on their own account so as to alter the structure of their assets and liabilities in different currencies. These banks serve as dealers or market makers, buying and selling currencies at quoted exchange rates. The trading between banks occurs in what is often referred to as the interbank market (the middle part of Figure 3.2). The commercial banks usually serve as market dealers. There are around 2,000 dealer institutions that essentially make up the global foreign exchange market. A small number of market dealers are **market makers**, buying and selling one or more particular currencies at quoted exchange rates. Dealers making a market in foreign exchange stand ready to quote bid and offer (ask) prices on major currencies, earning their profit by buying at their bid price and selling at a slightly higher offer price. In order to make a profit from this activity, the market maker must manage the firm's own inventory and position very carefully, and accurately perceive the short-term trends and the prospects of the market. In addition to the commercial banks, other financial institutions such as merchant banks are engaged in buying and selling currencies both for proprietary purposes and on behalf of their customers in finance-related transactions. Those banks are not market makers in the interbank market. Instead of maintaining significant inventory positions, they buy from and sell to larger banks to offset retail transactions with their own customers. The interbank market is the most important part of the whole foreign exchange market because it makes up more than 80% of all foreign exchange transactions.

Foreign exchange brokers are the intermediary who acts as agent for one or both parties in the transaction and, in principle, do not commit capital (the middle left of Figure 3.2). Foreign exchange brokers rely on the commission or fees received for the service provided. Brokers do not put their own money at risk and usually serve three important purposes in the foreign exchange market. First, foreign exchange brokers typically have many lines of communication open to various foreign exchange dealers, and they provide information to dealers on the best available prices. Therefore, a broker is a precious source of information for the traders in markets where one or two basis points can mean a difference of thousands of dollars on a contract. For example, if the market price of the British pound is $1.3504, a broker's offer may be $1.3503. For a ten million pound deal, the broker's price can save a dealer $1,000. Second, a broker brings buyers and sellers together and contributes to market efficiency. Third, he makes it possible for traders to remain anonymous when revealing their identity would put them at a disadvantage. For example, if the U.K. central bank wants to dispose of an accumulated position in euros without signaling its activity to the market, it can use a broker to maintain anonymity. One disadvantage of dealing though a broker is that a small brokerage fee is payable which is not incurred in a straight bank to bank deal.

Businesses such as multinational corporations are the major nonbank participants in the foreign exchange market as they exchange cash flows associated with their multinational operations (see middle right of Figure 3.2). Others include hedge funds, mutual funds for investment or speculative purposes. Since these firms usually buy and sell a large quantity of foreign currencies, they will directly enter into the interbank market.

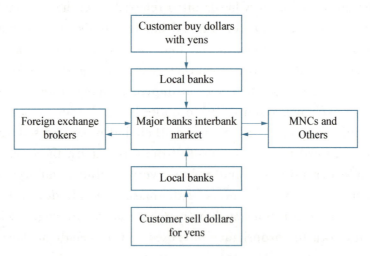

Figure 3.2 Foreign Exchange Market Structure

Central banks are not indifferent to changes in the external value of their currency, they frequently intervene to buy and sell their currencies in a bid to influence the rate at which their currency is traded. As a matter of fact, a lot of central banks participate in their nation's foreign exchange market to some degree, and their operations can be of great importance to those markets. Therefore, the motive of the central banks is not to earn a profit as such, but rather to influence the foreign exchange value of their currency in a manner that will benefit the interests of their citizens. Foreign exchange market intervention is not the only reason central banks buy and sell foreign currencies. Many central banks are also their governments' bank. They buy and sell foreign currencies for their governments as well as public sector enterprises. A central bank also may seek to accumulate, allocate among currencies, or reduce its foreign exchange reserve positions. When central banks buy and sell foreign exchanges, they go directly to the interbank market.

Speculators and arbitragers seek to profit from trading in the market itself. They operate in their own interest, without a need or obligation to serve clients or to ensure a continuous market. Where dealers seek profit from the spread between bid and ask in addition to what they might gain from changes in exchange rates, speculators seek all of their profit from exchange rate changes. Arbitragers try to profit from simultaneous exchange rate differences in different markets. The difference between a speculator and an arbitrager is that the former takes the risks while the latter makes the riskless profit. Since investment to and from overseas has expanded far more rapidly than trade. Institutional investors, insurance companies, pension funds, hedge funds, and other investment funds have become major participants in foreign exchange market. Some of them are speculators at some time and arbitragers at some other time.

Electronic Foreign Exchange Trading (eFX)

Until the 1980s, most foreign exchange trading was done over the phone. However, since the introduction of the internet, most foreign exchange trading is now executed electronically. Although the largest currency transactions are still handled by humans via telephone, the use of computer trading has grown dramatically in the past two decades. It is possible that the old telephone-based system will eventually be supplanted by pure electronic trading. Electronic trading platforms may offer multiple quotes from a number of foreign exchange dealers and/or can house an **electronic communication network** (**ECN**). An ECN electronically collects and matches buy and sell orders, and it display the best available prices.

In such a system, traders sit before the computer screens, key an order into his or her computer terminal, indicating the amount of a currency, the price, and an instruction to buy or sell. If the order can be filled from other orders outstanding, and it is the best price available in the system from other traders, the deal will be made. If a new order cannot be matched with outstanding orders, the new order will be entered into the system and traders in the system from other institutions will have access to it. Another trader may accept the order by pressing a "buy" or "sell" button and a transmit button.

Because of the electronic foreign exchange trading, it is possible that a pension fund trades with a hedge fund, so that banks lose their traditional role of market makers. Trades are often totally anonymous. Because the market price for a particular currency is visible for all participants on the platform, electronic trading ensures price transparency. Another advantage of electronic trading is the possibility of **straight-through processing** (**STP**). A foreign exchange trade takes place from placement of the order to settlement and even entry in accounting systems in an automated fashion without errors induced by faulty paperwork. Electronic trading has greatly enhanced the liquidity of the foreign exchange market and reduced trading costs.

Spot Exchange Market, Exchange Rate Quotations, and Foreign Exchange Arbitrage

Spot Exchange Market

Foreign exchange spot market is for spot transactions. Most transactions in our daily life are spot transactions. You go to a supermarket and pick up the goods you need, and then pay the store by cash or **Alipay** or credit card. This is a spot transaction because the deal is executed on the spot. In currency transactions, when two parties agree to exchange currency and execute the deal immediately, it is referred to as a spot transaction. Unlike the spot transaction in the supermarket, foreign exchange spot transactions do not require *immediate* settlement, or payment "on the spot". By convention, the settlement date, or **value date**, is the second business day from the deal date (or trade date) on which the transaction is agreed to by the two traders. If the deal is made on January 25, the value date would be January 27, assuming January 27 is a normal business day.

The exchange rate agreed to by the two parties in the spot transaction is called spot exchange rate. The **spot exchange rate** is the current market price, the rate at which a foreign exchange dealer converts one currency into another currency on a particular moment.

A spot transaction represents a direct exchange of one currency for another, and when executed, leads to transfers through the payment systems of the two countries whose currencies are involved.

For example, the Mitsubishi Bank in Tokyo will agree on January 25 to sell $10 million for Japanese yen to City Bank in New York at the rate of, say 103 yen per dollar, for value January 27. On January 27, City Bank will pay ¥1,030 million for credit to Mitsubishi Bank's account at a bank in U.S., and Mitsubishi Bank will pay $10 million for credit to City Bank's account at a bank in Japan. The execution of the two payments completes the transaction.

The spot exchange market for some particular currencies such as U.S. dollar, Euro, Japanese yen, and pound is very liquid, meaning those currencies are easily bought and sold. The more buyers and sellers there are for a currency, the more liquid the market for that currency is. In contrast, the spot markets for some currencies of less developed countries are much less liquid. An illiquid currency is found to be hardly bought and sold in a timely fashion and the bid-ask spread is usually large because the number of willing buyers and sellers is limited.

Direct and Indirect Quotes

We have already known that the foreign exchange rate is the price of two currencies. A **foreign exchange quotation (or quote)** is a statement of willingness to buy or sell at an announced rate. Quotations are usually designated by traditional currency symbols like "$" "£" "€" "SFr", etc. The International Organization for Standardization (ISO) has set standard code for currency abbreviations in recent decades. **Exhibit 3.1** provides a list of some of the ISO currency abbreviations used to represent the different currencies. In most cases, the abbreviation is the ISO two-digit country code plus a letter from the name of the currency.

Exhibit 3.1 Currencies and Currency Symbols and Codes

Country or region	Currency	Symbols	ISO Currency Code
Argentina	Peso		ARS
Australia	Dollar	$, A$	AUD
Brazil	Real	R$	BRL
Canada	Dollar	$, C$	CAD
Chile	Peso	$	CLP
China	Yuan	¥	CNY
Hong Kong	Dollar	$, HK$	HKD
Taiwan	Dollar	NT$	TWD
Czech Republic	Koruna	Kc	CZK
Denmark	Krone	Kr	DKK
Egypt	Pound	£	EGP
European Union	Euro	€	EUR
Hungary	Forint	Ft	HUF
India	Rupee		INR
Indonesia	Rupiah	Rp	IDR
Israel	Shekel		ILS
Japan	Yen	¥	JPY
Kuwait	Dinar		KWD
Malaysia	Ringgit	RM	MYR
Mexico	Neuvo Peso	$	MXN
New Zealand	Dollar	$	NZD
Norway	Krone	kr	NOK

(Continued)

Country or region	Currency	Symbols	ISO Currency Code
Philippines	Peso		PHP
Poland	Zloty		PLZ
Russia	Ruble	R	RUR
Saudi Arabia	Riyal	SR	SAR
Singapore	Dollar	S$	SGD
South Korea	Won	W	KRW
South Africa	Rand	R	ZAR
Sweden	Krona	kr	SEK
Switzerland	Franc	Fr	CHF
Thailand	Baht		THB
United Kingdom	Pound	£	GBP
United States	Dollar	$	USD
Vietnam	Dong		VND

For example, the code for the U.S. dollar is USD, the British pound is GBP, the Japanese yen is JPY, and the Swiss franc is CHF. To make things simple, in examples throughout the book, we usually use traditional symbols for the major currencies. At other times, though, we use ISO codes to illustrate the units involved in different transactions.

In this book, we will use the following notation for exchange rate. In general, $S^{d/f}$ will refer to an exchange rate, that is the price of one unit of foreign currency f in terms of the domestic currency d. In other words, the currency in the numerator is the domestic currency and the currency in the denominator is the foreign currency. Thus, the exchange rate of C$1 = U.S.$0.80 is expressed as $S^{U.S.\$/C\$} = 0.80$. In this example, the U.S.$ is regarded as domestic currency and the C$ refers to the foreign currency.

$S^{U.S.\$/C\$} = 0.80$ can also be written as U.S.$0.80/C$. Notice that we treat the slash symbol (/) as a divisor in a ratio to indicate the amount of the currency d (here the U.S. dollar) that is necessary to purchase one unit of the currency f (here the Canadian dollar). Sometimes the hyphen symbol (–) can also be treated as a divisor. For example, euro-dollar exchange rate refers to the dollar price in terms of euro; dollar-pound exchange rate means the number of dollars needed to exchange one British pound. It clearly pays to be careful to remember how the exchange rate is being quoted so you will not be confused when you are reading the textbook or are required to calculate some specific problems later.

Exchange rate quotes come in two forms: direct and indirect quotes. A **"direct" quote** is the amounts of domestic currency per unit of foreign currency. An **"indirect" quote** is the amounts of foreign currency per unit of domestic currency. Most countries adopt direct quotes while a few countries such as the United Kingdom and former colonies of Great Britain use indirect quotes. The euro is normally quoted indirectly; that is, in the euro zone, countries are used to quoting the price of euro in terms of other currencies.

For example, a direct quote for the Canadian dollar would be U.S.$0.80/C$ in the United States. Conversely, in Canada, a direct quote for the U.S. dollar would be C$1.25/U.S.$ which is the reciprocal of U.S.$0.80/C$. Obviously, the direct quote from the U.S. perspective is an indirect quote from the Canadian viewpoint, and the indirect quote from the U.S. perspective is a direct quote from the Canadian viewpoint. Therefore, direct and indirect quotes are reciprocals, and either can easily be determined from the other.

European and American Quotes for the U.S. Dollar

Since the U.S. dollar is the most frequently traded currency in the foreign exchange market, it is common practice among currency dealers worldwide to both price and trade currencies against the U.S. dollar. Interbank quotations that include the U.S. dollar are conventionally given in **European terms**, which state the foreign currency price of one U.S. dollar, such as A$1.28/U.S.$, SFr0.89/U.S.$. This convention is used for all interbank dollar quotes except those involving the euro and British pound. From the perspective of American people, the European term is equivalent to the indirect quote.

A quote of the U.S. dollar price per foreign currency unit is called **American terms**. For example, the exchange rate of U.S.$1.35/£ or U.S.$0.80/C$ refers to the number of dollars it takes to purchase one unit of pound sterling or Canadian dollar. The American term is also a direct quote if you are in the United States. It should be noted that the terminology European and American quotes are not possible for transactions that do not include the U.S. dollar.

Foreign exchange rates are quoted in all major financial newspapers such as *Wall Street Journal* and *Financial Times*. **Exhibit 3.2** is derived from *The Wall Street Journal* of January 15, 2021 and displays part of the foreign exchange rates. The table gives the quotes of U.S. dollar verses other currencies in two ways. The U.S. dollar per currency is the price of other currencies in terms of the U.S. dollar. This is the American quotes, also direct quotes form the U.S. perspective. The U.S.$ equivalent is the dollar price in terms of the other currencies. It is the European quotes, or indirect quotes from the viewpoint of American people. For example, 0.0117 of the first row under the "U.S. dollar per currency" column means that you must give $0.0117 in exchange for one Argentina peso on Friday. Equivalently, it takes 85.7216 Argentine pesos to purchase one U.S. dollar. This rate is shown under the "currency per U.S. dollar" column on the right side.

Exhibit 3.2 U.S. Dollar Currency Quotes in Late New York Trading
(Friday, January 15, 2021)

Country or region/ Currency	U.S. Dollar per Currency		Currency per U.S. Dollar	
	Friday	Thursday	Friday	Thursday
Argentina peso	0.0117	0.0117	85.7216	85.6525
Brazil real	0.1889	0.1924	5.2930	5.1971
Canada dollar	0.7851	0.7910	1.2738	1.2643
Mexico peso	0.0505	0.0507	19.7061	19.7140
Australian dollar	0.7702	0.7780	1.2984	1.2853
China yuan	0.1543	0.1544	6.4808	6.4746
Hong Kong dollar	0.1290	0.1290	7.7537	7.7534
Taiwan dollar	0.03572	0.03573	27.99	27.99
India rupee	0.01367	0.01368	73.16115	73.07675
Indonesia rupiah	0.000071	0.0000711	14,020	14,055
Japan yen	0.00963	0.00963	103.87	103.80
Malaysia ringgit	0.2477	0.2478	4.0365	4.0360
New Zealand dollar	0.7132	0.7224	1.4021	1.3843
Singapore dollar	0.7514	0.7551	1.3309	1.3243
South Korea won	0.0009056	0.0009124	1,104.27	1,096.07
Vietnam dong	0.00004335	0.00004336	23,066	23,065
Czech koruna	0.04614	0.04648	21.674	21.514
Denmark krone	0.1624	0.1634	6.1595	6.1201
Euro	1.2080	1.2157	0.8278	0.8226
Russia ruble	0.01360	0.01364	73.519	73.292
Sweden krona	0.1191	0.1204	8.3968	8.3077
Swiss franc	1.1222	1.1263	0.8911	0.8879
Turkey lira	0.1339	0.1357	7.4689	7.3719
U.K. pound	1.3584	1.3688	0.7362	0.7306
Egypt pound	0.0639	0.0638	15.6616	15.6622
Kuwait dinar	3.3022	3.2989	0.3028	0.3031
Saudi Arabia riyal	0.2666	0.2666	3.7512	3.7515
South Africa rand	0.0657	0.0662	15.2312	15.0946

Source: *Wall Street Journal*, January 16, 2021.

Bid and Ask Quotes

In the foreign exchange market there are always *two* prices for every currency — the **bid quote** is the price at which a buyer of that currency wants to buy and the **ask quote** (also called **offer quote**) is the price at which a seller of that currency wants to sell. A market maker is expected to quote simultaneously for his customers *both* a price at which he is willing to sell and a price at which he is willing to buy standard amounts of any currency for which he is making a market. For example: For a U.S. resident, a direct quote for the Swiss franc might be

$1.1222/SFr Bid and $1.1232/SFr Ask

Apparently, the dealer bid low and ask high, or buy low and sell high in order to make profits. That is: the dealer is willing to buy francs (and sell dollars) at $1.1222/SFr (less dollars to buy francs) or sell francs (and buy dollars) at $1.1232 (more dollars to sell francs). In other words, the dealer is buying low and selling high. The difference between bid and ask price for the dealer in this example is $0.0010/SFr.

In countries using the indirect quotes, the dealer's bid price is higher than the ask price. We know that the indirect quotes state the price of one unit of domestic currency in foreign currency terms. In this case, an indirect Swiss franc quote to a U.S. resident might be

SFr0.8911/$ Bid and SFr0.8903/$ Ask

Remember the dealer buys and sells foreign currency. For Americans the foreign currency is Swiss franc, not the dollar. The dealer is willing to buy franc at the price of SFr0.8911 (the customer gives SFr0.8911 in exchange for one dollar, in other words, the dealer requires more francs when it sells dollar) and sell franc at the price of SFr0.8903 (the customer takes one dollar to purchase SFr0.8903, or the dealer gives less francs when it buys dollar). Therefore, the dealer is still buying low and sell high!

The rule for determining the currency that is being quoted is as follows:

- When the bid quote is lower than the offer quote, the dealer is buying and selling the currency in the denominator of the quote. In the previous first quote, $1.1222/SFr is lower than $1.1232/SFr, the dealer is buying and selling the Swiss franc (denominator currency).
- When the bid quote is higher than the offer quote, the dealer is buying and selling the currency in the numerator of the quote. In the previous second quote, SFr0.8911/$ is higher than SFr0.8903/$, the dealer is still buying and selling the Swiss franc, but the franc is in the place of numerator.

Bid-Ask Spread and Bid-Ask Margin

The dealer's **bid-ask spread** is the differential between bid and ask prices. It reflects the dealer's gain of buying and selling foreign exchanges. Like the previous example, $1.1222/SFr Bid and $1.1232/SFr Ask, the bid-ask spread is $0.0010/SFr. A larger bid/ask spread generates more revenue for commercial banks, but represents a higher cost to individuals or firms that engage in foreign exchange transactions. Economists like to use basis points to describe the difference between the bid and ask price. Usually the last digit of a quotation is referred to as a **basis point** or a point. Hence, a point is equal to one percent of one percent or 0.0001 for most currencies. In our example, the spread here is 10 points (0.0010) which is 0.1 percentage point. The bid-ask spread can also be expressed as a percent of the **middle price** (the average of the bid and ask price), known as the **bid-ask margin,** which is:

$$\text{Bid-ask margin} = (\text{Ask price} - \text{Bid price})/\text{Middle price} \times 100 \tag{3.1}$$

In this example, the bid-ask margin is

$$(1.1232 - 1.1222)/1.1227 \times 100 = 0.089\%$$

For most currencies, bid and offer quotes are presented to the fourth decimal place — that is, to one-hundredth of one percent, or $1/10,000^{th}$ of the numerator currency unit. However, for a few currency units that are relatively small in absolute value, such as the Japanese yen, quotes may be carried to two decimal places, 1/100 of the numerator currency unit. So one point for Japanese yen refers to one percent or 0.01.

There are many factors influence the bid-ask spread. The most important factors are the trading volume and competition. Currencies that have large trading volume are more liquid because there are numerous buyers and sellers at any given time. So the bid-ask spread is usually small. The more intense the competition, the smaller the spread quoted by banks. The establishment of electronic communication network (ECN) is a form of competition against foreign exchange dealers, and it has forced dealers to reduce their spread in order to remain competitive.

Cross Rates

For currencies that are traded frequently like the U.S. dollar, euro and the Japanese yen, the system is fairly straightforward. But how do we know the rate of the Vietnamese dong for the Polish zloty? The IMF records exchange rates for 152 countries, which means that there are (152 × 151) / 2 = 11,476 different pairs of possible exchange rates. Most of these possibilities are likely never to come up for a trade and many only once in a blue moon. If they do come up, however, how can the trader arrive at a price?

The answer is that all currencies are quoted against the U.S. dollar. Knowing the price of any two currencies against the dollar means that the price of one currency for the other can easily be found. The exchange rate between two currencies not involving the dollar is called the **cross rate**. So a cross rate is a rate calculated from two known bilateral exchange rates. Here again we see the importance of the vehicle currency — the U.S. dollar. For 152 member countries, there would be a total of 151 exchange rates to be dealt with (i.e., one exchange rate for the U.S. dollar against each of the others). Use of the dollar as a vehicle currency greatly reduces the number of exchange rates that must be dealt with in a multilateral system.

Now let's take some examples to see how cross rates are calculated.

(1) If the exchange rate of $S^{SFr/\$} = 0.8887 - 92$, and the exchange rate of $S^{¥/\$} = 103.55 - 65$, what is the $S^{¥/SFr}$ bid and ask cross rate?

Before we answer this question, let's suppose you are a bank's customer and have one Swiss franc, how much Japanese yen can you buy with one Swiss franc?

Since you don't know the exchange rate of yen relative to franc, you have to buy U.S. dollar first with the Swiss franc using the bank's dollar ask price of 0.8892 SFr/$, you get $1.1246 (1/0.8892). Second, you sell the dollars for Japanese yen at the bank's dollar bid price of ¥103.55/$. You then get ¥116.45 ($1.1246 × ¥103.55/$). The bank is selling yen and buying franc, so ¥116.45/SFr is the bank's bid price for franc.

By the same token, you can calculate the bank's franc ask price which is ¥116.63/SFr. The formula for cross-rate calculation is as follows:

$$S_b^{z/x} = S_b^{z/y} / S_a^{x/y} \quad (3.2)$$
$$S_a^{z/x} = S_a^{z/y} / S_b^{x/y} \quad (3.3)$$

Where

$S_b^{z/x}$: the bid rate of currency x verses currency z

$S_a^{z/x}$: the ask rate of currency x verses currency z

Applying **Equation 3.2** and **Equation 3.3**, the Swiss franc bid price is:

$$\text{Bid of } S^{¥/SFr} = 103.55/0.8892 = 116.45$$

and the Swiss franc ask price is:

$$\text{Ask of } S^{¥/SFr} = 103.65/0.8887 = 116.63$$

(2) If the $S^{\$/£}$ is 1.3668–74 and the $S^{¥/\$}$ is 103.55–65, what is the $S^{¥/£}$ cross rate? We need follow the same logic as in the previous question. You take one pound to buy $1.3668, and then sell the dollar for yen which is ¥141.53 ($1.3668 × ¥103.55/$). So,

$$\text{Bid of } S^{¥/£} = 1.3668 \times 103.55 = 141.53$$
$$\text{Ask of } S^{¥/£} = 1.3674 \times 103.65 = 141.73$$

Cross rates often appear in the form of a matrix in newspapers, as shown in **Exhibit 3.3**. The currency column refers to one unit of that currency and the country row represents the units of currency of that country. Here, to find the value of the British pound relative to the Swiss franc, we simply locate the intersection of the pound column and the Switzerland row. The cross rate is given as 1.2153 which means one pound can exchange for 1.2153 Swiss franc. In like manner, the cross exchange rates of other key currencies can be read directly from the table.

Exhibit 3.3　Key Currency Cross Rates

(Thursday, January 21, 2021)

	Dollar	Euro	Pound	Sfranc	Peso	Yen	CAD
Canada	1.2615	1.5302	1.7262	1.4194	0.064520	0.012185	—
Japan	103.56	125.61	141.68	116.52	5.2929	—	82.07
Mexico	19.5565	23.7248	26.7508	22.0118	—	0.188934	15.4990
Swiss	0.8889	1.0779	1.2154	—	0.045430	0.008582	0.7045
U.K.	0.7315	0.8868	—	0.8228	0.037382	0.007058	0.5793
Euro	0.8247	—	1.1276	0.9277	0.042150	0.007961	0.6535
U.S.	—	1.2126	1.3671	1.1250	0.051134	0.009656	0.7927

Source: *Wall Street Journal*, January 21, 2021.

Changes in Exchange Rates — Appreciation and Depreciation

The previous section explained how exchange rates are quoted at one point in time. Now, we turn to the topic of how to describe changes in exchange rates that occur over time. The first thing to remember about describing changes in exchange rates is that they are relative prices. Consequently, there are always two ways to describe the same situation. When an exchange rate changes, one currency either gains or loses value relative to another currency. If a currency gains value relative to another currency in the foreign exchange market, the currency appreciates. If a currency loses value relative to another currency, it depreciates. Therefore, **appreciation** of a currency refers to the rise in the price of the currency and **depreciation** of a currency means the price of the currency falls in the foreign exchange market. The appreciation and depreciation of a currency is usually measured in percentage terms.

For example, if the U.S. dollar-Japanese yen exchange rate changes from $0.0095/¥ to $0.0092/¥, it means that fewer U.S. dollars have to be taken to get one Japanese yen, so the dollar appreciates against yen, or the yen depreciates against the dollar. But what is the percent decrease in the dollar value of the Japanese yen and what is the percent increase in the yen value of the U.S. dollar? Percentage changes in currency values are asymmetric, which means the percent decrease in yen not equal to the percent increase in dollar. For example, If the number of students majoring in finance increases from 1,000 to 1,500, it is a 50% increase in the number of the students whose main subject is finance. If the number of students falls from 1,500 to 1,000, it is an approximately 33% decrease in the number of students majoring in finance.

When we talk about appreciation or depreciation of a particular currency, we usually put the currency in the place of the denominator in the given exchange rate. In the above example, we were talking about the value of the Japanese yen. Since a unit of Japanese yen now can buy fewer dollars than before, the yen depreciates against the dollar. We can use the following formula to calculate the percent decrease in the dollar value of a Japanese yen:

$$\text{Percentage change in the value of the currency in denominator} = (\text{Ending rate} - \text{Beginning rate}) / (\text{Beginning rate}) \quad (3.4)$$

Applying the **Equation 3.4**, we get:

$$(\$0.0092/¥ - \$0.00095/¥) / \$0.0095/¥ = -0.0316, \text{ or } -3.16\%$$

The negative sign indicates depreciation, so the yen depreciates against the dollar by about 3.16%. For annual percentage change, it is

$$-3.16\% \times 4 = -12.64\%$$

If we want to know the changes in value of the dollar, we can use the reciprocal of the given exchange rate, that is, the value of the dollar changes from ¥105.26/$ [1/($0.0095/¥)] to ¥108.70/$ [1/($0.0092/¥)]. Thus, we put the dollar in the place of the denominator in the exchange rate. We then apply the **Equation 3.4** and get the appreciation rate of the dollar which is:

$$(¥108.70/\$ - ¥105.26/\$) / (¥105.26/\$) = 3.268\%, \text{ or } 13.07\% \text{ p.a.}$$

This problem can also simply be solved by applying the following formula:

$$\text{Percentage change in the value of the currency in numerator} = (\text{Beginning rate} - \text{Ending rate}) / (\text{Ending rate}) \quad (3.5)$$

In our example, the beginning rate is $0.0095/¥ and the ending rate is $0.0092/¥, the change in value of the U.S. dollar is then by applying **Equation 3.5**:

$$(\$0.0095/¥ - \$0.0092/¥) / \$0.0092/¥ = 3.26\%$$

The dollar appreciates relative to the yen by 3.26%, The annual percentage change rate is:

$$3.26\% \times 4 = 13.04\% \text{ p.a.}$$

Foreign Exchange Arbitrage

Although the popular press often uses the term arbitrage to refer to speculative position, arbitrage is more strictly defined as a profitable position obtained with no net investment and no risk. This type of "no money down and no risk" opportunity sounds too good to be true. In the high-stakes international currency markets, it usually is too good to be true once trading costs are included. Arbitrage opportunities are exploited just as quickly as they disappear, as market forces drive prices back toward equilibrium.

Foreign exchange arbitrage means buying one currency in one place and selling it in another place at the same time to make riskless profits. If the process is taking place in two places, it is a **spatial arbitrage**. When the process is taking place in three places, it is called **triangular arbitrage**.

The following example illustrates the spatial arbitrage:

If in New York, U.S. dollar per Danish krone rate is $S^{\$/Dkr} = 0.1584 - 94$, and in London, the dollar price in terms of the krone is $S^{Dkr/\$} = 6.3520 - 40$, and assume a trader has $1million line of credit and both markets are open without restrictions against buying and selling currencies. The trader finds the Danish krone is cheaper in London because the reciprocals of 6.3520–40 is 0.1574–73. The trader can buy Danish krone in London and sell it in New York, the no money down and no risk arbitrage profits will be:

$1,000,000 × Dkr6.3520/$ = Dkr 6,352,000 (sell dollar for krone in London)
Dkr6,352,000 × $0.1584/Dkr = $1,006,157 (sell krone for dollar in New York)
Profits: $1,006,157 – $1,000,000 = $6,157

if there are not any other fees.

Like the example shows, such arbitrage is practical only if the participants have instant access to quotes and executions. The trader must know the krone/dollar rates are quoted differently in two different markets. When he knows the difference, he should be able to execute the buying and selling orders. It means there is no any kind of restrictions on the foreign exchange transactions in both markets. Also the trader can conduct such arbitrage without an initial sum of money, other than his bank's credit standing, because the trades are offset by electronic means before the normal settlement two days later.

The triangular arbitrage is a process that keeps cross-rates (such as euros per British pound) in line with exchange rates quoted relative to the U.S. dollar. It is a little more complex and involves three or more currencies and/or markets.

Suppose you are given exchange rates for currencies d, e, and f. The **no-arbitrage condition for triangular arbitrage** in the currency markets is

$$S^{d/e} \times S^{e/f} \times S^{f/d} = 1 \tag{3.6}$$

Chapter 3   THE FOREIGN EXCHANGE MARKET

If this condition does not hold within the limits of transactions costs, then there is an opportunity for a riskless profit through triangular arbitrage.

For example: Suppose the following exchange rates hold among U.S. dollars, pounds, and euros:

$$S^{\$/€} = 1.3524$$
$$S^{\$/£} = 1.6010 \implies £0.6246/\$$$
$$S^{€/£} = 1.1766$$

The product of the three spot rates is less than 1:

$$S^{\$/€} \times S^{€/£} \times S^{£/\$} = (\$1.3524/€)(€1.1766/£)(£0.6246/\$) = 0.9939 < 1$$

Thus, these rates are not in equilibrium and there is an arbitrage opportunity so long as transactions costs are not too high.

Suppose you start with €1 million and simultaneously make the following transactions in a *round turn* (that is, buying and then selling each currency in turn):

Buy £ with € (€1,000,000) / (€1.1766/£) = £849,906.51
Buy $ with £ (£849,906.51) × ($1.6010/£) = $1,360,700.32
Buy € with $ ($1,360,700.32) / ($1.3524/€) = €1,006,137.47

The profits will be:

€1,006,137.47 − €1,000,000 = €6,137.47

This is the only way that you can make money. If you go the wrong way on your round turn, you will lose your money. How can you tell which direction to go on your round turn?

Here is a rule for determining which currencies to buy and sell in triangular arbitrage:
If $S^{d/e} S^{e/f} S^{f/d} < 1$, then $S^{d/e}$, $S^{e/f}$, or $S^{f/d}$ must rise.
→ Buy the currencies in the denominators with the currencies in the numerators.
If $S^{d/e} S^{e/f} S^{f/d} > 1$, then $S^{d/e}$, $S^{e/f}$, or $S^{f/d}$ must fall.
→ Sell the currencies in the denominators for the currencies in the numerators.

If the given exchange rates are not in the format of $S^{d/e} S^{e/f} S^{f/d}$, they should be altered to be consistent with the standard format. Like the previous example, the dollar/pound exchange rate was given $S^{\$/£} = 1.6010$, we changed the rate to be £0.6246/\$. Therefore, because the given three exchange rates are in the form of $S^{\$/€}$, $S^{€/£}$, and $S^{£/\$}$, we can tell whether there are discrepancies among the given exchange rates.

Obviously, in perfectly competitive financial markets, it is impossible to earn arbitrage profits for very long. If the euro price of the pound were not equal to the euro price of the U.S. dollar multiplied by the U.S. dollar price of the pound, arbitrage activity would immediately restore equality between the quoted cross-rate and the cross-rate implied by two dollar quotes:

$$(Euros/Pound) = (Euros/Dollar) \times (Dollars/Pound)$$

Or, equivalently,

$$S^{\$/\euro} \times S^{\euro/\pounds} \times S^{\pounds/\$} = 1$$

In other words, the direct quote for the cross-rate should equal to the implied cross-rate, using the dollar as an intermediary currency.

Before we finish this section, two important things about triangular arbitrage are worth mentioning. First, the transactions must all be conducted simultaneously if you try to make profits. Because it is not physically possible to do all three transactions simultaneously, there is some risk involved in any attempted triangular arbitrage because prices might change between transactions. If more and more traders buy lower priced currency and sell higher priced currency, market forces will drive the value of lower priced currency up and put the value of higher priced currency down. In other words, the condition for triangular arbitrage no longer exists. It is not possible to make riskless profits in this situation. Second, the arbitrage need not start by using a specific currency, it could start from any of the currencies. In our previous example, we found that three exchange rates related to U.S. dollar, British pound and euro are not aligned with each other. We started by using euro to purchase pounds. Actually, the triangular arbitrage would be profitable starting from pound or dollar, as long as you go the correct way on your round turn to conduct these transactions.

The Forward Foreign Exchange Market

Forward Market and Forward Exchange Rate

Forward foreign exchange market is for forward foreign exchange transactions. It means the rates and the amounts of the deal are agreed on today but settlement occurs sometime later than two days in the future. For example, a Japanese trader who has to pay $5,000,000 to the U.S. supplier at the end of June may decide on April 1 to buy $5,000,000 for delivery on June 30 at a forward exchange rate of ¥105/$. The deal is made on April 1 in terms of the amounts and the price, but the delivery of dollar and yen will be on June 30. This is a forward foreign exchange transaction.

The forward market like the spot market is an over-the-counter market. Forward contracts are usually big contracts and used only by large businesses. In some cases, the minimum is $1 million or equivalent and sometimes it must be $5 million at least. So they are not generally used by small businesses and consumers. The two parties involved in a forward contract can negotiate for just about any maturity but most banks supply regular quotes on maturities of 30, 60, 90, and 180 days. In some cases, it is possible to get forward exchange rates for a few days to several years into the future. Very long-dates forward contracts are rare because they tend to have a large bid-ask spread and are relatively expensive.

As mentioned previously, one of the functions of foreign exchange market is to minimize the exchange rate risks faced by the MNCs, exporting, importing firms and the like, and banks are willing quote forward exchange rates for their corporate and institutional customers. However, such simple forward contracts, called outright forward contracts, are a relatively unimportant component of the foreign exchange market. In fact, a Bank for International Settlements survey (2019) found that only about 15% of all transactions in the foreign exchange market are outright forward contracts. The survey also found that forward contracts are much more often part of a package deal, called a swap. In fact, about 49% of foreign exchange market transactions are swaps. A swap transaction involves the simultaneous purchase and sale of a certain amount of foreign currency for two different dates in future. We'll discuss the swap transactions shortly.

Many of the large dealers that serve as intermediaries in the spot market also serve the forward market. The liquidity of the forward market varies among currencies. The forward market for U.S. dollar and euro is very liquid because many MNCs and institutional investors take forward positions to hedge their future cash flows in those currencies. In contrast, the forward markets for some currencies are less liquid because there is less international trade with those currencies. There are even some currencies for which there is no forward market.

The **forward exchange rate** can be defined as the rate to be paid for delivery of specific currency at some future date. The exchange of currencies in a forward contract takes place on the **forward value date**. The forward value date is related to today's spot value date. As we discussed before, a spot value date is two business days in the future for trades between the relative currencies. Exchange of currencies in a 30-day forward contract occurs on the calendar day in the next month that corresponds to today's spot value date, assuming that it is a business day. So, if today is July 28 and the spot value date is July 30, the forward value day for a 30-day contract is August 30. If the forward value date is a weekend or a bank holiday in either country, settlement of the forward contract occurs on the next business day. If the next business day moves the settlement of the forward contract into a new month, the forward value day becomes the *previous* business day. For example, in our previous example, it is possible that August 30 and 31 are weekend days. In that case, the value date would be August 29. This rule is followed except when the spot value day is the last business day of the current month, in which case the forward value day is the last business day of the next month (this is referred to as the *end-end rule*).

Regular quotes on forward contracts are limited to a relatively small number of currencies. The U.S. dollar, euro, the Japanese yen and the British pound make up a large part of the whole market. A common use of forward contracts is to eliminate uncertainty in commercial contracts arising from possible changes in the exchange rate. The same reasoning can be applied to investors who make forward contracts to lock in returns in domestic currency.

Swap Transactions

The unique feature of foreign exchange market nowadays is the predominance of trading in foreign exchange derivatives over spot transactions. Daily trading volume in foreign exchange swaps has been exceeding that of spot for years and by 2019 accounted for almost half of all trading in global foreign exchange market. Most of the trading of forward contracts happens in the swap market. A **swap transaction** is the simultaneous purchase and sale of a given amount of foreign exchange for two different value dates. We introduce foreign exchange swaps in this section. Chapter 5 will discuss another kind of swap transaction called "currency swaps". The swap transaction can effectively eliminate the foreign exchange risks which we will discuss shortly.

Spot against forward is the most common type of swap. It refers to an activity that a trader buys a currency in the spot market and simultaneously sells the same amount back to the same counterparty with a forward contract. For example, Walmart may set up a contract with Bank of America where Walmart buys 1 million euros now at \$1.20/€ and simultaneously sells 1 million euros to Bank of America 60 days from now at \$1.18/€.

Forward against forward is another type of swap transaction in which a trader conducts two forward transactions with the same counterparty but in opposite directions. For example, a trader sells RMB10,000,000 for dollars for delivery in 60 days at ¥6.4520/\$ and simultaneously buys RMB10,000,000 forward for delivery in 90 days at ¥6.4500/\$. This transaction is equivalent to borrow the dollar in 60 days and pay back the loan in 90 days. The difference between the buying price and the selling price is the interest the borrower must pay. Therefore, we can say that foreign exchange swaps are term loans of one currency collateralized with another currency, the interest rate implicit in swaps reflects aspects of funding liquidity conditions in the two currency pairs.

There has been a popular swap transaction in some emerging market economies since 1990s. It is called **non-deliverable forwards (NDFs)**. NDFs have the same characteristics as traditional forward contracts, except that they are settled only in U.S. dollars; the foreign currency being sold forward or bought forward is not delivered. For example, a currency dealer sells ¥10 million forward for dollars for delivery on, say, July 30 at ¥6.50/\$ and simultaneously agrees to buy the same amount back from the same counterparty on July 30. The exchange rate at which the dealer will use to buy back ¥10 million is the spot exchange rate available on July 30. If the spot exchange rate on July 30 is ¥6.45/$, the dealer takes the loss of $11,926. This is because he sells ¥10 million for $1,538,462 and buys ¥10 million back with $1,550,388. That means the dealer should pay $11,926 ($1,538,462 − $1,550,388) to his counterparty. This transaction need not deliver the RMB because the dealer buys and sells RMB simultaneously. The dollar-settlement feature reflects the fact that NDFs are traded offshore, just like RMB and NDFs are traded in Singapore and Hong Kong of China.

Pricing of NDFs reflects basic interest differentials, as with regular forward contracts, plus some additional premium charged by the bank for dollar settlement. If, however, there is no accessible or developed money market for interest rate setting, the pricing of the NDFs takes on a much more speculative element. Without true interest rates, traders often price on the basis of what they believe spot rates may be at the time of settlement.

Swaps are valuable to those who are investing or borrowing in foreign currency. For example, an insurance company that invests foreign bonds for six months can use a spot-forward swap to avoid foreign exchange risk. The company will buy foreign currency at the spot exchange rate. At the same time it can sell forward foreign currency. Since a known amount of the company's home currency will be received according to the forward component of the swap, no uncertainty from exchange rates is faced. In a similar way, those who borrow in foreign currency can buy forward the foreign currency needed for repayment of the foreign currency loan at the same time that they convert the borrowed foreign funds into their own currency on the spot market. The value of swaps to international investors and borrowers helps explain their substantial popularity.

Swaps are also popular with banks because it is difficult to avoid risk when making a market for many future dates and currencies. Swaps allow banks to exchange their surpluses and shortages of individual currencies to offset spot and forward trades with their customers and with each other. It should be no surprise that matching customer trades with appropriate swaps is a complex and dynamic problem.

Forward Premiums

Exhibit 3.4 illustrates the spot and forward quotations for RMB versus euro and U.S. dollar. Usually, the forward exchange rate is different from the spot exchange rate because of the differences in interest rates of the currencies. The quotation of forward rates can be given either outright or swap points. This table gave the outright forward quotes of the euro and the U.S. dollar.

Even though some forward contracts are outright, the convention in the interbank market is to quote all forward rates in terms of the spot rate and the number of **swap points** for the forward maturity in question. For example, 3-month forward euro and 1-month forward dollar could be given as shown in **Exhibit 3.5**.

Exhibit 3.4 Spot and Forward Quotes for Euro and the U.S. Dollar
(February 19, 2021)

Term	Euro: Spot and Forward (¥/€)		Dollar: Spot and Forward (¥/$)	
	Bid	Ask	Bid	Ask
Spot	7.8094	7.8670	6.4513	6.4787
1 month	7.8029	7.8911	6.4665	6.4995
3 month	7.8513	7.9402	6.4984	6.5319
1 year	8.0504	8.1441	6.6213	6.6577

Source: Bank of China, February 19, 2021, www.bankofchina.com.

Exhibit 3.5 90-Day Forward Euro Quote

	Bid	Ask
Spot	$1.2052/€	$1.2060/€
Forward (90 days) swap points	18	26

The spot rates quoted in this example is straightforward. The swap points are a set of points that must be either added to or subtracted from the current spot bid and ask prices to yield the actual 90-day bid and ask forward prices. The need to add or subtract depends on whether the two numbers in the swap points are ascending or descending. In other words, it depends on whether the first number in the swap points is larger than the second. If it is ascending, you add the points to the spot bid and ask prices to get the outright forward quotes; if it is descending, you subtract the points. Let's look at our example.

When the swap points are ascending, as they are in our example of 18/26, the swap points are added to the spot bid and ask prices so that the outright 90-day forward rate is as follows:

$$\$1.2052/€ + \$0.0018/€ = \$1.2070/€ \text{ (bid)}$$
$$\$1.2060/€ + \$0.0026/€ = \$1.2086/€ \text{ (ask)}$$

Exhibit 3.6 is the spot dollar price in terms of Japanese yen and the 30-day forward rate.

Exhibit 3.6 30-Day Forward Dollar Quotes

	Bid	Ask
Spot	¥103.50/$	¥103.55/$
Forward (30 days) swap points	6	4

As we discussed before, most currencies are usually quoted to four decimal points, so one basis point is the last digit of the quote which is 0.0001. In Exhibit 3.5, the 90-day forward euro bid quote is larger than spot quote by 18 points, so the outright quote should be \$1.2070/€. The outright euro ask quote is \$1.2086/€. However, the price of Japanese yen is quoted only to two decimal points; one point is 0.01 for Japanese yen. In our example, 6 and 4 points mean 0.06 and 0.04 respectively. It should be noted that the numbers have been reversed, swap points are 6/4 in this example. The rule tells us when the swap points are descending they should be subtracted from the spot rates. The implied outright bid and ask on the U.S. dollar for 30-day forward then should be:

¥103.50/\$ − ¥0.06/\$ = ¥103.44/\$ (bid)
¥103.55/\$ − ¥0.04/\$ = ¥103.51/\$ (ask)

The above two examples indicate that the bid-ask spread in the forward quote is larger than the spread of the spot quote. There are 8 basis points in the spot dollar/euro quote and 5 basis points in the spot yen/dollar quote. However, the spread of implied 90-day forward dollar/euro quotes is 16 basis points and the spread of 30-day yen/dollar quotes is 7 basis points. The longer the maturity is, the larger spreads are. The reason is that the market maker will find difficult to offset their positions in the interbank market. The longer the maturity, the less likely are unsolicited offsetting orders, and therefore the more likely the market maker is to face other market makers' spreads. Put it differently, the market maker's concern is for uncertainty between rates when buying and selling offsetting contracts.

The difference between the spot and forward rate is defined as **forward premium**. However, the forward premium may be either a positive or a negative value. If it is positive, it is called forward premium; if it is negative, it is a forward discount. In our previous example, the value of the euro in terms of dollar in the forward market is higher than in the spot market. So the euro is trading at a forward premium. A currency is trading at a **forward premium** when the value of that currency in the forward market is higher than in the spot market. As the euro's forward value is higher than the spot value, the euro is trading at forward premium. On the other hand, like the second example shows, the dollar is trading at a **forward discount** because the dollar's forward value against yen is lower than its spot value. Chapter 5 will discuss why the value of a currency is different in spot market than in forward market.

Because the forward premiums are related to the interest rates on the two currencies, the forward premiums are often quoted as an annualized percentage deviation from the current spot rate. This is the forward premium in percentage terms. The formula for forward premium of the foreign currency (the currency in the denominator) in percentage term is

$$\text{Forward premium of the currency (f)} = (360/N \text{ days}) [(F_t^{d/f} - S_0^{d/f})] / (S_0^{d/f}) \quad (3.7)$$

where

$S_0^{d/f}$: the spot exchange rate at time 0

$F_t^{d/f}$: the forward exchange rate matured at time t

N days: the number of days in the forward contract

Multiplying by 360/N days translates the periodic forward premium into an annualized rate with n-period compounding. For example, a 6-month (180 days) forward premium is annualized by multiplying the 6-month forward premium by 2 (360/180). Similarly, a 1-month forward premium is multiplied by 12 (360/30).

The forward premium of the domestic currency (the currency in the numerator) in percentage term can be calculated as:

$$\text{Forward premium of the currency (d)} = (360/N \text{ days}) [(S_0^{d/f} - F_t^{d/f})] / (F_t^{d/f}) \quad (3.8)$$

For example, $S^{\$/€} = 1.4464$, 95 days forward euro $F^{\$/€} = 1.4425$, the annualized forward discount for the euro is calculated by applying **Equation 3.7**:

$$(360/N \text{ days}) [(F_t^{d/f} - S_0^{d/f})] / (S_0^{d/f})$$
$$= (360/95) (\$1.4425/€ - \$1.4464/€) / (\$1.4464/€)$$
$$= (3.789474)(-0.002696) = -0.010785 \text{ or } 1.0218\% \text{ p.a.}$$

The annualized forward premium for the U.S. dollar in this example can be calculated by applying **Equation 3.8**:

$$(360/N \text{ days}) [(S_0^{d/f} - F_t^{d/f})] / (F_t^{d/f}) = (360/95)(1.4464 - 1.4425)/(1.4425) = 1.0245\% \text{ p.a.}$$

A 360-day year is used for most currencies, corresponding to the conventions for quoting interest rates. Exceptions to this convention include the British pound and the Chinese yuan, which are quoted on a 365-day year.

Foreign Exchange Risk and Hedging Strategies

Forward contracts are used to reduce the foreign exchange risk inherent in foreign currency payment or receipt. **Foreign exchange risk** refers to fluctuations in the domestic value of assets, liabilities, income or expenditure due to unanticipated changes in exchange rates. A firm with international operations finds its business activity and financial settlement affected by changes in foreign exchange rates of currencies in which it is dealing. Such firms must measure foreign exchange exposure and manage it so as to maximize the profits of the firm.

A great number of real world cases show that changes in exchange rates have a huge impact on a firm's profits or earnings. For example, Volkswagen, Europe's largest carmaker in January 2004 reported a 95% drop in 2003 fourth-quarter profits, which slumped from €1.05 billion to mere €50 million. For all of 2003, Volkswagen's operating profit fell by 50% from the record levels attained in 2002. There were many causes to explain the company's profit slump, but two of the factors were considered the most important ones. The first was the unprecedented rise in the value of the euro against the dollar during 2003. In 2002, the exchange rate between the U.S. dollar and euro was $1 = 1€. In late 2003, the euro increased its value by 25% from $1 = €1 to $1.25 = €1. This means that the Volkswagen would suffer 20% loss when they converted their U.S. dollar profits to the euro. The second cause was the company's decision to hedge only 30% of its foreign currency exposure, as opposed to the 70% it had traditionally hedged. In total, currency losses due to the euro's rise are estimated to have reduced Volkswagen's operating profits by some €1.2 billion.

Categories of Foreign Exchange Risk

Foreign exchange risk is usually divided into three main categories: transaction exposure, translation exposure, and economic exposure. **Foreign exchange exposure** is what *is* at risk. Foreign exchange exposure does not always result in losses. They may occasionally result in gains to firms because in some cases the exchange rates change favorably to the firms.

Transaction exposure is the extent to which the income from individual transactions is affected by fluctuations in foreign exchange values. Transaction exposure arises from the purchase or sale of goods and services when prices are stated in foreign currencies and the borrowing or lending of funds in foreign currencies. For example, suppose in 2020 an American importing company agreed to purchase 1,000 Haier refrigerators for $500 each for a total price of $500,000, with delivery scheduled for 2021 and payment due then. When the contract was signed in 2020 the RMB/dollar exchange rate stood at ¥6.55/$ so Haier company anticipated receiving ¥3.275 million ($500,000 × ¥6.55/$) for the 1,000 refrigerators when they are delivered. However, imagine that the value of the dollar depreciated against the RMB over the intervening period, so that one dollar only buys ¥6.40 in 2021 when payment is due. Now the total receipts in RMB are ¥3.2 million ($500,000 × ¥6.4/$), in decrease of ¥75,000! The transaction exposure here is $500,000, which is the company's account receivable of foreign currency. The company is exposed to losses due to an adverse movement in exchange rates between the time when the deal was signed and when the refrigerators were paid for.

Translation exposure is the potential change in the reported financial statements of a company due to changes in exchange rates (also called accounting exposure). Translation exposure arises as the parent firm translates the financial statements of its foreign subsidiaries back into its domestic currency using the generally accepted accounting principles of the parent country. Foreign subsidiaries of U.S. companies, for example, must restate local euro, pound, yen, and so on, financial statements into U.S. dollars so the foreign values can be added to the parent's U.S. dollar-denominated balance sheet and income statement. The resulting accounting gains or losses are said to be unrealized — they are "paper" gains and losses — but they are still important. Consider a European firm with a subsidiary in U.S. If the value of the dollar depreciates significantly against the euro this would substantially reduce the euro value of the U.S. subsidiary's equity. In turn, this would reduce the total euro value of the firm's equity reported in its consolidated balance sheet. This would raise the apparent leverage of the firm (its debt ratio), which could increase the firm's cost of borrowing and potentially limit its access to the capital market. This is exactly the case in 2002–2004. The dollar fell rapidly in value against the euro and many European firms in the U.S. suffered from significant translation exposure. Usually, performance evaluations and management compensation are often tied to accounting performance, so managers have a strong incentive to minimize their accounting exposures.

Economic exposure refers to potential changes in all (monetary or nonmonetary) future cash flows due to unexpected changes in exchange rates. It is concerned with long-term effect of changes in exchange rates on future prices, sales, and costs. Therefore, economic exposure measures the amount of potential gain or loss in the value of a firm due to the exchange rate fluctuations. This is distinct from transaction exposure, which is concerned with effect of exchange rate changes on individual transactions, most of which are short-term affairs that will be executed within a few weeks or months. Consider the effect of wide swings in the value of the dollar on many U.S. firms' international competitiveness. The rapid rise in the value of the dollar on the foreign exchange market in the 1990s hurt the price competitiveness of many U.S. producers in world markets. U.S. manufacturers that relied heavily on exports saw their export volume and world market share decline. The reverse phenomenon occurred in 2000–2004, when the dollar declined against most major currencies. The fall in the value of the dollar helped increase the price competitiveness of U.S. manufacturers in world markets.

Hedging with Forward Contracts

Changes in exchange rates can affect not only firms that are directly engaged in international trade but also purely domestic firms. Consider, for example, a Chinese motor vehicle manufacturer that sources only domestic materials and sells exclusively in China, with no foreign-currency receivables or payables in its accounting book. This seemingly purely domestic Chinese firm can be subject to foreign exchange risk if it competes against imports, say, from a Japanese motor vehicle manufacturer. When the Japanese yen depreciates against RMB, this is likely to lead to a lower RMB price of Japanese cars, boosting their sales in the Chinese car market, thereby hurting the Chinese manufacturer.

Changes in exchange rates may affect not only the operating cash flows of a firm by altering its position but also home currency values of the firm's assets and liabilities. Consider a Chinese firm that has borrowed the U.S. dollars. Since the RMB amount needed to pay off the dollar debt depends on the RMB/dollar exchange rate, the Chinese firm can gain or lose as the dollar depreciates or appreciates against the RMB. A classic example of the peril of facing currency exposure is provided by Laker Airways, a British firm pioneered the concept of mass-marketed, low-fare air travel. The company heavily borrowed U.S. dollars to finance acquisitions of aircraft while it derived more than half of its revenue in sterling. As the dollar kept appreciating against the British pound throughout the first half the 1980s, the burden of servicing the dollar debts became overwhelming for Laker Airways, forcing it to default.

Foreign exchange risk makes successful planning difficult. An individual or firm always tries to avoid or eliminate the foreign exchange risk. One of the strategies the financial managers usually take is the hedging. **Hedging** is the act of offsetting exposure to risk. The exposure to be hedged can arise from a commercial transaction, a foreign investment or a liability in foreign currency. The exposure can be a long position or a short position. A position is said to be long when foreign currency or a claim in foreign currency is owned. In other words, a **long position** in foreign exchange refers to the amounts of foreign exchange that will be received (account receivable in foreign currency). A long position is an asset for a company. A position is short when there is a liability in foreign currency. That is to say, a **short position** in foreign exchange means the amounts of foreign currency that will be paid (account payable in foreign currency). A short position is a liability for a company. For example, an export billed in foreign currency creates a long position for the exporting firm in the form of a claim in foreign currency for value of the merchandise. On the other hand, an import billed in foreign currency creates a short position for the importing company in the form of a liability for the amount of the purchase. Now let's discuss how to hedge a long position or a short position.

Hedging a long position

Hedging a long position involves selling foreign exchange forward. For example, a Chinese textile company that has just signed a contract for $1 million worth of jeans to be shipped to U.S. and paid for three months later. When the contract is signed the spot exchange rate is: $S^{¥/\$} = 6.50$.

The company has a long position in dollar which is the company's asset. The chief financial officer of the company fears a fall in the value of the dollar, which would reduce the company' income when the jeans are finally delivered and the dollar proceeds are converted into RMB. In order to cover the risk exposure his banker suggests that he sell $1 million three-month forward. The forward rate is happened to be : $F^{¥/\$} = 6.45$. This means that no matter what the spot exchange rate is in the future, the company will deliver $1 million to the bank and the bank will credit the company's account by ¥6.45 million. By selling the dollar revenue forward, the company can guarantee what its income will be in RMB.

Figure 3.3 illustrates the change in the company's risk exposure resulting from the forward transaction. The solid line represents the company's income in RMB before making the forward transaction. It depends on the level of the exchange rate. At higher values of the dollar, RMB income is higher. At lower dollar values, it is lower. The broken line represents the company's income after the forward transaction. In this case, income in RMB is insensitive to the level of the exchange rate. No matter what the value of the dollar is in the future, RMB income is the same. The forward transaction has effectively eliminated the foreign exchange risk. Notice that in this example, the company's long position on foreign currency (the dollar) is hedged by a short position in the forward contract because the company is going to sell the dollars.

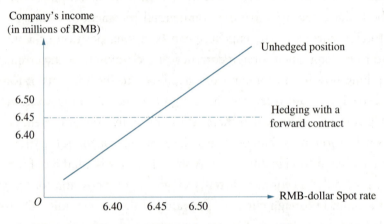

Figure 3.3 Hedging A Long Position

Eliminating foreign exchange risk has disadvantages as well as advantages. The main advantage is that if the value of the dollar falls, the company has no loss of income, which is guaranteed at ¥6.45 million. The disadvantage is that if the value of the dollar goes up, the company will not benefit from the appreciation. Furthermore, hedging the foreign exchange risk exposes the company to another kind of risk. Suppose that the exporter is not paid on time or that some of his merchandise is refused. The exporter will not have enough dollars to honor his forward contract. In order to make up the difference he will either have to roll over the forward contract at a new rate or buy dollars at the going spot rate. Either rate might be different from the ¥6.45/$ exchange rate of the forward contract. If the rollover rate is lower or the spot ask rate is higher, the company will make an unanticipated loss. Hedging in the forward market is a two-edged sword.

As a general rule of thumb, then, we can say that if the treasurer feels that there is a strong chance that the value of the dollar will fall and a weak chance that it will rise, the treasurer should hedge with a forward contract. In the opposite case where there is a strong chance that the dollar will appreciate and a weak chance that it will depreciate, he should not hedge.

Chapter 3　THE FOREIGN EXCHANGE MARKET

Hedging a short position

Hedging a short position involves buying foreign exchange forward. Consider a Chinese electronic appliance company that has just signed a contract to buy $1 million of desktops in three months from its Texas supplier in U.S. The current spot exchange rate is: $S^{¥/\$}$ = 6.50. The company has a short position or an account payable in dollars, which is a dollar liability.

The treasurer of the electronic appliance company fears that the dollar will appreciate and thus raise the cost of the merchandise in RMB when the time comes to pay for them. In order to avoid this undesirable eventuality, the treasurer goes to the company's banker and buys $1 million three-month forward. The forward rate is again: $F^{¥/\$}$ = 6.45.

In three months the Chinese company will deliver ¥6.45 million and receive $1 million, no matter what the exchange rate is. **Figure 3.4** illustrates the change in the company's risk exposure resulting from the forward transaction. The solid line represents the company's expenditure in RMB before making the forward transaction. It depends on the level of the exchange rate. At higher values of the dollar, RMB expenditure is higher. At lower dollar values it is lower. The broken line represents the company's expenditure after the forward transaction. Expenditure in RMB is insensitive to the level of the exchange rate. No matter what the value of the dollar is three months later, RMB expenditure is the same. The forward transaction has effectively eliminated the foreign exchange risk. This example indicates that a short position on foreign currency should be hedged by a long position in the forward contract.

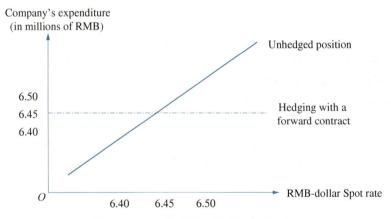

Figure 3.4　Hedging A Short Position

Here again, eliminating foreign exchange risk has disadvantages as well as advantages. The key advantage is that if the value of the dollar rises, the company has no increase in expenditure, which is guaranteed at ¥6.45 million. The disadvantage is that if the value of the dollar goes down, the company will not benefit from the depreciation. Furthermore, as we saw in the preceding example, hedging the foreign exchange risk exposes the company to another kind of risk. Suppose that delivery dates from the Texas supplier are not respected or that some of the merchandise is not up to standards and must be refused. Expenditure for the merchandise will be lower than expected, which will leave the company with dollar balances once the forward contract is consummated. When the dollar balances are converted back into RMB, the spot exchange rate might be higher or lower than the ¥6.45/$ exchange rate of the forward contract. If it is higher, the company will make an unanticipated gain. If it is lower, it will make an unanticipated loss. This kind of risk would not be present in the absence of the forward contract.

Just opposite to hedging a long position, if you strongly believe that the dollar will appreciate in the future, you should hedge your short position with a forward contract. Otherwise, if the chance for appreciation of the dollar is very week, it is not wise to use a forward contract as your hedging strategy.

Other Types of Exchange Rates

Nominal and Real Exchange Rate

Policy-makers and economists are very much concerned about analyzing the implications of exchange rate changes for an economy and its balance of payments. The exchange rate itself does not convey much information, and to analyze the effects and implications of exchange rate changes economists compile indices of the nominal and real effective exchange rates.

The nominal exchange rate is the exchange rate that prevails at a given date. The exchange rate published in a newspaper or magazine or some websites are all nominal exchange rates. The nominal exchange rate does not merely reflect changes in price levels in the relative countries. It is mainly determined by the demand and the supply of the relative currencies in the foreign exchange market. The nominal exchange rate just tells us how many units of another currency that one currency is able to exchange for.

The real exchange rate is the nominal exchange rate adjusted for relative changes in domestic and foreign price levels, that is, adjusted for inflation differential. Therefore, the real exchange rate reflects the purchasing power of a currency in terms of the goods and services the currency can actually buy in another country.

Suppose right now the RMB versus U.S. dollar spot exchange rate is $S_0^{¥/\$} = 6.5$. Expected inflation is $E[p^¥] = 10\%$ in China and $E[p^\$] = 3\%$ in the United States. If change in the nominal exchange rate merely reflects changes in the relative purchasing power of RMB and dollar, the expected future spot rate next year would be:

$$E[S_1^{¥/\$}] = S_0^{¥/\$} [(1+ E[p^¥]) / (1 + E[p^\$])] = (¥6.5/\$)(1.1/1.03) = ¥6.9417/\$$$

If next year the expected inflation rate is the same as the actual inflation rate and the exchange rate is ¥6.9417/$, then the nominal exchange rate equals the real exchange rate because the change in exchange rate matches the change in price level of the two countries. What if one year later the inflation estimates turn out to be accurate but dollar has appreciated to $S_1^{¥/\$} = 6.70$? Apparently, ¥6.70/$ is not the real exchange rate because it does not match the change in inflation rate. In nominal terms, dollar appreciates relative to RMB by 3.08% [(6.70 − 6.50)/6.50]. But, relative to the expected spot rate of ¥6.9417/$, dollar is undervalued. The undervalued currency is the currency whose value is lower than it is supposed to be. We'll discuss this topic in Chapter 5 in detail. The rate of undervaluation of dollar can be calculated by the following formula:

$$[(\text{Actual exchange rate}) - (\text{Expected exchange rate})] / (\text{Expected exchange rate})$$
$$= (¥6.70/\$ - ¥6.9417/\$)/(¥6.9417/\$) = -3.48\% \quad (3.9)$$

The real exchange rate captures changes in the purchasing power of a currency relative to other currencies by backing out the effects of inflation from changes in nominal exchange rates. The real exchange rate, say, of the f currency relative to the d currency, will be denoted $S_R^{d/f}$. It is defined to be the nominal exchange rate multiplied by the ratio of the price levels:

$$S_R^{d/f} = S_1^{d/f} / [(p^d)/(p^f)] \quad \text{or} \quad S_1^{d/f} \times [(p^f)/(p^d)] \quad (3.10)$$

where
$S_R^{d/f}$: real exchange rate
$S_1^{d/f}$: spot exchange rate of the currency d relative to the currency f at period 1
P^d: currency d's price index
P^f: currency f's price index

In the above example, the real exchange rate at the period one would be:

$$S_R^{¥/\$} = S_1^{¥/\$} \times (p^\$)/(p^¥)$$
$$S_R^{¥/\$} = ¥6.50/\$ \times (103)/(110) = ¥6.50/\$ \times 0.9364 = 6.0866$$

We can apply **Equation 3.10** to calculate the real exchange rate if one year later dollar has appreciated to $S_1^{¥/\$} = 6.70$ and the inflation index in China and U.S. is 110 and 103 respectively.

$$S_R^{¥/\$} = S_1^{¥/\$} \times (p^\$)/(p^¥)$$
$$S_R^{¥/\$} = ¥6.70/\$ \times (103)/(110) = 6.2736$$

Here, the real exchange rate of dollar indicates that the U.S. goods are more competitive on international markets than would be suggested by the nominal exchange rate. In real terms, dollar depreciates against RMB, that is, one unit of American goods or services can be exchanged into fewer Chinese goods or services now, so the U.S. goods and services are cheaper and will create an incentive for people to buy. Therefore, the competitiveness of U.S. export depends on the real exchange rate. Appreciation of the real exchange rate makes U.S. export more expensive to foreigners, reducing their competitiveness, while depreciation of the real exchange rate makes U.S. export seem cheaper to foreigners, improving their competitiveness.

Effective Exchange Rate

Since most countries of the world do not conduct all their trade with a single foreign country, policy makers are not so much concerned with what is happening to their exchange rate against a single foreign currency but rather what is happening to it against a basket of foreign currencies with which the country trades. **The effective exchange rate (EER)** is a measure of whether or not the currency is appreciating or depreciating against a weighted basket of foreign currencies. The effective exchange rate is also called "trade weighted" exchange rate, because it is computed by formulating a weighted average (reflecting the importance of each country's currency in international trade) of selected bilateral rates.

Exhibit 3.7 shows the nominal effective exchange rate indices from 1999 to 2020 for selected major developed countries. The nominal effective index simply calculates how the currency value relates to some given base period, but it is used in the formation of the real effective exchange rate index. The real effective exchange rate index tells how the weighted average purchasing power of the currency has changed relative to the selected base period.

Exhibit 3.7 Nominal Effective Exchange Rate Indices for Major Developed Countries 1999–2020 (Annual Averages)

	Australia	U.K.	Canada	Euro	Japan	U.S.
1999	100	100	100	100	100	100
2000	95.03	104.18	103.62	87.16	113.60	105.13
2001	88.20	102.26	100.87	87.62	103.34	110.71
2002	91.30	102.88	98.73	89.89	98.42	108.79
2003	102.02	99.02	107.70	100.48	100.37	97.77
2004	109.62	103.71	113.61	104.25	103.59	91.00
2005	112.80	102.29	121.61	102.86	100.22	89.30
2006	110.77	102.77	129.59	102.85	93.10	87.79

(Continued)

	Australia	U.K.	Canada	Euro	Japan	U.S.
2007	118.38	104.91	134.81	106.35	88.04	83.16
2008	115.27	91.46	133.36	110.19	97.83	79.40
2009	109.87	80.66	125.94	111.71	111.42	82.43
2010	126.57	80.71	138.75	104.54	117.57	80.59
2011	135.81	79.87	141.55	104.29	124.30	76.22
2012	138.40	82.81	141.33	98.64	125.49	78.02
2013	129.94	80.63	137.18	102.17	101.03	78.77
2014	121.73	85.51	128.18	102.42	93.20	79.99
2015	109.29	89.73	114.94	92.63	86.20	89.26
2016	110.03	79.99	111.77	95.27	98.92	91.11
2017	113.85	75.25	114.20	97.55	95.68	91.14
2018	108.66	75.80	113.16	100.03	95.32	88.95
2019	104.08	75.37	112.20	98.20	99.91	92.34
2020	102.79	74.96	110.69	99.74	101.62	91.66

Note: 1999 average = 100.
Source: European Central Bank (ww.ecb.europa.eu), January, 2021.

According to the definition of the effective exchange rate, it is a measure of a currency's strength and weakness against a basket of currencies. To construct an effective exchange rate, we need first choose a basket of currencies. For example, to construct the effective exchange rate of the euro, the European Central Bank used 19 currencies of its major trading partners as the currency basket. Second, we should select a base period which serves as a reference point in time. For example, Exhibit 3.7 uses 1999 as the base period. The value of each currency was set at 100 in the base period. Third, we should assign weights for each currency in the basket. The weights are a means of placing greater emphasis on the more important currencies in the currency basket and less emphasis on the least important currencies in the currency basket. Typically, economists determine the weights on bilateral trade flows.

The following example shows how to construct the U.S. dollar effective exchange rate from 2018 to 2019. For simplicity, we only select two of the top trading partners of the United States, the Canada and the Japan. The base year is 2018 with the value of 100. **Exhibit 3.8** gives the relative information.

Exhibit 3.8 Nominal exchange rates and trade volume to the U.S.

(millions of U.S. dollar)

Country	S (2018)	S (2019)	Export to U.S.	Import from U.S.
Canada	C$1.23/$	C$1.18/$	275	150
Japan	¥100/$	¥105/$	235	175

The weights assigned to the Canadian dollar and Japanese yen are determined by the importance of Canadian foreign trade to U.S. and the importance of Japanese foreign trade accounting for the total foreign trade of the United States. The Canadian exports to and imports from U.S. are $425 million ($275m + $150m), which accounts for 50.90% ($425m/$835m) of the U.S. total foreign trade. Therefore, the weight assigned to the Canadian dollar should be 50.90%. The Japanese exports to and imports from U.S. are $410m ($235m + $175m). It accounts for 49.10% of the U.S. total foreign trade. So the weight of the Japanese yen should be 49.10%. The weights always sum to 1.

The effective exchange rate is constructed by calculating each of the bilateral exchange rates relative to the base-year exchange rate. The C$/$ rate in 2018 was 1.23 and 1.18 in 2019, and the ¥/$ rate was 100 in 2018 and 105 in 2019. The dollar depreciated against the Canadian dollar but appreciated against the Japanese yen. Was the dollar "stronger" or "weaker" in general terms? In other words, since the value of the dollar in 2018 was set to 100, was the dollar value in 2019 below or above 100? That's what the effective exchange rate of the dollar will tell us.

As we know the value of the dollar in terms of Canadian dollar was 1.23 in 2018 and 1.18 in 2019, this means the value of the dollar in 2019 was 95.93% (1.18/1.23) of the 2018 value. By the same token, the value of the dollar in terms of Japanese yen in 2019 was 105% (105/100) of the 2008 value. The effective exchange rate for 2019 can be calculated as follows:

$$EER_{2019} = [(0.5090)(0.9593) + (0.491)(1.05)] \times 100 = 100.38$$

The value of 100.38 refers to the dollar index (effective dollar exchange rate). Because the value of the dollar was set 100 in 2018, the dollar index increased by 0.38% in 2019. In other words, the dollar was "stronger" generally even though it lost value relative to the Canadian dollar.

The real effective exchange rate index tells how the weighted average purchasing power of a currency has changed relative to the selected base period. The difference between the nominal effective exchange rate and real effective exchange rate is that the latter is adjusted for the effects of inflation. It means we have to convert each of the nominal exchange rates in the currency baskets we have chosen into the real exchange rate to compute the real effective exchange rate. So we also need the information about the changes in prices of the relative countries. We then would complete the remaining calculation as described earlier.

Summary

1. Foreign exchange is simply another country's money. The most important character of the foreign exchange is convertibility. Foreign exchange rate is the price of one currency in terms of another.
2. The foreign exchange market serves three main functions. One is to convert one currency into another (transfer purchasing power); the second is to provide international liquidity for international trade and investment (provide credit); the third is to minimize the exchange risk (minimize risk).
3. The foreign exchange market is the largest financial market in the world in terms of its trading volume. The core of the foreign exchange market is the interbank market. It is an informal, over-the-counter, around-the-clock market that includes the major commercial banks and some specialized brokers located in the principal financial centers throughout the world. They are linked by telephone and computer screens, and most use a special satellite communications network called SWIFT.
4. The interbank market is composed of dealers (traders) and brokers. The role of the dealer and the broker is essentially different. The dealer usually operates out of the foreign exchange trading room of a major bank and is essentially a market-maker, standing ready to buy and sell foreign currencies on a more or less continuous basis. The broker is an intermediary between traders, bringing buyers and sellers together and contributing to market efficiency. Brokers also serve as a source of information for traders and make it possible for traders to remain anonymous when revealing their identity would put them at a trading disadvantage.
5. The electronic foreign exchange trading is very popular nowadays. It is possible that the old telephone-based system will be supplanted by pure electronic trading. An electronic communication network (ECN) collects and matches buy and sell orders, and it displays the best available prices.
6. The spot exchange market is for spot transactions. By convention, the settlement date or "value date" is the second business day from the "deal date".
7. Foreign exchange rates can be quoted in two ways: (a) the number of units of domestic currency for one unit of foreign currency known as the direct quotes, or (b) the number of units of foreign currency for one unit of domestic currency known as the indirect quotes. Most countries use direct quotes. The Euro Zone, the United Kingdom, and a few of former British colonies use indirect quote.

8. European quote is the foreign currency price of one U.S. dollar. American quote is the U.S. dollar price per foreign currency unit. European quote and American quote must involve the U.S. dollar.
9. The bid quote is the price at which the bank wants to buy; while the ask quote is the price at which the bank wants to sell. Costs or gains on foreign exchange transactions are in the form of bid-ask spreads. They are usually expressed as "points". The spread can also be expressed as a percentage term known as the bid-ask margin.
10. A cross rate is a bilateral exchange rate that does not involve the U.S. dollar.
11. If a currency gains value in the foreign exchange market, the currency appreciates; if a currency loses value in the foreign exchange market, the currency depreciates. The appreciation and depreciation of a currency are usually measured by the percentage change.
12. Percentage changes in currency values are asymmetric. The value of the foreign currency in the denominator of an exchange rate quote changes according to the formula: [(Ending rate − Beginning rate)] / (Beginning rate).
13. The no-arbitrage condition for triangular arbitrage in the currency market is that the product of the three exchange rates equals to 1.
14. Forward exchange market is for forward transactions. Forward exchange rate is the price to be paid for delivery of a currency in a future date. Determination of the value date for a forward contract begins by finding today's spot value date.
15. A swap transaction is the simultaneous purchase and sale of a given amount of foreign exchange for two different value dates. Foreign exchange swaps usually take the forms of spot-forward, forward-forward, and non-deliverable forwards (NDFs).
16. Forward exchange rate can be quoted outright or by swap points. Interbank market conventionally quotes forward rates in terms of spot rate and the number of swap points. Swap points can be added to or subtracted from the spot rate to construct the forward rate. If the swap points are ascending, the swap points are added to the spot rate; if the swap points are descending, the swap points are subtracted from the spot rate.
17. When a currency's forward rate is higher than the spot rate, the currency is traded at forward premium. When its forward rate is lower than the current rate, it is traded at the forward discount. Forward premiums make domestic currency cash flows differ from what they would be at the spot rate and the bid-ask spread accentuates the difference.
18. The bid-ask spread of the forward rate is larger than that of the spot rate. The longer the maturity is, the larger the spread is. Market dealers' concern is for uncertainty between rates when buying and selling offsetting contracts.
19. Changes in exchange rates can dramatically alter the profitability of foreign trade and investment deals. Financial managers must understand the potential risks the firms

face when they are dealing with foreign currencies. The three types of exposure to foreign exchange risk are transaction exposure, translation exposure, and economic exposure.
20. Transaction exposure refers to accounts receivable or accounts payable in foreign exchange. It results from changes in exchange rates after transactions are initiated, but before they are settled.
21. Translation exposure is the potential for accounting-derived changes in owner's equity to occur because of the need to "translate" foreign currency financial statements of foreign subsidiaries into a single reporting currency to prepare worldwide consolidated financial statements.
22. Economic exposure measures the change in the present value of the firm resulting from any change in future operating cash flows of the firm caused by an unexpected change in exchange rates. The change in value depends on the effect of the exchange rate change on future sales volume, prices, and costs.
23. Many techniques are available to cover or hedge exposure to risk of exchange rates. The simplest and most common technique involves using a forward contract.
24. A long position in foreign exchange (account receivable in foreign currency) can be hedged by selling foreign exchange forward. A short position (account payable in foreign currency) can be hedged by buying foreign exchange forward.
25. Hedging has its disadvantages because, although it does eliminate adverse moves in the exchange rate, it also eliminates the possibility of benefiting from favorable moves.
26. Real exchange rate is the nominal exchange rate adjusted for relative changes in domestic and foreign price levels. So the real exchange rate captures changes in the purchasing power of a currency relative to other currencies by backing out the effects of inflation from changes in nominal exchange rates.
27. Policy-makers are more concerned what is happening to its own currency against a basket of foreign currencies with which the country has close trading relationship. The effective exchange rate is a measure of whether or not the currency is appreciating or depreciating against a weighted basket of foreign currencies.
28. To construct the effective exchange rate, three steps must be followed: to choose a currency basket; to choose a base year and to assign the weights for each currency in the basket.

Key Concepts and Terms

1. Alipay   支付宝

2. American term (American quote)   美式标价
3. Appreciation   升值
4. Arbitrager   套利者
5. Ask quote (ask price, selling price, offer price)   卖出价
6. Basis point   基点
7. Bid quote (bid price, buying price)   买入价
8. Bid-ask margin   用百分比表示的买卖差价
9. Bid-ask spread   买卖差价
10. Cross rate   交叉汇率
11. Depreciation   贬值
12. Direct quote   直接标价
13. Economic exposure   经济敞口
14. Effective exchange rate (EER)   有效汇率
15. Electronic communication network (ECN)   电子通信网络
16. Electronic foreign exchange trading (eFX)   电子外汇交易
17. European terms (European quotes)   欧式标价
18. Foreign exchange   外汇
19. Foreign exchange arbitrage   套汇
20. Foreign exchange broker   外汇经纪人
21. Foreign exchange dealer   外汇交易商
22. Foreign exchange market   外汇市场
23. Foreign exchange market turnover   外汇市场交易量
24. Foreign exchange rate   外汇汇率
25. Foreign exchange risk   汇率风险
26. Forward against forward   远期对远期的掉期交易
27. Forward exchange market   远期外汇市场
28. Forward exchange rate   远期汇率
29. Forward discount   远期升水
30. Forward premium   远期贴水
31. Forward value date   远期起息日,远期交易中双方交割约定货币的日期
32. Hedging   对冲,或套期保值
33. Indirect quote   间接标价
34. Long position   多头
35. Market dealer   市场经销商
36. Market maker   做市商
37. Middle rate   中间汇率
38. Nominal exchange rate   名义汇率
39. Non-deliverable forwards (NDFs)   非交割远期交易

40.	Real effective exchange rate	实际有效汇率
41.	Real exchange rate	实际汇率
42.	Short position	空头
43.	Spatial arbitrage	两地套汇
44.	Speculator	投机商
45.	Spot against forward	即期对远期的掉期交易
46.	Spot exchange rate	即期汇率
47.	Spot transaction	即期交易
48.	Straight-through processing (STP)	直通式交易程序
49.	Swaps	掉期，外汇交易的一种，与同一对手方进行即期–远期交易或远期–远期交易
50.	Swap points	掉期基点，即用基点表示的即期汇率与远期汇率的差
51	Transaction exposure	交易敞口
52.	Translation exposure	转换敞口
53.	Triangular arbitrage	三角套汇
54.	Value date	起息日，外汇交易双方货币交割日
55.	Vehicle currency	载体货币
56.	SWIFT (Society for Worldwide Interbank Financial Telecommunications)	全球同业银行金融电信协会

Questions

1. Define the foreign exchange and foreign exchange rate.
2. What are the three main functions of the foreign exchange market?
3. Why does most interbank currency trading worldwide involve the U.S. dollar?
4. How do we distinguish a dealer from a broker in the foreign exchange market?
5. Discuss the role of foreign exchange brokers in the foreign exchange markets.
6. How is a foreign exchange speculator different from an arbitrager?
7. Explain the European and American quotes.
8. Take an example to show what cross exchange rate is.
9. Explain the situation where the bid quote is higher than the ask quote.
10. What conditions must be satisfied for arbitragers to make profits in currency arbitrage?
11. What is an appreciation of the RMB relative to the U.S. dollar? What happens to the yuan price of the dollar in this situation?
12. Discuss the difference between the spot and forward market.

13. How are the swap points related to the forward exchange rates?
14. Who are the participants in the forward exchange market? What advantages does this market afford these participants?
15. What are the pros and cons to take the advantage of a forward contract?
16. What is meant by a currency trading at a discount or at a premium in the forward market?
17. Compare and contrast the transaction, translation and economic risk exposure.
18. What is a real exchange rate? What is the difference between a nominal exchange rate and a real exchange rate?
19. What does the effective exchange rate measure?
20. How the effective exchange rate is constructed?

Chapter 4
INTERNATIONAL MONETARY SYSTEM

LEARNING OBJECTIVES

- Discuss the concept of international monetary system.
- Examine the characteristics, pros and cons, and the fall of gold standard.
- Learn the mechanism of the Bretton Woods System and why it collapsed.
- Understand the floating exchange rate system and its characteristics.
- Learn the various exchange rate arrangements adopted by many countries nowadays.
- Analyze the pros and cons of the fixed and floating exchange rate systems.

International transactions in trade and investment must conduct in a global environment that is rationally organized. Since every country uses its own currency, households, firms, governments must be able to exchange foreign currencies in order to purchase foreign goods, services and investment products. A rational system for clearing and settling these transactions must be placed into operation. This system is what is called international monetary system. So we can say that the international monetary system is the global environment within which international trade and investment and other economic activities can operate smoothly. It is actually an institutional framework within which international settlements are made and the exchange rates among currencies are determined.

This chapter begins with the explanation of the definition of international monetary system. The next section introduces a brief history of the international monetary system from the days of the classical gold standard to the present time. The gold standard and Bretton Woods System are the typical fixed exchange rate system under which the foreign exchange rate is fixed or pegged by government decree. The Bretton Woods System was regarded as a very successful international monetary system after World War II. After 1973, major developed countries have widely adopted floating exchange rate system. The free floating exchange rate system means the exchange rate is purely determined by the market forces, so the currency values fluctuate from minute to minute. The following section describes various other exchange rate systems chosen by emerging market economies and other developing countries including crawling peg, currency boards and no separate legal tender system. Finally, we compare the two most important exchange rate systems — the fixed and floating exchange rate system.

Definition of the International Monetary System

International monetary system is broadly defined as a complex set of conventions, rules, procedures and institutions that govern the conduct of financial relations between nations. Usually the system needs to determine an international currency as a medium of exchange in international transactions, how the international currency is related to the currencies of different countries, how balance of payments disequilibrium is resolved and the consequences that the adjustment process will have on the countries involved. Different systems have different ways to deal with those issues.

The international monetary system is based on the exchange rate systems adopted by individual countries. An **exchange rate system** is a set of rules governing the value of a country's currency relative to other foreign currencies. The choice of fixed or floating or other exchange rate system depends on the macroeconomic goals a country tries to achieve because there is a very close connection between exchange rate system and domestic monetary policy. Like a country's monetary system, the international monetary system must provide an international currency for facilitating international trade and investment. Three kinds of the money have been used as an international currency.

Commodity money such as gold and silver were widely used in the early days. However, as the volume of international trade expanded in the wake of the Industrial Revolution, a more convenient means of financing international trade was needed. Shipping large quantities of gold and silver around the world to finance international trade seemed impractical. The solution adopted was to arrange for payment in bank notes or drafts and for governments to agree to convert the bank notes into gold on demand at a fixed rate.

Commodity-backed money refers to mainly the bank notes which are backed by commodities like gold or silver. The bank notes can be converted into gold or silver, which means the government cannot easily increase its supply.

Fiat money is inconvertible money that is made legal tender by a government decree. Fiat money is backed by nothing; the only thing that gives the money value is the faith placed in it by the people that use it. Fiat money is money because the government says they are, not because they are backed by physical commodities. When the government is unable to repay

Chapter 4 INTERNATIONAL MONETARY SYSTEM

all its debt in real values, fiat money with unlimited credit creation is a perfect solution. Once that confidence is gone, money irreversibly becomes worthless.

Now we briefly review the history of the international monetary system. It helps you to understand how alternative exchange rate systems affect asset values across national borders. This is essential knowledge for managing the value and financial risks of an individual investment portfolio or a multinational corporation.

The Gold Standard (1876-1944)

The gold standard was a commitment by participating countries to fix the prices of their domestic currencies in terms of a specified amount of gold, that is, to announce the **gold par value** (or **gold parity**). National money and other forms of money (bank deposits and notes) were freely converted into gold at the announced rate. The first full-fledged gold standard was established in Great Britain in 1821, when bank notes from the Bank of England were made fully redeemable for gold.

The Classical Gold Standard (1876-1914)

The period from 1876 to 1914 was known as the classical gold standard. During that time the majority of countries adhered to gold. It was also a period of unprecedented economic growth with relatively free trade in goods, labor, and capital.

The gold standard was a domestic standard, regulating the quantity and growth rate of a country's money supply. Because new production of gold would add only a small fraction to the accumulated stock and because the authorities guaranteed free convertibility of gold into nongold money, the gold standard assured that the money supply and, hence, the price level would not vary much. But periodic surges in the world's gold stock, such as the gold discoveries in Australia and California around 1850, caused price levels to be very unstable in the short run.

The gold standard is an important beginning for a discussion of international monetary system because when each currency is defined in terms of its gold value, all currencies are linked in a system of fixed exchange rates. Therefore, the gold standard was also an international standard — determining the value of a country's currency in terms of other countries' currencies. Because adherents to the standard maintained a fixed price for gold, rates of exchange between currencies tied to gold were necessarily fixed. The gold standard is a typical fixed exchange rate system because the exchange rate is quite stable. A **fixed exchange rate** means that the value of a currency is fixed to something else. Under the gold standard, the value of a currency was fixed to gold. A fixed exchange rate does not necessarily mean the exchange rate never changes. It only means that the flexibility of the exchange rate is limited to a narrow range, called a **parity band**, around the chosen fixed rate, called the **par value**. For example, as the **Figure 4.1** shows the United States fixed the price of gold at $20.67 per ounce; Britain fixed the price at £4.2474 per ounce. The exchange rate between dollar and pound — "par exchange rate" — necessarily equaled $4.8665 per pound. Therefore, $4.8665/£ was the par value or mint par of exchange rate.

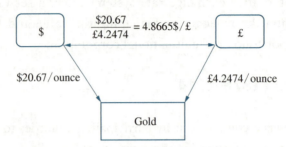

Figure 4.1　Exchange Rate Determination under the Gold Standard

If the dollar/pound rate deviated from the par exchange rate, arbitrage opportunity would exist. This is because three conditions should be met for a real gold standard. First, the gold coinage was unrestricted which means people could bring the gold to a mint and ask for making gold coins. Second, the banknotes could be freely converted into gold and vice versa. Third, gold could be freely exported or imported. Those conditions guaranteed that the exchange rate between currencies were necessarily stable. For example, if the U.S. dollar versus the British pound rate were $5/£ instead of $4.8665/£, an arbitrager could pay $20.67 for one ounce of gold in America. He then could sell the gold in England for £4.2474. The £4.2474 would have exchanged on the foreign exchange market for £4.2474 × 5$/£, or $21.237, earning a profit of $0.567. Here we ignore the transportation costs of gold. Everyone would be selling pounds in the foreign exchange market but no one would be buying pounds. The excess supply of pounds would make the exchange rate fall to $4.8665/£, the point at which the arbitrage opportunity disappears.

In reality, dollar/pound rate in the foreign exchange market would just move around the par exchange rate plus and minus the transportation costs and other fees. Suppose that the fee to transport 1/4.2474 ounce of gold from England to the United Sates is 1% of the pound exchange rate which is $0.048665. The dollar/pound exchange rate would then fluctuate between $4.915165/£ (4.8665 + 0.048655) and $4.817835/£ (4.8665 − 0.048665). The rate of $4.915165/£ is the U.K. **gold import point** (the U.S. gold export point) and the rate of $4.817835/£ is the U.K. **gold export point** (the U.S. gold import point). If the exchange rate in the foreign exchange market is above $4.915165/£, the U.S. residents who owed pound debts would prefer paying gold; on the other hand, if the exchange rate is below $4.817835/£, those who had dollar debts would like to pay gold instead. The gold export and import points are actually the parity band of the exchange rate fluctuations. This example indicates why the exchange rate under the gold standard was pretty stable as long as the gold par value of the relative currencies remained unchanged. It remained in a range or band centered on the ratio of the mint parity values.

Because exchange rates were fixed, the gold standard caused price levels around the world to move together. This co-movement occurred mainly through an automatic balance of payments adjustment process called the price-specie-flow mechanism.

The Balance of Payments Adjustment under the Gold Standard

The great strength claimed for the gold standard was that it contained a powerful mechanism for achieving balance of payments equilibrium by all countries. A country is said to be in balance of payments equilibrium when the income its residents earn from export is equal to the money its residents pay to other countries for import (the current account of its balance of payments is in balance). The following example shows how the mechanism worked.

Suppose a technological innovation brought about faster real economic growth in the United States. With the supply of money essentially fixed in the short run (bank notes need to be backed by a gold reserve of a minimum stated ratio), this caused the U.S. prices to fall. Prices of the U.S. export then fell relative to the prices of import. This caused the British (and other countries) to demand more the U.S. exports and Americans to demand fewer imports. A U.S. balance of payments surplus was created, causing gold (specie) to flow from the United Kingdom (and other countries) to the United States. The gold inflow increased the U.S. money supply, reversing the initial fall in prices. In the United Kingdom (and other countries) the gold outflow reduced the money supply and, hence, lowered the price levels. The net result was balanced prices among countries and thus balanced balance of payments in the United States.

The fixed exchange rate also caused both monetary and nonmonetary (real) shocks to be transmitted via flows of gold and capital between countries. Therefore, a shock in one country affected the domestic money supply, expenditure, price level, and real income in another country.

In practice, actual flows of gold were not the only, or even necessarily the most important, means of settling international debts during this period. The United Kingdom at that time, like the United States today, was the political and financial power and the pound sterling served as an international money. International trade was commonly priced in pounds, and trade between other countries was often paid for with pounds.

For the gold standard to work fully, central banks were supposed to play by the **rules of the game**. In other words, they were supposed to raise their discount rates — the interest rate at which the central bank lends money to member banks — to speed a gold inflow, and lower their discount rates to facilitate a gold outflow. Thus, if a country was running a balance of payments surplus, the rules of the game required it to allow a gold outflow (that is, lower the discount rate) until the ratio of its price level to that of principal trading partners was restored to the par exchange rate.

For example, Bank of England played by the rules over much of the period between

1870 to 1914. Whenever Great Britain faced a balance of payments deficit and the Bank of England saw its gold reserve declining, it raised its bank rates (discount rate). By causing other interest rates in the United Kingdom to rise as well, the rise in the bank rate was supposed to cause holdings of inventories to decrease and other investment expenditures to decrease. These reductions would then cause a reduction in overall domestic spending and a fall in the price level. At the same time, the rise in the bank rate would stem any short-term capital outflow and attract short-term funds from abroad.

Performance of the Gold Standard

The great virtue of the gold standard was that it assured long-term price stability. The quantity of money supply under the gold standard depended directly on the quantity of gold reserves the monetary authorities had. Since the supply of gold was rather constant and no one could increase its quantity at will, the money supply was stable and couldn't get out of control. Prices may still rise and fall with swings in gold output and economic growth, but the tendency is to return to a long-term stable level. One statistics show that the annual inflation rate was 0.1 percent between 1880 and 1914 while the average was 4.2 percent between 1946 and 1990. People today often look back on the gold standard as a golden era of economic progress. It is common to hear arguments supporting a return to the gold standard. Such arguments usually cite the stable prices, economic growth, and development of world trade during this period as evidence of the benefits provided by such an orderly international monetary system.

Another virtue of the gold standard is that it does not need a central bank. Like we mentioned previously, the central bank only needed to abide by the rules of the game under the gold standard. The rules of the game were clear and simple. The function of central banks was just to maintain the gold par value which is the amount of money needed to buy one ounce of gold. They raised discount rates when their gold reserves declining and lowered discount rates when BOP had a surplus. A lot of countries such as Canada and the United States did not have central banks until the early 1900s.

But because economies under the gold standard were so vulnerable to real and monetary shocks, prices were highly unstable in the short run. A measure of short-term price instability is the coefficient of variation, which is the ratio of the standard deviation of annual percentage changes in the price level to the average annual percentage change. The higher the coefficient of variation is, the greater the short-term instability will be. For the United States between 1879 and 1913, the coefficient was 17.0, which is quite high. Between 1946 and 1990 it was only 0.8.

Moreover, because the gold standard gives government very little discretion to use monetary policy, economies on the gold standard are less able to avoid or offset either monetary or real shocks. Real output, therefore, is more variable under the gold standard. This can explain that some times in the history some governments simply abandoned the gold standard in order to pursue certain national objectives. Since the government could not have discretion over monetary policy, unemployment was higher during the gold standard. It average 6.8 percent in the United States between 1879 and 1913 versus 5.6 percent between 1946 and 1990.

Finally, any consideration of the pros and cons of the gold standard must include a very large negative: the gold is always such a scarce resource that rapid growth in international trade and investment can be seriously hampered for the lack of sufficient monetary reserves. If we adopt gold standard today, we will face severe deflationary pressures. At the same time, the resource cost of producing gold and the cost to manage a gold standard are huge. Milton Friedman estimated the cost of maintaining a full gold coin standard for the United States in 1960 to be more than 2.5 percent of GNP. In 1990 this cost would have been $137 billion.

The Gold Exchange System (1919-1944)

The gold standard worked adequately until the outbreak of World War I. The war caused Great Britain, France, Germany, and Russia to suspend redemption of banknotes in gold and impose embargoes on gold exports. Germany, Austria, Russia and other countries experienced hyperinflation. Those events caused the main industrialized countries to suspend operation of gold standard and threw the international monetary system into turmoil. During the World War I and the early 1920s, currencies were allowed to fluctuate over fairly wide ranges in terms of gold and in relation to each other. A lot of countries used "predatory" depreciation of their currencies as a means of gaining advantages in the world export market. International speculators were very active in the financial market. They sold the weak currencies and bought the strong currencies, causing the weak currencies to fall further and the strong currencies stronger.

As major countries began to recover from the war and stabilize their economies, they attempted to restore the gold standard. The United States had experienced little inflation and thus returned to a gold standard by June 1919. But high inflation in Europe during the 1920s prohibited restoration of the gold standard because differential inflation among the world's trading nations made it difficult to determine appropriate exchange rates. In 1925, England returned to a gold standard at the old prewar pound per gold exchange rate, even though prices had risen since the prewar period.

So a gold exchange standard was instituted in which U.K. and U.S. held only gold reserves while other countries could hold gold, the British pounds, and the U.S. dollars as reserves. Under this system, the British pound, the U.S. dollar and gold could be used to settle international imbalances. This was a modified gold standard, because U.K. and U.S. traded gold only with foreign central banks, not private citizens. The gold exchange standard lasted until 1931, at which time England withdrew from the system under pressure from massive demands on its reserves as a result of an unrealistically high pound value. Despite coordinated international efforts to rescue the pound, British gold reserves continued to fall to the point where it was impossible to maintain the gold standard. To maintain the competitiveness of their products on world markets, many other nations such as Sweden, Austria, and Japan followed England in getting off gold. The United States got off gold in 1933 after experiencing a spate of bank failures and outflows of gold. France abandoned the gold standard in 1936 because of the flight from the French franc.

From 1934 to the end of World War II, exchange rates were theoretically determined by each currency's value in terms of gold. As a matter of fact, paper standards came into being when the gold standard was virtually abandoned. In trying to stimulate domestic economies by increasing exports, country after country adopted competitive devaluation policies. Governments also resorted to foreign exchange controls in an attempt to manipulate net exports in a manner that would help them for economic development. Since the inconvertibility of the most currencies, currency speculation during this period was rampant, causing wild fluctuations in exchange rates. In sum, no coherent international monetary system prevailed during this period with profoundly detrimental effects on international trade and investment. As a result, the volume of international trade declined to a very low level with the protectionist policies adopted by many countries.

Bretton Woods System (1944–1973)

Bretton Woods Agreement

In 1944, at the height of World War II, representatives from 45 countries met at Bretton Woods, New Hampshire, to design a new international monetary system. The motivation behind creating a new international monetary system was the desire to avoid the breakdown in international monetary relations that had occurred in the 1930s. The 1930s were marked by major trade imbalances which in turn led to the adoption of widespread trade protectionism, the adoption of deflationary policies, competitive devaluations and the abandonment of the gold exchange standard. There was general consensus that fixed exchange rates were desirable.

The Bretton Woods Agreement reached in 1944 at Bretton Woods conference created the **International Monetary Fund (IMF)**. The IMF was responsible for coordinating the world monetary system. Its main function was to pool international reserves of member nations that could be loaned on a short-term basis to those member nations experiencing a shortage of foreign exchange reserves. Such loans are subject to IMF conditions regarding changes in domestic economic policy aimed at restoring balance of payments equilibrium. Two other important institutions that arose at the end of the war were the International Bank for Reconstruction and Development known today as the World Bank and the **General Agreement on Tariffs and Trade (GATT)**. The World Bank financed postwar reconstruction and assisted in economic development with funds for social capital projects such as dams, ports, and other social infrastructure. The function of the GATT, founded in 1948, was to promote the reduction of trade barriers and settle trade disputes among member nations.

The foreign exchange rate arrangement under this agreement was a pegged, but adjustable, exchange rate as **Figure 4.2** depicts. First, each nation fixed the value of their currencies to the U.S. dollar. For example, the gold parity of the British pound was 3.58134 gram of fine gold, and the par value of the U.S. dollar was 0.888671 gram of fine gold. Thus the U.S. dollar per sterling rate was fixed at 3.58134/0.888671 = 4.0306$/£. The gold parity of Deutsch mark was set at DM147.00 per ounce of fine gold, and the mark-dollar exchange rate was then fixed at DM4.20/$ (DM147.00/$35.00).

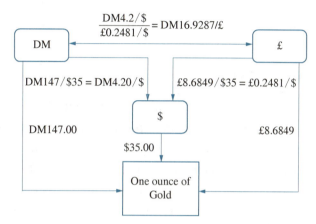

Figure 4.2   Bretton Woods Exchange Rate System

Second, the dollar was the anchor of the system. The U.S. dollar was thus called the **anchor currency** to which other currencies were tied. The U.S. monetary authority promised to convert the dollar possessed by other monetary authorities into gold at the mint parity of $35 to one ounce of gold. Therefore, the system established the link between the U.S. dollar and gold, and the link of other nations' currencies to the U.S. dollar. Other nation's currencies indirectly linked to gold, because their U.S. dollar reserves could be converted into gold at mint parity.

Third, the **parity band** which was the width of the floating range of the par value was within 1% on either side. That is, for example, if one British pound is equal to $4.0306, then, the width of the floating range of the pound should be between $4.070906 and $3.990294 (plus and minus 0.040306).

Forth, if the exchange rate deviated from the parity band, the monetary authorities should intervene in the foreign exchange market to maintain the pegged value. For example, if dollar/pound rate began to float near or slightly above the ceiling ($4.070906/£), the Bank of England had to be prepared to sell pounds for dollars on the foreign exchange market so that the increased demand for dollars would cause the pound price to fall. If the rate fell to the floor, $3.990294/£ in this case, the central bank had to sell dollar reserves into the market so that the rate would increase back toward par. Thus, Bretton Woods

System required central banks of member countries keep enough foreign exchange reserves to maintain the par value.

Finally, the pegged value was adjustable. It means when a nation's balance of payments moved away from its long term equilibrium position, the nation could re-peg its exchange rate via devaluation or revaluation polices. Member nations agreed in principle to defend existing par values as long as possible in times of BOP disequilibrium. They were expected to use fiscal and monetary policies first to correct payments imbalances. But if reversing a persistent payments imbalance meant severe disruption to the domestic economy in terms of inflation or unemployment, member nations could correct this fundamental disequilibrium by repegging their currencies up to 10% without permission from the IMF and by greater than 10% with the fund's permission.

Devaluation and Revaluation

In Chapter 3 we discussed the appreciation and depreciation of a currency relative to other currencies. When the market forces drive the value of a currency up and down, we describe it with the terms appreciation and depreciation. **Devaluation** refers to a fall in the value of a country's currency by government decree; while **revaluation** is the rise in the price of a currency by law. Under the fixed exchange rate system, a currency's par value is announced by the government. Therefore, the currency value is basically fixed like the gold standard system. But if a country runs persistent payments deficit, it may be necessary to devalue its currency's exchange value to correct a BOP deficit. On the other hand, if a country abounds with BOP surplus, the government may revalue its currency's exchange rate to counteract a BOP surplus.

The purpose of devaluation and revaluation is to change relative prices so that it can change the domestic and foreign expenditures between domestic goods and foreign goods. By raising the home price of the foreign currency, devaluation makes the home country's exports cheaper to foreigners in terms of the foreign currency, while making the home country's imports more expensive in terms of the home currency. Expenditures are diverted from foreign to home goods as home exports rise and imports fall. Revaluation discourages the home country's exports and encourages its imports, diverting expenditures from home goods to foreign goods.

Before implementing a devaluation or revaluation, the government officials must decide (1) if an adjustment in the official exchange rate is necessary to correct BOP disequilibrium, (2) when the adjustment will occur, and (3) how large the adjustment should be. Exchange rate decisions of government officials may be incorrect — that is, ill-timed and of improper magnitude.

The Triffin Dilemma

The Bretton Woods System ran smoothly and looked successful for almost two decades after the World War II. The system provided the world economy with a stable exchange rate arrangement. It promoted economic growth of many nations and a rapid increase in world trade. The Bretton Woods System was not without its shortcomings, however. Since there was a limit to the U.S. gold stock, the dollar would not increase in value relative to gold, but it could always decrease in value. When U.S. experienced long term deficit of its international balance of payments, it would be very difficult for U.S. to maintain the dollar's mint parity to gold.

Well before the eventual demise of Bretton Woods System, Robert Triffin (1960) had predicted an eventual loss of confidence in the system. Triffin argued that there was an inherent contradiction in the gold-dollar standard. For the Bretton Woods System to function successfully it was essential that confidence was maintained in the U.S. dollar; so long as central banks' knew that dollars could be converted into gold at $35 per ounce they would willingly hold dollars in their reserves. Triffin pointed out that as international trade grew, so would the demand for international reserves, namely the U.S. dollars. To meet the demand for these reserves the Bretton Woods System depended on the U.S. running deficits, with other countries running surpluses and purchasing dollars to prevent their currencies appreciating. Hence, over time, the stock of the U.S. dollar liabilities to the rest of the world would increase and this rate of increase would be higher than the annual addition to the gold reserves resulting from gold-mining activities. As a result, the ratio of the U.S. dollar liabilities to gold held by the U.S. Federal Reserve would deteriorate until eventually the convertibility of dollars into gold at $35 per ounce would become de facto impossible.

As it became apparent that the U.S. authorities would not be able to fulfill their convertibility commitment, Triffin predicted that central banks would begin to anticipate a devaluation of the dollar rate against gold. In anticipation of this, central banks would start to convert their reserves into gold and stop pegging their currencies against the dollar leading to an inevitable breakdown of the system. In brief, the Triffin dilemma was that U.S. could run neither BOP deficit nor surplus under the Bretton Woods System. This is because continued U.S. BOP deficit would undermine the Bretton Woods System, yet if U.S. took measures to curb its deficit this would lead to a shortage of world reserves which would undermine the growth of world trade and exert deflationary pressures on the world economy. Just as Mr. Triffin predicted, the fact that U.S. was unable to fulfill the convertibility commitment contributed to the eventual collapse of the Bretton Woods System.

Decline of the Bretton Woods System

The system was well-designed for the immediate post-war international economy. Through the 1950s and into the 1960s, the international economy outgrew the system. Because of fast growth in European and Japanese economic development, the world demand for international reserves grew more rapidly than world gold supplies, and foreign countries happily accumulated interest-bearing dollar international reserves without converting them into gold at the U.S. Federal Reserve. On the other hand, American dollars were being spent overseas, in the form of foreign aid, defense spending, investment, trade, and tourism. This outpouring of dollars into the international economy was not reciprocated by an equal inflow of currency. This brought about a deficit in the capital account, resulting in a balance of payments deficit. The U.S. dollar's strength began declined.

To control the balance of payments deficit, the federal government adopted a number of measures to help bring about equilibrium beginning in the late 1950s. Foreign aid was tied to purchases of goods and services in the United States, so that aid outflows could be counteracted. Duty-free allowances were reduced for American tourists returning from travels abroad. Government agencies reduced their overseas spending. The Federal Reserve lowered the ceiling on bank loans to foreigners. A number of other measures were taken, including the creation of a **gold pool** funded by the central banks of several industrial nations to intervene in the London gold market to maintain the official price of gold.

The countermeasures of the 1950s and early 1960s had proven insufficient to remove the deficit. All the methods of reducing the balance of payments deficit were in opposition to the economic goals that Kennedy administration had articulated. Reducing federal spending might have eroded the United States' position as an important international power in the post-war cold-war international political scene. Kennedy's economists were also reluctant to raise interest rates, especially on long-term investments, since such an action might have discouraged domestic entrepreneurs, thus slowing growth. The third option, to devalue the currency, was not possible under the Bretton Woods System, since, as the anchor of the monetary system, the American dollar was the only currency that could not be devalued or revalued, even in a state of fundamental disequilibrium.

The problem of the American balance of payments deficit was becoming more pressing, and increased military spending in Vietnam was exacerbating the difficulties. Nevertheless, none of the remedy policies were able to even stop the growth of the capital account deficit, let alone reverse the trend. By 1964, the capital account deficit had increased tremendously, pushing the balance of payments further into deficit despite the $2.4 billion increase in the current account balance.

The U.S. Dollar Crises

The fact that more currency was flowing out of the United States than was coming in would cause a severe problem. As these dollar claims became larger and larger relative to the size of the U.S. gold reserves, though, foreign confidence in the dollar-gold parity understandably fell. The market began to predict a devaluation of the dollar in terms of gold, which increased the incentive of individuals and central banks to hold gold, not dollars. If individual foreign countries exercised their right to convert their dollar claims into good or foreign exchanges, the Federal Reserve's gold or foreign exchange reserves were in danger of being seriously depleted. Since holding a dollar represented guarantee that one could exchange it for foreign currency or for gold at any time, such a depletion of official reserves could cause a crisis of confidence and a massive panic. The **dollar crisis**, a run on the dollar, in which large numbers of people attempted to sell their dollars to the Federal Reserve, could occur, causing the Fed to approach insolvency.

There were two serious American dollar crises in the 1960s. The first occurred in the early months of 1965. Among the contributing factors were the worsening situation in Vietnam; the rumor that the United States intended to eliminate the gold reserve requirement against Federal Reserve deposits and notes, and French verbal attacks on the role of the dollar in the international monetary system. In March, 1965, the price of gold peaked at $35.17 an ounce and the United States had to find a way to bring the price back down to $35.00 in order to maintain the dollar's value in the Bretton Woods System. The Congress freed about $4.9 billion worth of gold in order to meet potential international claims on American gold reserves.

The second crisis occurred in 1968, when there was a drastic increase in purchases of gold. The seven major industrial countries (members of the gold pool) could not maintain the market price of gold at $35 an ounce, so they gave up their efforts (the gold pool was officially closed in that year), except for the United States, which agreed to continue selling gold to governments at $35 an ounce. In order to support this commitment, the U.S. Congress freed more gold ($10.7 billion) from currency reserves. On the other hand, to partially alleviate the pressure on the dollar as the international reserve currency, the IMF created an artificial international reserve called the special drawing rights (SDRs) in 1969.

Special Drawing Rights (SDRs)

The SDR was created as a supplementary international reserve asset allocated to IMF members. The SDR is neither a currency nor a claim on the IMF. Rather, it is a potential claim on the freely usable currencies of the IMF members. SDRs can be exchanged for these currencies. The purpose of the SDR was to support the Bretton Woods fixed exchange rate system. IMF member countries needed more official reserves to support the domestic exchange rate. However, at that time, the supply of gold and U.S. dollars was insufficient for the rapid growth of world trade. The SDR provided more liquidity to the world markets and allowed countries to continue to expand trade. The SDR does not exist as notes and coins, but has value because all member countries of the IMF have agreed to accept it.

The SDR was initially defined as equivalent to 0.888671 grams of fine gold — which at the time, was also equivalent to one U.S. dollar. After the collapse of Bretton Woods System, the SDR was redefined as a basket of currencies.

The SDR basket is reviewed every five years to ensure that the basket reflects the relative importance of currencies in the world's trading and financial systems. The reviews cover the key elements of the SDR method of valuation, including criteria and indicators used in selecting SDR basket currencies and the initial currency weights used in determining the amounts (number of units) of each currency in the SDR basket. These currency amounts remain fixed over the five-year SDR valuation period but the actual weights of currencies in the basket fluctuate as cross-exchange rates among the basket currencies move.

On October 1, 2016, Chinese Renminbi (RMB) joined the U.S. dollar, euro, Japanese yen, and British pound sterling in the SDR basket. The value of the SDR was set according to the sum of the values of each of the five currencies, as **Exhibit 4.1** shows.

Exhibit 4.1   The Composition of the Value of One SDR

Currency	Weights Determined in the 2015 Review	Fixed Number of Units of Currency for a 5-year Period Starting from OCT 1, 2016
U.S. dollar	41.73	0.58252
Euro	30.93	0.38671
Chinese yuan	10.92	1.0174
Japanese yen	8.33	11.900
Pound sterling	8.09	0.085946

Source: International Monetary Fund, March 24, 2020, www.imf.org.

The IMF has allocated a total of SDR204.2 billion (equivalent to about U.S.$318 billion), including three general allocations and a one-time special allocation. The first SDR9.3 billion was allocated in 1970–1972. The second allocation of SDR12.1 billion occurred in the period of 1979–1981. The third allocation of SDR161.2 billion which was by far the biggest allocation was on August 28, 2009. A special one-time allocation of SDR21.5 billion took effect on September 9, 2009 to correct for the fact that members that had joined IMF after 1981 had never received an allocation. In March 2021, the IMF considered a new SDR allocation equivalent to U.S.$650 billion to provide additional liquidity to the global economic system by supplementing the reserve assets of the 190 member countries[1]. The purpose of this allocation was to support the global recovery from COVID-19 crisis. It would also be a powerful signal of the IMF membership's determination to do everything possible to overcome the worst recession since the Great Depression.

---

1 IMF news release, March 23, 2021, www.imf.org.

The Breakdown of the Britton Woods System

Several efforts were made to maintain the stability of the exchange rate system during 1960s. It included 1960's gold pool, the intervention of the central banks of Germany and France in foreign exchange market in 1969. All those efforts turned out to be ineffective and did not stop the speculation built up by the continual U.S. balance of payments deficit, the expansionary monetary policy and inflation. One statistic showed that the U.S. official reserve assets, primarily gold, fell to about $12 billion in 1971, whereas the U.S. liquid liabilities to all foreigners rose to more than $88 billion at the same time[1]. Obviously, if those debts were presented to the U.S. government in return for gold, the entire U.S. reserves of gold could be depleted. Eventually, in August 1971, as the U.S. trade deficit continued to expand, the United States suspended the convertibility of the dollar into gold or other reserve assets. President Richard Nixon announced an emergency 10% tariff on all U.S. import as an interim measure until U.S. trading partners agreed to revalue their currencies against the dollar. He also announced some domestic policies designed to stabilize the U.S. inflation rate; these included price and wage controls. The world's exchange rate system was in disarray. Consequently, international trade between nations also fell into a chaotic state.

Smithsonian Agreement (Dec. 1971)

The immediate response of foreign governments to the Nixon measures was along the lines sought by the U.S. administration. Foreign governments allowed their exchange rates to float and agreed to a further liberalization of trade barriers. In a bid to restore the pegged exchange rate system, the G10 nations met in December at the Smithsonian Institute in Washington to reach an agreement called **Smithsonian Agreement**. The agreement tried to tackle the problem of the overvalued dollar by devaluing it against gold from $35 to $38 and revaluing currencies against the dollar by an average of 8%. In addition, the margin by which other currencies could fluctuate against the dollar was widened from ±1% to ±2.25%. In return for the revaluation of other currencies, the U.S. agreed to remove its 10% import tariffs. In 1972, the U.S. trade deficit nearly tripled from 1971, and speculative flows of currencies continued, resulting in the international monetary crisis of February 1973.

After the Smithsonian agreement, several industrial countries led their currencies float. During that period, the official desire for fixed exchange rates had remained strong, but any hopes of a return to fixed parities were overtaken by events. The first cause was that the U.S. government switched to advocacy of floating rates. It was reluctant to intervene on the foreign exchange market when the dollar exchange rate moved favorable to the U.S. economy. The second cause was that the **oil crisis** hurt both developed and developing countries. In 1973, OPEC quadrupled the price of oil which had a huge impact on the

---

[1] Bureau of Economic Analysis, International Investment Position Statistics, www.bis.gov.

world economy and effectively ended any hopes of restoring a fixed exchange rate system. The huge oil price rise caused the developed countries such as Japan and the United Kingdom suffered significant balance of payments deficits during the period of 1973 and 1975. Less-developed countries were also hard hit by the soaring oil prices. Their costs of importing oil were increased dramatically. Their export earnings were reduced tremendously because of the recession in the industrialized countries.

In February 1973, the U.S. dollar was devalued again because of the selling pressure on the world market. The price of gold was further raised from $38 to $42 per ounce. By March 1973, major currencies like Japanese yen, British pound and Deutsch mark began to float against each other. The decline and fall of the Bretton Woods System was completed. The world entered the new era of floating exchange rate system.

Floating Exchange Rate System (1973–Now)

The **floating exchange rate** is the rate free to go wherever the market equilibrium is. The government lets the market to determine the exchange rate. Although major developed countries adopt floating exchange rate system, they nonetheless have a variety of tools at their disposal to influence the path of exchange rates. For example, they can use domestic monetary policy (by varying the money supply or interest rates under their control); they can attempt to restrict capital movements; or they can tax or subsidize international trade to influence the demand for foreign currency; or they can simply direct foreign exchange intervention — that is, the sale or purchase of foreign exchanges by central banks. Therefore, there are two kinds of floating exchange rate: clean float and managed float. **Clean float rate** refers to the exchange rate solely determined by the market forces. The clean float is also called free float. In some countries, the exchange rates are basically determined by the supply and demand in the foreign exchange market. The governments, however, often try to have a direct impact on the exchange rates through official intervention. In this case, the countries are said to adopt **managed float rate** system. The managed float is sometimes called the **dirty float**.

The Jamaica Accord (1976)

Although the world was operating under a floating exchange rate system, it was illegal from the viewpoint of the IMF, because the constitution of the IMF forbade floating rates. In January 1976, the members of the IMF amended the constitution of the IMF, thus formally legitimized the new floating exchange rate system. The key elements of *the Jamaica Accord* include: (1) Member countries were basically free to choose any exchange rate system they wanted; (2) Gold was abandoned as a reserve asset; (3) The conference aimed at increasing the importance of SDRs in international reserves, and there was a declaration that the SDR should become the principal reserve asset. After *the Jamaica Accord*, the

IMF continued its role of helping countries cope with macroeconomic and exchange rate problems, albeit within the context of a radically different exchange rate regime.

The Plaza Agreement (1985) and the Louvre Accord (1987)

The Jamaica Accord amended the constitution of the IMF to allow, among other things, each member nation to determine its own exchange rate arrangement. Thus a new era of floating exchange rate system occurred. Actually, the floating rate system is not a true flexible exchange rate system. It is a managed float system (dirty float), which is a system of flexible exchange rates but with periodic intervention by monetary authorities.

This can be proved by the two events in the 1980s. First, *the Plaza Agreement* in 1985 was to reduce the speculation for the U.S. dollar. The U.S. economy experienced high inflation and high employment in the 1980s. The high U.S. interest rates attracted international capitals from all over the world. As a result, the dollar had a relentless substantial appreciation from 1980 to 1985. The dollar nominal effective exchange rate appreciated by around 50% and even more in real terms. The group of five (France, Germany, Japan, the United Kingdom, and the United States) met at the Plaza Hotel in New York in September, 1985 to reach *the Plaza Agreement*. The purpose was to intervene collectively to drive down the value of the dollar. The efforts by the central bankers of the group five appeared to achieve its goal and the dollar did depreciate against the major currencies within the next two years. Second, *the Louvre Accord* of 1987 was, on the other side, to declare that the monetary authorities would cease to drive down the value of the dollar, because the dollar had fallen to the same price where it had started in 1981. G7 countries would only intervene in the foreign exchange market as needed to ensure stability. The dollar decline had ended by the following year.

The Creation of the Euro

The most important international monetary development of the last half of the 20th century is the **European Economic and Monetary Union (EMU)**, which aimed for economic and monetary union within EMU countries. EMU was a single-currency area within the European Union (EU) single market, now known as the euro zone, in which people, goods, services, and capital were supposed to move without restrictions. To achieve this objective, participating countries traded their currencies for the euro (€).

It is long time ago that the European Union desired for exchange rate stability in the member countries. One reason these countries desired monetary stability was that most western European countries are not only quite open to foreign trade but their main trading partners are also their neighboring countries, making costs of exchange rate variability particularly acute within Europe. Another reason the EU countries wanted to limit exchange rate fluctuations was to facilitate the operation of a common market for agricultural products. Finally, the desire for stable exchange rates in Europe should also be viewed as an integral part of the wider drive toward economic, monetary, and political union between European countries in the EU.

The timetable for EMU was established in the 1991 *Treaty of Maastricht* and included the following dates:

- *January 1, 1999.* The euro replaced the **European Currency Unit (ECU)** in the European exchange rate mechanism, becoming a unit of account but not yet a physical currency. ECU was a basket currency constructed as a weighted average of the currencies of member countries of the European Union back to 1979. Beginning in 1999, the exchange rates of participating countries were pegged to the euro at that time.
- *January 1, 2002.* The euro began public circulation alongside national currencies.
- *July 1, 2002.* The euro formally replaced the currencies of participating countries.

To prepare for the EMU, *the Maastricht Treaty* called for the integration and coordination of the member countries' monetary and fiscal policies. The EMU would be implemented by a process called convergence. Before becoming a full member of the EMU, each member country was originally expected to meet the following convergence criteria:

- Inflation rates should not be more than 1.5% above that of the three members of the EU with the lowest inflation rates during the previous year.
- Long-term interest rates should not be more than 2% above that of the three members of the EU with the lowest interest rates.
- Budget deficits should be no higher than 3% of gross domestic product.
- Government debt should be less than 60% of gross domestic product.

Originally, only 11 countries met the convergence criteria. Up till now there are 19 countries that use the euro. The euro began trading on world currency markets in 1999. It had a parity of $1.17/€ against the U.S. dollar and many economists expected it to strengthen. But contrary to expectations the first few years of its existence the value of the euro slid steadily following its introduction. However, the euro has since made a dramatic recovery and the U.S. dollar has declined in value in part due to concerns about the need to correct an ever-widening U.S. current account deficit.

Even though many prominent economists think that Europe is not particularly well suited to be a monetary union, substantial academic research documents sizable economic benefits following the introduction of the euro in terms of price convergence, lower costs of capital, and increased trade. The euro's future looks to be bright because of the various safeguards that have been put in place to ensure that it will be a sound low-inflation currency.

Currency Turmoil and Crises Post-1990

The Mexican Peso Crisis of 1995. During December 1994 and January 1995, the

Mexican peso lost 40% of its value against the U.S. dollar because of the political turmoil. International mutual funds had invested more than $45 billion in Mexico securities during a three-year period prior to the peso crisis. After the Mexico new president devalued the peso against the dollar by 14%, investors started to sell pesos as well as Mexican stocks and bonds. A capital flight from Mexico resulted from the panic among international investors. The Mexican stock market also fell 50% in peso terms during this time. The Peso crisis not only adversely affected the Mexican economy, but also led to significant falls in many other developing countries' stock markets and currencies, and this process of contagion from the Mexican markets to other developing countries gave rise to the so-called "Tequila effect". U.S. and IMF assisted the Mexico to overcome the crisis, so the crisis was relatively short-lived and in 1996 the Mexican economy rebounded strongly.

The Asian Contagion of 1997. In May 1997, the Thai baht came under pressure as speculators bet against the currency, which was pegged to a currency basket that included the U.S. dollar. As the property and stock market bubbles began to burst there was a rush on the part of international investors to exit Thailand. The substantial capital outflows made the country's foreign currency reserves severely depleted as the Bank of Thailand defended the currency. The foreign exchange reserves fell from nearly $40 billion in December 1996 to less than $10 billion by July 1997. On July 2, 1997, Thailand allowed the baht to float. By the end of 1997, the baht had lost nearly 50% of its value against the dollar.

The "Asian contagion" soon spread to Indonesia and South Korea. By the end of January 1998, the rupiah had lost more than 75% of its value against the dollar, and Indonesia's stock market fell by 33% near the end of 1997. The South Korea won lost nearly 44% against the dollar and the Korean stock market lost more than 50% of its value between September 1997 and September 1998.

The Fall of the Russian Ruble in 1998. Russia embarked on a painful transition toward a market-based economy after the breakup of the Soviet Union in 1991. Russia's difficulties during this transition included hyperinflation, an undeveloped banking system, widespread tax avoidance, corruption, and huge budget deficits. In 1998, the ruble came under speculative pressure as investors reassessed the viability of emerging market investments following the Asian crisis of 1997. By July 1998, Russia found it is difficult to refinance its dollar debt as it matured. In August, Russia was forced to abandon its exchange rate peg and defaulted on more than $40 billion of debt.

2002 Argentina Peso Crisis. The overvalued Argentina peso contributed to a severe depression beginning in 1998. The Argentina government had financed its large budget deficits with foreign currency debt, accumulating a balance of more than $150 billion. The government was forced to devalue the peso in 2002 and eventually allowed the peso to float. As of January 2003, 40% of Argentina's population was living in poverty, unemployment was approaching 20%, and Argentina owed $10 billion to the IMF.

Exchange Rate Systems in Practice

Since 1973, exchange rates have become much more volatile and less predictable than they were before. Governments around the world pursue a number of different exchange rate policies. Today's international monetary system is a mixture of all currency regimes. These range from a pure "free float" where the exchange rate is determined by market forces to a pegged system that has some aspects of the Bretton Woods System of fixed exchange rates.

Exhibit 4.2 surveys the current arrangements in place across the world, using the information from the International Monetary Fund (IMF). The IMF distinguishes four types, 10 categories of the exchange rate arrangements adopted by its 189 members plus three other territories. As the table shows, the exchange rate system can be split up into roughly three broad categories: currencies that have fixed exchange rates, no separate legal tender and currency board, currencies that have pegged exchange rates (conventional peg, crawling peg, etc.), and currencies with floating exchange rates (free floating and managed floating).

Exhibit 4.2　Classification of Exchange Rate Arrangements

Type	Categories				
Hard pegs	No separate legal tender	Currency board			
Soft pegs	Conventional peg	Pegged rate within bands	Stabilized arrangement	Crawling peg	Crawl-like arrangement
Floating regimes	Floating	Free floating			
Residual	Other managed arrangement				

Source: *2019 IMF Annual Report*, 2020, www.imf.org.
Note: This methodology became effective February 2, 2009, and reflects an attempt to provide greater consistency and objectivity of exchange rate classifications across countries and improve the transparency of the IMF's bilateral and multilateral surveillance in the area.

Exhibit 4.3 provides the information of world exchange rate arrangements by those member countries from the year of 2014 to 2019. As of 2019, 16.1% of the IMF members (31 countries) allowed their currencies to float freely. Another 35 countries (18.2%) intervened in only a limited way (the managed float). 24 countries, account for 12.5% of IMF members, now have no separate legal tender of their own. They have adopted a foreign currency as legal tender within their borders, typically the U.S. dollar or the euro. 89 countries (46.4%) belong to the categories of soft peg, in which 42 member countries (21.9%) used conventional peg system under which they pegged their currencies to U.S.

dollar, euro, composite currency or other indicators. 13 countries (6.8%) are classified as "other managed". For those countries, it is usually difficult to maintain a more clearly defined exchange rate arrangement especially during volatile foreign exchange market conditions. China belongs to this group. Here we are going to examine the mechanics and implications of several exchange rate systems.

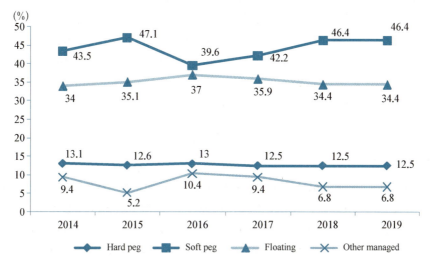

Exhibit 4.3   Exchange Rate Arrangements, 2014–2019

(Percent of countries as of end-April)

Source: *Annual Report on Exchange Arrangements and Exchange Restrictions 2019,* IMF, www.imf.org.
Note: Includes 189 countries and three territories: Aruba, Curacao and Sint Maarten, and Hong Kong SAR of China.

Crawling Pegs

The **crawling peg** is an exchange rate system in which a country pegs its currency to another nation's currency, but allows the parity value to change at regular time intervals. It is a compromise between fixed and floating rates. Central bank interventions in the foreign exchange market may occur to maintain the temporary fixed rate. However, central banks can avoid interventions and save reserves by adjusting the fixed rate instead. Suppose that the Mexico central bank sets the par value at 10 Mexican pesos to 1 U.S. dollar and allows plus and down 3% fluctuations around the par value between 10.3 pesos and 9.7 pesos. If in the foreign exchange market, the dollar approaches 10.3 pesos, the Mexico central bank sells dollar for peso. On the other hand, if the peso/dollar exchange rate stays near 10.3 for a long time even after the market intervention, the Mexico central bank can then adjust the par value to 10.3 pesos per dollar with the new limit points at 10.6090 and 9.9910.

Since crawling pegs are adjusted gradually, they can help eliminate some exchange rate volatility without fully constraining the central bank with a fixed rate. The crawling peg system has been used primarily by nations having high inflation rates. Some developing countries, mostly South American, have recognized that a pegging system can operate in an inflationary environment only if there is provision for frequent changes in the par values. For example, in the 1990s, Mexico had fixed its peso with the U.S. dollar. However, due to the significant inflation in Mexico, as compared to the U.S., it was evident that the peso would need to be severely devalued. Because a rapid devaluation would create instability, Mexico put into place a crawling peg exchange rate adjustment system, and the peso was slowly devalued toward a more appropriate exchange rate.

The crawling peg differs from the system of adjustable pegged rates. Under the adjustable peg, currencies are tied to a par value that changes infrequently (perhaps once every several years) but suddenly, usually in large jumps. The idea behind the crawling peg is that a nation can make small, frequent changes in par values, perhaps several times a year, so that they creep along slowly in response to evolving market conditions.

Currency Boards

In most countries today, the monetary authority is a central bank. A typical central bank today is a wholly government-owned body, separate from the ministry of finance that has a monopoly of issuing notes and coins. A typical central bank today has a high degree of discretionary power: it is constrained by no monetary rule, such as a binding commitment to a particular exchange rate or inflation rate.

Among the other monetary systems that once were widespread were currency boards. Unlike the rest of the monetary system, which have all but vanished, currency boards have enjoyed a revival of interest since about 1990. A few countries have established currency board-like systems, and others have debated whether to have currency boards. As the IMF survey shows that 11 countries or regions adopted currency boards system in 2019.

A currency board is a monetary authority that issues notes and coins convertible into a foreign anchor currency or commodity (also called the reserve currency) at a truly fixed rate and on demand. An orthodox currency board typically does not accept deposits. A currency board can operate in place of a central bank or as a parallel issuer alongside an existing central bank; cases of parallel issuer have been quite rare, though.

Currency boards supply currency on the basis of 100 percent foreign exchange reserves in order to honor the commitment of exchanging domestic currency for anchor currency at a fixed exchange rate. Hong Kong of China established the currency board system in 1983 to defend the value of its currency — Hong Kong dollar. If the currency board in Hong Kong of China issues one Hong Kong dollar, and the fixed exchange rate it maintains is HK$7.5 per U.S. dollar, anybody who wants to obtain HK$7.5 from the currency board has to give it $1, and anybody who has Hong Kong dollars issued by the currency board can require it to give up $1 for every HK$7.5. As reserves, a currency board holds low-risk, interest-bearing bonds and other assets denominated in the anchor currency. A currency board's reserves are equal to 100 percent or slightly more of its notes and coins in circulation, as set by law. A currency board generates profits from the difference between the interest earned on its reserve assets and the expense of maintaining its liabilities — its notes and coins in circulation. It remits to the government all profits beyond what it needs to cover its expenses and maintain its reserves at the level set by law. An orthodox currency board has no discretion in monetary policy; market forces alone determine the money supply.

Currency boards can confer considerable credibility on fixed exchange rate regimes. The most vital contribution a currency board can make to exchange rate stability is by imposing discipline on the process of money creation. This results in greater stability of domestic prices, which, in turn, stabilizes the value of the domestic currency. The developing countries are likely to choose the currency boards. This is because central banks in some developing countries are incapable of retraining nonpolitical independence and instill less confidence than is necessary for the smooth functioning of a monetary system. They are answerable to the prerogatives of populism or dictatorship and are at the beck and call of political changes. The bottom line is that central banks should not be given the onerous responsibility of maintaining the value of currencies. This job should be left to an independent body whose sole mandate is to issue currency against a strict and unalterable set of guidelines that require a fixed amount of foreign exchange or gold to be deposited for each unit of domestic currency issued.

No Separate Legal Tender (Dollarization)

Some nations take an even more dramatic approach to exchange rate arrangement by allowing the currency of another nation to serve as legal tender. The no **separate legal tender system**, like currency board was used by small developing nations. This kind of system is also called "dollarization" because the U.S. dollar is widely adopted as legal tender in those countries. Other currencies can also be used in such kind of exchange rate system such as euro and Australian dollar. Many of the economies opting for dollarization already use foreign tender in private and public transactions, contracts, and bank accounts; however, this use is not yet official policy, and the local currency is still considered the primary legal lender. By deciding to use the foreign tender, individuals and institutions are protecting against possible devaluation of the local exchange rate. This is called partial dollarization. And the partial dollarization has existed for years in many Latin American and Caribbean countries where U.S. is a major trading partner and a major source of foreign investment. On the other hand, full dollarization means the elimination of the domestic currency and its complete replacement with the U.S. dollar. In that case, the central bank would sell foreign exchange reserve (mostly U.S. Treasury notes) to buy dollars and exchange all outstanding domestic currency notes for dollar notes. The U.S. dollar would be the sole legal tender. Full dollarization system has been adopted by some small countries in Latin America, Africa and southeastern Europe.

Advantages of the no separate legal tender

There are some compelling reasons for a country to decide to give up so much control over its economy and adopt full dollarization system.

First, full dollarization system implies that sound monetary and exchange rate policies no longer depend on the intelligence and discipline of domestic policymakers. Their monetary policy becomes essentially the one followed by U.S., and the exchange rate is fixed forever. The inflation rate in the domestic country will be tied to that of the issuing country. The low inflation rate reduces the risk of devaluation and the local interest rates will no longer contain a devaluation premium. The full dollarization thus removes any currency volatility against the dollar and would theoretically eliminate the possibility of future currency crises. Countries with a high inflation and financial instability often find the potential offered by dollarization to be quite attractive.

Second, there are savings in administrative and transaction costs of having to convert the local currency into dollars for trade and financial purposes.

Third, full dollarization reduces country risk, thereby providing a stable and secure economic stability and investment climate. The diminished risk encourages both local and foreign investors to invest money into the country and the capital market. The result is an increased economic activity, a more stable capital market, the end of sudden capital outflows, and a balance of payments that is less prone to crises.

Last but not least, full dollarization can improve the global economy by allowing for easier integration of economies into the world's market.

Note that dollarization is not the same as a monetary union like the euro zone. All the participating countries of a euro zone take part in monetary policy decisions and all share in the revenue that comes from printing euros. Europe's national banks still operate as lenders of last resort in making euro loans. In sum, a monetary union is shared governance; dollarization is not.

Disadvantages of the no separate legal tender

There are some substantial drawbacks to adopting a foreign currency as a country's legal tender. When a country gives up the option to print its own money, it loses its ability to directly influence its economy, including its right to administer monetary policy and form of exchange rate system. The country that adopts no separate legal tender system essentially accepts the monetary policy of the currency issuing country's central bank. If the business cycles of the no separate legal tender country do not coincide with those in the currency issuing country. The former cannot count on the letter to come to its rescue.

The central bank loses its ability to collect "**seigniorage**", the profit gained from issuing currency (the printing of monies costs less than the actual value of the notes). The dollarized country needs to replace the local currency with the foreign legal tender and thus hands over the seigniorage benefit of issuing its own currency to the foreign government.

In a fully dollarized economy, the central bank also loses its role as the lender of last resort for its banking system. It may still be able to provide short-term emergency funds from held reserves to banks in distress; it would not necessarily be able to provide enough funds to cover the withdrawals in the case of a run on deposits.

Another disadvantage for a country that opts for full dollarization is that its securities must be bought back in the U.S. dollars. If the country does not have a sufficient amount of reserves, it will either have to borrow the money by running a current account deficit or find a means to accumulate a current account surplus.

Finally, because a local currency is a symbol of a sovereign state, the use of foreign currency instead of the local one may damage a nation's sense of pride.

Arguments for Fixed and Floating Exchange Rates

The breakdown of the Bretton Woods system has not stopped the debate about the relative merits of fixed versus floating exchange rate systems. Although the contemporary international monetary system is typically referred to as a "floating rate system", it is clearly not the case for the majority of the world's nations. As we discussed earlier, only 31 countries of 192 countries covered adopt the free floating exchange rate system. A complete pure floating exchange rate system does not really exist. In reality, central banks intervene episodically in the foreign exchange market. That is, they buy and sell their own currencies to attempt to affect their values. Disappointment with the system of floating rates has led to renewed debate about the merits of fixed exchange rates. In this section, we review the pros and cons of floating versus fixed exchange rates. The arguments we list seem likely to circulate continuously as debate continues over the "ideal" system. It should become clear from the arguments we present that either system has it weaknesses. You can reach your own judgment on whether a country should adopt fixed or floating exchange rate system.

The Key Arguments for Floating Exchange Rates

The case in support of floating exchange rates has three main elements: automatic balance of payments adjustments, monetary policy autonomy and economic stability.

Automatic balance of payments adjustments

One advantage claimed for floating rates is their simplicity and easier balance of payments adjustments. Floating rates allegedly respond quickly to changing supply and demand conditions, clearing the market of shortages or surpluses of a given currency. Under the Bretton Woods System, if a country developed a permanent deficit in its balance of payments that could not be corrected by domestic policies, this would require the IMF to agree to a devaluation of the deficit country's currency. This means that the deficit country would experience a recession to reduce income or prices. Under the floating rate system, the currency of the deficit country will simply depreciate to the level at which there is no excess supply of the depreciating currency. After the depreciation, the exports are cheaper and the imports are more expensive. The deficit country then automatically restores to the balance of payments equilibrium. The proponents of the floating rate system claim that it provides a less painful adjustment mechanism to imbalanced BOP than does fixed exchange rate. Put differently, the adjustment mechanism works more smoothly under the floating rate system than it does under the fixed rate system.

Monetary policy autonomy

It is argued that under fixed rate system, a country's ability to expand or contract its money supply as it sees fit is limited by the need to maintain exchange rate parity. Monetary expansion can lead to inflation, which puts downward pressure on fixed exchange rates. Similarly, monetary contraction requires high interest rates (to reduce the demand for money). Higher interest rates lead to inflows of money from abroad, which puts upward pressure on fixed exchange rates. Thus, to maintain exchange rate parity under fixed rate system, countries are limited in their ability to use monetary policy to expand or contract their money supplies.

Advocates of floating exchange rate system argue that removal of the obligation to maintain exchange rate parity would restore monetary control to the governments. The governments can use monetary and fiscal policies to pursue whatever economic goals they attempt to achieve. If a government faced with high unemployment wants to increase its money supply to stimulate domestic demand and reduce unemployment, it could do so unencumbered by the need to maintain its exchange rate. While monetary expansion might lead to inflation, this would lead to depreciation in the country's currency. If the purchasing power parity theory is correct, the resulting currency depreciation on the foreign exchange markets should offset the effects of inflation. Although under a floating exchange rate system, domestic inflation would have an impact on the exchange rate, it should have no impact on businesses' international cost competitiveness due to exchange rate depreciation. The rise in domestic costs should be exactly offset by the fall in the value of the country's currency on the foreign exchange markets. Similarly, a government could use monetary policy to contract the economic growth without worrying about the need to maintain exchange rate parity.

Economic stability

Someone argued that floating exchange rates are more conducive to economic stability. The exchange rate is a variable which can easily rise or fall whereas domestic prices tend to be very difficult to reduce. Hence, if there is a loss of international competitiveness it is better to allow exchange rates to depreciate rather than maintain fixed exchange rates and require deflationary policies to restore international competitiveness. Since the domestic price level is resistant to downward pressure, it may require quite severe deflationary policies with associated high unemployment to induce the fall in domestic wages and prices necessary to restore international competitiveness.

The floating exchange rate insulates national economies from disturbance coming from abroad. A country could neither import foreign inflation nor export its home-grown domestic inflation under the floating rate system, for movements in the exchange rates would compensate at the border for disturbances originating on the other side.

For example, if China experiences high inflation, then the resulting increased Chinese demand for the U.S. goods and services will place upward pressure on the value of the U.S. dollar. As a second consequence of the high Chinese inflation, the reduced U.S. demand for Chinese goods and services will result in a reduced supply of the U.S. dollars on the foreign exchange market, which will also place upward pressure on the dollar's value. The appreciation of the dollar will make the U.S. goods and services more expensive for Chinese consumers. In U.S., the actual dollar price of goods may be unchanged. Even though Chinese prices have increased, U.S. consumers will continue to purchase Chinese goods and services because they can exchange their dollars for more RMB.

A country is more insulated from unemployment problems in other countries under floating exchange rate system. If China has high unemployment rate, Chinese consumers' income declines. They will thus reduce purchases of the U.S. goods and services and reduce their demand for the U.S. dollars. Such a demand shift could cause the dollar to depreciate against the RMB. This depreciation will make the U.S. goods and services cheaper for Chinese consumers than before, offsetting the reduced demand for these goods and services that may follow a reduction in Chinese income. As was true with inflation, a sudden change in unemployment will have less effect on a foreign country under floating rate system than under fixed rate system.

These examples illustrate that, in a freely floating exchange rate system, the problems experienced in one country will not necessarily be contagious. Exchange rate adjustments serve as a form of protection against "exporting" economic problems to other countries.

The Key Arguments for Fixed Exchange Rates

The case for fixed exchange rates rests on arguments about monetary discipline, stability, and the competitiveness in foreign trade.

Monetary discipline

The need to maintain a fixed exchange rate parity ensures that governments do not expand their money supplies at inflationary rates. If a country with a fixed exchange rate runs higher inflation than its trading partners, it loses competitiveness. The fear of this occurring should discourage over-expansionary fiscal or monetary policies, which in turn, should keep inflation down. Advocates of fixed rates argue that governments all too often give in to political pressures and expand the monetary supply far too rapidly, causing unacceptably high price inflation. Rigid adherence to the fixed exchange rate system involves a discipline on monetary authorities. Fixed rates provide an anchor for countries with inflationary tendencies. They have to keep their money supplies and inflation under control because inflation will eventually force devaluation.

Stability

Critics of a floating exchange rate system also argue that speculation can cause destabilizing speculation. By **destabilizing speculation** we mean that speculators in the foreign exchange market will cause exchange rate fluctuations to be wider than they would be in the absence of such speculation. For example, if foreign exchange dealers see a currency depreciating, they tend to sell the currency in the expectation of future depreciation regardless of the currency's longer-term prospects. As more traders jump on the bandwagon, the expectations of depreciation are realized. Such destabilizing speculation tends to accentuate the fluctuations around the exchange rate's long-term value. It can damage a country's economy by distorting export and import prices. Thus, advocates of a fixed exchange rate regime argue that such a system will limit the destabilizing effects of speculation.

Speculation also adds to the uncertainty surrounding future currency movements that characterizes floating exchange rate system. Floating rates have made business planning difficult, and they add risk to exporting, importing, and foreign investment activities. Advocates of the fixed exchange rate system argue that a fixed rate, by eliminating such uncertainty, promotes the growth of international trade and investment. Fixed rates encourage exporters and importers to engage in international trade without concern about exchange rate movements of the currency to which their home currency is linked. This is also true for foreign direct investment and portfolio investment. This benefits MNCs and the countries that need large amount of foreign funds to stimulate their economies.

Of course, this argument can be easily countered by noting that the currency risk under the floating rate system can be rather cheaply hedged and by noting that the stability offered by fixed exchange rate system appears more illusory than real. With fixed exchange rates speculators know in which direction an exchange rate will move, if it is to move. And so fixed-rate speculation is destabilizing, and because it provides one-way bets, may be profitable for speculators and costly for central banks and taxpayers. In fact, the 1990s witnessed a number of important currency crises where speculators successfully attacked pegged currencies.

Competitiveness in foreign trade

Countries prefer a fixed exchange rate system for the purposes of export and trade. By controlling its domestic currency a country can — and will more often than not — keep its exchange rate low. This helps to support the competitiveness of its goods as they are sold abroad. For example, let's assume a stronger U.S. dollar versus RMB exchange rate. Given that the dollar is much stronger than the RMB, a jean can cost a company five times more to produce in a U.S. company as compared to the company in China.

But the real advantage is seen in trade relationships between countries with low costs of production (like Thailand and Vietnam) and economies with stronger comparative currencies (the United States and European Union). When Chinese and Vietnamese manufacturers translate their earnings back to their respective countries, there is an even greater amount of profits that are made through the exchange rate. So, keeping the exchange rate low ensures a domestic product's competitiveness abroad and profitability at home.

The choice between the fixed and floating exchange rate system involves a trade-off between national policy autonomy and international economic integration. Research has shown that there are systematic differences between countries choosing to peg their exchange rates and those choosing floating rates. One very important characteristic is the country size in terms of GDP. Countries like industrialized nations that pursue their domestic economic goals prefer floating exchange rate system, because those countries tend to be more independent and less willing to subjugate domestic policies with a view toward maintaining a fixed rate of exchange with foreign currencies. Since foreign trade tends to constitute a smaller fraction of GDP the larger the country is, it is perhaps understandable that larger countries are less attuned to foreign exchange rate concerns than are smaller countries. On the other hand, most developing countries that commit to promoting international economic integration more likely prefer to adopt the fixed exchange rate system. Those countries' economy may heavily depend on international trade. The more open the economy, the greater the weight of tradable goods prices in the overall national price level, and therefore the greater the impact of exchange rate changes on the national price level. To minimize such foreign-related shocks to the domestic price level, the more open economy tends to follow a pegged exchange rate.

Summary

1. The exchange rate system is a set of rules established by a nation to govern the value of its currency relative to foreign currencies.
2. The international monetary system is defined as a set of conventions, rules, procedures and institutions that govern the conduct of financial relations between nations. It is based on the exchange rate system adopted by individual countries.

3. The gold standard is a monetary standard that pegs currencies to gold and guarantees convertibility to gold. It was thought that the gold standard contained an automatic mechanism (price-specie-flow mechanism) that contributed to the simultaneous achievement of a balance of payments equilibrium by all countries.
4. The gold standard broke down at the outbreak of World War I. There was a modified gold standard, the gold exchange system, after the war. The pound and the dollar were the international currencies and the international reserve currencies. This system lasted until 1931.
5. No coherent international monetary system prevailed during 1934 to the end of World II with profoundly detrimental effects on international trade and investment.
6. The Bretton Woods System of pegged exchange rates was established in 1944. The U.S. dollar was the central currency of this system; the value of every other currency was pegged to the value of the dollar. The dollar also served as the most important reserve currency in this system. Significant exchange rate devaluations were allowed only with the permission of the IMF.
7. The parity band under the Bretton Woods System was within 1% on either side. 1% above the parity is the ceiling, 1% below the parity is the floor. The monetary authorities of the relative countries were obligated to intervene the foreign exchange market if there currencies' exchange rates reached near ceiling or floor.
8. Since there was a limit to the U.S. gold stock, the dollar would not increase in value relative to gold, but it could always decrease in value. When the U.S. experienced long-term deficits of its international transactions, it would be very difficult for U.S. to maintain the dollar's mint parity to gold.
9. The Triffin Dilemma was that the U.S. could run neither BOP deficit nor surplus under the Bretton Woods System. This is because the continued U.S. deficits would undermine the Bretton Woods System, yet if U.S. took measures to curb its deficits this would lead to a shortage of international reserves which would undermine the growth of world trade and exert deflationary pressures on the world economy.
10. The SDR was created in 1969 as a supplementary international reserve asset allocated to IMF members. The SDR is neither a currency nor a claim on the IMF. Rather, it is a potential claim on the freely usable currencies of the IMF members. SDRs can be exchanged for these currencies.
11. The pegged exchange rate system collapsed in 1973, primarily due to speculative pressure on the dollar following a rise in the U.S. inflation and a growing U.S. balance of payments deficit.
12. Since 1973 the world has operated with a floating exchange rate regime, and exchange rates have become more volatile and far less predictable. Volatile exchange rate movements have helped reopen the debate over the merits of fixed and floating exchange rate system.

13. The managed floating exchange rate system means the exchange rates are basically determined by the market forces but with periodic intervention by the monetary authorities. *The Plaza Agreement* and *the Louvre Accord* are two examples of the managed floating (dirty float) exchange rate system.
14. Several currency turmoil and crises occurred during 1995 and 2002 including the Mexican Peso Crisis of 1995, the Asian Contagion of 1997, the Fall of Russian Ruble in 1998, and the 2002 Argentine Peso Crisis.
15. The European Economic and Monetary Union (EMU) was a single-currency area within the European Union (EU) single market, now known as the euro zone, in which people, goods, services, and capital are supposed to move without restrictions.
16. Before becoming a full member of the EMU, each member country was originally expected to meet the convergence criteria which are the requirements of a nation's inflation rate, interest rate, budget deficits and government debt.
17. In today's international monetary system, some countries have adopted floating exchange rates, some have pegged their currency to another currency such as the U.S. dollar, and some have pegged their currency to a basket of other currencies, allowing their currency to fluctuate within a zone around the basket.
18. The crawling peg system means that a nation makes small, frequent changes in the par value of its currency to correct a balance of payments disequilibrium. The term crawling peg implies that par value changes are implemented in a large number of small steps, making the process of exchange rate adjustment continuous for all practical purposes. The peg crawls from one par value to another.
19. A currency board is a monetary authority that issues domestic notes and coins convertible into a foreign anchor currency (the reserve currency) at a fixed rate and on demand.
20. No separate legal tender, also called dollarization is an exchange rate arrangement by allowing the currency of another nation to serve as legal tender. It helps the small countries to avoid the speculative attacks on the local currency and capital market. The small nations can achieve economic stability through dollarization.
21. The case for a floating exchange rate regime claims: (1) such a system gives countries autonomy regarding their monetary policy; (2) floating exchange rates facilitate smooth adjustment of trade imbalances; and (3) floating exchange rates are more conducive to economic stability.
22. The case for a fixed exchange rate regime claims: (1) the need to maintain a fixed exchange rate imposes monetary discipline on a country, (2) floating exchange rate regimes are vulnerable to speculative pressure. The uncertainty that accompanies floating exchange rates dampens the growth of international trade and investment. The fixed exchange rate system can eliminate such uncertainty and limit the destabilizing effects of the speculation. (3) keeping the exchange rates low can

improve the competitiveness in foreign trade.
23. There are systematic differences between countries choosing to peg their exchange rates and those choosing floating rates. Developed countries usually choose floating rates while developing countries prefer pegged rates.

Key Concepts and Terms

1. Anchor currency — 锚货币
2. Bretton Woods Agreement — 布雷顿森林协议
3. Bretton Woods System — 布雷顿森林体系
4. Clean float — 清洁浮动，净浮动（汇率）
5. Commodity money — 商品货币
6. Commodity-backed money — 商品担保货币
7. Convergence criteria — 趋同标准
8. Crawling peg — 爬行钉住（汇率）
9. Currency board — 货币局制度
10. Destabilizing speculation — 非稳定性投机
11. Devaluation — 法定贬值
12. Dollarization — 美元化
13. Dollar crisis — 美元危机
14. Euro — 欧元
15. European currency unit (ECU) — 欧洲货币单位
16. European Economic and Monetary Union (EMU) — 欧洲货币与经济联盟
17. Exchange rate system — 汇率制度
18. Fiat money — 法定货币，信用货币
19. Fixed exchange rate — 固定汇率
20. Floating exchange rate — 浮动汇率
21. General Agreement on Tariffs and Trade (GATT) — 关税与贸易总安排
22. Gold export point — 黄金输出点
23. Gold import point — 黄金输入点
24. Gold par value (Gold parity) — 黄金平价
25. Gold pool — 黄金总库
26. Gold Standard — 金本位
27. Gold exchange standard — 金汇兑本位
28. International Bank for Reconstruction and Development — 国际复兴与开发银行
29. International Monetary Fund (IMF) — 国际货币基金组织
30. International monetary system — 国际货币体系

31.	Jamaica Accord	牙买加协定
32.	Louvre Accord	卢浮协定
33.	Managed float	有管理的浮动汇率
34.	Maastricht Treaty	马斯特里赫特条约
35.	No separate legal tender	没有独立法定货币的汇率制度，如美元化制度
36.	Oil Crisis	石油危机
37.	Par value	平价汇率，中心汇率
38.	Parity band	平价波幅
39.	Pegged exchange rate	钉住汇率
40.	Plaza Agreement	广场协议
41.	Price-specie-flow mechanism	物价与现金流动机制
42.	Revaluation	法定升值
43.	Rule of the game	游戏规则
44.	Seigniorage	铸币税
45.	Smithsonian Agreement	史密森协议
46.	Special drawing right (SDR)	特别提款权
47.	Triffin Dilemma	特里芬悖论
48.	World Bank	世界银行

Questions

1. Describe the gold standard. What forced the gold standard to collapse?
2. Explain the exchange rate determination under the gold standard.
3. Why the exchange rates under the gold standard were stable?
4. What are the pros and cons of the gold standard?
5. Explain the mechanism that restores the balance of payments equilibrium under the gold standard system.
6. Define the fixed exchange rate and floating exchange rate system.
7. Describe the Bretton Woods system.
8. What factors contributed to the fall of Bretton Woods system?
9. Why did the Bretton Woods System break down according to Robert Triffin?
10. What are the advantages of fixed exchange rate and the floating exchange rate?
11. What are the main advantages for EMU countries to use euro?
12. List the pros and cons of the dollarization.
13. What is a currency board? What is the difference between a currency board and the dollarization?

14. What are the differences between a crawling peg system and a pegged exchange rate system?
15. Why do some countries use a crawling peg exchange rate system?
16. What are the potential benefits of a pegged currency system?
17. What does the anchor currency mean? List some anchor currencies nowadays that are actively used in some countries' exchange rate system.
18. If a small country in east Europe asks your opinion about whether they should join the euro-zone countries to adopt euroize exchange rate system. What advice would you give?
19. Do you think euro will survive?
20. What is the purpose of a currency devaluation? What about a currency revaluation?

Chapter 5
EXCHANGE RATE DETERMINATION AND FORECASTING EXCHANGE RATES

LEARNING OBJECTIVES

- Examine the model of market determined exchange rates, that is, in the short-run, the supply and demand for a currency determine the relative price of that currency.
- Explore the purchasing power parity theory, i.e., over the long-run, how price levels and changes in price level (inflation) in countries determine the exchange rate at which their currencies are traded.
- Discover the relationship between the forward exchange rate and interest rate, the so-called interest rate parity (IRP) and how the asset prices influence the short-run exchange rate movements.
- Distinguish between covered and uncovered interest arbitrage.
- Show how forward markets for currencies reflect expectations held by market participants about the future spot exchange rate (Forward Parity).
- Analyze the relationship between interest rate and inflation rate (Fisher equation, International Fisher equation, Real interest parity).
- Understand several methods of exchange rate forecasts.

Lots of people have an opinion about the likely course of exchange rates. Should you listen to them to try to turn a profit on changes in the exchange rate? The answer is surely no. To see why, let's look at a recent episode in economic history. In 2008, U.S. imports exceeded exports by nearly 5% of GDP (that's a really big current account deficit); the economy was faltering; the stock market was declining; but still the dollar was strong. Moreover, the Japanese Yen remained strong after more than a decade of stagnation and record low interest rates. Anyone who followed such matters would tell you that both the dollar and the yen should have depreciated. But having a good sense of what will happen over the long run doesn't help much in the short run. What the experts can't tell you is when the dollar will depreciate.

Exchange rates have broad implications both for countries and for individuals. Take the case of South Korea in the winter of 1998. As economic and financial turmoil spread through Asia starting in the summer of 1997, output and employment plunged. In South Korea, large industrial companies and financial institutions approached bankruptcy. From October 1997 to January 1998, the number of South Korea Won needed to purchase one dollar more than doubled, rising from 990 to 1900. The consequences were dramatic, both inside and outside the country. When the cost of buying won plummeted, South Korean products became much cheaper for foreigners to buy. At the same time, U.S.-made products became extremely expensive for South Koreans to buy. In fact, the crisis became so severe that many Korean students at U.S. colleges and universities had to go home. The price of a U.S. education, measured in Won, had doubled, and many Korean students just couldn't afford to continue.

This chapter focuses on the determination of exchange rates in both the short and long run. Because economists believe that the determinations of exchange rate fluctuations are rather different in the short run (a few weeks or even days), and long run (one, two, or even five, ten years). We will consider these time frames when analyzing exchange rates. We first examine a simple model of market determined exchange rates, that is, in the short run, the demand and supply of the relative currencies have tremendous influences on the exchange rates. We then discuss the exchange rates in the long run (purchasing power parity) and forces that drive its movement over an extended period, such as a year or more. Purchasing power parity is a useful tool to forecast the future exchange rates. The third section of this chapter explores the interest rate parity (IRP). It describes a no-arbitrage relationship between spot and forward exchange rates and the two nominal interest rates associated with these currencies. Interest rate parity is a critical equilibrium relationship in international finance. The fourth section introduces other parity conditions, mainly the Fisher Equation and international Fisher Equation. Finally, we briefly introduce some basic techniques of the exchange rate forecasts.

Exchange Rates Determination in the Short Run

To explain the short-run changes in exchange rates, we are going to use an analytical model of the supply of and demand for currencies in the foreign exchange market. These exchange rate flows reflect current and financial account transactions in a country's balance of payments. This model is also called **balance of payments approach**. The theory argues that the equilibrium exchange rate is determined by the net inflow (outflow) of foreign exchange arising from current account transactions matches the net outflow (inflow) of foreign exchange arising from financial account transactions.

The Demand for Foreign Exchange

Here, we pick Euro as the foreign exchange and Japanese Yen as the domestic currency in our analytical model. In other words, we will discuss the number of Japanese Yen that it takes to purchase one Euro. The demand for Euros in the foreign exchange market results from transactions of goods, services, investment instruments, speculations, and hedging needs of the people outside the Euro Zone. Therefore, the demand for Euros in the foreign exchange market is a **derived demand**; that is, Euros are not demanded because they have an intrinsic value in themselves, but rather because of what they can buy.

Suppose a Japanese student would like to attend a college in Germany. The school will accept payment only in Euros, so paying the tuition bill means exchanging Yens for Euros. The lower the ¥/€ exchange rate — the fewer Yens needed to buy one Euro — the cheaper the tuition bill will be from the viewpoint of a Japanese student. At a given Euro price, the fewer Yens needed to purchase one Euro, the cheaper are German-made goods and services. And the cheaper a good or service, the higher the demand for it. The same is true of investment. The cheaper the Euros — the lower the ¥/€ exchange rate — the more attractive are German investments and the higher is the demand for Euros with which to buy them. Thus *the demand curve for Euros slopes downward*. **Figure 5.1** depicts the demand curve for Euros.

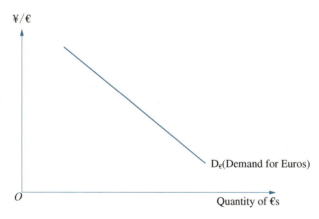

Figure 5.1   The Demand for Euros

The Supply of Foreign Exchange

In our model the supply of Euros is in essence the German demand for Japanese Yen. There are two reasons why German people who are holding Euros would want to exchange them for Yens. First, they plan to purchase goods and services produced in Japan, like a Japanese car, dinner in Tokyo, or tuition at a Japanese college; and second, they intend to invest in Japanese assets, such as bonds issued by the Japanese government, or shares in Honda, the Japanese manufacturer of cars and motorcycles.

Figure 5.2 shows the supply of Euros in the foreign exchange market. Just like any supply curve, it slopes upward. The higher the price a Euro commands in the market, the more Euros are supplied. And the more valuable the Euro, the cheaper are Japanese-produced goods, services, and assets relative to German ones in German markets.

To see why, suppose a German worker planning to buy a car. He has narrowed his options to a Japanese-made Honda Accord and a German-made Volkswagen Jetta. Price is important to him. Because the Accord is manufactured abroad, a change in the value of the euro will affect his decision. As the Euro increases in value, the price of the Honda Accord falls and he becomes more likely to buy the Accord. If he does, he will be supplying Euros to the foreign exchange market. What is true for his car purchase is true for everything else. The more valuable the Euro, the cheaper Japanese goods, services, and assets will be and the higher the supply of Euros in the ¥/€ market. Thus, *the supply curve for Euros slopes upward*, as shown in Figure 5.2.

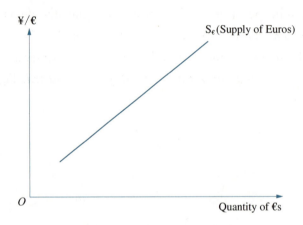

Figure 5.2　The Supply of Euros

The Equilibrium Exchange Rate

Since the foreign exchange market is merely a market which brings together those people who wish to buy a currency (which represents the demand) with those who wish to sell the currency (which represents the supply), then the spot exchange rate can most easily be thought of as being determined by the interaction of the supply and demand for the currency. **Figure 5.3** illustrates the determination of the ¥/€ exchange rate in the context of such a supply and demand framework. The figure depicts the supply and demand for Euros in the foreign exchange market. **The equilibrium exchange rate** is determined by the intersection of the supply and demand curves (labeled as S and D) to yield a ¥/€ exchange rate (labeled as E). At this exchange rate, the quantity demanded and the quantity supplied of the euros are equal, so the market reaches equilibrium. When the exchange rate is left to float freely it is determined by the intersection of the supply and demand curves. As a result, fluctuations in their value are the consequence of shifts in supply and demand.

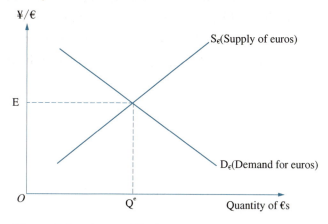

Figure 5.3 The Equilibrium Exchange Rate of Euros

Shifts in the Supply of and Demand for Foreign Exchange

If, at a given exchange rate, there is an increase in the demand for German goods and services which shifts the demand curve from D_1 to D_2 as depicted in **Figure 5.4**, and this increase in the demand for Euros leads to an appreciation of Euro on the foreign exchange market. **Figure 5.5** examines the impact of an increase in the supply of Euros due to an increased demand for Japanese exports and therefore Japanese Yen. The increased supply of Euros shifts the S_1 schedule to the right to S_2 resulting in a depreciation of euro. The essence of a floating exchange rate is that the exchange rate adjusts in response to changes in the supply and demand for a currency. If quantity supplied of Euros exceeds quantity demanded for Euros, the value of Euros falls on the foreign exchange market and vice versa. The question is what factors that cause the supply and demand schedules of currencies to change. These factors can be summarized as two main categories, the market fundamentals and the market expectations.

Market fundamentals refer to economic variables such as balance of payments, relative inflation rates and interest rate, national income and government economic policies, etc. Here we briefly summarize some basic reasons that the supply curve of foreign exchange will shift. Again, we take Euro as an example.

A rise in the supply of Euros Germen use to purchase foreign goods and services can be first caused by an increase in Germen's *preference* for foreign goods and services. If German people are attracted by Japanese electronic appliances or the scene of Fuji Mountain, they would exchange Euros for Yens, shifting the Euro supply curve to the right. A fall in the supply of Euros reflect the opposite direction. If Germen do not like foreign goods or services, the Euro supply curve will shift to the left.

Second, the supply of Euros increases because of an increase in Germen *income*. An increase in income raises consumption of everything, including importing goods and services. The more money Germen earn, the more foreign goods and services they will buy, and the more Euros they will exchange for foreign moneys, shifting the supply of Euros to the right. On the other hand, if Germen income decreases, they will spend less on everything, including imports, shifting the supply curve of Euros to the left.

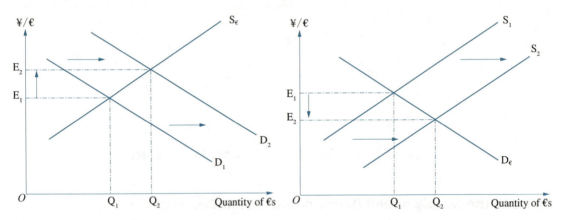

Figure 5.4　A Change in Demand (Increase in Demand for Euros)

Figure 5.5　A Change in Supply (Increase in Supply of Euros)

Third, change in *relative prices* due to inflation will change the supply of Euros. If inflation in Germany is higher than inflation in Japan, the prices of German goods and services will be higher. Germen will want to consume import substitutes. They will sell Euros, increasing the supply of Euros on the foreign exchange market. A fall in the supply of Euros may result from the higher prices of foreign goods and services. If inflation in Germany is lower than that in foreign countries, imports will be expensive. Thus, the supply of Euros shits to the left.

Market expectations result from the news or events about the economic variables and very importantly, the speculative opinion about future exchange rates. If the market reaches a consensus that Euros are going to lose value, people who have Euros will like to exchange them for Yens. To see why, assume that one euro is currently worth ¥130 and people expect it to move to ¥120/€ over the next year. If you exchange € 100 for Yens today, you will get ¥13,000. Reversing the transaction a year later, you will be left with € 108.33, an 8.33% return. Therefore, if people think the Euro will decline in value — it will depreciate — they will sell Euros, increasing the supply of Euros on the foreign exchange market. On the other hand, if people think the Euro will appreciate in the future, the supply curve of the Euro shifts to the left.

To understand shifts in the demand for Euros, all we need to do is review the list just presented, this time from the point of view of a foreigner. Anything that increases the preference of foreigners to buy German-made goods and services, or to invest in German assets, will increase the demand for Euros and shift the demand curve to the right. When the income in foreign countries increases, when foreign prices are higher than German prices and when people expect the Euro will appreciate in the future, all these factors lead to increase in demand, shifting the demand curve to the right (see **Figure 5.4**). **Exhibit 5.1** summarizes what we have discussed that increase the supply of and demand for Euros in the foreign exchange market.

Exhibit 5.1 Causes of an Increase in the Supply of and Demand for Euros

Increased Supply Shifts Supply Curve to the Right	Increased Demand Shifts Demand Curve to the Right
Increase in German preference for foreign goods, services, etc.	Increase in foreign preference for German goods, services, etc.
Increase in German income	Increase in foreign income
Increase in German prices	Increase in foreign prices
Expected depreciation of the Euro	Expected future euro appreciation

Foreign Exchange Market Intervention

The exchange rate is not necessarily determined by the market forces of demand and supply even under the floating exchange rate system. It seems that every country's central bank these days is involved in some sort of capital control over its currency. Besides standard monetary and fiscal strategies, these policies are used to keep the domestic currency under control and to keep a country's economic growth stable. One of the most frequently-used strategies by policy makers is direct foreign exchange market intervention. If the exchange rate changes frequently and violently, the monetary authorities would like to directly enter into the market to make up the difference between the supply and demand for the relative currencies, which means they will buy or sell currency in an attempt to affect demand or supply. This approach is called a **foreign exchange market intervention**. By intervening, the monetary authorities keep the exchange rate from changing violently and avoid the consequences of the unstable exchange rate. The more a country relies on exports and imports, the more important its exchange rate. Some governments frequently intervene in the foreign exchange market.

Figure 5.6 depicts the process of foreign exchange market intervention. Suppose that the People's Bank of China (PBOC) thinks the appropriate RMB/USD rate should be RMB¥6.50/$. If the present market rate is RMB¥6.30/$, the PBOC can buy U.S. dollars with RMB, thus increasing the demand for dollars. The original demand schedule now shifts rightward. The new equilibrium point E′ is reached with higher exchange rate. The PBOC

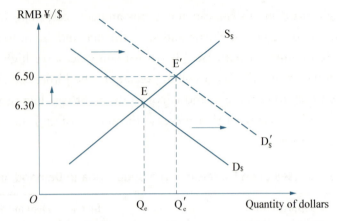

Figure 5.6　The Foreign Exchange Market Intervention

will stop intervening in the market because the exchange rate rises to RMB¥6.50/$.

Some countries try to maintain their home currency rates within some unofficial, or implicit boundaries. When the exchange rates fall below or rise above the benchmark value, the central bank would intervene to prevent that from occurring. In some cases, a central bank may intervene to insulate a currency's value from a temporary disturbance.

A lot of studies have found that government intervention does not have a permanent effect on exchange rate movements. To the contrary, in many cases the intervention is overwhelmed by market forces. However, during a period when a country experiences much economic or political instability, currency movements might be even more volatile without direct intervention.

Purchasing Power Parity (PPP)

In the previous section we explained how the exchange rate reaches equilibrium and why it changes according to the market forces. If we understand what determines exchange rates, we may be able to forecast exchange rate movements. Because future exchange rate movements influence export opportunities, the profitability of international trade and investment deals, and the price competitiveness of foreign imports, this is valuable information for an international business. Unfortunately, there is no simple explanation. The forces that determine exchange rates are complex, and no theoretical consensus exists, even among academic economists who study the phenomenon every day. Nonetheless, most economic theories of exchange rate movements seem to agree that three factors have an important impact on future exchange rate movements for a country's currency: the country's price inflation, its interest rate, and market psychology. In this section we look at one of the earliest and simplest models of exchange rate determination known as **Purchasing Power Parity (PPP) Theory**. PPP Theory has been advocated as a satisfactory model of exchange rate determination in its own right, and also provides a point of reference for the long-run exchange rate in many of the modern exchange rate theories.

The Law of One Price

The Theory of Purchasing Power Parity is generally attributed to the Swedish economist Gustav Cassel's writings in the 1920s. The starting point for understanding how long-run exchange rates are determined is the Law of One Price.

The **Law of One Price** states that identical products that are easily and freely traded in a perfectly competitive global market (free of transportation costs and barriers to trade) should have the same price everywhere, once the prices at different places are expressed in the same currency.

$$P^d = S^{d/f} \times P^f \tag{5.1}$$

where

P^d: the domestic price

P^f: the foreign price

$S^{d/f}$: the amount of domestic currencies per unit of foreign currency (exchange rate)

If the same commodities have different prices in different places, people will begin to take advantage of it by buying commodities in the cheaper market and then shipping them to and selling them in the more expensive market. People who buy in one market and sell in another are **commodity arbitragers**.

For example, if a sneaker retails for $80 in New York and sells for HK$640 in Hong Kong, the exchange rate between the Hong Kong dollar and the U.S. dollar should be HK$8/US$ (HK$640/US$80) according to the law of one price. Consider what would happen if the sneaker costs HK$600 in Hong Kong. At this price, it would pay a trader to buy sneakers in Hong Kong and sell them in New York (an example of commodity arbitrage). The trader initially could make a profit of US$5 on each sneaker by purchasing it for HK$600 (US$75) in Hong Kong and selling it for US$80 in New York (we are assuming away transportation costs and trade barriers). However, the increased demand for sneakers in Hong Kong would raise their price in Hong Kong, and the increased supply of sneakers in New York would lower their price there. This would continue until prices were equalized. Thus, prices might equalize when the sneaker costs HK$624 in Hong Kong and US$78 in New York (assuming no change in the exchange rate of US$1 = HK$8).

The proponents of PPP argue that the exchange rate must adjust to ensure that the Law of One Price which applies only to individual goods also holds international for identical bundles of goods.

In reality, we can see immediately that the Law of One Price fails almost all the time, because the same commodity or service sells for vastly different prices in different places. Reasons include transportation costs, tariffs, technical specification, and non-tradable goods or services.

Internal and External Purchasing Power of a Currency

Before we discuss the Theory of Purchasing Power Parity, let's first study several concepts related to the theory.

Purchasing Power refers to the amount of real goods and services each unit of money will buy. It is the reciprocal of price index. **Price index** (or **price level**) is an index number of the prices of goods of some given type. If only one good i is concerned, period 0 is the base period, and period t is the current period. The price index is given by P_{it}/P_{i0}. If a class of goods i = 1, 2, 3 ... N is concerned, the price index is a weighted average of the indices of their price. The weights are the values of the goods purchased in some period.

$$P_C = \left(\sum_i P_{it} q_{it}\right) / \left(\sum_i P_{i0} q_{i0}\right) \tag{5.2}$$

The purchasing power of a currency can be classified as internal purchasing power and external purchasing power. The **internal purchasing power** of a currency, say Renminbi, refers to the amount of goods and services that can be purchased with ¥1 in China. For example, if the price level in China is ¥20,000 for the average of a basket of goods and services, what is the purchasing power of ¥1,000,000? Since the purchasing power of ¥1 is the reciprocal of the price level which is 0.00005 (1/¥20,000), the purchasing power of ¥1,000,000 equals to 50 [¥1,000,000 × (1/20,000)] units of basket of goods and services.

The external purchasing power of Renminbi is the amount of goods and services outside China that can be purchased with ¥1, say, in the United States. Calculating the external purchasing power of ¥1 in the United States involves two steps. First, it is necessary to purchase some units of dollars with the yuan. Second, it is necessary to examine the purchasing power of those dollars in U.S.

As before, we assume the price level in China is ¥20,000 for the average of a basket of goods and services. Suppose the price level in U.S. is $5,000 for the same basket of goods and services and the exchange rate between yuan and dollar is ¥6.50/$. To calculate the external purchasing power, we first exchange one yuan for dollars, which is $0.1538 [1/(¥6.50/$)], then multiply the dollar's purchasing power 0.0002 (1/$5,000), the result is 0.00003076. In other words, the RMB's external purchasing power in U.S. is 0.00003076 units of a basket of goods and services. The external purchasing power of ¥1,000,000 in U.S. is then 30.76 (1,000,000 × 0.00003076) units of basket of goods and services. Obviously, the RMB's internal purchasing power is not equal to its external purchasing power. Why? After we examine the Theory of Purchasing Power Parity, you'll understand it.

Absolute Purchasing Power Parity

Since the Law of One Price fails so often, why do we bother with it? Because even with its obvious flaws, the Law of One Price is extremely useful in explaining the behavior of exchange rates over the long run, like 5, 10, or even 20 years. To see why, we need to extend the law from a single commodity to a basket of goods and services. The result is the Theory of Purchasing Power Parity, which means that one unit of a currency will buy the same basket of goods and services anywhere in the world. This idea may sound absurd, but let's look at its implications.

The **absolute purchasing power parity** describes the relationship between average price levels in each country and the equilibrium exchange rate. If the Law of One Price were true for all goods and services, the purchasing power parity exchange rate could be found from any individual set of prices. By comparing the prices of identical products in different currencies, it would be possible to determine the "real" or PPP exchange rate that would exist if markets were efficient. (An **efficient market** has no impediments to the free flow of goods and services, such as trade barriers). Therefore, the absolute PPP implies that exchange rate will adjust to equalize the internal and external purchasing powers of a currency. In our previous example, the RMB's internal purchasing power does not equal to its external purchasing power, because something is wrong with the exchange rate. According to the theory, a currency's internal purchasing power should be equal to its external purchasing power. That is to say:

$$1/¥20,000 = 1/S^{¥/\$} \times 1/\$5,000$$

Therefore, the equilibrium exchange rate between Renminbi and dollar suggested by PPP should be:

$$S^{¥/\$} = ¥20,000/\$5,000 = ¥4/\$$$

We can formalize and express absolute PPP as **Equation (5.3)**. Let $S^{d/f}$ denote the spot exchange rate; P^d the domestic price level and P^f the foreign price level. Then the absolute PPP is expressed as:

$$S^{d/f} = P^d / P^f \qquad (5.3)$$

The absolute PPP can be used to predict the exchange rate given the price levels in two countries. Equation 5.3 predicts that the yuan-dollar exchange rate should be equal to the ratio of the price level in China to the price level in the United States just like we have calculated.

It should be noted that the theory of absolute purchasing power parity implies that real exchange rate (discussed in Chapter 3) is always equal to one. The implication of this conclusion is straightforward. It is that purchasing power of a currency is always the same, regardless of where in the world you go.

Overvaluation and Undervaluation

Every year, the newsmagazine *The Economist* publishes its own version of the PPP theory, which it refers to as the "Big Mac Index." *The Economist* has selected McDonald's Big Mac as a proxy of a "basket of goods" because it is produced according to more or less the same recipe in about 120 countries. The Big Mac PPP is the exchange rate that would have hamburgers costing the same in each country. According to *The Economist*, comparing a country's actual exchange rate with the one predicted by the PPP theory based on relative prices of Big Macs is a test on whether a currency is undervalued or not. This is not a totally serious exercise, as *The Economist* admits, but it does provide us with a useful illustration of the PPP theorem.

The Big Mac index for July 2012 is reproduced in **Exhibit 5.2**. To calculate the index *The Economist* converts the price of a Big Mac in a country into dollars at current exchange rates and divides that by the average price of a Big Mac in America (which is $4.33). According to the PPP theory, the prices should be the same. If they are not, it implies that the currency is either overvalued or undervalued against the U.S. dollar.

Exhibit 5.2 The Big Mac Index

Country or region	Big Mac prices in local currency	in dollars	Implied PPP° of the dollar	Actual dollar exchange rate July 25th	Under(−)/ over(+) valuation against the dollar,%
United States	$ 4.33	4.33			
Argentina	Peso 19.0	4.16	4.39	4.57	−4
Australia	A$ 4.56	4.68	1.05	0.97	8
Brazil	Real 10.08	4.94	2.33	2.04	14
Canada	C$ 3.89	3.82	0.90	1.02	−12
Chile	Peso 2,050	4.16	473.71	493.05	−4
China	Yuan 15.65	2.45	3.62	6.39	−43
Hong Kong	HK$ 16.5	2.13	3.81	7.76	−51
Taiwan	NT$75.0	2.48	17.33	30.20	−43
Colombia	Peso 8,600	4.77	1,987.29	1,804.48	10
Costa Rica	Colones 1,200	2.40	277.30	501.02	−45

Chapter 5 EXCHANGE RATE DETERMINATION AND FORECASTING EXCHANGE RATES

(Continued)

Country or region	Big Mac prices in local currency	in dollars	Implied PPP♀ of the dollar	Actual dollar exchange rate July 25th	Under(−)/over(+) valuation against the dollar,%
Czech Rep.	Koruna 70.33	3.34	16.25	21.05	−23
Denmark	DK 28.5	4.65	6.59	6.14	7
Egypt	Pound 16	2.64	3.70	6.07	−39
Euro area♂	€ 3.58	4.34	1.21‡	1.21‡	0
Hungary	Forint 830	3.48	191.8	238.22	−19
Indonesia	Rupiah 24,200	2.55	5,592	9,482.50	−41
Israel	Shekel 11.9	2.92	2.75	4.08	−33
Japan	¥320	4.09	73.95	78.22	−5
Latvia	Lats 1.69	2.94	0.39	0.57	−32
Lithuania	Litas 7.80	2.74	1.80	2.85	−37
Malaysia	Ringgit 7.40	2.33	1.71	3.17	−46
Mexico	Peso 37.0	2.70	8.55	13.69	−38
New Zealand	NZ$ 5.10	4.00	1.18	1.27	−7
Norway	Kroner 43.0	7.06	9.94	6.09	63
Pakistan	Rupee 285	3.01	65.86	94.61	−30
Philippines	Peso 118.0	2.80	27.27	42.2	−35
Poland	Zloty 9.10	2.63	2.10	3.46	−39
Russia	Rubble 75.0	2.29	17.33	32.77	−47
Saudi Arabia	Riyal 10.0	2.67	2.31	3.75	−38
Singapore	S$ 4.40	3.50	1.02	1.26	−19
South Africa	Rand 19.95	2.36	4.61	8.47	−46
South Korea	Won 3,700	3.21	855.00	1,151	−26
Sri Lanka	Rupee 290	2.21	67.01	131.00	−49
Sweden	SKr 48.4	6.94	11.18	6.98	60
Switzerland	SFr 6.50	6.56	1.50	0.99	52
Thailand	Baht 82.0	2.59	18.95	31.70	−40

(Continued)

Country or region	Big Mac prices in local currency	in dollars	Implied PPP♀ of the dollar	Actual dollar exchange rate July 25th	Under(−)/ over(+) valuation against the dollar,%
Turkey	Lira 8.25	4.52	1.91	1.83	4
UAE	Dirhams 12.0	3.27	2.77	3.67	−25
U.K.	£2.69	4.16	1.61*	1.55*	−4
Ukraine	Hryvnia 15	1.86	3.47	8.09	−57
Uruguay	Peso 99.0	4.53	22.8	21.87	5
Venezuela	Bolivar 34	7.92	7.86	4.29	83

Source: "The Big Mac Index", *The Economist*, July 15, 2012.
♀: Implied PPP (purchasing power parity) = local price/price in the United States
♂: Weighted average of prices in Euro area
‡: Dollars per Euro
*: Dollars per pound

An **overvalued currency** is a currency in which the actual market-determined value is higher than the value predicted by an economic theory or model. An **undervalued currency**, on the other hand, is a currency in which the actual market-determined value is lower than that predicted by an economic theory or model. For example, as the Exhibit 5.2 shows, the average price of a Big Mac in China was RMB¥15.65 in 2012. Dividing this by the average price of a Big Mac in the United States gives RMB¥3.6143/$ (RMB¥15.65/$4.33), which is the implied PPP of the dollar (the fourth column in Exhibit 5.2). But on July 15, 2012, the actual dollar exchange rate was RMB¥6.39/$ (the fifth column), it suggests that the actual dollar value was overvalued against the yuan or the yuan was undervalued against the dollar. The degree to which the U.S. dollar was overvalued versus the yuan is calculated by the following formula:

$$\frac{\text{Actual exchange rate} - \text{Implied exchange rate}}{\text{Implied exchange rate}} \quad (5.4)$$

Therefore, the dollar was overvalued by:

$$(6.39 - 3.6143) / 3.6143 = 0.768 = 76.8\%$$

To calculate the undervaluation of the yuan we have two ways. First we can use the reciprocal of the above given exchange rate and then apply **Equation 5.4**:

$$(1/6.39 - 1/3.6143) /(1/3.6143) = -43.44\%$$

Second, the undervaluation of the yuan can be calculated by applying the **Equation 5.5** which is:

$$\frac{\text{Implied exchange rate} - \text{Actual exchange rate}}{\text{Actual exchange rate}} \qquad (5.5)$$

So, the yuan is undervalued by

$$(3.6143 - 6.39)/6.39 = -43.44\%$$

This is the value showed in the last column of Exhibit 5.2.

The Big Mac Index may be a good candidate for the application of the law of one price and measurement of under valuation or overvaluation. But as *The Economist* points out, the Big Mac Index is not perfect.

The index was never intended to be a precise predictor of currency movements, simply a take-away guide to whether currencies are at their "correct" long-run level. Curiously, however, burgernomics has an impressive record in predicting exchange rates: currencies that show up as overvalued often tend to weaken in later years. But you must always remember the Big Mac's limitations. Burgers cannot sensibly be traded across borders and prices are distorted by differences in taxes and the cost of non-tradable inputs, such as rents.[1]

Relative Purchasing Power Parity

The next step in the PPP theory is to argue that the exchange rate will change if relative prices change. Changes in exchange rate should be equal to the difference in prices change between the two economies. For example, imagine there is no price inflation in the United States, while prices in China are increasing by 10 percent a year. At the beginning of the year, a basket of goods costs $5,000 in the United States and ¥20,000 in China, so the yuan/dollar exchange rate, according to PPP theory, should be $1 = ¥4. At the end of the year, the basket of goods still costs $5,000 in the United States, but it costs ¥22,000 in China. Relative PPP theory predicts that the exchange rate should change as a result. More precisely, by the end of the year:

$$S_t^{¥/\$} = ¥22{,}000/\$5{,}000 = ¥4.4/\$$$

Thus, $1 = ¥4.4. Because of 10 percent price inflation in China, the dollar has appreciated against the yuan by 10 percent. One dollar will buy 10 percent more yuan at the end of the year than at the beginning.

---

1 "Happy 20th Anniversary", *The Economist*, May 25, 2006.

Figure 5.7 shows the relationship between the exchange rate and price level in the related countries (the theory of **relative purchasing power parity**). The purchasing power parity line (PPP line) is a 45 degree line. It shows that the percent change in the spot exchange rate for foreign currency should be equal to the percent difference in expected inflation rates if the relative PPP holds. For instance, if the inflation rate of the foreign currency (π^f) is lower than the domestic inflation rate (π^d) by 3%, the value of the foreign currency will increase by 3% compared to the domestic currency (point P in the figure). Therefore,

$$\% \Delta S_t^{d/f} = \pi^d - \pi^f \tag{5.6}$$

Where the $\% \Delta S_t^{d/f}$ is the percentage change in exchange rate of the foreign currency relative to domestic currency (d); and ($\pi^d - \pi^f$) is the inflation differential of the domestic currency versus the foreign currency.

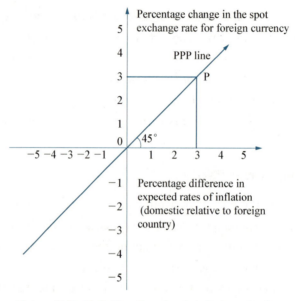

Figure 5.7 Relative Purchasing Power Parity

Now let's consider our preceding example again. Since the rate of Chinese inflation is higher than the rate of U.S. inflation by 10% ($\pi^¥ - \pi^\$ = 10\% - 0\% = 10\%$), the U.S. dollar will appreciate against the RMB by 10%. The new exchange rate should be equal to

$$S_t^{¥/\$} = 4 \times (1 + 10\%) = 4.4$$

Equation 5.6 provides a hint about exchange rate trends in the long run. That is: Currencies with relatively low inflation rates tend to appreciate in the foreign exchange market; while currencies with relatively high inflation rates tend to depreciate in the foreign exchange market. This is because inflation lowers the purchasing power of money. If the amount of inflation in the foreign country differs from the inflation rate in the domestic

Chapter 5 EXCHANGE RATE DETERMINATION AND FORECASTING EXCHANGE RATES

country, a change in the nominal exchange rate to compensate for the differential rates of inflation is warranted so that the loss of internal purchasing power due to domestic inflation equals the loss of external purchasing power due to foreign inflation and the change in the exchange rate. If the change in the exchange rate satisfies this warranted change, relative PPP is satisfied.

The theory of relative purchasing power parity can be used to predict long-run exchange rates. Consider the following example, if the CPI for the U.S. in 2019 was 101.4, and 103.2 in 2020, the CPI was 102.8 and 104.1 in U.K. respectively, and if the respective exchange rate was $1.4590/£ and $1.4105/£ in 2019 and 2020, was the pound correctly priced in 2020 according to relative PPP?

To predict the 2020 dollar/pound exchange rate we first calculate the inflation rate of both the U.S. and the U.K. The U.S. inflation rate in this period is 1.78% [(103.2/101.4) − 1]. The U.K. inflation rate at the same period is 1.26% [(104.1/102.8) − 1]. Second, we calculate the inflation rate differential. The U.K inflation is 0.52% (1.26% − 1.78%) lower than the U.S. inflation. The pound should appreciate against the dollar by 0.52% according to Equation 5.6. Therefore, the implied exchange rate between the dollar and the pound is:

$$\$1.4590/£ \ (1 + 0.52\%) = \$1.4666/£$$

In 2020, the actual pound value was $1.4150, and the implied value suggested by relative PPP should be $1.4666. So the pound was undervalued against the dollar according to Equation 5.4 by:

$$(\$1.4105/£ - \$1.4666/£)/\$1.4666/£ = -3.83\%$$

The relative purchasing power parity can also be expressed by the following formula:

$$S_1/S_0 = (P^d/P^f)_1 / (P^d/P^f)_0 \qquad (5.7)$$
$$\text{Or, } S_1 = S_0 \times [(P^d/P^f)_1 / (P^d/P^f)_0] \qquad (5.8)$$
$$\text{Or, } S_1 = S_0 \times [(P_1^d/P_0^d) / (P_1^f/P_0^f)] \qquad (5.9)$$

Where
  S_0: the exchange rate in base period
  S_1: the exchange rate in period 1
  P^d: the domestic price index
  P^f: the foreign price index

The previous question can be solved by applying Equation 5.9:

$$S_{2020} = S_{2019} \cdot [(P_{2020}^{U.S.}/P_{2019}^{U.S.}) / (P_{2020}^{U.K.}/P_{2019}^{U.K.})]$$
$$= \$1.4590/£ \times [(103.2/101.4) / (104.1/102.8)]$$
$$= \$1.4590/£ \times (1.01775/1.01265)$$
$$= \$1.4663\$/£$$

149

This is the implied exchange rate predicted by the relative PPP theory which is approximately the same as our previous answer.

Problems of PPP

Is PPP theory true in practice? Extensive empirical testing of PPP theory has yielded mixed results. While PPP theory seems to yield relatively accurate predictions in the long run, it does not appear to be a strong predictor of short-run movements in exchange rates covering time spans of five years or less. As a matter of fact, there are noticeable deviations from PPP in the short run. In addition, the theory seems to best predict exchange rate changes for countries with high rates of inflation and underdeveloped capital markets. The theory is less useful for predicting short-run exchange rate movements between the currencies of advanced industrialized nations that have relatively small differentials in inflation rates. The failure of PPP theory to predict exchange rates more accurately can be summarized as follows:

Transportation costs and trade barriers are significant and they tend to create significant price differentials between countries. So prices are allowed to differ between markets by up to the cost of transportation.

Restrictions on movement of goods (trade barriers) like **import tariffs** can also cause PPP violations. If a country has 15% import tariff, prices within the country will have to move more than 15% above those in the other countries. **Quotas**, which are limits on the amounts of different commodities that can be imported, generally mean that price differences can become quite sizable, because commodity arbitragers are limited in their ability to narrow the gaps.

Price discrimination still exists because of imperfect competition. Dominant enterprises may be able to exercise a degree of pricing power, setting different prices in different markets to reflect varying demand conditions. In this case, arbitrage must be limited. Enterprises with some marketing power may be able to control distribution channels and therefore limit the unauthorized resale (arbitrage) by differentiating otherwise identical products among nations along some line, such as design or packaging.

For example, even though the version of Microsoft Office sold in China may be less expensive than the version sold in the United States, the use of arbitrage to equalize prices may be limited because few Americans would want a version that was based on Chinese characters. The design differentiation between Microsoft Office for China and for the United States means that the Law of One Price would not work for Microsoft Office, even if transportation costs were trivial and tariff barriers between the United States and China did not exist.

Price indices are different in different countries. Many of the items that are included in the commonly used price indices do not enter into international trade. Some of the items are immovable or inseparable from the providers of their services, such as real estates, haircuts, medical services, housing, and the like. Therefore, one of the major problems is to decide whether or not the PPP theory is supposed to be applicable to both traded goods and non-traded goods, or applicable to only one of those categories. The wholesale price indices are normally dominated by traded goods, while the consumer price indices generally include both traded and non-traded goods. Whichever price index is employed, an overall problem is that PPP is only expected to hold for similar baskets of goods, but national price indices typically attach different weights to different classes of goods. Some goods and services are more important for some countries than for other countries. PPP requires that the goods and services in the price indices should have the same weight. It is unrealistic.

Even if PPP does not hold in most cases, it is still popular among academic studies and even among decision makers. The PPP theory at least provides us with currencies' long-run tendency in the foreign exchange market. In some cases, it is also useful in economic analysis. As we have learned from the Big Mac Index, one can use the implied exchange rate by PPP as a benchmark in deciding if a country's currency is undervalued or overvalued against other currencies.

Interest Rate Parity (IRP)

This section focuses another important factor that determines the short-run exchange rates. The **asset market approach** argues that the supply and demand for financial assets of a wide variety determine the exchange rates. Shifts in the supply and demand for financial assets alter exchange rates. Changes in monetary and fiscal policy alter expected returns and perceived relative risks of financial assets, which in turn alter exchange rates.

According to the asset market approach, investors consider two key factors when deciding between domestic and foreign investments: relative levels of interest rates and expected changes in the exchange rate itself over the span of the investment. So what is the relationship of forward exchange rate and interest rate?

Interest Rate and Forward Premium

Interest rate parity as a theory was first developed by J.M. Keynes in 1930s. Like purchasing power parity, interest rate parity is based on the Law of One Price. However, where PPP refers to the law of one price in the commodity market, interest rate parity refers to the Law of One Price in the securities market. When quoted in a common currency, identical securities should have the same price in all markets.

Interest rate parity states that the forward premium between two currencies is determined by the nominal interest rate differential between those currencies. **Figure 5.8** illustrates the relationship of the forward exchange rate and the interest rates between the two currencies.

Consider one unit of domestic currency that can be invested both in the domestic and foreign financial market. Suppose the domestic annual interest rate is i^d and the foreign annual interest rate is i^f. When one unit of the domestic currency is invested in the domestic financial market, it will become $(1 + i^d)$ at the end of the year. If one unit of the domestic currency is invested in the foreign market, it should first be converted into the foreign currency $(1/S^{d/f})$. It will become $(1/S^{d/f})(1 + i^f)$ at the end of the year, since the foreign interest rate is i^f. However, when you move from the domestic currency into foreign currency the investment in foreign financial market is not identical to the domestic investment because the exchange rate could change over the year of the investment. This means that you are exposed to exchange risk. A change in the value of the domestic currency versus the foreign currency would change the number of domestic currency you receive when you convert your foreign currency investment into domestic currency at the end of the investment. A depreciation of the foreign currency would reduce the number of domestic currency you receive, while an appreciation of the foreign currency would increase it. In order to render the two investments identical, the exchange risk must be eliminated. This can be done by making a deal to sell the proceeds of the foreign currency investment on the forward foreign exchange market. With the forward transaction the two investments are comparable and the return in the domestic currency on the foreign currency investment can effectively be calculated.

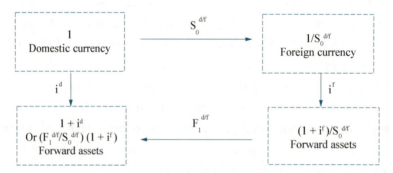

Figure 5.8 Relationship of the Forward Rate and the Interest Rate

According to the Law of One Price, the return should be equal no matter where you invest your domestic currency. If the expected returns on two similar financial instruments are different, one will move one instrument to another. In equilibrium, these rates would be equal. That is, we would have interest parity, in which interest rate equalization across nations would ensure that no such flow of funds would occur. Therefore, $(1 + i^d) = (1 + i^f) F^{d/f}/S^{d/f}$. Rearrange the equation, we get **Equation 5.10**:

$$(1 + i^d) / (1 + i^f) = F^{d/f}/S^{d/f} \tag{5.10}$$

This is the interest rate parity. The left side of the equation is the interest rate differential between the domestic and foreign financial instruments; and the right side is the forward

Chapter 5 EXCHANGE RATE DETERMINATION AND FORECASTING EXCHANGE RATES

premium.

There is a simplified version of the IRP. For the right part of the Equation 5.10, we use the fact that

$$F^{d/f}/S^{d/f} = (S^{d/f}/S^{d/f}) + (F^{d/f} - S^{d/f})/S^{d/f} = 1 + (F^{d/f} - S^{d/f})/S^{d/f}$$

to rewrite the parity condition as

$$1 + i^d = [1 + (F^{d/f} - S^{d/f})/S^{d/f}](1 + i^f)$$

Cross-multiplying the right part of the equation yields:

$$1 + i^d = 1 + (F^{d/f} - S^{d/f})/S^{d/f} + i^f + i^f[(F^{d/f} - S^{d/f})/S^{d/f}]$$

Because i^f and $(F^{d/f} - S^{d/f})/S^{d/f}$ are both typically small fractions, their product is approximately equal to zero. Making this approximation and subtracting 1 and i^f from both sides of the equation yields

$$(i^d - i^f) \approx (F^{d/f} - S^{d/f})/S^{d/f} \qquad (5.11)$$

Equation 5.11 or **Equation 5.10** is also called covered interest parity condition. Covered interest parity states that the difference between the domestic interest rate and the foreign interest rate on a similar financial asset should approximately equal the forward premium in percentage term.

Exhibit 5.3 shows how the calculation of the forward premium works in practice using the dollar-sterling exchange rate. It should be noted when the one-month forward premium is calculated, the annual interest rate should be divided by 12 so that the maturity of the interest rate is consistent with that of the forward premium. By the same token, the annual interest rate should be divided by 4 to calculate the 3-month forward premium. We apply Equation 5.10 to calculate the forward premiums in our examples.

The spot sterling exchange rate is 1.8277 dollars per pound.

The one-month forward exchange rate is calculated as:

$$F^{\$/£} = 1.8277 \times [(1 + 0.0159375/12) / (1 + 0.048125/12)] = 1.8228$$

The three-month forward exchange rate is calculated as:

$$F^{\$/£} = 1.8277 \times [(1 + 0.0171875/4) / (1 + 0.049375/4)] = 1.8132$$

The six-month forward exchange rate is calculated as:

$$F^{\$/£} = 1.8277 \times [(1 + 0.019375/2) / (1 + 0.050625/2)] = 1.7998$$

The one-year forward exchange rate is calculated as:

$$F^{\$/£} = 1.8277 \times [(1 + 0.0228125) / (1 + 0.0525)] = 1.7761$$

Exhibit 5.3 Dollar-Pound Forward Exchange Quotations and U.K. and U.S. Interest Rates

	Dollar-pound exchange rate	Sterling interest rate (%)	Dollar interest rate (%)
Spot rate	1.8277		
1 month	1.8228	4.8125	1.59375
3 month	1.8132	4.9375	1.71875
6 month	1.7998	5.0625	1.93750
12 month	1.7761	5.2500	2.28125

Covered Interest Arbitrage (CIA)

To understand why IRP must be used to calculate the forward exchange rate, consider what would happen if the forward rate was different to that calculated in the example; say it was $1.7861/£ instead of $1.7761/£ of the one-year forward dollar/sterling rate. In this instance, a U.S. investor with $100 could earn the U.S. interest rate and the payoff at the end of the year will be $102.28. What if the U.S. investor buys pounds spot (at $1.8277/£) and invest £54.71 ($100/1.8277) in England? He would have earning the U.K. interest rate of 5.25% giving him £57.58 (£54.71 × 1.0525) at the end of one year, which he would sell at a forward price of $1.7861/£ giving $102.85. Clearly, it pays a U.S. investor to invest in U.K. and sell pounds forward. With a sufficient numbers of investors doing this, the forward rate of the pound would depreciate until such arbitrage possibilities were eliminated. With a spot rate of $1.8277/£, only if the forward rate is at $1.7761/£ will the guaranteed yields in U.S. and U.K. time deposits be identical, since £57.58 times 1.7761 equals $102.27. Only at this forward exchange rate are there no riskless arbitrage profits to be made.

Figure 5.9 shows the covered interest rate parity. The vertical axis denotes the interest rate differential ($i^d - i^f$), and the horizontal axis represents the forward premiums (($F^{d/f} - S^{d/f}$) / $S^{d/f}$). The IRP line is a 45° line. Any point on the IRP line indicates the covered interest parity condition is satisfied. In other words, no-arbitrage condition exists. There is no way arbitragers can make riskless arbitrage profits since the market is in equilibrium. Any point above or below the IRP line means interest rate differential is greater or less than forward premium or discount. In this case, there is arbitrage opportunity. Arbitragers can borrow money from one place and invest in another place to make no-investment, no-risk profits.

We face the same problem here as in triangular arbitrage. When the interest rate differential is not equal to the forward premiums, we know there is arbitrage opportunity.

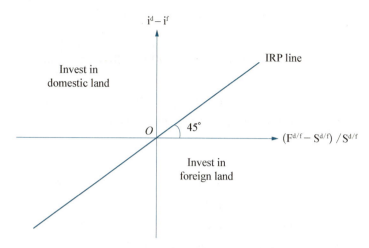

Figure 5.9 Covered Interest Rate Parity

But which currency do we borrow and which currency do we lend in order to take advantage of the market disequilibrium? Here is the rule of thumb for covered interest arbitrage:

- If interest rate differential is greater than forward premiums (or, if the intersection of interest rate differential and the forward premiums is above the 45° line), borrow money from foreign land, exchange borrowed money for domestic currency on the spot market, invest the borrowed money in domestic land, and sell the domestic currency for foreign currency on the forward market.
- If interest rate differential is less than forward premiums (or, if the intersection of interest rate differential and the forward premiums is below the 45° line), borrow money from domestic land, exchange borrowed money for foreign currency on the spot market, invest the money in foreign land, and finally sell the foreign currency for domestic currency on the forward market.

The following example shows when the covered interest parity does not hold, arbitrage opportunity will occur. Therefore, **covered interest arbitrage** refers to the activity of foreign exchange transaction resulting from the difference of the interest rates between two places, where the speculator moves funds from one place to another place and at the same time buys and sells foreign exchange on the foreign exchange market.

Suppose that Korean Won/U.S. dollar spot exchange rate is W1,200/$, forward rate is W1,165/$; The interest rate on U.S. government securities with one-year maturity is 7% and the interest rate on Korean government securities with one-year maturity is 5%, where should you invest and how much can you make from the covered interest arbitrage (ignoring the transaction fees)?

Since $i^{SK} - i^{US} = 5\% - 7\% = -2\%$

then $(F^{\$/£} - S^{\$/£}) / S^{\$/£} = (1,165 - 1,200)/1,200 = -2.92\%$,

you should move funds from U.S. to South Korea (interest rate differential < exchange rate differential). The steps of covered interest arbitrage are as follows:

1. Borrow $1million from the U.S. money market for one year, your obligation will be $1m × (1 + 7%) = $1.07 m.

2. Exchange dollars for Wons on the spot exchange market. This leaves you with a Won inflow today which is $1m × 1,200 = W1.200m.

3. Invest the Wons in Korean government securities for one year. Your payoff at the end of the investment will be: W1.200m × (1 + 5%) = W1,260 m.

4. Sell the expected W1,260m on the forward market. Your U.S. inflow will be 1,260/1,165 = $1.0815m.

Now you have $1.07 million obligation and dollar net inflow of $1.0815 at the end of the year. Your net profit is the difference of the two.

Net profit: $1.0815m − $1.07m = $0.015 m = $15,000 (ignoring transaction fees).

The above arbitrage will quickly affect both the financial market and foreign exchange market. **Figure 5.10** illustrates the changes in the money markets of the U.S. and South Korea. In U.S. the demand for dollar goes up, the demand curve shifts from $D^\$$ to $D^{\$'}$, the dollar interest rate moves up from i_0 to i_1 as left panel of Figure 5.10 shows. In South Korea, the supply of Won rises, the supply curve shifts rightward to $S^{W'}$, it pushes down the interest rate of the Won from i_0 to i_1 (see right panel of Figure 5.10).

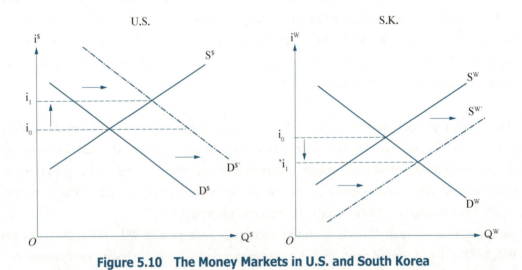

Figure 5.10 The Money Markets in U.S. and South Korea

Figure 5.11 describes the situation in foreign exchange market. In the spot exchange market, the Won is going to appreciate against the dollar since the demand for Won

Chapter 5 EXCHANGE RATE DETERMINATION AND FORECASTING EXCHANGE RATES

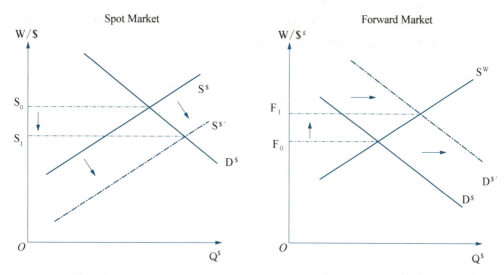

Figure 5.11 The Spot and Forward Markets for the U.S. Dollar

increases; the dollar will lose its value because of the increased supply. The supply curve of the dollar shifts rightward to $S^{\$'}$, and the spot dollar rate goes down from S_0 to S_1 (the left panel of Figure 5.11). In the forward exchange market, the increased demand for the U.S. dollar forces up the value of the dollar. The demand curve in the right panel of Figure 5.10 shifts from $D^{\$}$ to $D^{\$'}$, the forward rate goes up from F_0 to F_1. The value of Korean Won will be pushed down because of the increased supply. Both the money market and foreign exchange market will adjust until the covered interest parity holds.

Foreign exchange traders will tell you that interest rate differentials determine the forward premiums and not vice versa. Forward rates are almost entirely an interest rate play. If there is disequilibrium, exchange rates are much more likely to change than the interest rates.

Money Market Hedge

In Chapter 3 we discussed how to use forward market to hedge transaction risk exposures. When interest rate parity is satisfied, there is another equivalent way to hedge the transaction foreign exchange risks. That is, borrowing or lending the foreign currency coupled with making a transaction in the spot exchange market. This technique is also known as a **synthetic forward**. There are a number of reasons for using such hedges. First, it might be that the transaction is not large enough to warrant a forward contract, which typically has a denomination of at least $1 million. Second, some countries (certain developing countries) may not have forward exchange market. There is no way that you can take the advantage of a forward contract to hedge the currency exposures. Third, when you try to use a forward contract for a long time, it may cost you more since the bid-ask margin for a long-time forward contract widens substantially. Therefore, it may be advantageous to consider the **money market hedge**.

The general principal is that if you have an asset (account receivable) denominated in foreign currency, you need an equivalent liability in the money market to provide a hedge. On the other hand, if you have a liability (account payable) denominated in foreign currency, you need an equivalent asset in the money market to provide a hedge. We are going to take two examples to show how this technique works.

Hedging a foreign currency receivable (a long position on foreign currency)

Suppose a U.S.-based company, Aquatech, that manufactures, sells, and installs water purification equipment. On April 1, the company sold a system to the City of Nagasaki, Japan, for installation in Nagasaki's famous Glover Gardens. The sale was priced in yen at ¥20,000,000, with payment due in three months. The spot exchange rate is ¥105/$; the three-month forward exchange rate is ¥104.8694/$; the three-month yen interest rate is 1.5% p.a.; and the three-month dollar interest rate is 2% p.a..

Remember that because the Aquatech's underlying transaction gives it a yen-denominated account receivable, which is the company's foreign currency asset, the company is exposed to losses if it does nothing to hedge the transaction exposure and the yen depreciates relative to the dollar. In this case, the yen receivable will purchase fewer dollars when the City of Nagasaki pays. Aquatech can take the advantage of using a forward contract to eliminate the potential risk. It can sell the yen forward for dollars. The amount of dollars that will be received in 90 days is (¥20,000,000)/(¥104.8694/$) = $190,713.40.

Now consider the alternative money market hedge. Aquatech must acquire a yen liability that is equivalent in value to its yen asset. The company borrow the present value of its yen asset and use the yen that it receives from selling water purification system to pay off the principal and interest on its yen loan. To be hedged, the company convert the yen principal that is borrowed into dollars at the spot exchange rate. The present value of ¥20,000,000 at 1.5% p.a. is

$$¥20,000,000/(1 + 0.00375) = ¥19,925,280.20$$

By borrowing ¥19,925,280.20 for 3 months at 1.5% p.a., the company owes ¥20,000,000 in 3 months, which is the amount it receives for selling the equipment. The dollar revenue is found by selling the ¥19,925,280.20 for dollars in the spot market at ¥105/$, which is

$$(¥19,925,280.2)/(¥105/$) = $189,764.57$$

We can compare this revenue to the revenue available from the forward hedge in 3 months by taking the future value of the $189,764.57. The company can invest dollars at 2% p.a. Hence, the future value of the dollars received today is

$$189,764.57 \times (1 + 0.005) = \$190,713.39$$

Hence, at these interest rates and exchange rates, the money market hedging strategy is almost equivalent to the forward hedging strategy.

Hedging a foreign currency payable (a short position on foreign currency)

Micca Metals, Inc. is a specialty materials and metals company located in Detroit, Michigan. The company just purchased a shipment of phosphates from Australia for A$1,000,000, payable in 180 days. The current spot exchange rate is A$1.3025; the six-month forward rate is A$1.3057; the six-month Australian dollar interest rate is 2.5% p.a.; and the U.S. dollar interest rate is 2% p.a..

Micca Metals imports Australian raw materials so it has a short position on Australian dollar (Australian dollar-denominated account payable). The company is exposed to losses if it does not hedge the exposure and the Australian dollar appreciates against the dollar. In this case, the U.S. dollar cost of the Australian dollars would be higher when the payment is due. Micca Metals can simply sign a forward contract to eliminate this risk. The company takes a long position on Australian dollar at the forward rate of A$1.3057, the equivalent U.S. dollar will be

$$A\$1,000,0000/(A\$1.3057/\$) = \$765,872.71$$

Let's look at the alternative money market hedging strategy. Because Micca Metals has an Australian dollar liability, it must acquire an equivalent Australian dollar asset. It can do this by buying the present value of its Australian dollar debts at the spot exchange rate and investing these Australian dollars in a money market asset. Micca Metals then use the principal plus interest on this asset to offset its underlying Australian dollar liability at maturity. The present value of A$1,000,000 at 2.5% p.a. is

$$A\$1,000,000/(1 + 0.0125) = A\$987,654.32$$

This amount of Australian dollars must be purchased in the spot exchange market:

$$A\$987,654.32/(A\$1.3025/\$) = \$758,275.87$$

Notice that with money market hedge, the company has to pay today. To compare the money market hedge to the forward market hedge, we must take the present value of the $765,872.71 at 2% p.a.:

$$\$765,872.71/(1 + 0.01) = \$758,289.81$$

At these interest rates and exchange rates, the two strategies are basically equivalent. The dollar present value of the forward market strategy is only $13.94 more expensive.

Forward Parity and Uncovered Interest Rate Parity (UIP)

Sometimes people choose not to hedge (or "cover") the potential risks. When investors borrow in currencies exhibiting relatively low interest rates and convert the proceeds into currencies that offer much higher interest rates, they do not sell the higher yielding currency proceeds forward, choosing to remain uncovered and accept the currency risk of exchanging the higher yield currency into the lower yielding currency at the end of the period. This strategy is called **uncovered interest arbitrage**, or **carry trade**. "Carry" represents the interest rate differential between the high-yield and low-yield currencies. If the exchange rate does not change in value, the investor simply earns the carry.

In the 1990's, the so-called "**Japanese yen carry-trade**" was very popular. The Japanese yen's interest rates were extremely low (approximately 0.40% per annum) at that time. Investors, both inside and outside Japan, borrowed yens and then converted yens into other currencies like the U.S. dollars or Australian dollars. Because those currencies could bring much higher rates of return (5% per annum in the U.S. market). But a lot of investors did not cover their potential currency risks, they just waited until their dollar investment was due. What they did not expect was that Japanese yen appreciated significantly against the U.S. dollar by about 14% in the late 1999. These "uncovered" investors suffered sizable losses when they converted their dollars into yen to repay the yen they borrowed (They earned interest differential by 5% − 0.4% = 4.6%, but lost 14% on the exchange rate differential). The higher return does indeed come at higher risk.

Forward parity

The uncovered interest arbitrage is based on forward parity. The **forward parity** states that the forward exchange rates are unbiased predictors of future spot rates. That is,

$$E[S_t^{d/f}] = F^{d/f} \qquad (5.12)$$

When the forward rate is termed an "**unbiased predictor** of the future spot rate", it means that the forward rate overestimates or underestimates the future spot rate with relatively equal frequency and amount. That is to say, the distribution of possible actual spot rates in the future is centered on the forward rate. In other words, an unbiased predictor implies that the expected forecast error is zero. This hypothesis has two important implications. First, given your current information, you should expect the forecast error to be zero. Second, on average, the forecast errors of an unbiased predictor may sometimes be negative and sometimes positive, but they are not systematically positive or negative, and they will average to zero. Therefore, the unbiased predictor does not mean that the future spot rate will actually be equal to what the forward rate predicts. The forward rate may, in fact, never actually equal the future spot rate.

Speculation will make the forward exchange rate approximately equal to the expected future spot rate. For example, if $E[S_t^{d/f}] > F^{d/f}$, speculators will buy foreign currency forward. This will force up the forward rate, $F^{d/f}$, until it is no longer less than the expected future spot rate. Similarly, if $E[S_t^{d/f}] < F^{d/f}$, speculators will sell forward foreign currency. This pushes the forward rate down until it is no longer more than the expected future spot rate. Only when the Equation 5.12 holds is the forward rate in equilibrium in the sense that speculative pressures are not forcing the forward rate higher or lower.

But empirical studies shows the forward rates are not good predictors of future spot rates over short forecasting period.

Uncovered interest rate parity

Uncovered interest rate parity states that nominal interest rates reflect expected changes in exchange rates, and vice versa. Since interest rates are tied to the forward premiums and the forward premiums are a predictor of change in the spot rate, then

$$(1 + i^d) / (1 + i^f) = E[S_t^{d/f}] / S_0^{d/f} \tag{5.13}$$

$$(i^d - i^f) \approx (E[S_t^{d/f}] - S_0^{d/f}) / S_0^{d/f} \tag{5.14}$$

The uncovered interest rate parity is the hypothesis that the expected return on the uncovered foreign investment equals the known return from investing funds in the domestic money market. If uncovered interest rate parity is true, there is no compensation to the uncovered investor for the uncertainty associated with future spot rate, and expected returns on investments in different money markets are equalized. Equivalently, the speculative return on borrowing one currency and invest it in another market is expected to be zero, given current information.

If a nations' currency value is highly variable, the ability to predict its future value becomes more difficult. If this is the case, individuals will become less confident in their ability to accurately predict the spot rate. This makes the purchase of a foreign financial instrument a much riskier proposition. To induce investors to purchase a risky financial instrument, borrowers may have to offer a higher rate of return on the debt instruments they issue. In other words, the investors may require the risk premium for the more risky financial instruments. This means that in the Equation 5.14 the risk premium should be added to compensate individuals for the additional risk they undertake. That is:

$$(i^d - i^f) \approx (E[S_t^{d/f}] - S_0^{d/f}) / S_0^{d/f} + rp \tag{5.15}$$

where rp is the risk premium.

The risk premium can also reflect risks other than foreign exchange risk. The most common risk of those non-foreign-exchange-risks is the **country risk**, which is the risk due to the political and fiscal environment of the nation itself. A government with a considerable amount of external debt may eventually default on that debt, so holding its bonds is a risky proposition. Investors would risk losing the return on their funds, and perhaps their principal as well. Changes in government leadership may lead to increased taxes on foreign investment or restricted outflows of foreign funds. Hence, risk premium may reflect both foreign exchange risk and country risk.

For example, assume the spot exchange rate of Mexican peso versus dollar is MXP12.00/USD. The interest rate on one-year Mexican government bonds is 8.2% and the interest rate on U.S. treasury bonds with the same maturity is 5%. The international investors may require the risk premium because of the country risk if investing in Mexico. Suppose the required risk premium is 2%, then the expected future spot rate can be calculated by applying Equation 5.15 as follows:

$$E[S_t^{MXP/USD}] \approx \{[(8.2\% - 5\%) - 2\%] \times 12\} + 12 \approx MXP12.144/USD$$

Real Interest Rates and Real Interest Parity

The Fisher Equation

When setting required returns, investors demand a return to compensate them for risk. They also try to anticipate future inflation. The Fisher Equation, named after economist Irving Fisher, relates nominal interest rates (i) to real interest rates (r) and inflation rates (π).

$$(1 + i) = (1 + r)(1 + \pi) \tag{5.16}$$

If investors care about real (or inflation-adjusted) returns, then they will set nominal required returns to compensate them for their real required return and expected inflation. For example, if inflation in a particular country is expected to be 10 percent and investors require a real return of 3 percent on a 1-year government security, then the nominal required return on the government security should be

$$i = (1 + r)(1 + \pi) - 1 = (1.03)(1.10) - 1 = 0.133, \text{ or } 13.3\%$$

Realized real return is determined by the realized nominal return and inflation. If a bond yields 7% in a particular year and realized inflation is 5 percent, then the realized real return is

$$r = [(1 + i)/(1 + \pi)] - 1 = (1.07/1.05) - 1 \approx 0.019, \text{ or } 1.9\%$$

The Fisher Equation can alternatively be written as

$$i = (1 + r)(1 + \pi) - 1 = r + \pi + r\pi \tag{5.17}$$

If real interest rates and inflation rates are low, then the cross-product term $r\pi$ is small and

$$i \approx r + \pi \qquad (5.18)$$

In the example, with r = 0.019, and π = 0.05, the nominal required return i ≈ 0.019 + 0.05 = 6.9%, which is close to the exact answer of 7.0%.

The International Fisher Equation and Real Interest Parity

When Fisher Equation is applied to international environment, it is the international Fisher Equation or Fisher Open. We know interest rate parity includes the ratio $(1 + i^d) / (1 + i^f)$. From the Fisher Equation, each of the nominal interest rate compensates for a required real return r and expected inflation E[π]. The interest rate differential of the two countries is expressed by $(1 + i^d) / (1 + i^f)$. Substituting the Fisher Equation in the numerator and denominator leads to

$$(1 + i^d) / (1 + i^f) = [(1 + r^d)(1 + E[\pi^d])] / [(1 + r^f)(1 + E[\pi^f])] \qquad (5.19)$$

Real interest parity asserts that real required returns on comparable assets are equal across currencies, so that

$$r^d = r^f \qquad (5.20)$$

This is a consequence of the Law of One Price applied to real rates of return in different currencies. If real interest parity holds, then $(1 + r^d)$ and $(1 + r^f)$ in Equation 5.19 cancel and the nominal interest rate differential reflects the expected inflation differential, that is:

$$(1 + i^d) / (1 + i^f) = (1 + E[\pi^d]) / (1 + E[\pi^f]) \qquad (5.21)$$

This relation is the **International Fisher Equation** or **Fisher Open**. It states that interest rate differential reflects the expected inflation rate differential between the two countries. The International Fisher Equation suggests that foreign currencies with relatively high interest rates will depreciate because the high nominal interest rates reflect expected high inflation.

Suppose that investors in Australia expect a 4% rate of inflation over the next year and require a real rate of return 3% over the next year; the nominal interest rate on 1-year government notes would be approximately 7%. If a Japanese investor required the same real rate of return for one year, then the differential in nominal interest rates between Australia and Japan would represent their respective inflation differentials. For example, assume that the nominal interest rate in Japan is 8%. If the Japanese investor requires 3% real return, then the expected inflation rate in Japan over the next year would be 5%. According to the relative PPP theory, the Japanese yen would be expected to depreciate by the expected inflation differential of 1% (Japan's inflation is 1% higher than that in Australia). If the exchange rate changes as expected, Australian investors that attempt to capitalize on the higher Japanese interest rate would earn a return similar to what they could have earned in their own country. This is because when the Australian investors convert the Japanese yen into Australian dollar at the end of the investment, they would get fewer Australian dollars.

International Parity Conditions

Now we complete the circuit of international parity conditions relating exchange rates, real and nominal interest rates, and inflation rates among the different currencies. It may be helpful to compare those related theories of international finance. **Figure 5.12** summarizes the main theme of each theory. Note that all those theories are based on the Law of One Price and all relate to the determination of exchange rates. Yet, they differ in their implications. The interest rate parity and forward parity focus on why the forward rate differs from the spot rate and how much the difference should be at a specific point in time. In contrast, the relative purchasing power parity and international Fisher Equation both focus on how a currency's spot rate will change over time. Whereas PPP theory suggests that the spot rate will change in accordance with the inflation differential between two countries, the international Fisher Equation suggests that it will change in accordance with the nominal interest rate differential (and therefore in accordance with the expected inflation rate differential) between two countries. The Fisher Open relies on the Fisher Equation to determine how the differential in expected inflation rates between two countries can be measured based on the prevailing nominal interest rate differential, and then it applies PPP theory to predict how the exchange rate between the two countries will change based on the differential in expected inflation rates.

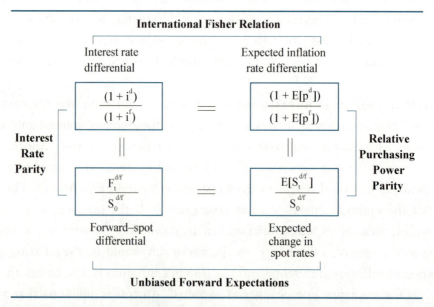

Figure 5.12 International Parity Conditions (Implications of Law of One Price)

Some generalizations about countries can be made by applying these theories. High-inflation countries tend to have high nominal interest rates (due to the Fisher Open). Their currencies tend to weaken over time (because of the PPP theory and the Fisher Open), and the forward rates of their currencies normally have large discounts (due to IRP and forward parity).

Exchange Rate Forecasting

We have already examined various factors that determine exchange rate movements. Even a clear understanding of how factors influence exchange rates does not guarantee that we can forecast how exchange rates will change, because forecasting exchange rates is very complex and tricky, especially in the short run. Foreign trade and investment involve risk. A major issue, as far as business is concerned, however, is whether forecasting exchange rates is feasible and, if so, how to do it. The managers of MNCs often actively manage the firm's currency risk exposures, hedging when exchange rates are expected to be unfavorable to MNC, accepting the exposure when exchange rates are expected to favor the MNC. This is an effective strategy if, and only if, the MNC can successfully forecast exchange rate movements.

There are two schools of thought regarding the exchange rate forecasts. The efficient market school argues that the international parity relations are an elegant set of simple equilibrium relationships between the prices of goods and services, interest rates, and the spot and forward exchange rates. Although they are highly stylized and depend on some demonstrably unrealistic assumptions, they constitute a powerful theoretical framework for understanding and explaining the international financial environment and the underlying forces that determine exchange rates and why they vary. For this reason they form the basis for much of the economic analysis involved in exchange rate forecasting. Understanding and interpreting the relationships among them are an important part of the exercise.

Efficient market hypothesis argues that in an efficient market, currencies are correctly priced based on available information or the prices reflect all available public information. According to efficient market hypothesis, forward exchange rates are the unbiased predictors of future spot rates. This does not mean the predictions will be accurate in any specific situation. It means inaccuracies will not be consistently above or below future spot rates; they will be random. Therefore, it is not possible to consistently "beat the market" and earn excess returns in an efficient market. If efficient market hypothesis holds, exchange rate forecasting can be done on the market conditions.

The other school of thought, the **inefficient market school** believes the foreign exchange market is inefficient. They think the currencies in the foreign exchange market are not correctly priced and the forward exchange rates will not be the best possible predictors of future spot exchange rates. In other words, the international parity conditions are not reliable because of the inefficient market. Therefore, other forecasting techniques are needed to predict the changes in exchange rates. Those techniques or models do not rely directly on the predictions embodied in parity conditions that we have just discussed. They can be split into two main categories: fundamental analysis and technical analysis. Now we briefly describe several popular forecasting methods in turn.

Market-Based Exchange Rate Forecasts

Market-based exchange rate forecasts are the simplest technique for forecasting exchange rate movements. It focuses on the parity conditions we have learned in this chapter. The forward exchange rate usually indicates whether a currency depreciates or appreciates in the near future. Currencies sold at a forward discount do tend to depreciate while those sold at a premium tend to appreciate. The forward parity, interest rate parity and relative purchasing power parity can be used to forecast the long-run exchange rate movements.

The beauty of market-based forecasts is that anyone with access to a financial newspaper can make them, so it is costless to generate forecasts. Unfortunately, these forecasts do not work well in the short term. But in the long run, cross-currency inflation and interest rate differentials begin to impose themselves and forecasts based on the parity conditions begin to dominate the current spot rate as predictors of nominal exchange rates.

Fundamental Analysis

Fundamental analysis considers macroeconomic variables and policies that are likely to affect a currency's value. It constructs sophisticated econometric models for predicting exchange rate movements. Those models are statistical estimations of economic theories. The models attempt to incorporate the fundamental variables that underlie exchange rate movements such as trade and investment flows, industrial activities, inflation rates, income levels, and the like.

Fundamental analysts believe that changes in key economic variables will induce changes in future exchange rates in approximately the same patterns as in the past. The formulation of an econometric model requires specifying independent variables like previous quarterly changes in interest rates or inflation rates that influence the dependent variable (for example, quarterly percentage change in a currency's value). Therefore, publicly available information is crucial for model constructors. Fundamental analysts must also identify the nature of the relationship (for example, linear, exponential) that best explains the dependent variable. The established models determine the direction and degree to which a currency's exchange rate is affected by each independent variable.

However, the link between currency values and fundamental information can be difficult to establish. First, obtaining reliable information such as inflation rates or interest rates is not easy. Second, factors that affect exchange rates cannot always easily be quantified.

Third, the precise timing of a factor's effect on a currency's exchange rate may be unclear. For example, inflation rate changes may not have their full impact on a currency's value until three or six months in the future. Fourth, exchange rates may respond to fundamental variables with a lag, or only in the long run.

Unfortunately, researchers found that the fundamental analysis failed to more accurately forecast exchange rates than the market-based exchange rate forecasts models. The fundamental analysis is best suited for forecasting long-run exchange rate trends. This is because exchange rates in the short run are influenced by many factors that change on a minute-to-minute basis, resulting in considerable short-term volatility.

Technical Analysis

Technical analysts look for specific exchange rate patterns. Technical analysis is similar to technical analysis of stock prices. They believe the past patterns of exchange rate movements are the predictors of the future exchange rates. Once the beginning of a particular pattern has been determined, it automatically implies what the short-run behavior of the exchange rate will be. Clearly, the technical analysis is based on the premise that history repeats itself. However, if the pattern of currency values over time appears random, then technical analysis is not appropriate.

Technical analysis encompasses a variety of charting techniques involving a currency's price, cycles, or volatility. A common starting point for technical analysis is a chart where a trading period's opening, high, low, and closing prices are plotted. Prices are plotted on the charts on a daily basis, and the charts are also created on a weekly, monthly, and yearly basis. Traders watch for new highs and lows, broken trend lines, and patterns that are thought to predict price targets and movements.

Technical analysts construct models to find recurring exchange rate patterns to issue sell or buy instructions if exchange rates deviate from their past pattern. Because technical analysis follows the market closely and because patterns in exchange rate movements may be more predictable over short-run, it is used to forecast the very short-run exchange rate movements. Determining an exchange rate pattern is useful only as long as the market continues to consistently follow that pattern. Because such patterns are likely less reliable for forecasting long-run such as a quarter, 1 month or 1 year, technical analysis are less useful for forecasting exchange rates in the distant future.

Furthermore, a technical analysis model that has worked well in one particular period may not work well in another period. Unless historical trends in exchange rate movements can be identified, examination of past movements will not be useful for indicating future movements.

But technical analysis is often dismissed by the academic literatures. Because exchange rates movement are random. Nevertheless, technical analysis has always been popular among practitioners such as the professional traders. If a trader knows that other traders use technical analysis it can be rational for the trader to use technical analysis too. If enough traders use technical analysis, the predictions based on it can become self-fulfilling to some extent, at least in the short run.

Summary

1. In the short run, the value of a currency depends on supply of and demand for the currency in the foreign exchange market.
2. The demand for foreign exchanges in the foreign exchange market is a derived demand; that is, the foreign currencies are not demanded because they have an intrinsic value in themselves, but rather because of what they can buy.
3. When people in a country, say, Germany wish to purchase foreign goods and services or invest in foreign assets. They must supply Euros to the foreign exchange market.
4. The more foreign currency that can be exchanged for one Euro, the greater will be the supply of Euros. That is, the supply curve for Euros slopes upward.
5. Foreigners who wish to purchase German-made goods and service or invest in German assets will demand Euros in the foreign exchange market.
6. The fewer units of foreign currency needed to buy one Euro, the higher the demand for Euros. That is, the demand curve for Euros slopes downward.
7. Anything that increases the desire of Germen to buy foreign-made goods and services or invest in foreign assets will increase the supply of Euros (shift the supply curve for euros to the right), causing the Euro to depreciate.
8. Anything that increases the desire of foreigners to buy German-made goods and services or invest in German assets will increase the demand for Euros (shift the demand curve for Euros to the right), causing the Euro to appreciate.
9. The Law of One Price holds that in competitive markets that are free of transportation costs and barriers to trade, identical products sold in different countries must sell for the same price when their price is expressed in the same currency.
10. There are two versions of the purchasing power parity (PPP). The absolute PPP theory states that the internal purchasing power of a currency should be equal to its external purchasing power; in other words, the price of a basket of particular goods should be roughly equivalent in each country and thus it is an application of the Law of One Price.
11. The relative PPP theory predicts that the exchange rate will change if relative prices change (because of inflation). The currency with relative high inflation will depreciate while the currency with low inflation will appreciate in the spot market.
12. The PPP theory is most appropriate for forecasting exchange rates in the long run,

in the short run it is a poor forecaster because of the transportation costs and trade barriers, price discrimination and price indices' discrepancy.
13. Interest Rate Parity (IRP) states that on free money markets the forward discount or premium on the foreign exchange market is equal to the relative difference between the interest rates on the two currencies. The empirical evidence shows that there is a strong tendency for interest rate parity to hold and that on the Euro currency markets it is equivalent to a technical fact.
14. If IRP holds then covered interest arbitrage is not feasible, because any interest rate advantage in the foreign country will be offset by the discount on the forward rate. Thus covered interest arbitrage would not generate higher returns than would be generated by a domestic investment. If the forward premiums deviate substantially from the interest rate differential, then covered interest arbitrage is possible.
15. Covered interest arbitrage involves borrowing in one currency, selling the borrowed currency on the spot market, investing the proceeds of the sale, and simultaneously buying back the borrowed currency on the forward market. In this manner, the investor is not exposed to fluctuation in the foreign currency's value.
16. When interest rate parity holds, there are two equivalent way to hedge transaction exchange risk exposure, the forward hedge and the money market hedge.
17. The money market hedge is also called synthetic forward, a strategy that is borrowing or lending the foreign currency coupled with making a transaction in the spot exchange market.
18. Uncovered interest parity is based on the forward parity. Forward parity states that the forward rate will be approximately equal to the expected future spot rate because of the speculation. Uncovered interest parity claims that the nominal interest rates reflect the expected changes in exchange rates and vice versa.
19. The uncovered interest arbitrage, or carry trade refers to an investment strategy. Investors borrow low yield currency and invest the proceeds in high yield currency. "Carry" represents the interest rate differential between the high-yield and low-yield currencies. If the exchange rate does not change in value, the investor simply earns the carry.
20. According to Fisher Equation, each of the nominal interest rate compensates for a required real return and expected inflation. That is: $i \approx r + \pi$, where i the nominal interest rate, r the real interest rate and π the inflation rate.
21. Real interest parity asserts that real required returns on comparable assets are equal across currencies. This is a consequence of the Law of One Price applied to real rates of return in different currencies.
22. If real interest parity holds, then substituting the Fisher Equation in the interest rate parity leads to the international Fisher Equation which states that the nominal interest rate differential reflects the expected inflation differential.

23. According to the efficient market school, prices reflect all available public information. If the foreign exchange market is efficient, forward exchange rates should be unbiased predictors of future spot rates. Therefore, a company cannot beat the market by investing in forecasting services.
24. The international parity conditions form the basis for most market-based exchange rate forecasting.
25. Assuming the inefficient market school is correct that the foreign exchange market's estimate of future spot rate can be improved, on what basis should forecasts be prepared? One adheres to fundamental analysis, while the other uses technical analysis.
26. Fundamental analysis draws on economic theory to construct sophisticated econometric models for predicting exchange rate movements. The variables contained in these models typically include relative money supply growth rates, inflation rates, interest rates and balance of payments statistics.
27. Technical analysis uses price and volume data to determine past trends, which are expected to continue into the future. It is used to forecast the very short-run exchange rate movements. It is less useful for forecasting exchange rates in the distant future.

Key Concepts and Terms

1. Absolute purchasing power parity — 绝对购买力平价
2. Asset market approach — 资产市场分析法
3. Balance of payments approach — 国际收支分析法
4. Big Mac index — 汉堡包价格指数
5. Carry trade — 差额交易，指利用利差或汇差赚取超额利润的投资策略
6. Commodity arbitrager — 商品套利者
7. Country risk — 国家风险
8. Covered interest parity — 抛补套利平价
9. Covered interest arbitrage — 抛补套利
10. Derived demand — 衍生需求
11. Efficient market — 有效市场
12. Efficiency market hypothesis — 有效市场假说
13. Equilibrium exchange rate — 均衡汇率
14. External purchasing power — 外部购买力
15. Fisher Equation — 费雪方程式

16.	Foreign exchange market intervention	外汇市场干预
17.	Forward parity	远期平价
18.	Fundamental analysis	经济基本面分析预测法
19.	Import tariffs	进口关税
20.	Inefficient market school	非有效市场学派
21.	Internal purchasing power	内部购买力
22.	International Fisher Equation (or Fisher Open)	国际费雪方程式
23.	Interest rate parity	利率平价
24.	Law of One Price	一价定律
25.	Market expectations	市场预期
26.	Market fundamentals	市场基本面，即基本经济变量
27.	Money market hedge	货币市场套期保值
28.	Overvalued currency	高估货币
29.	Price discrimination	价格歧视
30.	Price index	价格指数
31.	Price level	价格水平，通常以价格指数表示
32.	Purchasing power	购买力
33.	Purchasing power parity (PPP)	购买力平价
34.	Quotas	配额制，一般指进口配额
35.	Real interest parity	实际利率平价
36.	Real interest rate	实际利率
37.	Relative purchasing power parity	相对购买力平价
38.	Synthetic forward	合成远期
39.	Technical analysis	技术分析法
40.	Uncovered interest arbitrage	不抛补套利
41.	Uncovered interest parity	不抛抵补套利平价，非抛补套利平价
42.	Undervalued currency	低估货币

Questions

1. Why is the demand for foreign exchange called the derived demand?
2. List several factors that would shift foreign exchange demand curve and supply curve.
3. What is the equilibrium exchange rate? Take an example to show why the equilibrium exchange rate changes.
4. Define the internal and external purchasing power of a currency.
5. Explain the relationship between the Law of One Price and PPP. Based on the PPP, what is the general forecast of the values of currencies in highly inflated countries?

6. Explain why you agree or disagree with each of the following statements:
   a. A country's currency will appreciate if its inflation rate is high than that of its trading partners.
   b. A country whose interest rate is much lower than that of other countries can expect the exchange value of its currency to appreciate.
   c. A country's currency will appreciate if it increases tariffs on all foreign goods.
7. If a currency becomes overvalued in the foreign exchange market, what will be the likely impact on the home country's trade balance? What if the home currency becomes undervalued?
8. Why is it not a good idea to speculate on short-run exchange rate movements using the predictions of purchasing power parity?
9. What are some limitations of the purchasing power parity theory?
10. Describe how you would calculate a one-year forward exchange rate of dollar per Euro if you knew the current spot exchange rate and the interest rate of one-year bond denominated in dollar and Euros. Explain why this has to be the market price.
11. Describe a covered interest arbitrage and an uncovered interest arbitrage. Why does the covered transaction make a guaranteed profit and why the "uncovered" does not?
12. Someone suggests you to invest in Mexican bonds with yield of 10%, 5% above your country's bonds with the same risk characteristics. Should you do it? What factors should you consider in making your decision?
13. Are arbitrage activities good or bad to foreign exchange market? Why?
14. Both Japan and Canada adopt floating exchange rate system. You note that the three-month interest rate on a Canadian bond is higher than the three-month interest rate on a comparable Japanese bond of equal risk. Assuming money market arbitrage, what would you expect to happen to the value of the Canadian dollar relative to the Japanese yen over the next three months?
15. Why would investors consider covered interest arbitrage in a foreign country where the interest rate is lower than their home interest rate?
16. What is a money market hedge? How is it constructed?
17. Suppose you are the CFO of an exporting company selling industrial equipment abroad. Describe your foreign exchange risk and how you might hedge it with a money market hedge.
18. What does the International Fisher Equation say about interest rate and inflation differentials?
19. Your friend strongly believes the efficient market hypothesis. If you ask him what will be the yuan-dollar exchange rate next year, which methods would he probably use to predict the exchange rate movements?
20. Which methods do currency forecasters use to predict future changes in exchange rates?

Chapter 6

FINANCIAL DERIVATIVES FOR CURRENCY RISK MANAGEMENT

LEARNING OBJECTIVES

- Compare the forward contracts with the futures contracts.
- Examine the features of the futures market.
- Understand the marking to market procedure for futures contracts.
- Define the call and put option.
- Examine the option payoff profiles.
- Learn how currency options are quoted and used for hedging and speculation purposes.
- Introduce direct financing and parallel loan by MNCs.
- Explore the currency swap, interest rate swap, and other types of swaps on swap markets.

One of the most important developments in international financial markets over the last three decades is the phenomenal growth of trading in financial derivatives. **Financial derivatives** are financial instruments whose values are derived from an underlying asset such as a stock or a currency. The development and growth of financial derivatives market resulted from the price volatility. One of the Chicago futures exchanges, the Chicago Mercantile Exchange (CME), began trading currency futures contracts in 1972 in response to the dramatic increase in currency risk following the 1971 collapse of the Bretton Woods System. Since then, the turnover of financial derivatives for currency risk management has increased at an astonishing growth rate. Financial managers and international investors found ways to use derivatives as hedging strategies to reduce foreign exchange risks. However, many traders believed that they could earn significant short-term profits by speculating with derivatives. At the same time, some traders learned that such derivatives speculations can turn out to be wrong and they suffered sizable losses. So the financial derivatives are a powerful tool in the hands of careful and competent financial managers. They can also be very destructive devices when used recklessly.

The financial managers and international investors must understand some basics about the features and structure of the financial derivatives. We will cover three common foreign currency financial derivatives in this chapter, foreign currency futures, foreign currency options and currency swaps. The first section begins by analyzing the differences and similarities between the forward contract and futures contract. It then discusses the unique features of the futures contracts, how futures contracts are quoted and used as a hedging strategy and a tool for speculation. The second section introduces currency options, we distinguish the call option from the put option, analyze the option payoff profiles and show how to hedge and speculate with option contracts. Finally, we learn the basics of the currency swap, interest rate swap and other types of swap contracts on swap markets.

Currency Futures

Development of Futures Markets

The introduction of futures markets was originally due to the violent fluctuations of commodity prices such as the prices of crops. Futures contracts are relative newcomer compared to spot and forward contracts which have been around as long as recorded history, first appearing in Europe in medieval times. Organized exchanges serviced the rice market at Osaka, Japan, in the early 1700s. This market bore many similarities to present-day futures markets. Rice futures contracts were standardized according to weight and quantity, traded through a futures exchange clearing house, and had a specified contract life. The Chicago Board of Trade (CBOT), the first organized futures exchange was created in 1848 and around 1865 the first "modern" futures contracts were developed. Chicago still remains the world's leading futures center today.

The first currency futures market was opened on June 16, 1972. The Chicago Mercantile Exchange (CME), now known as CME Group, introduced the futures contracts for the pound sterling, the Canadian dollar, the German mark, the Japanese yen, the Mexican peso, the Swiss franc and the Italian lira. Many other currency futures contracts were initiated later. In 1982 London opened the London International Financial Futures Exchange (LIFFE) which in 2001 was merged with the Amsterdam, Paris, and Belgium Exchanges to create Euronext. Since then Euronext has also merged with the Lisbon Stock Exchange and the New York Stock Exchange (NYSE). In 1985, the CME and the Singapore International Monetary Exchange (SIMEX) began offering interchangeable contracts that could be traded on either exchange. This relationship expands the trading hours of these contracts and increases their flexibility as speculative and hedging instruments. In addition to the above exchanges, many other exchanges have been established to trade currency futures.

Forwards VS. Futures

Forward markets for foreign exchange have existed for several decades. With the astonishing growth of derivative markets, we have seen an explosion of growth in forward markets for other instruments. It is now just as easy to enter into forward contracts for a stock index or oil as it was formerly to trade foreign currencies. Forward contracts are also extremely useful in that they facilitate the understanding of futures contracts.

A **currency futures contract** is very similar to a currency forward contract. It is an agreement between two parties to buy or sell a specified amount of two currencies at a given date in the future time at a predetermined price (exchange rate). But a futures contract has its own characteristics. A futures contract is a forward contract that has standardized terms, is traded on an organized exchange, and follows a daily settlement procedure in which the losses of one party to the contract are paid to the other party, etc. Therefore, these two contracts are different in several ways and it is useful to examine these differences.

Trading location and counterparty

The first major difference between currency forward contracts with futures contracts is that forward contracts are bought and sold on over-the-counter market, whereas futures contracts are traded on an organized exchange. The two parties involved in a forward contract always know each other. Participants are banks that deal with each other, as well as other major commercial entities. Access for individuals and smaller firms is quite limited. Since the forward markets have no physical facilities or buildings like the stock exchanges or futures exchanges, forward contracts are traded through direct communications among major financial institutions. In contrast to forward contracts, the trading for futures contracts takes place on the floor of an organized futures exchange. All contracts on a futures exchange are between a member of the exchange and the exchange itself. In other words, the two parties in a futures contract are unknown to one another. Retail clients buy futures contracts from futures brokerage firms, which in the United States must register with the Commodity Futures Trading Commission (CFTC) as a futures commission merchant (FCM). Legally, FCMs serve as the principals for the trades of their retail customers. Consequently, FCMs must meet minimum capital requirements set by the exchanges and fiduciary requirements set by the CFTC. In addition, if an FCM wants to trade with CME Group, it must become a clearing member.

Trading amounts

As mentioned in Chapter 3, forward contracts are big contracts with minimum $1million or equivalent. Forward contracts can be tailored to a client's specific needs which means that the trading amounts are negotiated by two parties. The trading amounts of futures contracts, on the other hand, are standardized. The standardized amounts are relatively small compared to a typical forward contract. For example, the size of a British pound futures on the International Monetary Market (IMM) at the CME Group is worth only £62,500. If larger positions are desired, one merely purchases more contracts. The small contract sizes allow individuals and smaller firms to participate in the futures market. Importantly, the small contract sizes facilitate trade and enhance market liquidity.

Maturities

The two parties involved in a forward contract can negotiate for just about any maturities, and active daily trading occurs in contracts with maturities of 30, 60, 90, 180 and 360 days. CME Group contracts mature on the third Wednesday of March, June, September, and December. Therefore, the maturity date is also standardized. The last trading day for a futures contract is typically two business days before the maturity day of the contract, usually Monday.

Default risk

The major problem with forward contracts is the **default risk,** that is, one party of the forward contract fails to comply with the terms of the contract. As we know, the forward contracts are pure credit instruments to which no parties are bound. Whichever way the price of the spot rate of exchange moves, one party has an incentive to default. For example, if the forward rate is \$1.35/£, and the spot rate is \$1.40/£ when the contract expires, the party who sell the pound has a strong incentive to default. This is simply because he will lose money if he executes the contract. If the amount of the forward contract is £500 million, his instant loss will be \$250,000. Obviously, the party who sells the pound prefers to sell the pound in the spot market. If the future spot rate turns out to be \$1.30/£, the party who buys the forward pound has an incentive to default because he can get cheaper dollar on the spot market. The default risk tends to limit the forward market to only very high-grade financial and commercial institutions.

The futures contracts are guaranteed by the exchange on which they are traded. When a futures contract is purchased or sold, the purchaser or seller must deposit some assets into a margin account. And the clearing house in the exchange use a process called marking to market to ensure any future losses on the contract will be covered, thus relieving the gaining party of a futures contract the risk of default by the losing party and relieving the need to evaluate the creditworthiness of the counterparty. We'll discuss the margin account and marking to market shortly.

Delivery

The process of delivery is different between the forward and futures contracts.

Delivery is always made on forward contracts unless the contract is swapped for some other currency or date of maturity. For most futures contract, especially those that involve physical commodities such as gold, cotton and so on, the physical delivery of the commodity would be a cumbersome process. To avoid getting involved in the actual delivery process most traders will therefore enter into what is known as reversing trade prior to the maturity of the contract. That is, if a trader originally took long (meaning he will purchase the currency), he can take short (meaning he will sell the currency) to offset his position on the exchange before expiration date. For example, if trader A agreed to purchase Euros (take long on euros) at the price of \$1.30/€ one month ago, he finds that the present price of the Euro is \$1.35/€. Trader A may not actually wish to receive euros. Hence, at some date prior to expiry he may take out reversing trade to liquidate his position. He can then sell Euros (take short on euros) to lock in his profits. As far as the exchange concerned trader A will have no net position in the futures market since it has an identical futures contract to both receive and deliver the Euros. If the contract was originally short, or sold, the trader expects the market to decline and, thus, the contract can be bought at a lower price and a profit can be made, the trader then buys an offsetting contract on or before contract expiration date. It is extremely rare when a futures contact is physically delivered, usually an occurrence when the trader forgets to take out a reversing trade before expiration date.

Costs

It costs nothing for any party to enter into a forward contract except the bid and ask exchange rate. Retail customers must pay a commission to their broker to buy or sell a futures contract. The commission covers reversing trade, meaning the customer can make a complete buy/sell or sell/buy transaction with the commission he has paid.

Exhibit 6.1 summarizes what we have discussed about the differences between currency forwards and currency futures contracts.

Exhibit 6.1   Differences between Currency Forward and Futures Contracts

	Forward contracts	Futures contracts
Trading location and counterparty	Over-the-counter market two parties know each other, usually banks, financial institutions and large companies	Organized exchanges two parties are unknown to one another. They just know their counterparty is the clearing member
Trading amounts	Negotiated by two parties, usually \$1 million minimum	Standardized, for example, The British pound futures is worth £62,500

(Continued)

	Forward contracts	Futures contracts
Maturities	Negotiated, any days after the three days when the deal is made	Fixed maturity day set by the exchanges
Default risk	One party has the incentive to default when the future spot rate is unfavorable to him	Futures contracts are guaranteed by the margin account and marking to market
Delivery	Nearly all the forward contracts need physical delivery of the related currencies	Rarely delivered upon; settlement often takes place through purchase of offsetting position
Costs	No charges for entering a forward contract except bid-ask spread	Commission charged for a complete buy/sell or sell/buy transaction

Characteristics of Futures Contracts

Futures contracts have the following three characteristics.

Standardized contracts

First, the futures contracts are standardized contracts in terms of the traded currencies, the amount of each contract and the expiration date of the contract. Not all of the currencies have futures contracts. The traded currencies were originally limited in number. But for now, CME Group offers 53 foreign exchange futures contracts on 40 different currency pairs. This product offering covers all major currencies, including cross rates, and a wide range of emerging currencies such as RMB, the Mexican peso, the Brazilian real, and the Russian ruble. For each currency there is a specified amount of a contract rather than for a tailor-made sum. **Exhibit 6.2** lists 20 currency futures contracts (all currencies against the U.S. dollar) available at the CME.

Exhibit 6.2 Currency Futures Contracts Traded at the CME

Currency	Units per contract
Australian dollar	100,000
Brazilian real	100,000
British pound	62,500
Canadian dollar	100,000
Chinese yuan	1,000,000
Czech koruna	4,000,000
Euro	125,000

(Continued)

Currency	Units per contract
Hungarian forint	30,000,000
Indian rupee	5,000,000
Israeli shekel	1,000,000
Japanese yen	12,500,000
Korean won	125,000,000
Mexican peso	500,000
New Zealand dollar	100,000
Norwegian krone	2,000,000
Polish zloty	500,000
Russian ruble	2,500,000
South African rand	500,000
Swedish krona	2,000,000
Swiss franc	125,000

For some currencies, the CME offers "E-mini" futures contracts, which specify half the number of units of a typical standardized contract. The typical currency futures contract is based on a currency value in terms of U.S. dollars. However, futures contracts are also available on some cross rates, such as the exchange rate between the Euro and Japanese yen, British pound and Australian dollar, etc.

Maturities are based on a quarterly cycle of March, June, September and December, and each contract has a precise delivery date. CME Group[1] contracts expire on the third Wednesday of the contract month. The last trading day is on the second business day immediately preceding the expiration day (usually Monday).

Margin account

Second, futures contracts are traded on an exchange. Only commission houses registered as member firms are allowed to trade on the exchange. Clients who seek access to the market must do so through a commission house by opening an account called margin account. All orders are then executed through the commission house.

The trader must deposit some assets into a **margin account** to fulfil the **initial margin requirement** when he takes a position on a futures contract. The assets in the margin

---

[1] CME Group, www.cmegroup.com.

account act as a **performance bond** because they may be confiscated if the trader loses money in the trade. As futures prices change, one party to the contract experiences profits, and the other party experiences losses. The daily profits and losses are deposited to and subtracted from the margin accounts of the respective parties. In 2020, initial margin on the CME Group were about 3% to 12% depend on the size of the contract and the volatility of the currencies. The initial margin is usually set high enough so that the cost and inconvenience of frequent small payments can be avoided as the futures price is marked to market each day. Small losses are simply deducted from the initial margin until a predetermined minimum, called the **maintenance margin**, is reached. At this point, the commission house issues a **margin call** requesting the client to deposit the funds necessary to bring the margin back to the initial level.

Marking to market

Third, contracts are settled through the exchange's clearing house. The clearing house is the ultimate counterparty of the futures contracts' clients. The clearing house records each traded contract. It manages settlement of day-to-day operations through a process called marking to market, and guarantees delivery at the contract's maturity. This feature of the futures contracts provides a remedy for the default risk inherent in forward contracts.

Marking to market means that profits and losses are paid every day at the end of trading and is equivalent to closing out a contract each day, paying off losses or receiving gains, and writing a new contract. Marking to market is analogous to what happens during a poker game. At the end of each hand, the amount wagered is transferred from the losers to the winner. In financial parlance, the account of each player is making to market. Alternative methods of accounting are too complicated, making it difficult to identify players who should be excused from game because they have run out of money. For similar reasons, the clearing house marks futures accounts to market every day. Doing so ensures that sellers always have the money to make delivery and buys always can pay. As in poker game, if someone's margin account falls below the minimum, the clearing house will sell the contracts, ending the person's participation in the market.

An example will help you understanding how marking to market works. Suppose on Tuesday morning in November a client takes a long position in a Swiss franc futures contract at a price of $1.10/SFr. The amount of a Swiss franc futures contract is for SFR125,000, so the client will pay $137,500 for SFR125,000 when the contract expires. The client is required to deposit $3,300 as initial margin in his margin account. The clearing house sets the maintenance margin at $3,000 which means a margin call will be issued if the money deposited in the margin account is less than $3,000. Just like the spot exchange rates change all the time, the futures price will change accordingly. Now assume at the end of the day the price has risen to $1.12. The clearing house settles the client's account by the closed price of the Swiss franc futures. Since the price now is up, the client is long in the Swiss franc contract, money is put into his margin account. The value of a long position when it is settled can be calculated by the following formula:

$$\text{Value of a long position} = \text{Contract size} \times (\text{Spot} - \text{Futures}) \quad (6.1)$$

The value of the client's position at the end of the day is:

$$\text{SFR}125{,}000 \times (\$1.12/\text{SFR} - \$1.10/\text{SFR}) = \$2{,}500.$$

The client receives $2,500 and is the owner of a new contract the price of which is now $1.12/SFR. His margin account is $5,800 ($3,300 + $2,500) at the end of Monday.

On Wednesday evening, if the price has fallen to $1.09 and therefore the client takes loss. The total loss is the changes in exchange rate times the contract size:

$$\text{SFR}125{,}000 \times (\$1.09/\text{SFR} - \$1.12/\text{SFR}) = \${-}3{,}750$$

He now owns a contract the price of which is $1.09. But the dollar on his margin account falls to $2,050 ($5,800 − $3,750) which is below the maintenance margin. Since the value of his margin account drops, the clearing house will issue a margin call to ask the client to deposit $1,250 more and bring the account's balance back up to the initial $3,300. If the client fails to do so, the contract will be cancelled, and the client loses all the money left in his margin account.

Suppose that on Thursday, the dollar price of the Swiss franc futures contract rises again by $0.05/SFR, to $1.14/SFR. This is new daily settle price of the contract, and it affects the client's margin account again. This time he makes profits of

$$\text{SFR}125{,}000 \times (\$1.14/\text{SFR} - \$1.09/\text{SFR}) = \$6{,}250$$

and his margin account has the balance of $9,550 ($3,300 + $6,250).

This process continues every day, until the maturity date of the contract. On the last trading day of this franc futures contract, two business days remain before delivery. Trading the futures contract stops. Arbitrage guarantees that the futures price at the maturity of the contract will be equal to the spot exchange rate on that day because both the futures price and the spot price are ways of purchasing francs with dollars for delivery in 2 business days. Hence, if on the Monday before the third Wednesday of December, the spot price is $1.13/SFR, the futures price will have risen by

$$\$1.13/\text{SFR} - \$1.10/\text{SFR} = \$0.03/\text{SFR}$$

The client will make a profit of $3,750 ($0.03/SFR × SFR125,000). His payoff on Wednesday will be:

$$\$3{,}300 + \$3{,}300 + \$3{,}750 = \$10{,}350$$

The clients' accounts are making to market at the end of each day and clients are subject to margin calls if their position deteriorates. Therefore, the margin account and daily marking to market efficiently overcome the default risk incorporated in the forward contracts. It makes client defaults a rare occurrence and reinforce the overall financial soundness of the exchange.

Because futures contracts are making to market each day, a futures contract can be viewed as a bundle of consecutive one-day forward contracts. Each day, the previous day's forward contract is replaced by a new one-day forward contract with a delivery price equal to the closing price from the previous day's contract. At the end of each day, the previous forward contract is settled and a new 1-day forward contract is created. The purchaser of a futures contract buys the entire package. For example, a 3-month futures contract contains 90 renewable 1-day forward contracts. The clearing house renews the contract daily until expiration, so long as the maintenance margin is satisfied.

The size and timing of the cash flows from the futures contact depend on the time path of the futures price, but the net gain or loss is the same as the forward contract. This is the reason futures and forwards are near substitutes and share the same risk profiles.

For every futures contract bought, there is a sold, one person's loss is always another person's gain. Buyer and seller are like two people playing poker. How much each player wins or loses depends on how the game is progresses, but the total amount on the table doesn't change. This is so-called **Zero Sum Game**. Maintenance margins and price limits for futures contracts are determined by the exchanges and vary by contract and by exchange.

Futures Quotations

Financial newspapers provide information on many of the currency futures traded on the different exchanges. **Exhibit 6.3** presents several currencies futures quotations from *The Wall Street Journal*. These futures contract are all traded on Chicago Mercantile Exchange. The contract size for Japanese yen is ¥12,500,000, for Canadian dollar CAD100,000, and for British pound £62,500. All contracts are quoted in U.S. dollars per currency.

The quotation itself is straightforward. The first column refers to the month that each particular contract expires. **Open** means the opening price of the Japanese yen, Canadian dollar and British pound futures on the day, i.e., the price at which each currency was first sold when the CME opened in the morning. Depending on overnight events in the world, the opening price may not be identical to the closing price from the previous trading day. The **high**, **low** and **settle** columns indicate the contract's highest, lowest, and closing prices for the day. These figures provide an indication of how volatile the market for each currency was during the day. **Change** indicates the change in the closing price from the previous day's settle. For example, for the Japanese yen futures contract due in March 2021 "−0.0019" under the change column shows that the closing price on January 29 was 0.0019 lower than the settled price of the previous day which was January 28. In other words, the closing price of January 28 was $0.009513/¥. You should be careful about the

Chapter 6 FINANCIAL DERIVATIVES FOR CURRENCY RISK MANAGEMENT

Exhibit 6.3 Futures Quotations for Major Currencies

(February 19, 2021)

	Open	High	Low	Settle	Change	Open Interest
Japanese Yen (CME) – ¥12,500,000; dollars per ¥100						
March	.9464	.9504	.9468	.9481	.0019	186,761
June	.9472	.9512	.9468	.9490	.0018	559
Canadian Dollar (CME) – CAD 100,000; $ per CAD						
March	.7887	.7941	.7865	.7924	.0037	153,646
June	.7886	.7940	.7866	.7923	.0037	4,585
British Pound (CME) – £62,500; $/£						
March	1.3980	1.4039	1.3953	1.4015	.0039	168,325
June	1.3974	1.4041	1.3957	1.4019	.0039	3,595
Swiss Franc (CME) – CHF125,000						
March	1.1165	1.1200	1.1151	1.1158	−.0004	49,223
June	1.1191	1.1227	1.1180	1.1185	−.0005	768
Euro (CME) – €125,000; $/€						
March	1.2098	1.2151	1.2088	1.2122	.0030	664,467
June	1.2124	1.2173	1.2111	1.2145	.0030	6,350

Source: *Wall Street Journal*, February 21, 2021.

yen's quotes, because it is quoted as dollars per ¥100. The **open interest** is the outstanding number of contracts obligated for delivery.

Each contract starts with zero open interest and during the early days of the opening of a futures contract open interest in the contract slowly builds up as the number of new contracts increases. However, eventually open interest in the contract peaks. Thereafter, as the expiry date of the contract nears, the number of traders involved in reversing trades increases so that open interest rapidly declines until the expiry date when open interest falls to zero.

Consider the March futures contract of the Canadian dollar. The opening price of the contract on January 29, 2021 was $0.7887/C$. The price was up to $0.7924/C$ when the exchange closed. The highest price of this March expired contract was $0.7941/C$ and the lowest price was $0.7865/C$ during the day. The clearing house will use $0.7924/C$ settle price to settle clients' margin accounts. There are 153,646 outstanding contracts supposed

183

to be executed when they expire.

The following example explains the reversing trade and indirectly describes why the number of open interest falls as the maturity date nears.

Assume that on January 19 a client sold a Japanese yen futures contract expired in March 2021 when the CME opened. By selling this futures contract, the client was obligated to sell ¥12,500,000 for $118,300 [($0.9464/¥/100) × 12,500,000] on the third Wednesday of March 2021. If the client no longer wanted to maintain such a short position on Japanese yen before the maturity date, he could make a **reversing trade** to close out the contract. That is, he could buy an identical Japanese futures contract so that he neither had to actually deliver nor actually received the Japanese yen. For example, on March 17, one week before the maturity day, the client found that yen futures price dropped to, say, $0.009350/¥, he could buy a yen futures contract due on March 24 at the price of $0.009350/¥. On March 24, the client had two yen futures contract, one was to buy yen and another was to sell yen. For the long position on yen he should pay

$$\$0.009350/¥ \times ¥12,500,000 = \$116,875$$

For the short position on yen he would receive

$$(\$0.009464/¥) \times 12,500,000 = \$118,300$$

The client bought low and sold high and made a profit. The exchange would then credit $1,425 ($118,300 − $116,875) on the client's margin account.

The Pricing of Currency Futures Contracts

Since currency futures are very similar to currency forward contracts, it is not surprising that covered interest parity is crucial to the determination of currency futures prices. Put differently, the interest rate differential between the two currencies determines the futures price. Therefore, the futures price should be equal to the forward price. The reason is simple: if the futures price were not the same as the forward price, then it would be possible to make a risk-free profits by engaging in offsetting forward and futures transactions. If the current forward price of Euro were below the futures contract price, someone could buy Euros at the low price with a forward contract and simultaneously sell Euros in a futures contract. Of course, the two contracts should have the same maturity dates. Exercise of the forward and futures contract when the two contracts mature would yield a profit equal to the difference between the forward and futures price. The arbitrage activities will eventually have the forward and futures prices equal.

Currency Futures Contracts Used for Hedging or Speculation

Currency futures contracts allow the transfer of risk between buyer and seller. This transfer can be accomplished through hedging or speculation. The following example shows how to use a futures contract for hedging risk exposure.

The CFO of Texas Instruments Incorporated in the U.S. is considering ways to hedge a 100 million Danish krone (DKR) obligation due in September. The CFO knows that the Danish krone exchange rate usually follows the euro, and there is a strong chance that the euro appreciates against the dollar in the coming months. Euronext in Frankfurt trades Danish krone/U.S. dollar futures contracts that expire in September and have a contract size of $50,000. The price of the dollar futures contract now is DKR1.25/$. To cover the transaction exposure, the company could sell September dollar futures contracts, taking a short position. By selling September contracts, the Texas Instrument locks in the right to sell dollars at a set price.

Texas Instruments Inc. sells 1,600 September futures contract for 100 million Danish krone at the price of DKR1.25/$ [(100 million/1.25) / (50,000) = 1,600]. The value of a short position is calculated by applying Equation (6.2):

$$\text{Value of a short position} = -\text{Contract size} \times (\text{Spot} - \text{Futures}) \qquad (6.2)$$

So the value of the short position at maturity — at the expiration of the futures contracts in September — is then (assume the spot exchange rate at maturity is DKR1.20/$):

$$-\$50{,}000 \times (1.20 - 1.25) \times 1{,}600 = \$4{,}000{,}000$$

The short position on the dollar makes 4 million dollar profits for the Texas Instruments. The profits earned from the futures contracts compensate for the loss in the future spot market. The seller of a futures contract — the Texas Instrument, in this case — can guarantee the price at which the dollars are sold. The other party to this transaction might be an Danish importer who is planning to purchase U.S. made goods in the future and wishes to insure against possible dollar exchange rate increases. Buying a futures contract fixes the price that the importer will need to pay. In this example, both sides use the futures contract as a hedge. They are both hedgers.

Exporters, importers, international investors, multinational companies are all possible hedgers in the currency futures markets. Anyone who owns an account receivable in foreign currency is the seller of a futures contract, taking short position. They want to stabilize the revenue they receive when they sell. Anyone who owes an account payable in foreign currency wants to buy futures to take long position. They require the foreign currency to make a payment, so they buy the futures contract to reduce risk arising from fluctuations in the exchange rates.

Currency futures contracts can also be used to speculate. Speculators bet on price movements to make a profit. Sellers of futures are betting that prices will fall, while buyers are betting that prices will rise. It should be noticed that futures contracts provide an easy way for speculator to profit from price declines. If a speculator believes Mexican peso will appreciate against the U.S. dollar, he could buy a peso futures contract, taking a long position. If he anticipates the peso will depreciate against the dollar, he could take a short position, selling pesos for dollars. When the future spot exchange rate turns out to favor the speculator's expectation, he gains; otherwise, he suffers speculative loss. Futures contracts are popular tools for speculation because they are cheap. A speculator needs only a relatively small amount investment — the margin — to purchase a futures contract that is worth a great deal. Margin requirements of 10 percent or less are common. In the case of our previous Swiss franc futures contract, CME requires an initial margin of only $3,300 per contract. That is, an investment of only $3,300 gives the speculator the same returns as the purchase of SFR125,000 (which is equivalent to $137,500 according to the futures' price of $1.10/SFR). It is as if the speculator borrowed the remaining $134,200 without having to pay interest.

To see the impact of this kind of leverage on the return to the buyer and seller of a futures contract, recall from the previous example that a rise of $0.03/SFR in the price of the franc futures contract meant that the long position/buyer gained $3,750, while the short position/seller lost $3,750. With a minimum initial margin of $3,300 for one contract, this represents a 113.64% gain to the futures contract buyer and a 113.64% loss to the futures seller. In contrast, if the client purchased the SFR125,000 on the spot market with $137,500, he would have gained $3,750 on an $137,500 investment, which is a return of just 2.73%. Speculation, then, can use futures contracts to obtain very large amounts of leverage at a very low cost.

Drawbacks of Futures Contracts

The major problem of the futures contract is the mismatch in terms of the amount and timing of the exposures. In most cases, the size of the futures contracts cannot exactly match with the position to be hedged. The users of the futures contracts can only partly hedge their exposed positions.

There are only a few maturity dates available for the futures contracts. The infrequent maturity dates make it unlikely that the futures contracts will correspond perfectly with the maturity of the cash flow to be hedged. If a firm expects to receive Canadian dollar payment at the end of November, it has to decide which contract they will purchase: the contract with the maturity date in September or December? Either one leaves the firm of open exposure.

For businesses, futures contracts are often considered inefficient and burdensome because the futures position is making to market on a daily basis over the life of the contract. Although this does not require the business to pay or receive cash on a daily basis, it does result in more frequent margin calls from its financial service providers than the business typically wants.

Currency Option

The option market was first developed in the early 1980s. It is another major feature of the international financial landscape. For the forward or futures contracts, making a profit or taking a loss depends on the future spot exchange rate. In other words, the return of a forward or futures contracts depends on the investor's prediction on the future spot exchange rate. If the trend of exchange rate movements is clear, the forward and futures contracts enable investors to avoid potential loss. What if the change in exchange rates is ambiguous, i.e., there is an equally strong chance for exchange rate moves up and down? In this case, it is less appropriate to hedge by a forward or futures contract. The reason for this is that the advantage of avoiding the loss is offset by the disadvantage of missing out on the gain. An option contract makes it possible to take advantage of potential gains while limiting downside risk. Proper use of options requires a clear understanding of their nature and the elements that determine their price. Currency options are traded primarily over the counter by money center banks, but they are also traded on organized exchanges. Two of the largest exchanges are the NASDAQ OMX PHLX, which was formed in 2008 when the Philadelphia Stock Exchange was purchased by NASDAQ OMX, and the International Securities Exchange, which is a subsidiary of EUREX.

This section will discuss some basics of the option contracts. We'll first define option contracts and introduce some terminologies used in option trading. Second, we categorize the option contracts, including calls and puts, American style and European style options. Third, we learn how to read option quotes and understand the option markets. Fourth, we analyze the option value, that is the intrinsic and time value of an option contract. They are important determinants in option pricing. Fifth, we'll examine the use of options in risk management and the speculation.

Terminologies Used in Option Contracts

A **currency option** is like a forward or futures contract in that it allows two parties to exchange currencies according to a prearranged date, amount, and rate of exchange. In a forward or futures contract, both parties have to fulfil their obligations. Unlike a forward or futures contract, an **option** gives the owner of the contract the right but not the obligation to buy or sell a currency at a predetermined price sometime in the future. The owner of an option contract is usually called the **holder** who buys the contract. The predetermined price is called **strike price** or **exercise price** which is the exchange rate for buying and selling a currency. If an option contract specifies the right to buy €125,000 at \$1.30/€ (strike price), then the holder of the contract can decide either execute or cancel the contract when it expires. In other words, the holder has the choice to buy or not to buy the Euro. For example, if the future spot exchange is above \$1.30/€, the holder will exercise the option; otherwise he will abandon the option. The option holder has to pay the **writer** (who issues the contract) for the right he is given. The price paid by the holder to the writer for an option is known as the **option premium** or **option price**.

Therefore, the fundamental difference between option and forward/futures contracts comes down to choice. The holder of an option has the choice; while the writer of an option has the obligation. Once the option is offered, it is the writer's obligation to fulfill the contract. In the above example, if the future spot rate goes down, say $1.25/€, the holder can abandon the contract because he will get cheap euro on the spot market. If the spot rate at the expiration rises to $1.35/€, the holder can force the writer to deliver the Euro at the price of $1.30/€. In this case, the writer has the obligation to fulfill the contract.

Call Option and Put Option

There are two types of options — calls and puts.

A currency **call option** is the right to buy the underlying currency at a strike price and on a specified date. The **underlying currency** is the currency to be granted by an option contract. The currency to be exchanged for the underlying currency is called **counter currency**. For example, a British pound option implies that the pound is the underlying currency. If it is priced by the U.S. dollar, the dollar is the counter currency. The holder of a call option takes a long position on the underlying currency.

A currency **put option** is the right to sell the underlying currency at a strike price and on a specified date. The holder of a put option takes a short position on the underlying currency.

We can summarize the concept of calls and puts as: The right to buy is called a **call**, while the right to sell is called a **put**. The buyer (**holder**) of an option pays the seller (**writer**), a certain sum, called the **option premium**, for the right to buy or sell at the prescribed price (**strike price**) in the future time.

American VS. European Options

If the holder of an option contract decides to engage in the transaction at the time specified in the option contract, he is said to have "exercised" his option. If the right can be exercised at any time during the life of the option it is called an **American option**. It means the holder can buy or sell the underlying currency any time prior to the contract expires. If an American option is exercised prior to the maturity date, the holder is said to have engaged in early exercise. If the right can be exercised only at the option's expiration date, it is called a **European option**. In this case, the holder can buy or sell the underlying currency only at the maturity of the contract.

Option Quotations

Currency option quotations are available daily in CME Group internet and in other major exchanges internet in large cities. **Exhibit 6.4** shows two typical option quotations on CME Group. The first is a pound sterling option with the contract size of £62,500 and the second is a Japanese yen option with the contract size of ¥12,500,000. Both options traded on CME are American options and can be exercised at any time prior to maturity. Let's examine the pound option and show how to read the quotations. The option premiums are quoted in cents per pound. The first column is the different strike prices. The quotations for the strike prices are unusual, and the user should be aware of current futures prices to ensure a correct interpretation of the units. Most currencies, such as the euro, are quoted in 1/100 cent per unit. So if the euro strike price is 12,030, which corresponds to an exchange rate of $1.2030/€. But the strike prices for the pound are quoted in 1/10 cent per pound, as 1,390 corresponds to an exchange rate of $1.390 per pound. The strike prices for the Japanese yen are in 1/10,000 cent per yen, as 9,709 corresponds to an exchange rate of $0.00970/¥. The column under the "Calls-Settle" and "Puts-Settle" lists the closing prices (option premium) for different contracts respectively. For example, "2.478" refers to 2.478 U.S. cents, which is the premium cost of the pound call option at a strike of $1.380/£ expiring in May, 2021.

Exhibit 6.4 Currency Option Quotations

British Pound (CME)
Contract GBP62,500, quoted in cents per pound

Strike price	Calls–Settle			Puts–Settle		
	March	May	August	March	May	August
1380	2.478	3.312	4.233	0.420	1.245	0.213
1385	2.085	—	—	0.547	—	—
1390	1.731	2.666	3.613	0.683	1.589	2.519
1395	1.411	—	—	0.862	—	—
1400	1.138	2.082	3.051	1.089	2.004	2.957
1405	0.898	—	—	1.349	—	—

Japanese Yen (CME)
Contract JPY12,500,000, quoted in cents per ¥100

Strike price	Calls–Settle			Puts–Settle		
	March	May	August	March	May	August
9259	—	—	0.7	—	—	0.1
9346	—	0.5	—	—	—	0.5
9434	0.4	0.8	0.3	0.9	0.4	—
9524	0.8	0.3	0.8	0.5	—	0.6
9615	—	0.9	0.4	—	0.7	0.3
9709	—	0.6	0.1	—	0.5	—

Source: www.cmegroup.com, January 21, 2021.

To check your understanding of the information provided in Exhibit 6.4, let's consider two examples of the purchase of a pound call option and a yen put option contract.

1. Suppose you purchase a pound call option contract with a strike price of "1380", and an August 2021 maturity was quoted at 4.233 cents per pound. Because the strike price is expressed in cents per pound, we can convert it to dollars per pound, or \$1.38/£ (1,380/1,000), and a similar transformation of the option price gives \$0.04233/£ (4.233/100). For a contract size of £62,500, this option would cost:

$$\$0.04233/£ \times £62,500 = \$2,645.63$$

2. Consider a Japanese yen put option contract with a strike price 9,615, and a maturity in May, which costs 0.7 U.S. cents per 100 yen. The strike price 9,615 represents \$0.009615/¥ (9,615/1,000,000). If we want to express the option price in dollars per yen, we must first divide by 100 to convert from cents per 100 yen to cents per yen, and then we must divide by 100 again to convert from cents per yen to dollars per yen. Hence, the cost of the option goes from 0.7 cents per 100 yen to 0.007 cents per yen, or \$0.00007/¥. Consequently, the buyer of the contract would pay

$$(\$0.00007/¥) \; ¥12,500,000 = \$875$$

to the writer of the contract at the initiation of the deal. Because the contract is an American option, the holder of the contract would have the right, but not the obligation, to sell ¥12,500,000 at the strike price of \$0.009615/¥ in May or before, and the writer would be obligated to purchase the yen at that price at any time before the May maturity.

Markets in Currency Options

The Philadelphia Stock Exchange (PSE) is the first organized exchange to trade the standardized currency options. Exchange-traded options are conducted by floor brokers. A customer calls his broker to place an order to purchase a specific option on a particular currency. The broker owns a specific "seat" on an exchange which allows him to trade various option contracts. A seat on the CME's Index Option Market (IOM) sold for \$400,000.

CME Group and the NASDAQ OMX PHLX both trades standardized option contracts. The contract specify different amount of the underlying foreign currency. For example, in CME Group, the option contract size for major currencies is basically the same as the size of futures contracts. But in NASDAQ OMX PHLX, the contract size is much smaller. For example, 10,000 units of foreign currency for the Australian dollar, the British pound, the Canadian dollar, the Euro, the Swiss franc, and the New Zealand dollar; 100,000 units of foreign currency for the Mexican peso, the Norwegian krone, the South African rand, and the Swedish krona; and 1,000,000 Japanese yen. The expiration months are March, June, September, and December plus 2 nearest future months. The last trading day is the third Friday of the expiring month. The exercise style is European. The settlement of all the contracts is in dollars.

Today, most currency options are traded on the over-the-counter market by banks and banks' clients. That is, transactions are done in a dealer network and are not listed on any centralized exchange. Options traded on organized exchanges are standardized contracts, whereas over-the-counter options are tailored to fit the needs of the customers. Typical OTC options use the European exercise convention. In the OTC market, options are written by commercial and investment banks. If a customer wishes to purchase an OTC option, he will normally call a bank, specify the currencies, maturity, strike price and ask for the premium. The bank will normally take a few minutes to a few hours to price the option and return the call. OTC options are also typically written for much larger amounts than exchange-traded options, and a much broader range of currencies is covered.

The OTC option contracts have several disadvantages. First, there is a considerable amount of counterparty risk that concerns both bank traders and corporate treasures. The holder of the option runs the risk of default on the part of the writer whereas exchange-traded options are guaranteed by the exchange. For this reason, only high-graded financial institutions or large companies tend to be an option writer in the OTC market. Second, the contract could be mispriced because of the relatively small number of buyers and sellers. Third, the secondary market for OTC contracts is severely limited because of the customized contract characteristics. Therefore, they lack the liquidity that is a vital part of exchange-traded options.

Intrinsic Value of the Option

Options differ from all other financial derivatives in that the option holder has the choice of executing the contract or abandoning the contract. The option holder will exercise his right only when exercising is profitable, which means only when the contract has value. **Figure 6.1** plots the dollar value of a purchased Mexican peso call option as a function of the spot rate of exchange between dollars and pesos at expiration. The strike price of this peso call option is $0.0508/Mex$. The time subscripts t on the call option value and on the

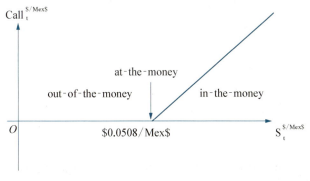

Figure 6.1 The Intrinsic Value of a Call Option

spot exchange rate are reminders that these are values at expiration.

If the future spot rate is above the exercise price $0.0508/Mex$, this Mexican peso call option will be exercised. In this case, the option is said to be **in-the-money**. If a call option is in-the-money, it has intrinsic value. The **intrinsic value** is the gain that would be realized if an option was exercised immediately. So the intrinsic value for a call option is the difference between the future spot rate and strike price as Equation 6.3 and Equation 6.4 indicates:

$$\text{Call option intrinsic value when exercised} = S_t^{d/f} - K^{d/f}, \text{ if } K > S_t^{d/f} \quad (6.3)$$

$$\text{Call option intrinsic value when exercised } 0, \text{ if } S_t^{d/f} \leq K \quad (6.4)$$

$S_t^{d/f}$ is the spot exchange rate at time t, $K^{d/f}$ is the strike price. In our example, suppose the future spot rate turns out to be $0.0520/Mex$, the intrinsic value of this Mexican peso call option is:

$$\$0.0520/\text{Mex}\$ - \$0.0508/\text{Mex}\$ = \$0.0012/\text{Mex}\$$$

A call option for which the spot exchange rate is below the strike price is called **out-of-the-money**. In that case, the option has no intrinsic value, or the intrinsic value is zero. For example, if the spot rate is $0.0500/Mex$ or $0.0490/Mex$ which is less than the strike price, the option has no intrinsic value. The intrinsic value under those exchange rates is ZERO!

If the future spot rate equals the strike price, the call option is **at-the-money** with no intrinsic value.

Figure 6.2 graphs the dollar value of a Mexican peso put option at expiration. Currency put options are options to sell the underlying currency (in this case, the Mexican peso), so these options are in-the-money when the strike price is higher than the future spot exchange rate. The intrinsic value of a put option is calculated as:

$$\text{Put option intrinsic value when exercised} = K^{d/f} - S_t^{d/f}, \text{ if } S < K \quad (6.5)$$

$$\text{Put option intrinsic value when exercised} = 0, \text{ if } S_t^{d/f} \geq K \quad (6.6)$$

If the spot rate at time t is $0.0500/Mex$, the intrinsic value of this peso put option is:

$$\$0.0508/\text{Mex}\$ - \$0.0500/\text{Mex}\$ = \$0.0008/\text{Mex}\$$$

A put option for which the spot exchange rate is above the strike price is called **out-of-the-money**. In that case, the option has no intrinsic value, or the intrinsic value is zero no matter what future spot exchange rate is as long as it is above the strike price.

If the future spot rate equals the strike price, the put option is **at-the-money** with no intrinsic value.

An important point should be made here. Because the options can either be exercised or expire worthless, we can conclude that the intrinsic value depends only on what the holder

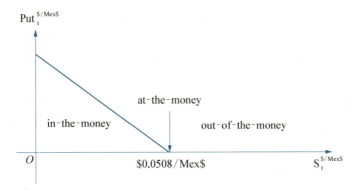

Figure 6.2 The Intrinsic Value of a Put Option

receives if the option is exercised. This means that someone holding an option will never make any additional payment to exercise it, so the intrinsic value must be greater than or equal to zero — the intrinsic value cannot be negative.

Time Value of the Option

An option premium is made up of two parts. The first is the intrinsic value which is the gain that would be realized if an option was exercised immediately. The second, the fee paid for the potential benefit from buying the option, we will call the time value of the option to emphasize its relationship to the time of the option's expiration. So the **time value** of an option is the option premium less the intrinsic value. The time value reflects the fact that an option may have more ultimate value than its intrinsic value.

$$\text{Time value of an option} = \text{Option premium} - \text{Intrinsic value} \qquad (6.7)$$

Now let's take an example to explain the time value of an option. Consider an at-the-money European call option on Euro with the strike price of \$1.2050/€ that expires in three months. Remember the European option can be exercised only at the expiration and that an at-the-money option is one for which the spot exchange rate equals the strike price. In this case, both equal \$1.2050/€. Since the intrinsic value of this call option is zero, all value resides entirely in the option's time value. Assume that, over the next 3 months, the price of the Euro will either rise or fall by \$0.05 with equal probability. That is, there is a probability of 1/2 the price will go up to \$1.2100/€, and there is a probability of 1/2 it will fall to \$1.2000/€. What is the value of this call option?

You should keep in mind that the call option is worth something only if the price goes up. If the price falls to \$1.2000/€, you will allow the option to expire without exercising it. For a call option, then, we need to concern ourselves with the upside, and the expected value of that payoff is the probability, 1/2, times the payoff, \$0.05, which is \$0.025. This is the time value of the option.

Now think about what happens if, instead of rising or falling by \$0.05, the Euro price will rise or fall by $0.10. This change increases the standard deviation of the Euro price. In the terminology used in options trading, the Euro price **volatility** has increased. The **volatility** here means the expected average change, up or down, in the price or yield of the underlying currency. Doing the same calculation, we see that the expected payoff is now $0.05. As the volatility of the Euro price rises, the option's time value rises with it.

At expiration, the value of an option equals its intrinsic value. An option holder, even if the option is out-of-the-money, will still have chance that at some time prior to expiry changes in the spot exchange rate will move the option into the money or further increase the value of the option if it is already in-the-money. This potential benefit is represented by the option's time value. The longer the time to expiry, the bigger the likely payoff when the option does expire and, thus, the more valuable it is.

The likelihood that an option will pay off depends on the volatility, or standard deviation, of the price of the underlying currency. Why? Think about an option on a currency whose price is simply fixed — that is, whose standard deviation is zero. This option will never pay off, so no one would be willing to pay for it. Add some variability to the price, however, and there is a chance that the price will rise, moving the option into the money. That is something people will pay for. Thus, the option's time value increases with the volatility of the price of the underlying currency. For example, after Denmark initially rejected *the Maastricht Treaty* and European exchange rate mechanism was nearly abandoned in 1992, the currency markets became extremely volatile. As a result, currency options trading volume was extremely heavy. Taking this analysis one step further, we know that regardless of how far the price of the underlying currency falls, the holder of a call option cannot lose more. In contrast, whenever the price rises higher, the call option increases in value. Increased volatility has no cost to the option holder, only benefits.

Hedging Transaction Risks with Option Contracts

Now we turn to the use of options in managing transaction exchange risk. Firms with long or short foreign exchange positions can use currency options to minimize their transaction risk exposure. Like we discussed before, option contracts differ from forward and futures contracts. As future spot exchange rate moves away from the strike price, option values follow a one-way path. Currency call option holders gain when the future spot rate rises above the strike price, but cannot lose more than the option premium as the spot rate falls below the strike price. Put option holder gain as the future spot rate falls below the strike price, but lose, at most, the option premium as the spot rate rises. It is this asymmetry that gives options their unique role as a disaster hedge. We first examine an call option used as a hedging strategy.

A call option payoff profile

Suppose today is February 22, a large U.S. importing company has signed a contract with a Japanese exporter for purchasing ¥200 million of sporting goods. Payments are expected to be made on June 20 which coincides with June expiration date for foreign currency options on CME Group. Even though the financial manager of the firm fears that the Japanese yen appreciates against the dollar in the following months, he is not too sure that this will actually happen. He has several strategies which can be used to cover the potential exchange risk.

The following information is available to the financial manager:

Spot exchange rate: $S^{\$/¥} = 0.009410$

Forward exchange rate: $F_{4m}^{\$/¥} = 0.009664$

Futures price on Japanese yen (Maturity date: June 20): = $0.009664/¥

June yen option quotes in ¢/¥100:

Strike	Call	Put
9434	2.3	0.9
9524	1.8	1.6
9615	1.4	2.3

One of the strategies that the financial manager can use to eliminate this exposure is to sell dollars and buy Japanese yen at the forward exchange rate with an expiration date on June 20. The company will pay $1,932,800 for ¥ 200 million on that day. The futures contract has the same result as the forward contract. The disadvantage of the forward contract or the futures contracts is that the firm cannot benefit from the possible appreciation of the dollar.

Now the manager is considering how it might hedge this transaction using foreign currency options. The first thing to determine is which type of option provides a hedge. Because he has an account payable in Japanese yen, the transaction risk is that the dollar depreciates against the Japanese yen. If he does not hedge, it will have loss when he purchases the ¥200 million on the spot market in June. The appropriate option hedge gives the manager the right, but not the obligations, to buy yens in 120 days at a strike price determined by the option contract. Therefore, the financial manager must purchase a yen call option.

Let's work with a strike price of $0.009434/¥, which costs ¢0.023/¥. The company is going to purchase ¥200 million. The size of the yen option on CME is ¥12,500,000, so the company needs 16 (¥200 million/¥12,500,000) yen option contracts to fully cover its transaction exposure. And the option premium the company must pay now is:

$$12{,}500{,}000 \times 16 \times (¢0.023/¥)/100 = \$46{,}000$$

Figure 6.3 displays the profit or loss at the expiration of the Japanese yen call option as a function of the possible future spot exchange rate. The profit or loss of these contracts depends on the future spot exchange rate. If the spot exchange at the expiration is the same as or below the strike price ($0.009434/¥), the manager can let the calls expire without exercising them, thus losing on the premium of $46,000. If the future spot rate is above the strike price, the company will exercise the option. The amount of the dollars he will deliver to the CME is the cost of exercising the option.

$$\text{Cost of exercise} = (¥12,500,000) \times 16 \times (\$0.009434/¥) = \$1,886,800$$

If the spot yen reaches $0.009664/¥ on the expiration date, the yens would cost financial manager $1,932,800 on the spot market ($0.009664/¥ × ¥200 million). So he can exercise the options and pay $1,886,800, for a savings of $46,000. That amount just covers the option premium he paid. He then breaks even in this option contract! The price of $0.009664/¥ is the break-even exchange rate for this particular contract. The break-even exchange rate for a call option is the sum of the option strike price and option premium. That is:

$$\text{Call break-even exchange rate} = \text{Strike price (K)} + \text{Premium Cost} \tag{6.8}$$

If the spot exchange rate on the expiration day is up to, say, $0.0097/¥, those contracts will bring the net profit of $7,200, which is shown by point A in Figure 6.3. If the future

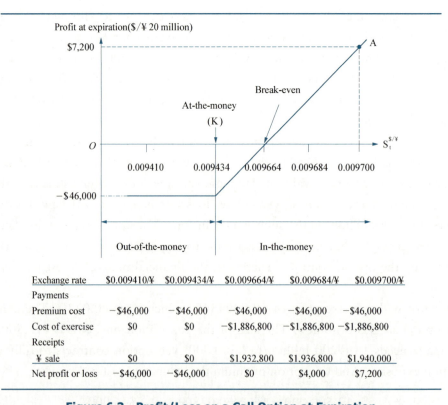

Figure 6.3　Profit/Loss on a Call Option at Expiration

Chapter 6 FINANCIAL DERIVATIVES FOR CURRENCY RISK MANAGEMENT

spot exchange rate is between the strike price and the break-even exchange rate, the option holder is partially compensated. We can see from the graph that the premium is partially offset. It should be noted that the financial manager should analyze the opportunity cost of investing the call premium of $46,000 at the risk-free Treasury Bill rate and deduct income on such an investment from $46,000 to determine his net savings.

A put option payoff profile

Our next example shows how to use a put option to hedge transaction risk. Suppose an American mutual fund is considering a withdrawal of its £5 million investment from the U.K. capital market. The maturity date of those securities is in December. The treasurer of the mutual fund is planning to use option contract to cover the potential risk.

To hedge this transaction using currency options, he must choose the type of option that provides a hedge. Because the mutual fund is going to receive £5 million, the transaction risk is that pound weakens relative to the dollar which decreases the dollar payoffs. To hedge, the treasurer should buy the option that gives him the right, but not the obligation, to sell pounds in December — a pound put option.

Figure 6.4 shows profit or loss at the expiration of a currency put option as a function of

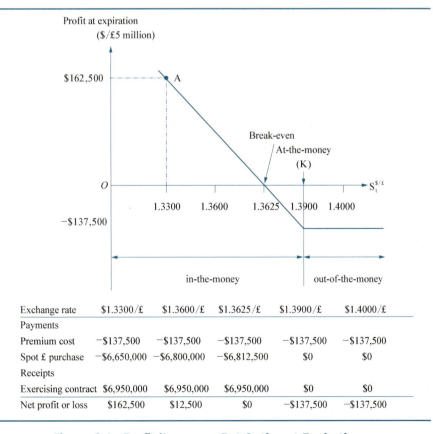

Figure 6.4 Profit/Loss on a Put Option at Expiration

the future spot exchange rate. Consider a NASDAQ OMX PHLX "British pound Dec 1390 put" selling at ¢2.75/£. Options traded on NASDAQ OMX PHLX are European options which can be exercised only at maturity.

The terms and conditions of this quote are as follows:

$K^{\$/£}$ = 1.390 (strike price)

Contract size = £100,000

Current put option price = ¢2.75/£ (premium)

Expiration date: third Friday in December

The treasurer should purchase 50 (£5m/100,000) pound put option contracts. The premium he will pay for 50 pound put option contracts is:

$$\text{Premium cost} = (£100,000) \times (50) \times (\$0.0275/£) = \$137,500$$

The contract is out-of-the-money if the future spot rate is equal to or greater than $1.39/£. The mutual fund loses whole amount of the premium of $137,500. If the spot exchange rate is lower than the break-even rate of $1.3625/£ ($1.39/£ − $0.0275/£), the transaction will generate a net profit. The break-even exchange rate for a put option is calculated by:

$$\text{Put break-even exchange rate} = \text{Premium Cost} - \text{Strike price (K)} \qquad (6.9)$$

If the spot exchange rate is $1.33/£, the treasurer exercises the put options and receives $6,950,000. The net profit from the transaction is $162,500 ($6,950,000 − $6,650,000 − $137,500) which is shown in Figure 6.4 by point A.

In contrast to forward and futures contracts, option payoffs are asymmetric. The previous example of call options shows that if the value of the dollar rises, the firm with a yen call option let the contract expire. The company captures the full benefit of the higher value of the dollar without any further gain or loss from the call option contracts. If the dollar depreciates against the yen, the firm is compensated by the contract. On the other hand, the example of put option indicates that if the value of pound goes up, the holder of the put option abandons the contracts and captures the benefits of the pound appreciation. If the value of pound goes down, the put option holder is compensated by the contracts. Because of the characteristic shape of an option's payoff profile, currency options are used as a form of insurance or "disaster hedge" against unfavorable changes in the value of a currency. When used to hedge currency risk, currency options allow the option holder to participate in gains on one side of the strike price while limiting losses on the other side.

Speculating with Option Contracts

Options can be used for speculation as well. Say that you believe that Euro exchange rate is going to rise over the next few months. There are three ways to bet on this possibility.

The first is to purchase some Euros outright, hoping that the value of these euros will be up. This is expensive, because you will need to come up with the resources to purchase the Euros. A second strategy is to buy a futures/forward contract, taking the long position. If the Euro exchange rate goes up, you will make a profit. As we saw in the previous section, this is an attractive approach, since it requires only a small investment. But it is also very risky, because the investment is highly leveraged. Both the Euro purchase and the futures/forward contract carry the risk that you will take a loss, and if the Euros depreciate substantially, your loss will be large.

The third strategy for betting that euros will appreciate is to buy a call option. If you are right and Euros do appreciate, the value of the call option will rise. But if you are wrong and Euros depreciate, the call will expire worthless and your losses will be limited to the option premium you paid for it.

In the same way that purchasing a call option allows you to bet that the price of the Euro will rise, purchasing a put option allows you to bet that the price of the Euro will fall. Again, if you are wrong, all the lost is the price paid for the option. In the meantime, the option provides a cheap way to bet on the movement in the price of underlying currency. The bet is highly leverage, because a small initial investment creates the opportunity for a large gain. But unlike a futures contract, a put option has a limited potential loss.

But keep in mind that the writer of the options can take a large loss. Some writers are pure speculators, because they are willing to take the risk for an option premium and bet that prices will not move against them. Another group of people who are willing to write options are insured against any losses that may arise. They are primarily dealers (or market makers) who engage in the regular purchase and sale of the underlying currency. Because they are in the business of buying and selling, market makers both own the underlying currency so that they can deliver it and are willing to buy the underlying currency so that they have it ready to sell to someone else. If you own the underlying currency, writing a call option that obligates you to sell it at a fixed price is not that risky. These people write options to obtain the premium paid by the buyer.

Currency Swaps and Interest Rate Swaps

Like other derivatives, swaps are contracts that allow traders to transfer risks. A **currency swap** involves the exchange of principal and interest in one currency for the same in another currency. It is considered to be a foreign exchange transaction and is not required by law to be shown on a company's balance sheet. A forward contract is a simple form of a swap. Whereas a forward contract leads to the change of only principal at a future date, swaps typically involve exchanges of both principal and interests during the life of the contract.

Background of the Currency Swaps

When the MNCs finance their businesses for their foreign subsidiaries, they can borrow from the mother country and exchange for the currencies they need. They face the currency risk however. One of the alternatives that they can use to cover the risk is to raise debt directly in the foreign market, but the MNCs have disadvantage compared to the local companies. For example, if a German subsidiary of a U.S. multinational company needs to issue a Euro-denominated bond since it could make payments with Euro inflows to be generated from existing operations. However, this firm is not well known to investors that would purchase these bonds. Even though they do consider buying these bonds, they may require high return. On the other hand, the local companies have established reputations and their information costs are relatively low. It is often the case that the local companies' borrowing costs are lower than that of the foreign companies in the domestic financial markets.

During the 1970s, the United Kingdom implemented foreign exchange controls. All cross-border currency transactions involving pounds were taxed. This made it expensive for both U.K.-based MNCs and foreign-based MNCs to transfer funds to or from their foreign subsidiaries. In the pursuit of a new funding method that could get around the foreign exchange taxes, the so called parallel loan (or back-to-back loan) was created.

A **parallel loan** is a funding method by which two borrowers can exchange the type of funds each one can most easily raise for the type of funds each really wants. For example, Volkswagen (VW) can easily raise Euro funds in German financial market, but it needs pound sterling to finance its operation in U.K.; a British firm, British Petroleum (BP), may have exactly the opposite problem. **Figure 6.5** presents a possible parallel loan arrangement.

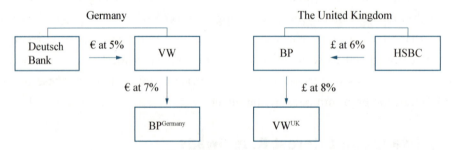

Figure 6.5 A Parallel Loan between VW and BP

VW borrows Euros from Deutsch Bank at the interest rate of 5% and then lends the Euro to German subsidiary of BP at 7% annual interest rate. Similarly, BP raises sterling funds from HSBC at the interest rate of 6% and then lends pounds to VW in U.K at 8%. Both VW and BP earn 2% of the face amount in annual interest.

The advantages of the parallel loan are: First, it successfully gets around the U.K. foreign exchange tax, because neither VW nor BP needs cross-border foreign exchange transactions. The euros raised by VW can be sent directly to BP within the Germany, just as pounds raised by BP can be sent directly to VW within the United Kingdom. Second, both companies save the cost of currency transactions and more importantly, reduce exposure to currency risk. Third, both companies enjoy relative low borrowing costs through the parallel loan. The benefits of parallel loan are especially valuable for MNCs with exposures in multiple currencies.

The parallel loan has several disadvantages. First is the default risk. If one party defaults, the other party does not release from its obligation to the banks. Second, both companies' outstanding liabilities are increased. The increased outstanding liabilities impair the ability of the parent firm to raise additional debts. Third, the parallel loan is time-consuming and expensive to establish. it is very difficult to find a partner (counterparty) for the currency, amount, and timing desired. When parallel loans were first introduced, MNCs usually asked for help from the investment banks. Investment banks acted as brokers rather than dealers. The absence of dealers able to make a market in parallel loans resulted in high search costs and slow growth.

Currency Swaps

A swap contract can correct the problems of the parallel loan. It releases each party from its obligation should the other party default on its obligation. Most countries treat swaps as off-balance-sheet transactions, which means the loan under a swap contract is not capitalized on the balance sheet. Thus, the swaps do not create the appearance of high levels of debt on the firm's consolidated balance sheet. The first currency swap was arranged by two U.S. banks — Continental Illinois and Goldman Sachs in 1976. A Dutch MNC Bos Kallis and a British MNC ICI Finance were the two parties in this agreement. Since then, the swap market has grown by leaps and bounds. One of the main reasons for the phenomenal growth of the swap market has been that they enable participants to raise funds more cheaply than would otherwise be the case.

The swap markets are facilitated by over-the-counter trading rather than trading on organized exchanges. Swap contracts are less standardized than other financial derivatives such as futures or options. Thus, a telecommunications network is more appropriate than an exchange to work out specific provisions of swaps.

The most common form of currency swap is the currency coupon swap which is a fixed-for-floating rate nonamortizing currency swap, traded primarily through international commercial banks. A **nonamortizing loan** means the entire principal is repaid at maturity and only interest is paid during the life of the loan. Currency swaps also come with **amortizing loans** in which periodic payments spread the principal repayment throughout the life of the loans. Currency swaps can be structured as fixed-for-fixed, fixed-for-floating, or floating-for-floating swaps of either the nonamortizing or amortizing variety.

Commercial banks are very active in the swap markets. They are the market dealers

Exhibit 6.5 JP Morgan-Chase Currency Coupon Swaps Quotes

Currency Coupon Swaps (£/$)		
Maturity	Bid (in £)	Ask (in £)
1 year	0.91%	0.94%
2 years	1.36%	1.40%
3 years	1.65%	1.69%
4 years	1.96%	2.01%
5 years	2.26%	2.31%

Note: Semi-annual interest payments.
All quotes against 6-month dollar LIBOR flat.

and quote the swap prices on a daily basis. **Exhibit 6.5** is a typical swap quotation by JP Morgan-Chase Bank. The quote is for a nonamortizing fixed-for-floating currency coupon swap between British pound (£) and U.S. dollar with semiannual interest payments on maturities of one to five years.

For example, a U.K. subsidiary of U.S. based multinational company needs a two-year 1 million pound sterling loan with fixed interest payment. The company can reach a swap agreement with JP Morgan-Chase. It receives £1 million from the bank and pays interest at 0.70% (1.40%/2) every six months. According to the swap agreement, the company gives the equivalent U.S. dollar of the £1 million to the bank and receives the interest at the 6-month dollar LIBOR rate. The two parties swap the related currencies at the end of the contract. LIBOR is the acronym for London Inter Bank Offered Rate. This is the rate at which banks lend to each other. LIBOR is used as a benchmark for variable-rates loans within the U.K. and internationally.

The swap bank makes profit by the bid-ask spread. The above quotes show the spread is 3 to 5 basis points.

An example of a currency swap

Assume AT&T has $100 million of 3-year debt at a floating rate of 6-month ($) LIBOR flat. The U.K. subsidiary of AT&T needs fixed-rate British pound for daily operations. The firm reaches a swap agreement with JP Morgan-Chase. According to the swap contract, JP Morgan Chase agrees to pay AT&T's floating-rate dollar debt in exchange for a fixed-rate sterling payment from AT&T. Suppose the spot exchange rate is $S^{\$/£} = 1.40$. At this spot rate, $100 million is approximately equal in value to £71.43 million.

JP Morgan Chase receives fixed-rate pound interest payments at a rate of 1.69% p.a. on the principal amount of £71.43 million. JP Morgan Chase pays the floating 6-month LIBOR Euro-dollar rate. **Figure 6.6** shows the cash flow of this transaction.

Chapter 6 FINANCIAL DERIVATIVES FOR CURRENCY RISK MANAGEMENT

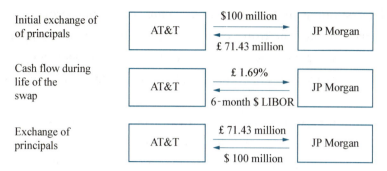

Figure 6.6 A Currency Swap between AT&T and JPMorgan-Chase

JP Morgan Chase gives AT&T the £71.43 million it requires while the AT&T gives JP Morgan Chase the $100 million as the initial exchange of principal. Next is the periodic exchange of interest payments by the two parties, AT&T pays JP Morgan-Chase 0.845% (1.69%/2) sterling interest every six months, while JP Morgan-Chase pays Eurodollar LIBOR to AT&T at the same time. Finally after three years two parties have the final exchange of principal. AT&T pays JP Morgan-Chase £71.43 million back while JP Morgan-Chase will pay AT&T $100 million back.

In effect the currency swap has enabled the AT&T to raise the £71.43 million it required at 1.69% p.a. fixed rate, thus saving it over what it would cost to raise the funds itself in the United Kingdom. The swap contracts have also enabled MNCs who face currency risk to hedge their long-term foreign exchange exposures. Prior to the development of swap markets most firms used the forward contracts to hedge the foreign exchange risk. However, most forward contracts are for less than one year. In order to hedge a 3-year position a firm would have to take out an annual forward contract for each of the next three years.

Interest Rate Swaps

An **interest rate swap** is a variant of the currency swap in which two parties make a series of interest payments to each other, with both payments in the same currency. One payment is variable, and the other payment can be variable or fixed. In an interest rate swap, the principal is called notional principal because it is in the same currency and needn't be exchanged. **Notional principal** is used only to calculate interest payments. Only the difference check between the interest payments is exchanged when interest payments are due.

At first, interest rate swaps were arranged by the counterparties themselves. However, in the 1980s, international banks entered the swaps market as intermediaries. The intermediary bank or swap dealer arranges the swap and transfers the interest rate payments. A counterparty may not know who is the other counterparty. The intermediary bank actually incurs some of the financial risk of the swap. In addition, banks themselves may enter an interest rate swap for asset/liability management purposes.

The swap serves to alter the firm's cash flow obligations, as in changing floating-rate payments into fixed-rate payments associated with an existing debt obligation. The swap itself is not a source of capital, but rather an alteration of the cash flows associated with payment.

The most common type of interest rate swap, indeed the most common type of all swaps, is a swap in which one party pays a fixed rate and the other pays a floating rate interest pegged to an interest rate index, such as 6-month LIBOR. Commercial banks will tailor the terms of interest rate to customers' needs. They also make a market in interest rate swaps and provide current market quotations. For example, Citigroup might quote prices on a U.S. dollar coupon swap as shown in **Exhibit 6.6**. The quotes are for nonamortizing debt and fixed-for-floating dollar rates. The floating rate is pegged to 6-month dollar LIBOR. Interests are settled every six months. The Citigroup quotes a fixed-rate bid-ask spread semiannual in basis points (bps) above U.S. Treasuries versus six-month dollar LIBOR flat. For instance, the quote for a 3-year swap with semiannual payments is 3-year T + 15 bps bid and 3-year T + 37 bps ask. 3-year Treasury notes are currently yielding 2.85%, the interest rate swap bid-ask spread quotation is:

$$0.0285 + 0.0015 = 3\% \text{ bid}$$
$$0.0285 + 0.0037 = 3.22\% \text{ ask}$$

This means the Citigroup will pay semiannual fixed rate dollar payments of 3% against receiving 6-month dollar LIBOR flat, or it will receive semiannual fixed-rate dollar payments at 3.22% against paying 6-month dollar LIBOR flat.

Exhibit 6.6 Citigroup Interest Rate Swaps Quotes

Coupon Swaps ($s)			
Maturity	Fixed Rate (bid)	Fixed Rate (ask)	Current TN Rate
2 years	2 yr TN + 10bps	2 yr TN + 25bps	2.05%
3 years	3 yr TN + 15bps	3 yr TN + 37bps	2.85%
4 years	4 yr TN + 20bps	4 yr TN + 43bps	3.45%
5 years	5 yr TN + 30bps	5 yr TN + 55bps	4.05%

Note: This schedule assumes nonamortizing debt and semiannual rates.
  The bank pays or receives fixed rates.
  All quotes are against 6-month dollar LIBOR flat.
  TN = U.S. Treasury note rate.

An example of an interest rate swap

Consider Exxon-Mobil that enters into a 5-year $50 million interest rate swap with Citigroup. The initiation date is June 15. Exxon-Mobil will pay Citigroup fixed payments a rate of 4.05% plus 55 basis points on December 15 and June 15 during the next 5 years. So Citigroup will have a cash inflow on December 15, the first payment date, of

$$(\$50,000,000) \times [(0.0405 + 0.0055)/2] = \$1,150,000$$

The swap calls for Citigroup to make payments to Exxon-Mobil based on 180-day LIBOR on the 15th of December and June for the next 5 years. The payment is determined by LIBOR at the beginning of the settlement period. Payment is then made at the end of the settlement period. Thus, the payment on December 15 is based on LIBOR on the previous June 15. Suppose the dollar LIBOR on June 15 is 4.4%, then on December 15, the first payment date, Citigroup will pay Exxon-Mobil:

$$(\$50,000,000) \times (0.044/2) = \$1,100,000$$

The two parties agree to net the payments in order to reduce the flow of money, which reduces the default risk. Therefore, only the difference of $50,000 is paid by Exxon-Mobil to Citigroup on December 15. So if LIBOR exceeds the fixed rate, Citigroup will be obligated to make a payment to Exxon-Mobil.

The swaps market has been experienced phenomenal growth since their introduction in the early 1980s. Interest rate and particularly currency swaps can become quite valuable. The reasons for so many parties enter into swaps are first, that borrowers and investors may desire to structure their cash flows and take on credit risks in a manner that is not conveniently arranged with existing financial instruments. Second, companies use swaps to manage their long-term exposure to currency and interest rate risks. Third, interest rate swaps are also used by banks as a form of asset/liability management and they enable the expansion of securities markets into minor currency areas of trading. Fourth, swaps have become an attractive source of off-balance sheet earnings for commercial and investment banks, although some banks have had their common stock penalized in the market because of extensive interest rate swap transactions.

But at the same time, swaps can be the source of large trading losses, especially when they are being used for speculative purposes. For example, in 1998, the hedge fund Long Term Capital Management (LTCM) lost $1.6 billion on trades in the swap markets, and it lost more than $4 billion in total, causing the Federal Reserve Bank of New York to organize a $3.6 billion bailout of LTCM counterparties to prevent a crisis. The LTCM crisis proved that the counterparty risk of swaps can be substantial, and the same marking-to-market techniques that are used in the futures market have become common in the swap market to mitigate these risks.

Other Types of Swaps

Swaps are designed with the intention of reducing the risk of unexpected changes in a financial price, such as currency values, interest rates, or commodity prices. Therefore, swaps can be traded on any financial asset or liability. There are a lot of customized swaps created for a wide variety of other assets and in a wide variety of combinations.

Commodity swap is a swap in which exchanged cash flows are dependent on the price of an underlying commodity. It is usually used to hedge against the price of a commodity. The two parties can swap two different commodities or the same commodity. The first commodity swap was a fixed-for-floating oil price swap engineered by Chase Manhattan Bank in 1986. The vast majority commodity swaps involve petroleum. Usually airline companies who consume a lot of oil might use commodity swaps to lock in the price of oil. It pays a financial institution the fixed price of oil. In return the financial institution pays the company floating oil price.

Swaps can be arranged for any commodity that has a reliable reference price. These prices can be futures prices or spot prices reported by well-known exchanges or specific organizations such as Platt's.

Equity swap is a swap which involves the exchange of interest payments for payments linked to the degree in a stock index. This type of swap arrangement may be appropriate for portfolio managers of insurance companies or pension funds that are managing stocks and bonds. The swap would enhance their investment performance in bullish stock market periods without requiring the managers to change their existing allocation of stocks and bonds. For example, mutual funds manager A has invested in S&P 500 stock index and pension funds manager B has a portfolio of T-bonds. Now manager A thinks the stock market will be weak next year and likes his investment in bond market. manager B, on the other hand, wishes to get into stocks market. Two managers could reach an equity swap in which manager A pays manager B the S&P 500 index return and manager B pays manager A the returns from his T-bonds portfolio.

Swaption (Swap Option) is the option to enter into an interest rate swap. In exchange for an option premium, the buyer gains but not the obligation to enter into a specified swap agreement with the issuer on a specified future date. The agreement will specify whether the buyer of the swaption will be a fixed-rate receiver (like a call option on a bond) or a fixed-rate payer (like a put option on a bond). For example, a financial manager of an MNC knows that in three months' time the company has to fund a big investment project with 5-year floating rate notes but will want to swap into fixed interest payments. The manager could sign a call swaption giving him the right to receive 3-month LIBOR and pay fixed rate for five years starting in three months. The financial manager wants to fix the rate at 6%. If three month later the fixed rate for a 5-year interest swap is higher than 6% he will exercise the option and obtain the swap for 6%. If it is lower than 6% he will abandon the swaption and sign a interest rate swap on the current terms.

Credit-default swap (CDS) is a credit derivative that allows lenders to insure themselves against the risk that a borrower will default. The buyer of a CDS makes payments — like insurance premiums — to the seller, and the seller agrees to pay the buyer if an underlying loan or security defaults. The CDS buyer pays a fee to transfer the risk of default — the credit risk — to the CDS seller.

The CDS was very popular before the 2008 financial crisis and many of the contracts were speculative in nature. Substantial amounts of CDS were written on subprime mortgages so it is said to have contributed to the 2008 financial crisis. In September 2008, the Federal Reserve Bank of New York arranged an $85 billion secured credit facility to American International Group (AIG), the largest insurance company in the world, was on the verge of collapse because it had sold several hundred billion dollars' worth of credit-default swaps.

Summary

1. Financial derivatives are financial instruments that have returns based on the expected future price movements of an asset to which it is linked — called the underlying asset — such as a currency or a share. Derivatives transfer risk from one person to another. Traders may use derivatives to hedge against foreign exchange risk, interest rate risk and other risks. They also may use derivatives to try to earn profits based on speculations about future movements in the price of underlying assets, such as foreign exchange rates, interest rates and so on.
2. A futures contract is an agreement between two parties to exchange a specified amount of two currencies at a given date in the future at a predetermined exchange rate.
3. Futures contracts are different from forward contracts in six aspects: Trading location and counterparty, trading amounts, maturities, default risk, delivery and costs.
4. Futures contracts have their own characteristics. The smaller size of the contract and the possibility of liquidating a position quickly and cheaply in an organized market are advantageous to small users as well as those with steady streams of income and expenditures. Futures contracts also reduce the risk of default relative to forward contracts through the following conventions:
    - An exchange clearinghouse takes one side of every transaction.
    - An initial and a maintenance margin are required.
    - Futures contracts are marked to market on a daily basis.
5. The price of the futures, like the forward price, is determined by interest rate differential between the relative currencies.
6. Futures contracts are commonly used in hedging transaction risk. If a firm has account receivable in foreign currency, it will take a short position on the foreign

currency in a futures contract. If a firm has an account payable in foreign currency, it will take a long position on the foreign currency.

7. Futures contracts are also popular tools for speculation because speculators need only a relatively small amount investment, which is the margin, to purchase a futures contract that is worth a great deal. In other words, speculators can use futures contracts to obtain very large amounts of leverage at a very low cost.

8. The disadvantages of the futures contracts are the limited number of traded contracts and delivery dates. It also causes the mismatch between the contract size and the actual currency risk exposure.

9. A currency call option is the right to buy the underlying currency at a specified price and on a specified date. A currency put option is the right to sell the underlying currency at a specified price and on a specified date.

10. If the right can be exercised at any time during the life of the option it is called an American option. If the right can be exercised only at the option's expiration date, it is called a European option.

11. The buyer of the option pays the seller, or "writer", a certain sum, called the option premium, for the right to buy or sell at the prescribed price.

12. The intrinsic value of an option is the difference between strike price and the spot exchange rate when the contract is exercised. When an option contract has intrinsic value, it is called in-the-money. When an option contract has no intrinsic value, it is called out-of-the-money. When the future spot rate of exchange is equal to the exercise price, the option contract is called at-the-money. The intrinsic value of at-the-money option is zero. All options have time value before the expiration date.

13. The volatility or the standard deviation of the underlying asset is an important factor for determining the time value of an option.

14. A short position on foreign exchange can be hedged by buying a call on foreign exchange and a long position can be hedged by buying a put on foreign exchange.

15. Options markets offer special opportunities for hedging and speculation. They are especially suited to situations where wide swings in the exchange rate are expected. Speculation on a sharp price rise involves buying calls while speculation on a sharp fall involves selling puts. Speculation on price stability involves selling calls or puts.

16. A currency swap is an agreement between two parties to exchange initial principal amounts of the two currencies and pay interest on the currency they initially receive, and to reverse the exchange of initial principal amounts at a fixed future date. The principal amounts are equivalent at the prevailing spot exchange rate.

17. Prior to currency swaps, there were parallel loans MNCs widely used to solve the financing problems. The parallel loan is a funding strategy by which two parties can exchange the type of funds each one can most easily raise for the type of funds each really wants.

18. Currency swaps solve the problem of foreign exchange risk when financing cannot be obtained in the currency in which the cash flows are generated.
19. Interest rate swaps are exchanges of liabilities in the same currency but are based on two different interest rates. That is, two parties exchange their interest payment obligations on two different kinds of debt instruments, one bearing a fixed interest rate and the other a floating interest rate. The cash flows associated with interest rate swaps are based on the notional principal, which is the conceptual amount of the outstanding debt.
20. The most common form of interest rate swap is the fixed-for-floating interest rate swap. The swap can also involve two floating rates in which interest obligations involving basis points are swapped.
21. Swaps can be traded on any financial asset or liability. A lot of customized swaps are created for a wide variety of other assets and in a wide variety of combinations. Commodity swaps, equity swaps, swaptions, and credit-default swaps are just few of them.

Key Concepts and Terms

1. American option — 美式期权
2. Amortizing loan — 分期偿还贷款
3. At-the-money — 平值状态，期权到期时市场价格与期权执行价相等的期权
4. Call option — 买入期权，看涨期权
5. Chicago Board of Trade — 芝加哥期货交易所
6. Chicago Mercantile of Exchange — 芝加哥商品交易所
7. Commodity swap — 商品互换
8. Counter currency — 对等货币，指衍生产品中购买或出售标的货币时支付或换回的另一种货币
9. Credit-default swaps — 信用违约互换
10. Currency futures contracts — 货币期货合约
11. Currency options — 货币期权
12. Currency swaps — 货币互换，货币掉期
13. Default risk — 违约风险
14. Equity swap — 权益互换
15. Financial derivatives — 金融衍生产品
16. Forward contracts — 远期合约
17. Initial margin — 初始保证金

18.	Interest rate swap	利率互换
19.	Intrinsic value	内在价值
20.	In-the-money	价内状态，指具有内在价值的期权合约
21.	Margin account	保证金账户
22.	Margin call	追加保证金
23.	Maintenance margin	维持保证金
24.	Marking to market	逐日盯市
25.	Nonamortizing loan	到期一次付清贷款，指贷款期内只支付利息，本金到期一次性付清的贷款
26.	Option holder	期权持有人，期权买主
27.	Option premium (option price)	期权价格
28.	Option writer	期权出售者
29.	Out-of-the-money	价外状态，指内在价值为零的期权合约
30.	Parallel loan (back-to-back loan)	平行贷款，背对背贷款
31.	Put option	卖出期权，看跌期权
32.	Standardized contract	标准化合约
33.	Strike price (exercise price)	期权执行价
34.	Swaption (Swap option)	互换期权
35.	Time value	时间价值
36.	Underlying currency	标的货币
37.	Volatility	波动率，指价格波动的标准差
38.	Zero sum game	零和游戏

Questions

1. What are financial derivatives? What is the main reason for the development and growth of financial derivatives?
2. How do currency forward and futures contracts differ with respect to maturity, settlement, and size and timing of cash flows?
3. What is the primary role of the exchange clearinghouse in currency futures market?
4. Explain the relationship between initial margin and maintenance margin?
5. How does a futures contract eliminate default risk?
6. Why are the futures contracts popular tools for speculation?
7. What is the difference between a call option and a put option?
8. How do American options differ from European options?
9. What are the differences between exchange-traded and over-the-counter currency options?

10. In what sense is a currency call option also a currency put option?
11. What is meant if an option is "in the money", "out of the money", or "at the money"?
12. What determines the intrinsic value of an option? What determines the time value of an option?
13. What are the benefits to use currency options and what are the disadvantages for currency options?
14. Suppose the average premium on foreign currency calls has decreased and the average premium on foreign currency puts has increased. How would you explain this?
15. An importer is expected to pay foreign currency 6 months later. He hesitates to a forward or futures contract to hedge the transaction exposure. Instead, he tries to buy a call option on the foreign currency. What is the possible reason that the importer prefers the option contract?
16. What is a parallel loan? What are the pros and cons of a parallel loan?
17. How are swaps related to forward contracts?
18. What is a fixed-for-floating rate nonamortizing currency swap?
19. What is notional principal? What is the function of notional principal?
20. What is the difference between currency swap and interest rate swap?

Chapter 7
INTERNATIONAL FINANCIAL MARKETS

LEARNING OBJECTIVES

- Examine the basics of financial market including functions, characteristics and classifications.
- Understand the international money market and popular financial instruments available in this market.
- Introduce the origins and development of the Eurocurrency market, the features and instruments of the market.
- Explore the international capital market and compare the domestic bond, foreign bond, Eurobond and global bond.
- Learn the basics of international equity market.

The foreign exchange market and the derivatives market we have examined in previous chapters are parts of the international financial markets. Firms and investors change one currency for another in foreign exchange markets. They use the derivatives markets to hedge foreign exchange risk exposure or interest rate risks. In this chapter we study other parts of the international financial markets, i.e., the non-derivatives markets. Due to astonishing growth in international trade and investment and reduction of barriers on capital movements, various international activities of banks (the so called "**international banking**") have evolved fairly rapidly during the past several decades. In addition to traditional international banking, new activities were initiated by a large number of international banks.

As we know, access to cheapest capital in global market is one of the prerequisites for a multinational corporation to maximize shareholders' wealth. The sources of funds for an MNC (and its subsidiaries) can be mainly categorized as two parts: cash that is internally generated by the MNC and cash that is externally provided from the debt markets or the equity markets. Financing and investing in international financial markets are both technical and difficult. This is because international financial markets have different regulation, instruments, terminology and techniques. Those differences will have important consequences for risk, returns and the cost of doing business. Financial managers are required to have a thorough technical knowledge of the international money market, capital market and equity market, the financial instruments available on a particular market, trading practices, taxes and regulations in different financial markets and so on.

This chapter focuses some basics of international financial markets, the popular instruments in money market and capital market. We'll describe the various funding sources for debt that are available to MNCs in an increasingly globalized world and to examine what makes MNC choose particular options, particularly the most important international financial market: the Eurocurrency market and Eurobond market. We introduce the origin of the Eurocurrency and Eurobond markets, basic attributes of those two markets and several instruments available in those markets. Finally, we discuss the international equity market. This section mainly introduces world's major equity markets in both developed and developing countries, including the U.S., Japan, the U.K. and emerging stock markets.

Introduction to Financial Market

Financial markets are markets for transactions of financial assets and liabilities. One party transfers funds in financial markets by purchasing financial assets previously held by another party. Financial markets facilitate the flow of funds and thereby facilitate financing and investing by households, firms, and government agencies. They are the economy's central nervous system, relaying rand reacting to information quickly, allocating resources, and determining prices. The markets and their many different instruments vary by source of funding, pricing structure, maturity, and subordination or linkage to other debt and equity instruments. For example, stock exchanges trade company shares and government debt; the money market trades short-term loans and deposits; the foreign exchange market trades different currencies, specialized markets trade financial derivatives; the gold market is for buying and selling gold. The most important characteristic of a financial asset is its liquidity. **Liquidity** refers to the ease with which you can capture an asset's value. Liquid assets can be quickly converted into their cash value.

There are many ways to categorize financial markets. **National financial market** is regarded as an internal market or domestic market because the financial assets or liabilities traded on this market are issued in the domestic currency; the trading practices follow the domestic conventions and are regulated by domestic authorities. **International financial market** refers to an external market where the financial contracts are placed outside of the borders of any single country and can be regulated by more than one country or by none at all. According to the maturities of the financial assets or liabilities, the financial market can be classified as money market and capital market. **Money market** is the market for trading financial assets and liabilities with maturities less than one year. The **capital market** trades financial contracts with maturities more than one year.

International Money Market

The international money market developed to accommodate the needs of MNCs. First, many MNCs borrow short-term funds in different currencies to pay for imports denominated in those currencies. Second, MNCs that need funds to support local operations may consider borrowing in a nonlocal currency that exhibits lower interest rates. This strategy is especially appropriate for firms expecting future receivables denominated in that currency. Third, MNCs may consider borrowing in a currency that they anticipate will depreciate against their home currency, as this would enable them to repay the short-term loan at a more favorable exchange rate. In this case, the actual cost of borrowing would be less than the interest rate quoted for that currency.

The typical international money markets are foreign exchange market, bank, government, corporate notes and international commercial paper markets. Money markets facilitate the flow of short-term funds. The most important financial intermediary in money markets is the commercial bank. This is the case for almost every country. The instruments in the money markets have a relatively high degree of liquidity simply because they can be easily bought and sold. Most firms and financial institutions maintain some holdings of money market instruments for this reason. On the other hand, money market instruments tend to have a low expected return but also a low degree of risk. International money market can be classified as short-term credit market, short-term securities market and discount market.

Short-term Credit Market

Short-term credit market is basically an interbank market. It operates at the wholesale level. The market provides short-term loans with the maturities from one day to one year. The market is facilitated by electronic funds transfer systems. The interest rates charged are those offered by major banks to each other in the interbank market. Major newspapers publish those rates every day. The international money market interest rates for some major currencies are shown in **Exhibit 7.1**.

Exhibit 7.1 International Money Market Interest Rate Quotations
(January 15, 2021)

	Short term	7 Days' notice	One month	Three month	Six month	One year
Euro	(−0.74)–(0.44)	(−0.71)–(−0.41)	(−0.70)–(−0.40)	(−0.65)–(−0.35)	(−0.67)–(−0.37)	(−0.67)–(−0.37)
Sterling		0.45–0.55	0.70–0.80	0.78–0.88	0.82–0.97	0.89–1.04
Swiss Franc						
CAD						
U.S. Dollar	0.18–0.38	0.03–0.23	0.06–0.26	0.14–0.34	0.16–0.36	0.22–0.32
Japanese Yen	0.10–0.05	0.11–0.06	0.05–0.04	0.35–0.25	(0.20)–(−0.10)	(−0.15)–(0.15)

Source: *Financial Times*, January 18, 2021.

Short-term Securities Market

This is a market for transactions of various kinds of short-term securities. The main securities include treasury bill, commercial paper, negotiable certificate of deposit, repurchase agreement and bankers' acceptance.

Treasury bill is a government short-term debt instrument. The typical treasury bill is the U.S. Treasury bill which is sold weekly through an auction and represents about one-third of the government's outstanding negotiable debt. T-bills bear no formal interest, but are promised to pay on maturity date, issued at a discount on their par value (the face value). The maturities of T-bill are typically three-month, six-month and one-year. One-year T-bill is issued on a monthly basis. The par value of the T-bill is $1,000 and in multiples of $1,000 thereafter. T-bills are regarded as highly liquid financial assets because of their short maturity and strong secondary market.

Commercial paper is an unsecured, short-term debt issued only by a well-known creditworthy corporation. It is usually issued at a discount. Commercial paper is often regarded as a reasonable substitute for Treasury bills, certificates of deposit, etc. The minimum denomination of commercial paper is usually $100,000. Most commercial papers are in multiples of $1 million denominations. Small investors can only invest in commercial paper indirectly through money market funds. Maturities are normally between 20 and 45 days but can be as short as one day or as long as 270 days. In most cases, commercial paper is held until maturity by investors. More than one-third of all commercial paper is held by money-market mutual funds (MMMFs), which require very short-term assets with immediate liquidity. Most commercial paper is used exclusively for short-term financing. For the most part, commercial paper is a very safe investment because the financial situation of a company can easily be predicted over a few months. Speculative-grade commercial paper does exist, but not because it was originally issued as such.

Negotiable certificate of deposit (NCD) is generally issued by large commercial banks and other depository institutions with a minimum face value of $100,000. Negotiable means that they can be bought and sold in the financial markets, just like bonds and commercial papers, thus providing investors with some liquidity. NCDs are bought most often by large institutional investors. Institutions often use these as a way to invest in a low-risk, low interest security. Maturities on NCDs range from two weeks to one year. Because NCDs can be resold, they have become an important source of bank financing. When a bank needs funds, it can issue NCDs, in addition to commercial paper and more conventional bonds.

Repurchase agreement is usually called repo. It is also an important source for financing. A dealer or holder of government securities (usually T-bills) sells the securities to a lender and agrees to repurchase them at an agreed future date at an agreed price. **Figure 7.1** shows how repurchase agreement works. They are usually very short-term, from overnight to 30 days or more. A repo is like a loan backed by the securities. If the borrower defaults on the loan, the lender has claim to the securities. Therefore, risks are relatively low in this market. A dealer can over-collateralize a deal by delivering securities with a market value of 102 percent or so of the amount borrowed. In addition, the collateral behind a repo is marking-to-market and the dealer can be required to furnish more collateral if security values decline.

There are also variations on standard repos. A **reverse repo** is the complete opposite of a repo. In this case, a dealer buys government securities from an investor and then sells them back at a later date for a higher price. A **term repo** is exactly the same as a repo except the term of the loan is more than 30 days. Repos are popular because they can virtually

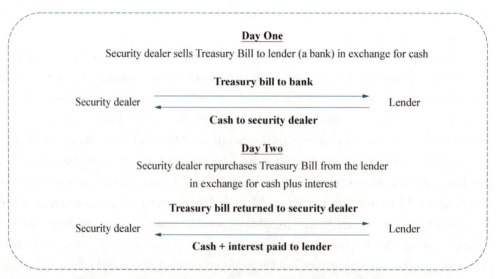

Figure 7.1 Mechanics of an Overnight Repurchase Agreement

eliminate default risk. The primary participating borrowers in the repo market are security dealers, while the primary lenders are commercial banks and nonfinancial corporations.

Banker's Acceptance is a short-term credit instrument created by a non-financial firm and guaranteed by a bank to make a payment. It is a form of promissory note, commonly used in international trade. If an exporter does not know an importer's credit standing, he usually prefers that a bank act as a guarantor. In other words, a time draft issued by the importer must be accepted by a bank. If a bank stamps "ACCEPTED" on the time draft, he obligates payment at a specified point in time. Exporters who hold acceptance usually sell it at discounts in the secondary market to obtain cash immediately.

Financial instruments in short-term securities market are usually perceived to be very safe, especially when they are rated high by rating agencies. But those instruments are exposed to exchange rate risk when the currency denominating the securities differs from the investor's home currency. Specifically, the return on investment in international short-term securities market will be reduced when currency denominating the securities weakens against the home currency. This means that, even for securities without credit risk, investors can lose money because of exchange rate risk.

Discount Market

Discount is a reduction from a bill of exchange or other drafts when it is purchased before its maturity date. The party that purchases (discounts) the bill pays less than its face value and therefore makes a profit when it matures. Discount market consists of banks, discount houses, and bill brokers. The discount houses primarily operate in the United Kingdom. They play a central role in England money market. They make markets, that is, they buy, sell and discount bill of exchanges, promissory notes and other short-term high-quality instruments at which they are prepared to deal. In addition, discount houses receive deposit money in the form of call money.

Call money is short-term deposits received by discount houses mainly from clearing banks and payable upon call. Call money accounts are secured by assets of discount houses in most instances. Depending on maturity, there are several types of call money: (1) overnight money which is payable automatically the next day; (2) day-to-day money which has no fixed maturity and is payable upon call; (3) notice money, which requires an advance notice, either two days or seven days; (4) time money, which has a fixed maturity.

Commercial banks or discount houses can rediscount a short-term negotiable debt instrument at the central bank's discount window. When there is low liquidity in the market, banks or discount houses can generate cash by rediscounting drafts.

Eurocurrency Market

The most important international money market is the Eurocurrency market which is a market for transactions of financial assets and liabilities denominated in Eurocurrencies. The banks dealing in Eurocurrencies are called Euro banks. A **Eurocurrency** is a currency held in a country other than the country the currency is issued. For example, a U.S. dollar deposit held in London or Paris or some other countries other than the United States is a Eurodollar deposit. A Japanese yen loan in Zurich is a Euroyen loan. The use of the prefix Euro is somewhat misleading because it does not necessarily mean that those currencies must be held in a European country. A Eurocurrency actually means an "offshore" currency.

Eurodollar is the most important Eurocurrency which accounts for approximately 60%–65% of all Eurocurrency activity, followed by the Euro-Euro, Euro-Swissfranc, Euro-Sterling and Euro-Yen.

Eurocurrencies are generally in the form of variable-rate time deposits with maturities of less than one year. So the Eurocurrency market is part of the international money market. The participants in the Eurocurrency market are governments, financial institutions, MNCs and international institutions such as IMF, World Bank and European Investment Bank as well as private investors. Developed countries act both lenders and borrowers of funds, while many less-developed countries are borrowers in this market.

Brief History of the Eurocurrency Market

The Eurocurrency originated from the Eurodollar. As tension between the U.S. and the former Soviet Union increased during the Cold War in 1950s, the Russian feared that U.S. might freeze Soviet Union's funds in U.S. banks. Also in 1957, the Bank of England introduced restrictions on U.K. banks' ability to lend sterling to foreigners and foreigner's ability to borrow sterling. This induced U.K. banks to turn to the U.S. dollar as a means of retaining London's leading role in the financing of world trade. In 1958 the abolition of the European Payments Union and restoration of convertibility of European currencies meant that the European banks could now hold U.S. dollars without being forced to convert these dollar holdings with their central banks for domestic currencies. All these three factors provided the initial demand and supply of Eurodollars.

The main reason for the Eurodollar market to prosper was the increased regulation of domestic banking activities by the U.S. authorities. **Regulation Q** introduced in 1963 by the Federal Reserve Bank imposed a 5.25% ceiling on the rate of interest that U.S. banks could pay on savings and time-deposit accounts. European banks were not subject to this regulation and, consequently, could pay higher rates for dollar deposits than U.S. banks. This induced American banks to set up overseas branches to take these dollar deposits. In the same year, the **Interest Equalization Tax (IET)** was introduced to discourage non-residents from borrowing in the United States. It was a tax on U.S. residents' earnings on foreign securities. To compensate for the tax, foreign borrowers were obliged to pay higher interest rates, which raised the cost to foreigners of borrowing dollars in U.S. The

IET led foreign borrowers to borrow funds on the Eurodollar market. A further measure to discourage U.S. banks from lending to non-residents was the **Voluntary Foreign Credit Restraint Guidelines** which were issued in 1965 and became mandatory in 1968. The Guidelines were restrictions placed on non-domestic uses of domestically generated funds. Under these restrictions, many U.S. firms with plans for overseas projects simply shifted their financing needs to the Eurodollar market.

The increased regulation of U.S. domestic banks gave a boost to the development of Euro banking activities to circumvent the effects of these controls. Many U.S. banks decided to set up foreign branches and subsidiaries to escape the banking regulations. More importantly, they gave a competitive edge to Euro banks which are not subject to such regulations. It is this competitive edge which is the fundamental reason for their rapid and sustained growth. Unlike domestic banks, because Euro banks are free of regulatory control they are not required to hold reserve assets. This gives them a competitive advantage over domestic banks which are required to hold part of their assets in zero or low interest liquid funds to meet official reserve requirements.

There were other reasons for the rapid growth of the Eurocurrency market. After 1973 oil crisis the OPEC countries deposited large amounts of dollars on the Eurodollar markets. Oil-importing countries, on the other hand, faced huge BOP deficit problems, and they needed funds to finance their deficits. Eurodollar markets thus played an important intermediary role in recycling funds from the surplus OPEC countries to the deficit oil importing countries. In 1970s and the early 1980s, many developing countries borrowed funds in the Eurocurrency market. Rapid growth of world trade also contributes to the development of the Eurocurrency market. More companies have excess working balances in a foreign currency on which they seek high rates of return, while others require short-term borrowing facilities at competitive rates of interest.

Credit Expansion through the Eurocurrency Markets

The following example shows how the Eurocurrency market expand credits. Suppose that a Chinese exporter sells $1 million of merchandise to an American firm. The American importer pays for the purchase by drawing a $1 million check on his checking account in Bank of America, New York. The Chinese exporter deposits the check in a time deposit account in HSBC Hong Kong Branch. Here HSBC Hong Kong Branch is an Euro bank because it takes U.S. dollar deposit. The above two transactions are shown in **Figure 7.2**.

From the U.S. perspective, ownership of $1 million demand deposits has been transferred from the U.S. importing company to an Euro bank, the HSBC Hong Kong Branch, but the U.S. banking system is not affected because the $1 million still remains in the United States. $1 million Eurodollar is created in Hong Kong. The reason is that the deposit in Hong Kong exists in addition to the dollars deposited in U.S.

Now assume that HSBC Hong Kong Branch makes $1 million loan to a local firm.

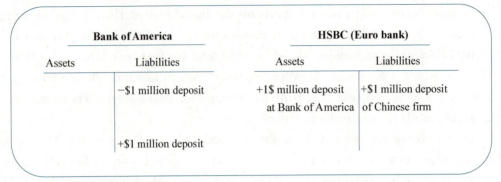

Figure 7.2 Transfer of U.S. Dollar from a U.S. Bank to an Euro bank

The firm deposits the proceeds of the loan in Bank of China, Hong Kong Branch. The transactions are shown in **Figure 7.3**.

Bank of America		HSBC		Bank of China	
Assets	Liabilities	Assets	Liabilities	Assets	Liabilities
−$1 million deposit of HSBC		−$1 million deposit at Bank of America		+$1 million deposit at Bank of America	+$1 million deposit of local firm
+1 million deposit of Bank of China		+1 million loan to local firm			

Figure 7.3 Loan by HSBC to a Local Firm

There are now $2 million worth of Eurodollars in the system. The whole process could be restarted as long as the funds are redeposited with another Euro bank. If the local firm uses the funds to pay various bills due or finance a project instead, $1 million will eventually injected into the American economy and thereby returned to the U.S. banking system. Therefore, no more Eurodollars will be created.

When a Eurocurrency deposit is transferred between and among banks, as shown in Figure 7.2 and 7.3, the deposit denominated in U.S. dollar never leaves the United States. Only the ownership of the deposit was transferred. Thus, expansion or decline of Eurocurrency volume has little or no effect on the money supply of specific countries.

This is a highly simplified example of the way the Euro banking system creates credit. In reality, there are leakages occur in the above process like we mentioned. Another example that dollars can "leak" from the Euro banking system is that the sale of dollars for another currency. In the above example, if the Chinese exporter sells dollars to HSBC for RMB, the dollars are most likely to "leak" from the system.

Characteristics of the Eurocurrency Market

There are several characteristics of this market. The first is that the market lacks the central bank's regulation. Since Eurocurrency transactions are outside the jurisdiction of any single country, they are not subject to the rules that governmental agencies impose on national credit markets. This allows the Eurocurrency markets to avoid domestic interest rate regulations, reserve requirements, and other barriers to free flow of capital. The banks on the Eurocurrency market are not required to hold reserve assets. This gives them a competitive advantage over domestic banks which are required to hold part of their assets in the central bank to meet official reserve requirements. The banks on the Eurocurrency market are then able to hold less money in the form of low-interest reserves enabling them to pay a higher interest rate on deposits and charge a lower rate on loans. Corporations and financial institutions with access to the Eurocurrency market can typically obtain lower cost funds or store funds at higher interest rates than is possible in domestic credit markets.

Second, the market uses the London Inter Bank Bid Rate and Offer Rate (LIBOR) as a benchmark rate. About 50% of Eurocurrency transactions occur through London banks. Consequently, LIBOR is the most frequently quoted rates. The bid rate is a Eurocurrency bank is willing to pay its customers and the offer rate is the bank demands for making a loan. The difference of the bid and ask is called interbank spread and is typically one-eighth percent for large interbank transactions in major currencies. For corporations and investors, the spread of the bid and ask is a little bit larger but it is still very small compared to many domestic market practices. **Exhibit 7.2** lists some LIBOR for major currencies reported in the Financial Times.

Exhibit 7.2   LIBOR for Major Currencies

	Over night	One month	Three month	Six month	One year
U.S. Dollar	0.08675	0.12888	0.22563	0.25125	0.32575
Euro	−0.58843	−0.59486	−0.55314	−0.53457	−0.49614
Sterling	0.03563	0.02838	0.03113	0.03950	0.07713
Swiss Franc		−0.81280	−0.76120	−0.72100	−0.60760
Japanese Yen		−0.06083	−0.07567	−0.05400	0.03950

Source: *Financial Times*, January 18, 2021.

The LIBOR has been a widely accepted interest rate since 1984. The reference rate varied depending upon the currency in which the debt obligation was created (due to variances in foreign exchange rates, differences in capital market liquidity, and other factors which can affect loan pricing); so, for example, there is EUROBOR (for debts denominated in Euro), JPYBOR (for Japan), HIBOR (for Hong Kong of China), SIBOR (for Singapore), SHIBOR (for China), and the like. But, far and away the greatest use of LIBOR has been in pricing the costs of debt denominated in U.S. dollars. After the discovery in the aftermath of the 2008 financial crisis of interest rate manipulation by the banks which "offered" the various rates, British authorities mandated that LIBOR cease being used as of the end of 2021, which means by the end of 2021, LIBOR for debt obligations in all currencies except USD LIBOR will no longer be published. The likely replacement in the United States is the **Secured Overnight Financing Rate (SOFA)**. SOFA is based on the rates investors offer banks for loans-based, bond-secured assets. These transactions take place on the U.S. Treasury's repurchase market.

Third, the structure of loans and deposits in the Eurocurrency market is that they are predominately of a short-term nature with some deposits being as short as one day (overnight loan) and the vast majority under six months. Furthermore, there is a close matching of the maturity structure of deposits and loans; typically if money is taken in for three months then it will be loaned out for three months. This is because Euro banks have to be wary of sudden large withdrawals of short-term funds. It is said the close matching of deposits and loans can also reduce risks to the banks due to interest rate fluctuations. The close matching of assets and liabilities stands in contrast to the balance sheets of domestic banks which usually accept short-term demand and time deposits and then engage in medium to long-term lending.

Instruments in Eurocurrency Market

Eurocredits or Euroloans refer to a short-term and medium-term bank loan denominated in Eurocurrency to corporations, sovereign governments, or international organizations. Most eurocredits are Eurodollar loans with the interest rate tied to the LIBOR. One of the features of a Eurocredit is that it can be mobilized quickly and easily. The documentation is standardized and simple and there is no waiting list to respect as there is in the Eurobond market. For example, the whole procedure takes only four to six weeks. The terms of a Eurocredit can be tailored to the borrower's specific needs. For example, standby credits make it possible for borrowers to mobilize a large loan just in case they need it. If they need to use it, they pay the interest and commissions just as they would on a normal loan. If they do not use it, they only pay the commissions and perhaps a small fee.

Borrowers usually prefer that loans be denominated in the currency of the country in which they receive their cash flows, which eliminates the borrower's exchange rate risk. However, the loan's interest rate depends on the currency in which the loan is denominated. In the Eurocurrency market banks still face the **interest-rate risk** which is the risk of mismatch between their maturities of the asset and liability. A bank's liabilities tend to be short term, while its assets tend to be long term. When interest rates rise, banks face the risk that the value of their assets will fall more than the value of their liabilities (reducing the bank's capital). Put another way, if a bank makes long-term loans, it receives payments from borrowers that do not vary with the interest rate. But its short-term liabilities — those with variable interest rates — require the bank to make larger payments when interest rates rise. So rising interest rates reduce revenues relative to expenses, directly lowering the bank's profits. Therefore, Euro banks commonly use floating rate loans to manage interest-rate risk. The loan rate floats in accordance with the movement of a market interest rate, such as LIBOR. For example, a loan that is denominated in a particular currency and is provided by a bank to an MNC might be structured with an interest rate that resets every six months to the prevailing LIBOR for that currency plus some percentage points.

Euro commercial paper (ECP) is an unsecured, short-term debt obligation issued at a discount by a bank or corporation in Eurocurrency market, denominated in a currency that differs from the corporation's domestic currency. Maturities are usually one, three and six months. Most Euro commercial papers are denominated in U.S. dollars. There are a number of differences between the U.S. and Euro commercial paper markets. The maturity of Euro commercial paper tends to be about twice as long as U.S. commercial paper. For this reason, the secondary market for large-denomination Eurocurrency certificates of deposit (CDs) with face value of $100,000 and up is more active than for U.S. commercial paper.

Floating rate notes (FRNs) are medium-term bonds that pay investors a regular interest linked to short-term interest rates like three or six month LIBOR. Sometimes the asset and liability maturities of Euro banks do not match. This can adversely affect a bank's performance during periods of rising interest rates, since it may have locked in a rate on its Eurocredit loans while its rate paid on short-term deposits is rising over time. To avoid this risk, Euro banks now commonly sell floating rate notes. Some FRNs guarantee a minimum interest rate. This can suit investor and issuer alike. The cost of issuance is key to the borrower.

Syndicated credit or **syndicated loan** is a loan offered by a group of lenders (called syndicate) who work together to provide funds for a single borrower. The borrower could be an MNC, a local or national government, an international organization. The loan may involve fixed amounts, a credit line, or a combination of the two. A syndicated credit is arranged by a lead bank (also called lead manager) on behalf of its client. The banks that provide the actual funding are called participating banks. The bank that receives the service payments from the borrower and distributes them to the participating banks is the paying agent.

Any given bank can play multiple roles. When a large company needs large amounts of capital, it deals with a lead bank. The lead bank seeks the participation of a group of banks, with each participant providing a portion of the total funds needed. This lead bank may be putting up a proportionally bigger share of the loan, or perform duties like dispersing cash flows amongst the other group members or administrative tasks. The main goal of a syndicated loan is to spread the risk of a borrower default across multiple lenders (such as banks) or institutional investors like pension funds or hedge funds. Because of the paying agent system, if the borrower defaults, the default is considered against all banks of the syndicate. This structure ensures that the borrower does not pay off the larger banks while ignoring the smaller debt holders.

Because syndicated loans tend to be much larger than standard bank loans, the risk of even one borrower defaulting could cripple a single lender. Borrowers who receive a syndicated loan incur various fees besides the interest on the loan. For example, **up-front cost** is typically a one-time fee of 1% to 2.5% of the total amount of the credit, which is paid to the lead manager and managing banks for organizing the syndicate and underwriting the loan; **commitment fee** is charged annually on the unused portion of the available credit extended by the syndicate. There is also a small fee paid to the paying agent bank to cover administrative expenses.

Syndicated loans are also used in the leveraged buyout community to fund large corporate takeovers with primarily debt funding. The syndicated loan is also known as "syndicated bank facility".

International Capital Market

Capital market is the market for trading financial assets and liabilities with maturities greater than one year such as bonds, mortgages, and stocks. Capital markets facilitate the flow of long-term funds. We focus our discussion mainly on the bond market in this section.

Bonds are bought and sold in enormous quantities every day. The trading volume in bonds on a typical day is many, many times larger than the trading volume in stocks. Publicly traded bonds are an important source of capital for companies and governments. One reason the bond markets are so big is that the number of bond issues far exceeds the number of stock issues. There are two reasons for this. First, a corporation would typically have only one common stock issue outstanding. However, a single large corporation could easily have a dozen or more note and bond issues outstanding. Beyond this, federal, state, and local borrowing is simply enormous. For example, even a small city would usually have a wide variety of notes and bonds outstanding, representing money borrowed to pay for things like roads, sewers, and schools. There are thousands and thousands cities in a country. Thus it is not difficult to imagine why the bond markets are so big.

The classification of a bond depends on its type of issuer, priority, coupon rate and redemption features. Here we just discuss domestic bonds and international bonds. International bonds can also be classified as foreign bonds, Eurobonds and global bonds.

Domestic bonds are issued by a domestic borrower, traded within the domestic market, and denominated in the domestic currency. Domestic bonds are regulated by the domestic government and are traded according to local conventions. For example, in the United

States, government bonds are traded in an over-the-counter (OTC) market through commercial and investment banks. Corporate bonds are traded over the counter by commercial banks as well as on the bond-trading floor of the New York Stock Exchange.

If the name of the bond owner is printed on the bond, it is a **registered bond**. Corporate and government bonds in Canada, Japan, and U.S. are issued as registered bonds. In countries requiring that bonds be issued in registered form, each issuer maintains a record of the owners of its bonds and directly sends interest of the bond to the owners. Registered bonds typically pay quarterly or semiannual interest.

The convention in European countries is to use bearer bonds. **Bearer bonds** are not registered and can be redeemed by the holder. The holder of the bearer bonds are required to clip coupons attached to the bonds and send them to the issuer to receive coupon payments. The principle advantage of bearer bonds is that they retain the anonymity of the bondholder. Bearer bonds are usually issued with annual coupons.

Bonds are sold at a discount meaning the bond's selling price is less than its face value. So if a bond is initially priced at 95 percent of par, the bond's initial price is $95. The price of a bond is determined by the prevailing interest rates on other similar financial assets and the time to maturity of the bond.

International bonds include foreign bonds, Eurobonds and global bonds.

Foreign bonds are issued in domestic market by a foreign borrower, denominated in domestic currency, marketed to domestic residents, and regulated by domestic authorities. Foreign bonds are usually underwritten and sold by brokers who are located in the country in which the bonds are issued. For example, a Chinese company issues dollar denominated bonds in America. This is foreign bonds in the eyes of Americans. The bonds must meet the security regulations of the United States and must be registered with the Securities and Exchange Commission (SEC). The Chinese company must also provide a prospectus disclosing detailed financial information to the prospective investors. There are special names for foreign bonds in some countries. For example, foreign bonds are known as Yankee bonds in the United States, Bulldog bonds in the United Kingdom, Samurai bonds in Japan, Panda bonds in China and the like.

Eurobonds are denominated in a currency different from the country where the bond is issued. Eurobonds are sold by international syndicates of brokers because they are generally sold simultaneously in a number of countries. For example, a dollar denominated bond sold outside the border of U.S. is a Eurobond or Eurodollar bond. A sterling bond sold in Japan is a Eurosterling bond. Eurobonds are bearer bonds, and the interest payments are free of withholding taxes. They are thus attractive to investors wishing to remain anonymous, for tax avoidance or other reasons.

Global bonds are bonds that can be offered within the Eurocurrency market as well as several other markets simultaneously. Unlike Eurobonds, global bonds can be issued in the same currency as the country of issuance. For example, a global bond could be both issued in the United States and denominated in U.S. dollars. Usually, borrowers must be large investment-grade borrowers and must borrow in actively traded currencies. A 10-year $1.5 billion offering by the World Bank in 1989 was the first global bond issued simultaneously in the U.S. market and in the Eurobond market. Global bond offerings enlarge the borrower's opportunities for financing at reduced costs. Purchasers desire the increased liquidity of the issues and have been willing to accept lower yields.

Major investors in the international bond market include institutional investors such as pension funds, insurance companies, money market mutual funds (MMMFs), hedge funds from many different countries. Institutional investors may prefer to invest in international bond markets, rather than in their respective local markets, when they can earn a higher return on bonds denominated in foreign currencies. Borrowers in the international bond market include large and mid-sized banks, MNCs, insurance companies and governments.

Eurobond Markets

Eurobond and Its Development

A Eurobond is a bond issued in a currency other than that of the country or market to which it is issued; i.e., a bond composed of claims in a particular currency but held outside the country of that currency. Eurobonds are identical in principle to Eurocurrencies and arose out of the Eurocurrency market. Eurobond market is part of the international capital market. The Eurobond segment of the international bond market accounts for approximately 80 percent of new offerings. As with many financial innovations, the Eurobond market was born and matured as borrowers and investors sought ways to circumvent government restrictions on cross-border capital flows.

The first Eurobond was issued in 1963. The Interest Equalization Tax (IET) in 1963 required the U.S. citizens who held dollar bonds issued by foreign entities in the United States pay taxes to the federal government. The purpose of the IET was to protect the balance of payments from excessive capital outflows and to preserve the scarce long-term capital supplied by domestic savers. Foreign borrowers began to issue U.S. dollar bonds outside of the United States. A further incentive for the growth of the Eurobond market was an interest withholding tax that was imposed on domestic U.S. bonds held by foreigners. The interest withholding tax made it inconvenient for foreign investors to own dollar-denominated bonds. Eurobonds that were not subject to taxation by the U.S. government were an attractive alternative for foreign investors wishing to avoid the interest withholding tax.

Although the IET was abolished in 1974 and withholding tax removed in 1984, the Eurobond market continued to prosper. Several thousand Eurobond issues now trade in the secondary market.

Firms in emerging market economies (EMEs) markedly increased their issuance of bonds in offshore markets after the 2008 financial crisis. Taking advantage of easy external financing conditions and investor appetite for higher yields, many EME firms raised funds through bond issue outside their jurisdictions. The major offshore markets are those of the European Union (Eurobonds) and the United States (Yankee bonds). By contrast, increases in offshore bond issuance by firms in advanced economies were more muted.

Characteristics of Eurobonds

Because Eurobond sales fall outside the regulatory domain of any single nation, Eurobonds are generally exempt from the rules and regulations that govern the issue of foreign bonds in a country. For example, the need to issue very detailed prospectuses and withholding taxes. Eurobonds have shorter maturities than other bonds on domestic markets. Dollar-denominated Eurobonds have traditionally been the most popular form of issue, although the dollar predominance is less than in the Eurocurrency loans market. The majority of Eurobonds have maturities from 4 to 7 years. Therefore, the Eurobond market is primarily a medium-term borrowing market.

Eurobonds are issued in bearer form, meaning that the name and country of residence of the owner is not on the certificate. The anonymity is one of the attractions to international investors who like to avoid open registration of their ownership. Bearer bonds are also tied to tax avoidance. Furthermore, Eurobonds are free of withholding taxes and Eurobonds interest is not always reported to tax authorities.

If a borrower needs to raise funds by issuing Eurobonds to the investors, he will usually contact an investment banker who is usually the lead manager of an underwriting syndicate. The **underwriting syndicate** is a group of investment banks, merchant banks and commercial banks that specialize in some phase of a public issuance. The group serves as an underwriter for the bond issue, that is, the **underwriter** will buy the bonds from the borrower at a discount from the issuing price. The bonds are then resold to other investors in the secondary market by the underwriter. The secondary market for Eurobonds is an over-the-counter market with principal trading in London.

The Eurobond market is constantly evolving and innovating to meet the changing preferences of both borrowers and investors of funds. Today Eurobonds come in a huge variety of different forms varying in the credit rating of the issuer, the maturity of the issue, the liquidity of the secondary market, the currency of denomination, whether of a fixed or variable rates and in specific features. This makes comparing different Eurobonds a complex issue.

The Types of Eurobonds

Straight fixed-rate bonds

Vast majority of the Eurobonds are straight bonds which pay fixed interest rate with repayment of principal upon maturity. During the life of the bond, fixed coupon payments, which are a percentage of the face value, are paid as interest to the bondholders. In contrast to many domestic bonds, which make semiannual coupon payments, coupon interest on Eurobonds is typically paid annually. The vast majority of new Eurobond offerings are straight fixed-rate issues.

A special category of straight fixed-rate bonds is zero coupon bonds, which are sold at a discount from face value and do not pay any coupon interest. At maturity, the investor receives the full face value. The U.S. dollar, Swiss francs, and Euro have been the most common currencies denominating straight fixed-rate bonds in recent decades.

Floating-rate notes

Increasingly popular are floating-rate notes (FRNs) which are Eurobonds on which the interest rate is adjusted every three to six months in line with changes in a key interest rate such as LIBOR. Floating-rate notes are typically medium-term bonds, with maturities between 1 and 10 years. Coupon payments on FRNs are usually quarterly or semiannual and in accord with the reference rate. Common reference rates are 3-month and 6-month LIBOR. Most companies pay a spread above the relevant LIBOR rate, which reflects the company's credit risk. If an investor needs to preserve the principal value of the investment when he likes to liquidate the investment prior to the maturity of the bonds, the FRNs are a good choice. FRNs are the second most common type of Eurobond issues.

Equity-linked bonds

Equity-linked bonds are associated with the right to acquire equity stock in the issuing company. It consists of two closely related bonds: convertible bond and bond with warrants. The first is a straight bond that can be directly convertible into a specified number of shares. The second has detachable warrants containing the acquisition rights, which grants the bondholder the right to purchase a certain amount of common stocks of the company at a specified price. Equity-linked bonds usually pay a below-market rate of interest with holders attracted by the potential gain on the possibility of a share price conversion.

The difference between the market value of the convertible bond and that of the straight bond involves the value of the conversion option. Companies often issue convertible bonds and warrants when it is difficult to assess the riskiness of the debt, such as when the firm is involved in projects with very uncertain cash flows or when investors are worried that managers may not act in their interests. The convertible bond gives investors a piece of the equity action when the projects turn out to be successful. While rapidly growing firms with heavy capital expenditures find the lower interest rates paid on these bonds to be particularly helpful, convertible bonds are not cheap debt because the firm also issues a valuable conversion option.

International Stock Market

Stocks are issued by firms that raise long-term funds. Stocks are purchased by investors that want to invest long-term funds and obtain partial ownership in firms. Stock markets are for trading company equities and derivatives at an agreed price. MNCs and domestic firms usually obtain long-term funding by issuing stock locally. They can also raise funds to float stock issues in international stock markets. The world capital markets experienced greater global integration during the last several decades. Nowadays many firms, especially the firms in emerging market economies, have obtained funds from developed foreign markets through international stock offerings. Two reasons can explain that firms decide to issue their stocks overseas. First, a firm can increase public awareness of the company and its products through international stock offerings. The name recognition of the company established in a new capital market paves the way for the firm to source new equity or debt capital from local investors as demands dictate. Second, having its stocks listed on foreign exchanges expands the investor base for the firm's stock, thus potentially increasing the market price of its stock because of increased demand. Additionally, greater market demand and a broader investor base improve the price liquidity of the stock.

Roughly one-third of the countries in the world has a stock market, and each of these markets has an index which measures the level of fluctuation in all stock values. Most are value-weighted indexes like the S&P 500. Listings of world's major stock market indexes are in newspapers such as *The Wall Street Journal* or *the Financial Times*, as well as online at web sites.

Those indexes in **Exhibit 7.3** give some sense of the behavior of stock markets during 2020. The index levels (in column 3) don't mean much, since the indexes themselves aren't comparable. Instead, the percentage changes in these indexes (in column 5) are important because they tell us how performed a particular market has. For example, the U.S. Nasdaq composite index increased 42.95% in the year of 2020. The Asia-Pacific region generally experienced healthy growth of their stock market. The stock index in South Korea, Japan and China increased 27.96%, 15.65% and 12.45% respectively.

The performance of all the world's stock markets is directly responsible for a significant amount of the world's economic condition — whether it be healthy, ailing, or trending sideways. In general, stock market growth is a leading indicator that the state of an economy is flourishing, while declining trends indicate of economic slowdown. For instance, rising stock prices tend to be associated with increased business investment and vice versa. Stock prices also affect the wealth of households and their consumption. Some commentators and economists suggest that stock markets often predict what will happen in the economy of that country around six months later.

We introduce four major stock markets in the world in this section, that is: the United States stock market, the Japanese stock market, the United Kingdom stock market and the

Exhibit 7.3 World Stock Market Index
(December 29, 2020)

Country or region	Index	Close	Change (%)	YTD Change (%)
U.S.	S&P 500	3740.25	0.13	15.42
	Nasdaq comp	12877.32	−0.17	42.95
	Dow Jones	30410.53	0.02	6.14
Canada	S&P/TSX comp	17561.78	−0.35	2.28
Brazil	Sao Paulo Bovespa	118837.95	−0.24	2.02
Mexico	S&P/BMV IPC	44713.13	1.89	1.01
France	CAC 40	5611.79	0.42	−7.05
Germany	DAX	13761.38	−0.21	3.18
Italy	FTSE MIB	22259.35	−0.13	−6.22
Spain	Ibex	8174.8	0.24	−15.73
U.K.	FTSE 100	6602.65	1.55	−13.56
Europe	FTSE Eurofirst 300	1547.30	0.75	−5.55
China	Shanghai Composite	3379.04	−0.54	12.45
Hong Kong	Hang Seng	26568.49	0.96	−5.87
India	BSE Sensex	47613.08	0.55	14.52
Japan	Nikkei 225	27568.15	2.66	15.65
Singapore	FTSE Straits Times	2848.14	0.28	−11.63
South Korea	Kospi	2820.51	0.42	27.96

Source: *Financial Times*, December 30, 2020.

emerging markets. **Exhibit 7.4** provides a summary of the world's major stock exchanges. Numerous other exchanges also exist. Stock markets in different countries differ in many ways. Their structures, trading practices, listing requirements, tax treatments and regulatory systems are all different. The United States has by far the largest equity market, with a total

Exhibit 7.4   World Major Stock Exchanges

Rank	Stock Exchange	Market Capitalization (billion dollars)
1	NYSE	30,923
2	NASDAQ	13,057
3	Tokyo Stock Exchange	5,679
4	Shanghai Stock Exchange	4,026
5	Hong Kong Stock Exchange	3,936
6	Euronext	3,927
7	London Stock Exchange	3,767
8	Shenzhen Stock Exchange	2,504
9	Toronto Stock Exchange	2,246
10	Bombay Stock Exchange	2,056

Source: www.yicai.com.

market capitalization of more than $44 trillion at the end of 2020. Japan was second at $5.7 trillion and China was third at $6.5 trillion. The list includes several emerging equity markets such as China, India, Brazil and South Africa. The new stock markets in emerging economies enable foreign firms doing business in those countries to raise large amounts of capital by issuing stock there.

U.S. Stock Markets

The U.S. stock markets are composed of several main stock exchanges: the New York Stock Exchange (NYSE), the NASDAQ, the American Stock Exchange (AMEX) and other smaller exchanges.

The NYSC was formed in 1792. Members trade stocks listed on the NYSE in a centralized continuous auction market at a designated location on the trading floor, called a post, with brokers representing their customers' buy and sell orders. A single specialist is the market maker for each stock. A member firm may be designated as a specialist for the common stock of more than one company, that is, several stocks can trade at the same post. But only one specialist is designated for the common stock of each listed company.

As explained earlier, specialists are dealers or market makers assigned by the NYSE to conduct the auction process and maintain an orderly market in one or more designated stocks. Specialists may act as both a broker and a dealer. In their role as a broker or agent, specialists transact customer orders in their assigned stocks, which arrive at their post electronically or are entrusted to them by a floor broker to be executed if and when a stock reaches a price specified by a customer (limit or stop order). As a dealer or principal, specialists buy and sell shares in their assigned stocks for their own account as necessary to maintain an orderly market. Specialists must always give precedence to public orders over trading for their own account.

Specialists balance buy and sell orders at the opening of the trading day in order to arrange an equitable opening price for the stock. They participate in the opening of the market only to the extent necessary to balance supply and demand. Although trading throughout the day via a continuous auction-based system, the opening is conducted via a single-priced call auction system, as determined by the specialists.

NYSE trading officials oversee the activities of the specialist and trading-floor brokers. Approval from these officials must by sought for a delay in trading at the opening or to halt trading during the trading day when unusual trading situations or price disparities develop.

In 2007 the New York Stock Exchange was merged with Paris-based Euronext, a pan-European stock exchange, to became the first international operator of major exchanges. It is the largest stock exchange in the world with approximately $31,000 billion market capitalization (see Exhibit 7.4). The organization of secondary markets for stocks and other securities is changing rapidly. More recently, **electronic communication networks (ECNs)** have enabled traders (or their brokers) to find counterparties who wish to trade in specific stocks, including those listed on an exchange.

The pace of structural change has accelerated dramatically in the past few years, driven by (1) ongoing technological advances in computing and communications and (2) increasing globalization. The former dramatically lowered the importance of a physical location of an exchange — as new technology allowed the rapid low-cost transmission of orders across long distances — while the latter encouraged unprecedented cross-border mergers of exchanges, integrating larger pools of providers and users of funds.

The main index tracking the performance of NYSE is the **Dow Jones Industrial Average Index.**

National Association of Security Dealers Automated Quotation System (**NASDAQ**) is the largest electronic screen-based equity securities trading market in the United States and second largest by market capitalization of $13,000 billion in the world. It is a virtual stock exchange, referred to as an over-the-counter or OTC market. There is no physical location for the Nasdaq, nor are there floor brokers on the Nasdaq. Therefore, Nasdaq is essentially a telecommunications network that links thousands of geographically dispersed market-making participants. Its electronic quotation system provides price quotations to market participants on Nasdaq-listed stocks. Although it maintains no central trading floor, Nasdaq functions as an electronic "virtual trading floor". One difference in the listing requirements for the NYSE and Nasdaq is that profitability is required for companies listed on NYSE but not on Nasdaq. The requirement for market capitalization also differs. The lower listing standards for Nasdaq permit smaller and newer companies to list. **NASDAQ Composite Index** is the index measuring the average performance of the stocks listed on the exchange.

In addition, there are several smaller regional exchanges in U.S, most notably the American Stock Exchange (AMEX), the Pacific Exchange and the Philadelphia Stock Exchange. Their listing requirements are less stringent than those of the NYSE Euronext and they encourage the registration of new companies as well as foreign ones.

The U.S. investment banks commonly serve as underwriters of the stock targeted for the U.S. market. Non-U.S. firms are able to place an entire stock offering within U.S. They also obtain equity financing by using **American Depository Receipts (ADRs)**, which are negotiable certificates issued by U.S. banks representing a specified number of shares in foreign stocks that are traded on U.S. exchanges. The bank holds the foreign stocks in its vault for its customers. The bank also serves as the transfer agent for the ADRs.

ADRs provide an opportunity for investors who want to invest in the shares of a foreign company to buy, hold, and sell their interests in these foreign securities without having to take physical possession of the securities, and while receiving dividends and exercising voting rights conveniently. A holder of an ADR can, at any time, request the underlying shares. Conversely, ADRs enable foreign companies with shares that have not been admitted to a U.S. stock exchange to obtain access to the U.S. public capital market. Usually, only shares traded on a recognized foreign stock exchange are represented by ADRs.

Japanese Stock Markets

The main stock exchanges in Japan are Tokyo Stock Exchange (TSE) and the Osaka Securities Exchange (OSE). Smaller stock exchanges operate in Nagoya and Hiroshima. TSE is the largest stock exchange in Japan. Stocks listed on the TSE are separated into the First Section for large companies, the Second Section for mid-sized companies and Mothers Section for high-growth startup companies.

The TSE is a continuous auction market where buy and sell orders directly interact with one another. The trading of shares is carried out under the "zaraba method", which is similar to an open outcry system. Prices are first established at the beginning of the trading session based on orders placed by regular members before the start of trading. The central book is kept by Saitori members who function solely as intermediaries between the regular members. They are not allowed to trade any listed stock for their own account, nor to accept orders from the investing public. After the opening price is established, Saitori members match orders in accordance with price priority and time precedence.

New public issues in Japan must be approved by the Japanese Ministry of Finance. The Japanese government takes an active role in determining which companies are allowed to issue securities to the Japanese market and in regulating trade in these issues. The main indices tracking TSE are Nikkei 225 Index, TOPIX Index and J30 Index. The Osaka Securities Exchange, on the other hand, mainly deals with derivative products. The Nikkei 225 Futures, introduced at OSE, is now an internationally recognized futures index.

U.K. Stock Markets

The London Stock Exchange (LSE) is the biggest equity market in Europe. LSE plays a vital role in maintaining London's position as one of the world's leading financial centers. One of the characteristics of the LSE is its internationalization. Over 60% of equity trading is the cross-border trading. It is also called the most international stock exchange. Trading in LSE was computerized by the so-called "Big Bang" in 1986. The Big Bang was the reform of British financial system in 1986. The major changes in LSE enacted on October 27, 1986 included the abolition of fixed commission rates charged by stockbrokers to their clients and the abolition of LSE rules enforcing a dual-capacity system. Since 1986 the Big Bang has also been associated with the globalization and modernization of the London securities market. Now trading on the LSE is computerized under the Stock Exchange Automated Quotations (SEAQ) system. Member firms are allowed to act as brokers or as dealers on their own account. The **FTSE 100** and **FTSE All Shares 750** indices are major indices tracking U.K. equities. The LSE plays special role in international finance because of London's role as an international center for currency and Eurocurrency trading.

Emerging Equity Markets

An emerging equity market is a stock market from a developing country. According to the International Finance Corporation, a developing country is one that has either a low ($725 or less per capita in 1994) or middle ($726 ~ $8,955) income[1]. Many emerging markets have grown significantly since 1980's as investors became aware of the benefits of international portfolio diversification. In Asia, China and India have become the world's fourth and seventh largest equity markets respectively. Other Asian countries such as Korea, Malaysia, India, Philippines and Turkey, etc. are all important emerging equity markets. Stock markets in Eastern and Central Europe, Africa, Latin America and Asia are, with few exceptions, still in their infancy. Wide disparities across countries still exist. Some countries have strict restrictions on foreign stock market participation and repatriation of income and

---

1 International Finance Corporation, "Emerging Stock Markets Factbook, 1996".

capital. Others have no restrictions.

Chinese mainland stock market consists of two exchanges — Shanghai Exchange and Shenzhen Exchange. Both were founded around 1990. The Hong Kong Stock Exchange has a much longer history and is considered a separate developed exchange. Chinese mainland stock market is already the second largest in terms of the market capitalization in the world. The huge rise in China's stock market capitalization highlights the extraordinary spread of market-based finance in a country once dominated by centralized-planed economy. In contrast, a stock market decentralizes economic decisions by allowing millions of investors to collectively determine the valuation of firms, thereby directing the allocation of capital.

Despite being one of the top stock markets in the world in terms of market capitalization, the Chinese stock market is far from well developed. For example, only 30% of the market capitalization of the listed companies is tradable (the remainder is mostly owned by government institutions). Since 2008, the regulatory authorities have allowed margin trading of stocks and stock lending, but short selling of stocks remains difficult. Day trading is not allowed. The history of futures and option contracts on stock market index is short. The Chinese market will likely remain underdeveloped until capital controls are lifted and the Chinese currency is fully convertible.

Summary

1. Financial markets are markets for transactions of financial assets and liabilities. They can be categorized according to different standards. The international money market is the market for short-term (usually less than a year) financial assets and liabilities. The capital market is the market for long-term (more than one year) financial assets and liabilities. The bond market is the most important source of capital for companies and governments.
2. Financial market provides liquidity. Liquidity refers to the ease with which you can capture an asset's value. Liquid assets can be quickly converted into their cash value.
3. International money markets are composed of short-term credit market, short-term securities market and discount market. The main instruments in international money markets include international bank credits, treasury bills, commercial papers, and negotiable certificates of deposits (NCDs), repos and banker's acceptance.
4. The Eurocurrency market is a typical international money market in which Eurocurrency, currency held in banks outside of the country where it is issued, is borrowed and lent by banks, corporations, governments and investors.
5. Eurocredit, Eurocommercial paper, floating rate notes, and syndicated credits are just part of the financial instruments traded on the Eurocurrency market.

6. The growth and development of the Eurocurrency market come down to the increased regulation on domestic banking practices by the U.S. authorities, OPEC countries' excess dollars and oil-importing countries' huge BOP deficits, and the rapid growth of international trade and investment.
7. The characteristics of Eurocurrency market are absence of regulatory interference, narrow spread of the bid and ask price of a loan and short-term nature of the loans in this market.
8. Bond market is the most important capital market. Bonds can be categorized according to the type of issuer, priority, coupon rate and redemption features. Domestic bonds and international bonds are classified according to the type of issuer. Domestic bonds are issued by domestic residents, while international bonds are issued by foreign residents.
9. There are three types of international bonds: foreign bond, Eurobond and global bond. Foreign bonds are issued in domestic market by a foreign borrower, denominated in domestic currency, marketed to domestic residents, and regulated by domestic authorities. Eurobonds are denominated in a currency different from the country where the bonds are issued. Global bonds are bonds that can be offered within the Eurocurrency market as well as several other markets simultaneously.
10. Eurobonds are issued in countries other than the one in whose currency they are denominated. They are not traded on a particular national bond market and, therefore, are not regulated by any domestic authority.
11. The Eurobond market is a major source of finance for top quality borrowers such as governments and government agencies of developed countries, international organizations, banks from developed countries and large corporations from developed countries.
12. The advantages to international equity issues are: Issuing internationally makes it possible to issue in larger amounts; it increases and diversifies the shareholder base; it improves the firm's image; it often offers less constraining listing procedures; and the secondary market on international issues is active and liquid, especially on the major international exchanges such as London and New York.
13. For investors, international equities offer the benefits of portfolio diversification and the possibility of favorable tax treatment.
14. The United States, Japan and the United Kingdom are the three major equity markets in the world. The three markets are different in many ways. The stock markets in emerging economies have experienced astonishing growth rate. They have become more and more important for investors all over the world.
15. Although Chinese stock market has become one of the top stock markets in the world, it is far from well developed. The Chinese market likely remain underdeveloped until capital controls are lifted and the Chinese currency is fully convertible.

Key Concepts and Terms

1. American depository receipts (ADRs) — 美国存股证
2. Banker's acceptance — 银行承兑汇票
3. Bearer bond — 不记名债券
4. Big Bang — 大爆炸金融改革
5. Bulldog bond — 斗牛犬债券
6. Call money — 通知存款
7. Capital market — 资本市场
8. Commercial paper — 商业票据
9. Commitment fee — 保证费用
10. Discount market — 贴现市场
11. Discount house — 贴现所
12. Domestic bond — 国内债券
13. Dow Jones Industrial Average Index — 道琼斯工业指数
14. Emerging equity markets — 新兴资产市场
15. Equity-linked bonds — 可转换股份债券
16. Euro bank — 经营欧洲货币的银行
17. Euro commercial paper (ECP) — 欧洲商业票据
18. Eurobond — 欧洲债券
19. Eurocredit (Euroloan) — 欧洲信贷，欧洲货币贷款
20. Eurocurrency — 欧洲货币
21. Eurodollar — 欧洲美元
22. Floating rate notes (FRNs) — 浮动利率债券
23. Foreign bond — 外国债券
24. Front-end fees — 先付费用
25. FTSE 100 — 英国富时100指数
26. Global bond — 全球债券
27. Interest equalization tax (IET) — 利息平衡税
28. Interest-rate risk — 利率风险
29. International banking — 国际银行业务
30. International bond — 国际债券
31. International financial market (external market) — 国际金融市场，外部市场
32. International Money Market — 国际货币市场
33. Lead bank (lead manager) — 牵头银行
34. London Inter Bank Bid Rate and Offer Rate (LIBOR) — 伦敦同业银行拆借利率
35. Liquidity — 流动性
36. National Association of Security Dealers Automated — 美国证券交易商协会自动

	Quotation System (NASDAQ)	报价系统
37.	NASDAQ composite index	纳斯达克综合指数
38.	National financial market (domestic market, internal market)	国内金融市场
39.	Negotiable certificate of deposits (NCDs)	可转让存单
40.	Nikkei 225 Index	日经225指数
41.	Osaka Securities Exchange	大阪证券交易所
42.	Panda bond	熊猫债券
43.	Registered bond	记名债券
44.	Regulation Q	Q字条例
45.	Repurchase agreement (Repo)	回购协议
46.	Reverse repo	反向回购协议
47.	Samurai bond	武士债券
48.	Secured overnight financing rate (SOFA)	担保隔夜融资利率
49.	Short-term credit market	短期信贷市场
50.	Short-term securities market	短期证券市场
51.	Straight fixed-rate bond	固定利率债券
52.	Syndicated credit (Syndicated loan)	辛迪加贷款
53.	Term repo	期限回购协议
54.	Tokyo Stock Exchange	东京股票交易所
55.	Treasury bill	国库券
56.	Treasury bond	政府债券
57.	Underwriter	证券承购商
58.	Underwriting syndicate	承购辛迪加
59.	Up-front cost	初始费，辛迪加贷款中借款人对贷款牵头银行发起大额贷款而支付的费用
60.	Voluntary foreign credit restraint guidelines	自愿国外信贷限制准则
61.	Yankee bond	扬基债券

Questions

1. What is the difference between a money market and a capital market?
2. Define liquidity.
3. What are the components of international money market?
4. What is the difference between the repo and banker's acceptance?
5. What is the most common type of U.S. Treasury debt?
6. What are the characteristics of a domestic bond? An international bond? A foreign

bond? A Eurobond? A global bond?
7. What is a zero coupon bond?
8. How often is the coupon payment on a Eurobond made? Name the two currencies most often used to denominate Eurobonds.
9. What are the benefits and drawbacks of offering securities in bearer form relative to registered form?
10. Why are Euroloans attractive to borrowers?
11. What is a Eurocurrency? How did the Eurocurrency market develop?
12. What is a syndicated loan? What is its purpose?
13. Why can the Eurocurrency markets offer more attractive borrowing and lending rates than the domestic markets for the same currencies?
14. Define the equity-linked bonds. What is the difference between an equity-linked bond and a straight bond?
15. What are the major investors and borrowers in international bond market?
16. When lenders are more optimistic about the future value of a currency than borrowers, what do you think this implies about the likelihood of debt denomination in that currency?
17. Why does the stock market experience dramatic structural change in the past few years?
18. What are ADRs? Why might it be easier for an investor desiring to diversify his portfolio internationally to buy depository receipts rather than the actual shares of the company?
19. Discuss any benefits you can think of for a company to (a) cross-list its equity shares on more than one national exchange, and (b) to source new equity capital from foreign investors as well as domestic investors.
20. Why is Chinese stock market regarded as an underdeveloped market?

Chapter 8
THE BALANCE OF PAYMENTS ADJUSTMENT

LEARNING OBJECTIVES

- Examine the elasticity approach to the balance of payments.
- Discover the effects of devaluation (depreciation) on the balance of payments.
- Understand Marshall-Lerner condition, J-curve effect and pass-through effect.
- Examine the absorption approach to the balance of payments.
- Identify policy instruments adopted by the government to tackle BOP imbalance, such as the absorption instruments and expenditure-switching instruments.
- Evaluate the impacts of devaluation on national income and absorption.

As discussed in the previous chapters, the balance of payments of a country reflects the supply and demand for the domestic currency on foreign exchange market. Under fixed exchange rate system, a country with BOP deficits usually has the pressure to devalue its currency, especially when the country runs persistent deficits on its international transactions. If the exchange rate is not allowed to change, the deficit country needs to make a series of adjustments on its domestic macroeconomic structure. On the other hand, a BOP surplus country has the pressure to revalue its currency. In some cases, the surplus nation also needs to change its domestic economic policies to reach external equilibrium. Under floating exchange rate system, major fundamental balance of payments disequilibrium is resolved through a change in exchange rates. It is usually the case that BOP deficit country's currency loses its value on foreign exchange market, while the surplus country's currency gains value on foreign exchange market.

In fact, no matter what exchange rate system is adopted, both the surplus country and the deficit country are required to reach the balance of payments equilibrium.

Because persistent balance of payments disequilibrium tends to have adverse economic consequences, there exists a need for adjustment.

This chapter examines two influential theories of the balance of payments adjustment in the early days. The elasticity approach to the balance of payments is concerned with how changing relative prices of domestic and foreign goods will change the status of the balance of payments. The theory provides an analysis of how devaluations will affect the balance of payments depending on the elasticities of supply and demand for foreign exchange and foreign goods and services. The absorption approach is a theory that emphasizes how domestic spending on domestic goods changes relative to domestic output. We start the chapter by defining the elasticities of export and import demand and supply. The elasticity model assumes domestic and foreign prices are fixed and changes in exchange rates have an impact on the current account position of a country. Will a devaluation (or revaluation) of the domestic currency lead to a reduction of a current account deficit (surplus)? Then we will learn the Marshall-Lerner Condition, J-curve Effect and pass-through effect of the elasticity approach. Finally, we analyze the absorption model which relates the BOP to income and spending. The model examines the effects of devaluation (revaluation) on domestic income and spending. The absorption approach has important implications for economic policies by the policy-makers.

Elasticity Approach (Relative Price Effects)

Elasticity of Supply of and Demand for Export and Import

Before examining the elasticity approach, we must first understand the concept of elasticity. Elasticity is the ratio of proportional change in one variable and proportional change in another. The elasticity of export (or import) demand is defined as the percentage change in the quantity of export (or import) demanded divided by the percentage change in the price of the export (or import). Algebraically, the elasticity of export demand is written as:

$$E_X = \triangle Q_X / \triangle P_X, \qquad (8.1)$$

The elasticity of import demand is written as:

$$E_M = \triangle Q_M / \triangle P_M. \qquad (8.2)$$

Where E_X: elasticity of export demand;
$\quad$ E_M: elasticity of import demand;
$\quad$ $\triangle Q_X$: percentage change in the quantity of exports demand;
$\quad$ $\triangle Q_M$: percentage change in the quantity of imports demand;
$\quad$ $\triangle P_X$: percentage change in the price of the exports;
$\quad$ $\triangle P_M$: percentage change in the price of the imports.

Suppose, for example, that when the price of imported laptops rises by 5%, the number of laptops imported falls by 10%. The elasticity of demand for imported laptops is calculated by applying **Equation 8.2**:

$$-10\%/5\% = -2$$

The minus sign shows the negative relationship between price and demand. It shows if price goes up by 1 percent, the quantity demanded goes down by 2 percent.

The elasticity of export (import) supply is defined as the same way. It is a measure of the responsiveness of the quantity supplied to a change in price.

If demand is elastic, E_X (or E_M) >1; the proportional rise in quantity is more than a proportional cut in price, so total spent rises as price falls. This is contrasted with inelastic demand, where E_X (or E_M) <1, so total spent falls as price falls. If supply is elastic, an increase in price increases supply more than in proportion. Inelastic supply means an increase in price increases supply less than in proportion. If E_X (or E_M) = 1, it denotes unitary elastic demand (supply), meaning that the percentage change in quantity demanded (supplied) just matches the percentage change in price.

Assumptions of the Elasticity Approach

The **elasticity approach** examines the effects of currency devaluation (depreciation) on a country's balance of payments. A BOP deficit country may improve its BOP status by lowering its relative prices (exchange rates), so that exports increase and imports decrease. The theory is based on the following assumptions.

Assumption 1: Assume that *there are no net capital flows* (KA = 0). Thus, the private supply and demand for foreign exchanges are determined entirely by the current account. Since current account is dominated by the trade subaccount, it implies that the balance of payments is simply sales of the export minus spending on the import.

Assumption 2: Assume that *domestic residents look only at prices expressed in domestic currency*. Thus, in the case of domestic consumers, the demand for import depends only on the price of the import expressed in domestic currency. In the case of domestic firms, the supply of exports depends only on the price of export expressed in domestic currency. Similarly, assume that *foreign residents look only at prices expressed in foreign currency* when choosing the demand for the home country's export (in the case of foreign consumers) or the supply of import to the home country (in the case of foreign firms). Changes in demand due to changes in income are ignored.

Assumption 3: Finally, assume for now that firms set a price for their product and then meet any forthcoming demand. In other words, assume that *supply is infinitely elastic*. This assumption implies that output levels are determined by demand, quantity supplied will not be affected by the changes in exchange rate.

If a country runs BOP deficit, the supply of the country's currency on foreign exchange market exceeds the demand for the country's currency. Or equivalently, the country's demand for foreign exchange exceeds its supply of foreign exchange. The goal of the devaluation is to bring the supply and demand for foreign exchange into equilibrium. Elasticity approach states that the key to the success of the devaluation depends on the price elasticities of demand for export and import.

The Effects of Devaluation or Revaluation

A devaluation on domestic currency will have two effects on the country's BOP. The first is the **price effect** which refers to the decreased quantity received of foreign exchanges after devaluation. This is because exports become cheaper measured in foreign currency and domestic residents will receive fewer foreign exchanges for the same amount of exports than before. Depreciation therefore makes domestic BOP worse. The second is the **volume effect**. It says that the depreciation leads the increase of the export volume because of the cheaper foreign price. In the meantime, imports decrease due to the expensive domestic price. The volume effect may improve the country's BOP.

For example, let's examine **Exhibit 8.1** which lists three possible scenarios after the RMB is devalued. Before devaluation the RMB/U.S. dollar exchange rate stands at ¥6.00/$ ($0.1667/¥), while after devaluation the RMB/dollar exchange rate is ¥7.00/$ ($0.1429/¥). The price of one unit of Chinese exports is ¥6 and the price of one unit of U.S. exports is $2. After devaluation, the RMB price of Chinese exports remains the same, but the dollar price of Chinese exports is decreased from $1 to $0.8571. The RMB price of U.S. exports rises from ¥12 to ¥14.

Exhibit 8.1 Devaluation and the Balance of Payments

Description	Volume	¥ Price	$ Price	Dollar Receipts (+) Payments (−)
Before devaluation the current account is in balance				
Chinese exports	12,000	¥6.00	$1.00	(+) $12,000
Chinese imports	6,000	¥12.00	$2.00	(−) $12,000
Current account				$0
Case 1 Devaluation leads to a current account deficit				
Chinese exports	13,200	¥6.00	$0.8571	(+) $11,314
Chinese imports	5,775	¥14.00	$2.00	(−) $11,500
Current account				−$186

(Continued)

Description	Volume	¥ Price	$ Price	Dollar Receipts (+) Payments (−)
Case 2 Devaluation leaves the current account unaffected					
Chinese exports	13,560	¥6.00	$0.8571	(+) $11,622
Chinese imports	5,811	¥14.00	$2.00	(−) $11,622
Current account				$0
Case 3 Devaluation leads to a current account surplus					
Chinese exports	13,800	¥6.00	$0.8571	(+) $11,828
Chinese imports	5,400	¥14.00	$2.00	(−) $10,800
Current account				$1,027

Before devaluation, China exports 12,000 units of goods and receives $12,000; it imports 6,000 units of goods from America and pays $12,000; so China's BOP attains balance. A devaluation on RMB may have three consequences for China's BOP. First, the devaluation leads to a BOP deficit because the price effect dominates the volume effect. The exports increase by 10% but the dollar receipts reduce to $11,314. In the meantime, the imports only decrease by 3.75%; and the dollar payment is $11,500. Therefore, the devaluation on RMB leaves a $186 deficit on China's BOP. Second, the devaluation leaves the current account unaffected. In this case, the elasticity of export demand is bigger than that in the first case; even the elasticity of import demand is slightly smaller. The dollar payment is equal to the dollar receipt. China's BOP is in equilibrium. Third, the devaluation leads to a current account surplus. The 10% reduction in the quantity of imports coupled with a 15% rise in the quantity of exports results in a $1,027 BOP surplus.

This example shows whether the China's BOP will be improved depends on the elasticities of export and import demand. The more elastic the export and import demand are, the more effective the devaluation is. The general rule that determines the actual outcome of the devaluation is called Marshall-Lerner Condition which will be discussed shortly.

The devaluation also has the so called **terms of trade effect**. The terms of trade refer to the number of units of imports that one unit of exports will buy (or vice versa) and can be calculated by dividing the price of exports by the price of imports. If, for example, the price of one unit of exports is ¥20 and the price of one unit of imports is ¥100, the terms of trade are ¥20/¥100 = 0.2. In other words, one unit of exports will buy 0.2 unit units of imports.

Suppose that supplies of exports can be increased without increasing costs in domestic currency and supplies of imports can be reduced without causing a fall in their foreign currency price. Then the price of exports in domestic currency will remain constant and their price in foreign currency will fall by the full amount of the devaluation while the foreign currency price of imports remains constant. In this case the terms of trade will deteriorate by the full amount of the devaluation. If, for example, the unit cost of exports is ¥6 and the value of the RMB goes from ¥6/$ to ¥7/$, the foreign currency value of an export unit goes from $1 to $0.8571 (6/7). With the foreign currency price of an import unit constant at $2 the terms of trade fall from 0.5 to 0.4286. Hence, the deterioration of the terms of trade due to a devaluation is maximum when supply elasticities are infinite — that is, when the exports and imports of the devaluing country are supplied at constant cost. It is minimum when the supply elasticities are zero — that is, when costs rise proportionately in the devaluing country or fall proportionately in the rest of the world.

Marshall-Lerner Condition

Assuming infinite supply elasticities for imports and exports, **Marshall-Lerner Condition** states that devaluation will always improve the trade balance if the sum of the demand elasticities for import and export is greater than one. That is:

$$E_X + E_M > 1 \tag{8.3}$$

If the sum of the demand elasticities is less than one, devaluation will worsen the trade balance. If the sum of the demand elasticities equals 1, the trade balance will be neither helped nor hurt. The Marshall-Lerner Condition may be stated in terms of the currency of either the nation undergoing a devaluation or its trading partner.

We can judge the theory on intuition. When the demand elasticity for imports is perfectly inelastic and the demand for exports is also perfectly inelastic, the trade balance will not improve. In this case, the import price goes up at the equivalent rate of the devaluation and the total value of imports always increases. Even though the export price falls the volume of export will not increase. Therefore, trade balance worsens. However, if the demand for import is elastic, then there will be a change in the quantity imported. The volume of import decreases. Similarly, an elastic demand for export will have a positive effect. As the foreign price of domestic export, the volume of export increases. The trade balance thus improves.

Empirical Evidence on Import and Export Demand Elasticities

The possibility that a devaluation may lead to a worsening rather than improvement in the balance of payments led to much research into empirical estimates of the elasticity of demand for export and import. During the 1940s and 1950s, there was considerable debate among economists concerning the empirical measurement of demand elasticities. Several early studies suggested low demand elasticities. Those findings led to the formation of the elasticity pessimist school of thought, which contended that currency devaluations and revaluations would be largely ineffectual in promoting changes in a nation's trade balance. From 1960s, most economists estimated the demand elasticities for most nations and found that the elasticities of demand were rather high. For example, a summary by Gylfason (1987) of 10 econometric studies undertaken between 1969 and 1981 has shown that the Marshall-Lerner Condition was fulfilled for all of the 15 industrial and 9 developing countries surveyed, and the results are shown in **Exhibit 8.2**. The results are based on estimates of the elasticities over a two-three-year time horizon. As such, while the table demonstrates clearly that a devaluation will improve the current account over such a time span, it does not preclude an initial J-curve Effect.

Exhibit 8.2 The Elasticity of Demand for Export and Import of 15 Industrial and 9 Developing Countries

	Elasticity of Export Demand	Elasticity of Import Demand	Sum
Industrial Countries			
Austria	1.02	1.23	2.25
Belgium	1.12	1.27	2.39
Canada	0.68	1.28	1.96
Denmark	1.04	0.91	1.95
France	1.28	0.93	2.21
Germany	1.02	0.79	1.81
Iceland	0.83	0.87	1.70
Italy	1.26	0.78	2.04
Japan	1.40	0.95	2.35
Netherlands	1.46	0.74	2.20
Norway	0.92	1.19	2.11
Sweden	1.58	0.88	2.46
Switzerland	1.03	1.13	2.16
United Kingdom	0.86	0.65	1.51
United States	1.19	1.24	2.43
Average	1.1	1.5	2.6
Developing Countries			
Argentina	0.6	0.9	1.5

(Continued)

	Elasticity of Export Demand	Elasticity of Import Demand	Sum
Brazil	0.4	1.7	2.1
India	0.5	2.2	2.7
Kenya	1.0	0.8	1.8
Korea	2.5	0.8	3.3
Morocco	0.7	1.0	1.7
Pakistan	1.8	0.8	2.6
Philippines	0.9	2.7	3.6
Turkey	1.4	2.7	4.1
Average	1.1	1.5	2.6

Source: Gylfason (1987), *European Economic Review*, vol. 31, p. 377.
Note: The above estimates refer to price elasticities over a 2–3 year period. Estimates are based upon the results of a number of different studies. Individual studies give differing estimates on the time periods involved, the econometric methodology employed and the particular data-set used.

The table shows that Sweden's export demand is most elastic. This measure indicates that when the prices of Swedish goods and services fall by 1 percent, other countries' demand for imported Swedish goods and services rises by 1.58 percent. The United Kingdom's import demand is least sensitive to the changes in prices of the import. When the prices of U.K. import increase by 1 percent, the U.K. demand for import decreases by only 0.65 percent.

J-curve Effect

The immediate effect of devaluation is a change in relative prices. Exports will rise because of the cheaper price in terms of the foreign currency; imports will fall due to the higher domestic price. For devaluation to take effect, time is required for change in prices to induce changes in the volume of export and import.

Figure 8.1 is the so called **J-curve Effect** which illustrates that in the beginning of the devaluation the trade balance may get worse for several months and then get better over the longer run. In other words, elasticities are lower in the short run than in the long run, in which case the Marshall-Lerner Conditions may not hold in the short run but may hold in the medium to long run.

The J-curve Effect shows that right after devaluation export and import volumes do not change much so that the country's export revenue declines and the import expenditure does not reduce leading to the current account balance deteriorating. However, after a time lag,

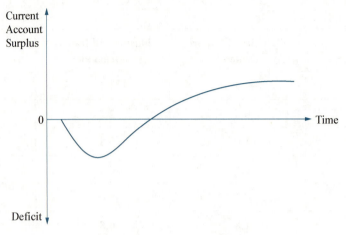

Figure 8.1 J-Curve Effect

perhaps about 18 months, the quantity of exports rises and the quantity of imports falls, and consequently the trade deficit starts to improve and eventually moves into surplus. In general, long-run elasticities (greater than two years) are approximately twice as great as short-run elasticities (0 ~ 6 months). Further, the short-run elasticities generally fail to sum to unity, while the long-run elasticities almost always sum to greater than unity.

J-curve Effect played a role for the U.S. current account during 1985–1987; the deficit initially rose in both absolute terms and as a percentage of U.S. gross national product, but after a lag of approximately two years it improved with long-run elasticities for import and export summing to 1.9 in excess of that required by the Marshall-Lerner Condition.

What factors might explain the time lags in a devaluation's adjustment process? There have been numerous reasons advanced to explain the slow responsiveness of the export and import volumes in the short run and why the response is far greater in the longer run. The most important reason is the **time lag** in consumer and producer responses. It means that both consumer and producer need time to respond to the changed situation.

Time is needed for foreign consumers to switch away from their domestically produced goods towards the export of the devaluing countries even though the prices are cheaper. On the other hand, after devaluation, the devaluing country's import are expensive so the domestic customers may switch away from foreign imported goods to domestically produced goods. It also takes time because consumers will be worried about issues other than the price change, such as the reliability and quality of domestic produced goods as compared to the foreign imports. They need time to find suitable alternatives to the relatively more expensive imported goods and services.

The same time lag exists for producers to respond to the price change. In short-run, the producers of the devaluing country may not have enough time to expand production of exports because of their limited capabilities. Therefore, it is unlikely that exports will increase dramatically at the beginning of the devaluation. As to imports, import orders are normally made well in advance and such contracts are not readily cancelled right after the devaluation. This is called **currency contract period**. The following description shows what the currency contract period is. Contracts are signed at time t_1. After the contracts are established, there is a currency devaluation at time t_2. Then the payments specified in the contracts are due at a later period t_3. The effects of such existing contracts on the balance of payments depend on the currency in which the contract is denominated. Some companies will be reluctant to cancel orders for vital inputs and raw materials which are necessary for making the products. For some firms, there are replacement lags in using up inventories and wearing out existing machinery before placing new orders.

Empirical evidence suggests that the trade-balance effects of devaluation do not materialize until months or even years afterward. Adjustment lags may be for several years. In 1967, the British balance of trade had a $1.3 billion deficit. The Bank of England devalued the pound by 14.3% at the end of 1967 and tried to improve its trade position. The initial impact of the devaluation was negative: in 1968, the British balance of trade deteriorated with a deficit of $3 billion. However, after a time lag, the imports gradually reduced and exports were start to rise. By 1969, the British balance of trade recorded a $1 billion surplus; by 1971, the surplus surged to $6.5 billion. The U.S. balance of trade had similar experiences during the 1980s and 1990s.

The Pass-through Effect of a Depreciation or Appreciation

Economists use the term **pass through effect** to describe the extent to which a depreciation (appreciation) of the currency leads to a rise (fall) in import prices in the short run. Pass-through is important because buyers have incentives to alter their purchases of foreign goods only to the extent that the prices of these goods change in terms of their domestic currency following a change in the exchange rate. This depends on the willingness of exporters to permit the change in the exchange rate to affect the prices they charge for their goods, measured in terms of the buyer's currency.

If there is complete pass-through, a 10% depreciation (appreciation) of the currency leads to a 10% rise (fall) in import prices. If RMB depreciates by 10%, complete pass-through implies the import prices in RMB rise by the full proportion of the RMB depreciation which is 10%. If, however, a 10% depreciation (appreciation) leads to only a 8% rise (fall) in the import prices, then there is only a partial pass-through effect, with the elasticity of exchange rate pass-through being 0.8. Empirical evidence suggests, however, that the more typical real world situation is partial pass-through with significant time lag. For example, in the United States, it is estimated that for every 10% change in the value of the dollar, both the import prices and the export prices change about 6%.

The main reason to explain the partial pass-through is that the producers are willing to cut profits or absorb losses in order to keep its market share. It is not easy for a firm to build up a share of foreign markets. This being the case, a foreign firm may be very reluctant to sacrifice market share in the devaluing country and might respond to reducing profit margin on its exports to the devaluing country. For example, during the 1980s, the U.S. dollar depreciated against the Japanese yen by more than 47%. Prior to the dollar depreciation, Japanese automakers enjoyed a super-normal 12% profit margin on their car sales to the U.S. market — nearly double that of U.S. automakers. After the dollar depreciation, the Japanese automakers kept profit margin thin, cutting their profits by $518 per vehicle. The dollar's depreciation was partly offset by the reducing prices of the Japanese cars.

The exporters of the devaluing country may seek to increase their profit margin so that prices do not fall proportionate to the devaluation in foreign markets. On the other hand, those foreign-import-competing industries may react to the threat of increased exports by the devaluing country by reducing prices in their home markets, limiting the amount of additional exports by the devaluing country.

Therefore, the partial pass-through effect on the price of imports in the short run also explains the J-curve Effect. It will dampen the size and complicate the dynamics and timing of the J-curve Effect. The prices of import do not rise as much as suggested by the devaluation, which makes the trades balance deteriorated in the very short run. However, as the exchange rate depreciation is increasingly passed on over time, this will gradually improve the BOP of the devaluing country.

The Absorption Approach (Income Effects)

The elasticity approach is based on the analysis of partial equilibrium. It focuses on the price effect of a devaluation (revaluation). This theory neglects devaluation induced effects on income and expenditure. It is regarded as the major defects of the elasticity approach. Sidney Stuart Alexander (1952) developed what is called the absorption approach. The theory studies the effects of price changes on the quantities supplied and demanded under the condition that the other relevant variables have been allowed to change. In other words, the absorption approach focuses on the fact that a current account imbalance can be viewed as the difference between domestic output and domestic expenditure (absorption). It poses the problems of balance of payments adjustment in a way which highlights their policy implications, and it allows for conditions of full employment and inflation.

Brief Description of the Absorption Approach

The elasticity approach assumes the relative price effects on the balance of payments. Once the exchange rate effects pass through to import and export prices, import should fall while export increase, stimulating production of goods and services and income at home. However, this does not always seem to occur. If a country is at the full employment level of output prior to the devaluation, then it is already producing all it can so that no further output can be forthcoming. What can happen in this case following a devaluation? The **absorption approach** takes into consideration variations in income and consumption. The theory assumes a country's BOP is the current account, i.e., no capital flows. It states that changes in real income (calculated by constant price) result in changes in a country's BOP. In other words, the balance of current account is viewed as the difference between what the economy produces and what it takes, or absorbs, for domestic use.

According to the theory of macroeconomics, a country's national income (Y) must be equal to its aggregate expenditure (E), that is:

$$\text{National Income (Y)} = \text{Aggregate Expenditure (E)} \tag{8.4}$$

Aggregate expenditure can be categorized into four groups in an open economy: consumption (C), investment (I), government expenditure (G), import and export (X − M). It can be expressed as the following:

$$\text{Aggregate expenditure (E)} = C + I + G + (X - M) \tag{8.5}$$

Since national income equals to aggregate expenditure, so:

$$Y = E = C + I + G + (X - M) \tag{8.6}$$

Rearrange Equation 8.6 yields

$$X - M = Y - C - I - G, \text{ or}$$
$$X - M = Y - (C + I + G) \tag{8.7}$$

(X − M) is the balance of trade which represents a country's current account (CA); Y is the national income, (C + I + G) are the aggregate expenditure on domestic goods and services. The absorption approach defines (C + I + G) as domestic absorption (A), so Equation 8.7 can be rearranged as follows:

$$CA = Y - A \tag{8.8}$$

Equation 8.8 says a country's BOP is the difference between the national income or output and domestic absorption. Then, if

CA > 0, BOP surplus; the country produces more output than it absorbs;

CA < 0, BOP deficit; the country's income is less than its absorption;

CA = 0, BOP balanced; the country national income equals to the total expenditure on domestic goods and services.

The absorption approach argues that a government should implement appropriate policies to erase a country's BOP deficit or surplus. If a country runs BOP deficit, it should adopt economic policies that increase domestic output or reduce domestic absorption. If a country has BOP surplus, it can use those policies to increase absorption or reduce total output.

Policy Instruments

The absorption approach suggests two policy instruments that government can use to tackle current account imbalance. Absorption instruments include fiscal and monetary policies. Expenditure-switching instruments refer to the controls on both trade and foreign exchanges.

Absorption instrument is the instrument that government can use to change a nation's absorption. If a country runs trade deficit, it can adopt restrictive fiscal and monetary policies to reduce domestic absorption. For example, the government can reduce the nation's absorption by cutting its own expenditures on goods and services, or by discouraging households and firms from consuming and investing through high tax rates. The restrictive monetary policy such as high interest rate also effectively limits domestic absorption. However, the restrictive fiscal and monetary policies may also reduce the total output. Even though any such policy will tend to reduce income and employment, it will have an additional attraction if the country is suffering from inflationary pressure as well as a balance of payments deficit. Of course, if a country is suffering from high unemployment, the contractionary fiscal and monetary policy are not appropriate. Moreover, because the total reduction in income and output required to correct a given deficit are larger than the proportion of the expenditure reduction falling on home-produced goods, and because different methods of expenditure-reduction may differ in this respect, the choice between alternative methods may depend on the inflationary-deflationary situation of the economy. Finally, because the accompanying reduction in income may lead to some reduction in the domestic price level, and a greater eagerness of domestic producers to compete with foreign producers both at home and abroad, absorption instrument may have incidental expenditure-switching effects. On the other hand, expansionary fiscal and monetary policies promote consumption and investment and thus increase total output. In most cases, the absorption instrument should be combined with expenditure-switching instrument to realize the goal of high output and low absorption.

Expenditure-switching instrument is the policy that the government can use to alter or switch expenditures among import and export. It seeks to correct a deficit by switching demand away from foreign towards domestic goods; and it depends for success not only on switching demand in the right direction, but also on the capacity of the economy to make available the extra output required to satisfy the additional demand.

The expenditure-switching instrument may be divided into two types, according to whether the policy instrument employed is general or selective: devaluation and trade controls. Devaluation aims at switching both domestic and foreign expenditure towards domestic output; controls are usually imposed on imports, and aim at switching domestic expenditure away from imports towards home goods, though sometimes they are used to stimulate export and aim at switching foreigners' expenditure towards domestic output.

If a country has trade deficit, it can impose trade restrictions on imports and encourage exports. The prices of import are raised up because of the tariffs. People may switch from expensive imports to relative cheap goods and services produced domestically. Tariffs and quotas are the common restrictions on imported goods and services; while the dumping and export subsidies are the usual way a government to help improve trade conditions. **Dumping** means a producer sells abroad at lower prices than at home. **Export subsidy** refers to the special tax exemptions and provision of capital at favored rates granted by a government to increase the volume of exports. The combination of absorption and expenditure-switching in some cases can effectively tackle the BOP disequilibrium.

The absorption approach also considers the impacts of currency devaluation (revaluation). Not like the elasticity approach, the absorption approach focuses on the impacts of devaluation on national income and absorption. It argues that currency devaluation will improve the devaluing country's trade balance only if total output exceeds its absorption level. It implies that the devaluing country should increase its total output, reduce its absorption, or do some combination of the two.

The Effects of Devaluation on National Income

The effects of a devaluation on the current balance will depend upon how it affects national income relative to how it affects domestic absorption. There are two cases faced by an economy: full employment and unemployment. If an economy is already at full employment, there are no unutilized resources available for additional production. Therefore, it is impossible to raise total output in this case. The only way in which devaluation can improve the trade balance is for the economy to somehow cut domestic absorption, freeing resources needed to produce additional export goods and import substitutes.

When an economy operates below full capacity, it can direct idle resources into the production of goods for exporting after devaluation if Marshall-Lerner Condition is fulfilled. The devaluation has the **employment effect** which means the devaluation brings more national income. In addition, the increased output will divert spending away from imports to domestically produced substitutes. The impact of the devaluation is thus to expand total output as well as to increase the domestic absorption. The question is whether devaluation improves a country's current account balance.

Since the absorption also rises because of the increased income, the increased absorption should be less than the increased income if current account improves. Otherwise the current account worsens. The **marginal propensity to absorb** is the ratio of additional absorb to the additional income. If this ratio is great than 1, additional absorb is greater than additional income, the current account is not likely to improve. Only if the marginal propensity to absorb is less than 1, the current account will get better. People may think that the marginal propensity to absorb is always less than unity. However, it is not necessary the case. For example, unemployed workers who obtain jobs are likely to have a high propensity to consume. They may decide to spend more than their income by borrowing against future prospective income. Similarly, as the economy expands firms' expenditure may exceed their revenues as they undertake significant investment in the expectation of high future profits. Hence, it is conceivable in the short run that the marginal propensity to absorb could be greater than unity, so that a rise in income leads to a deterioration in the current account.

Another effect of devaluation on national income concerns the **terms of trade effect**. Since the terms of trade deteriorate after devaluation, the real national income thus decreases because more units of exports have to be given to obtain a unit of imports.

Overall, the effects of a devaluation on the income of the devaluing country are ambiguous. Even if there are increased net export earnings, the negative terms of trade works to reduce national income.

The Effects of a Devaluation on Direct Absorption

For the moment, let us assume that the net effect of a devaluation on income is zero. This being the case, we must consider the effect of the devaluation on direct absorption. If the devaluation reduces direct absorption, then a devaluation will lead to an improvement in the current balance, whereas if direct absorption increases then the devaluation will lead to a deterioration of the current account. Let us now consider possible ways in which a devaluation can be expected to impact upon direct absorption.

The first and most important effect of a devaluation on direct absorption is the **income redistribution effect**. If Marshall-Lerner Condition is fulfilled, exporters and import-competing firms should experience an increase in income due to the expansion in export industries and import-competing industries. On the other hand, domestic consumers should experience a reduction in income because of the higher prices of import and substitutes. Overall, it is extremely difficult to say whether the income redistribution effect will raise or lower absorption. When the general price level rises, some people tend to reduce their consumption. Other people may like to absorb more.

The second effect of a devaluation on direct absorption is **real balance effect**, which is the effect on spending of changes in the ratio of money balances to income. As prices rise following devaluation, the real purchasing power of the money people already hold goes down. It is expected to make people more likely to save and less likely to spend their incomes. Also, people tend to sell bonds and stocks in an effort to maintain real cash balances. Thus the prices of stocks and bonds fall and the interest rates rise. The rise in interest rates causes a reduction in investment and consumption, so reducing direct absorption.

For the real balance effect to come into play, it must be emphasized that the authorities must not accommodate the increased money demand by increasing the money supply in line with the increased money demand. If they raise the money supply, this would leave the ratio of money to price index constant so that the real balance effect will not come into play.

Hence, the effects of a devaluation on absorption are ambiguous. Nonetheless, the absorption approach has some important lessons for policy-makers. Its central message is that raising domestic income relative to domestic absorption will improve the current account balance. In this respect, a devaluation is more likely to succeed if it is accompanied by economic policy measures that concentrate on raising income while constraining absorption.

Summary

1. A fundamental disequilibrium in BOP has perplexed governments all the time. Two traditional models to solve the problem are popularly known as the elasticity approach and absorption approach. Both models were created to answer the question in an open economy — will a devaluation (or revaluation) of the exchange rate lead to an equilibrium of the current account in BOP.
2. The elasticity approach looks at the impact of changes in exchange rate on the current account. The aim is to restore the equilibrium of the current account through the devaluation (or revaluation) of the domestic currency.
3. Elasticity is defined as the ratio between proportional change in one variable and proportional change in another. The elasticity of export (import) demand is the percentage change in the quantity of the export (import) demand divided by the percentage change in the price of the export (import). The same is true for the elasticity of export (import) supply.
4. The elasticity approach is based on three assumptions. First, there are no net capital flows; second, consumers look only at prices expressed in their domestic currency; third, the supply of exports and imports is infinitely elastic.
5. After the devaluation, prices of domestic exports fall in terms of the foreign currency. It means each unit of exports receives less units of foreign currency than before. This is the price effect of the devaluation and it clearly worsens the current account.
6. The decreased prices of domestic exports encourage foreign consumers to buy more domestic exports. Thus, a devaluation of the domestic currency brings increased volume of exports. At the same time, the increased prices of foreign imports lead to a decreased volume of imports. The volume effect of a devaluation contributes to improving the current account.
7. The impact of devaluation of a currency on terms of trade depends on supply elasticity. If supply elasticity is infinite — that is, when the exports and imports of the

devaluing country are supplied at constant costs, the deterioration of terms of trade is maximum. When the supply elasticity is zero, the deterioration is minimum.
8. The Marshall-Lerner Condition states that a devaluation of the domestic currency will improve the current account only if the sum of the elasticity of the demand for export and import is greater than unity assuming the elasticity of the supply of export and import is infinite.
9. J-curve illustrates that in the short run the Marshall-Lerner Condition may not be fulfilled but in the long run it may hold. That is to say, in a short period of time after the devaluation, current account may worse. Later, it gradually improves.
10. There are many reasons that can explain the J-curve Effect. The most important factor is the time lag in consumers and producers response to the devaluation. Empirical evidence suggests that the trade-balance effects of devaluation do not materialize until months or even years afterward.
11. Currency contract period is one of the reasons to explain the J-curve Effect. In some cases, import orders are normally made well in advance and such contracts are not readily cancelled right after the devaluation. Therefore, imports will not reduce immediately after the devaluation.
12. The pass-through effect describes the extent to which a x% of devaluation leads to a x% of rise in import prices. The empirical study shows the partial pass-through effect on the price of import in the short run will be to dampen the size and complicate the dynamics and timing of the J-curve Effect.
13. The absorption approach regards the current account imbalance as the difference between domestic output and domestic spending. The current account deficit means the expenditure exceeds the income, and vice versa.
14. Policy instruments the government can use to tackle the disequilibrium BOP are absorption instruments and expenditure-switching instruments. The former are generally the fiscal and monetary policies. The later are the administrative measures on trade and foreign exchanges.
15. If a country runs trade deficit, it can adopt restrictive fiscal and monetary policies to reduce domestic absorption. The restrictive fiscal policies include reduction in government spending and raising tax rates. The restrictive monetary policy refers to the high interest rates to encourage people save more instead of spending.
16. The expenditure-switching instrument seeks to correct trade deficit by switching demand away from foreign towards domestic goods. The success of this instrument depends not only on switching demand in the right direction, but also on the capacity of the economy to make available the extra output required to satisfy the additional demand.
17. One of the expenditure-switching instruments is devaluation. It aims at switching both domestic and foreign expenditure towards domestic output. Another is trade

controls. Trade controls are usually imposed on imports and aim at switching domestic expenditure away from imports towards home goods.

18. The absorption approach thinks that a devaluation has impacts on both the national income and direct absorption. The effects of a devaluation on income include employment effect and terms of trade effect. Whether those effects will raise or lower income depend on many factors, such as the marginal propensity to absorb.

19. The effects of a devaluation on direct absorption include income redistribution effect and real balance effects. Generally speaking, the effects of a devaluation on direct absorption are ambiguous. Nonetheless, the absorption approach has some important lessons for policy-makers. Its central message is that raising domestic income relative to domestic absorption will improve the current account balance. In this respect, a devaluation is more likely to succeed if it is accompanied by economic policy measures that concentrate on raising income while constraining absorption.

Key Concepts and Terms

1. Absorption approach — 吸收论
2. Absorption instrument — 吸收工具
3. Currency contract period — 货币合约期
4. Dumping — 倾销
5. Elasticity — 弹性
6. Elasticity approach — 弹性论
7. Elasticity of demand (supply) — 需求（供给）弹性
8. Employment effect — 就业效应
9. Expenditure-switching instrument — 支出转换工具
10. Export subsidy — 出口补贴
11. Income effect — 收入效应
12. Income redistribution effect — 收入再分配效应
13. Import tariff — 进口关税
14. Import quota — 进口配额
15. J-curve Effect — J曲线效应
16. Marginal propensity to absorb — 边际吸收倾向
17. Marshall-Lerner Condition — 马歇尔－勒纳条件
18. Pass-through effect — 传导效应
19. Price effect — 价格效应
20. Real balance effect — 实际余额效应
21. Real income — 实际收入

22. Terms of trade　　　　　　　　　　　　贸易条件
23. Terms of trade effect　　　　　　　　　贸易条件效应
24. Time lag　　　　　　　　　　　　　　时滞
25. Volume effect　　　　　　　　　　　　数量效应

Questions

1. Define the elasticity of export demand and the elasticity of import demand.
2. How does a currency depreciation or devaluation affect a nation's balance of trade according to the elasticity approach?
3. If volume effect dominates price effect after a devaluation, is the sum of elasticities of the export and import demand greater or less than 1?
4. What is Marshall-Lerner Condition? How can we use the Marshall-Lerner Condition to explain the J-curve Effect?
5. Define the terms of trade. How does a devaluation affect the terms of trade of the devaluing country?
6. What is J-curve Effect?
7. What is time lag? What factors might explain the time lags in a devaluation's adjustment process?
8. Explain the currency contract period.
9. How do elasticities of supply and demand for import and export affect the supply and demand for foreign exchanges?
10. What is complete pass-through and partial pass-through?
11. Explain the reasons of partial pass-through effect on the price of imported goods in the short-run.
12. Suppose that U.S. is considering devaluing its dollar against a foreign currency to improve the trade balance. What type of contracting would have a negative effect on the trade balance?
13. According to the absorption approach, does it make any difference whether a nation devalues its currency when the economy operates at less than full capacity versus at full capacity?
14. How can devaluation-induced changes in household money balances promote BOP equilibrium?
15. If Chinese government promotes an advertising campaign called "Buy Chinese products", what is the potential impact the campaign might have on China's balance of payments in the context of the absorption approach?
16. How does the absorption approach think of the terms of trade when a country

devalues its currency?
17. Is marginal propensity to absorb necessarily greater than 1? List several possible facts to prove your statement.
18. Explain the real balance effect of a devaluation.
19. Define income redistribution effect of a devaluation.
20. According to the absorption approach, what kind of economic policies should the government adopt when a nation runs BOP deficit with full employment?

Chapter 9

EQUILIBRIUM IN BALANCE OF PAYMENTS AND EXCHANGE RATE

LEARNING OBJECTIVES

- Examine the monetary approach to the balance of payments and the exchange rate.
- Show how the monetary policies influence a country's BOP and the adjustment process under different exchange rate system.
- Learn how the exchange rate is determined in a two-country monetary model.
- Examine the portfolio balance approach to the exchange rate determination.
- Understand the wealth identity and the relationship of each variable in the portfolio balance model.
- Know central bank's sterilized and non-sterilized intervention in the foreign exchange market.

Chapter 8 introduced two traditional approaches to balance of payments. Both elasticity and absorption approaches do not consider the monetary consequences of the devaluation (revaluation). Both theories also neglect the implications of capital movements for the balance of payments and exchange rates. In this chapter, we shall look at one of the most influential theories of the balance of payments adjustment and determination of exchange rates known as the monetary approach and another modern theory of the exchange rate determination — the portfolio balance of approach. The monetary theory was pioneered by Marina Whitman (1975), Jacob Frenkel and Harry Johnson (1976). The portfolio balance approach was established in 1983. The fundamental basis of the monetary approach is that the balance of payments is essentially a monetary phenomenon. Not only is the balance of payments a measurement of monetary flows, but such flows can only be explained by disequilibrium in the stock demand for and supply of money. On the other hand, the portfolio balance approach extends the monetary approach. It indicates the securities market plays an important role in the exchange rate determination because of the imperfect substitutability between domestic and foreign financial assets.

We will begin to learn the monetary model from the Cambridge Equation. The relationship between money supply and balance of payments will be examined. We'll analyze the model under the different exchange rate system and how the model works in a two-country situation. Second, the portfolio balance approach will be introduced through a wealth identity. We'll discuss the asset demand function, the effects of changes in money, domestic and foreign securities on the exchange rates. Finally, we will explain the sterilized and non-sterilized foreign exchange market intervention by the central bank.

The Monetary Approach

The basic premise of the monetary approach is that a monetary disequilibrium — that is, differences existing between the amount of money people wish to hold and the amount supplied by the monetary authority (the central bank) determines a country's balance of payments or changes in exchange rates. Put differently, if people demand more money than is being supplied by the central bank, then the excess demand for money would be satisfied by inflows of money from abroad or an appreciation of the currency. On the other hand, if the central bank is supplying more money than is demanded, the excess supply of money is eliminated by outflows of money to other countries or a depreciation of the currency. Thus the monetary approach emphasizes the determinants of money demand and money supply. The monetary approach can be analyzed separately for fixed and floating exchange rates. If the exchange rate is fixed, then the monetary approach pertains to the balance of payments. In such a case we call the approach the monetary approach to balance of payments. In contrast, if exchange rate is floating then the approach explains exchange rate movements and is called the monetary approach to exchange rates. We are going to explain the two approaches separately.

The Money Demand

The **monetary approach** postulates that changes in a country's BOP and the exchange rate are a monetary phenomenon. That is, BOP disequilibrium or exchange rate variations result from changes in the country's quantity of money supplied and demanded. The monetary approach begins with the Cambridge Equation, which is the **quantity theory of money** developed in the late nineteenth century.

The **Cambridge Equation** is written as follows:

$$M^d = k \times P \times y \tag{9.1}$$

where M^d is the demand for nominal money balances that people desire to hold, P is the domestic price level, y is real domestic income (calculated by constant price), and k is a parameter reflecting economic structure and monetary habits, namely the ratio of desired money balances to income (k > 0). Multiplying P by y yields the nominal income. This equation states that people hold a fraction of their nominal incomes as money balances.

The Cambridge Equation suggests that the demand for money is a positive function of the domestic price. A rise in the domestic price level will lead to an equally proportionate increase in the demand for money. The demand for money is also positively related to real domestic income; a rise in real income will, ceteris paribus, lead to an increase in the transactions demand for money.

The Money Supply

The domestic money supply in the economy is made up of two components:

$$M^s = m \times (D + R) \tag{9.2}$$

where M^s is the quantity of money supplied by the monetary authority, D is the domestic credits and R is the reserves of foreign currencies. The domestic credits and the foreign exchange reserves (D + R) constitute a country's **monetary base**. m is the **monetary multiplier**.

When the central bank conducts an open-market operation, that is: purchasing treasury bonds held by the public, it puts the domestic credits into circulation. Also, if central bank buys foreign exchanges on foreign exchange market, the central bank's monetary liabilities increase. Therefore, any increase in the domestic money supply can come about through either an open-market operation or a foreign exchange operation. The central bank plays a very important role in the determination of a country's money supply. It usually influences the quantity of money supplied through controlling the monetary base.

The Relationship between The Money Supply and The BOP

The equilibrium condition in money market is that the money demand equals the money supply, that is:

$$M^d = M^s \tag{9.3}$$

The money supply is composed of domestic credits and foreign exchange reserves as Equation 9.2 indicates. Now we substitute **Equation 9.2** into **Equation 9.3**.

$$M^d = m \times (D + R) \tag{9.4}$$

Suppose m = 1, R = M^d − D, that is to say, if money demand exceeds nominal money supply, foreign exchange reserve is positive, and BOP has surplus; if nominal money supply exceeds money demand, foreign exchange reserve is negative, BOP runs deficit.

Therefore, the monetarists view balance of payments surplus and deficit as monetary flow due to stock disequilibrium in the money market. A deficit in the balance of payments is due to an excess of the money supply in relation to money demand, while a surplus in the balance of payments is monetary flow resulting from an excess demand for money in relation to the stock money supply. Thus the balance of payments disequilibrium is merely a reflection of the disequilibrium in the money market. In this sense the monetary flows are the "autonomous" items in the balance of payments while the purchases and sales of goods/services and investments (long, medium and short-term) are viewed as the accommodating items, this is completely the reverse of the Keynesian approach which views the current account items as the autonomous and capital account and reserve changes as the accommodating items. This different way of looking at the balance of payments statistics is sometimes contrasted by saying that Keynesians look at the balance of payments statistics from the "top down" (that is, the current account) while the monetarists look from the "bottom up" (the change in reserves).

Monetarists observe that the overall balance of payments can be thought of as consisting of the current account balance, financial and capital account balance and changes in the authorities' reserves. That is:

$$BOP = CA + KA + \triangle R = 0$$

so that:

$$CA + KA = - \triangle R \tag{9.5}$$

where CA is the current account balance, KA is the financial and capital account balance and $\triangle R$ is the change in the authorities reserves. If the recorded $\triangle R$ in the balance of payments accounts is positive, this means that the combined current account and capital account are in deficit. This implies that reserves have fallen as the authorities have purchased the home currency with foreign currency reserves. If the recorded R is negative, the combined current account and capital account is in surplus. The adjustment mechanism that ensures the equilibrium of money supply and money demand will vary with the exchange rate system. With fixed exchange rates, money supply adjusts to money demand through international flows of money via balance of payments imbalances. With floating exchange rates, money demand will be adjusted to a money supply set by the central bank via exchange rate changes. Those two cases will be analyzed subsequently.

Monetary Approach under Fixed Exchange Rate System

Now we substitute the equation for the Cambridge Equation and the money supply Equation 9.2 into the Equation 9.3 to yield:

$$k \times P \times y = m \times (DC + R) \tag{9.6}$$

Monetary approach assumes the purchasing power parity holds. The domestic price level (P) in Equation 9.5 can then be replaced by the product of foreign price level times the exchange rate ($S^{d/f}P^f$). That is:

$$k \times S^{d/f}P^f \times y = m \times (DC + R) \tag{9.7}$$

Equation 9.7 is used by monetarists to explain how key variables affect a country's balance of payments and the exchange value of its currency. Now let's analyze the effects of a devaluation under fixed exchange rate. The immediate effect of a devaluation of the exchange rates is to make domestic goods more competitive compared with foreign goods. There is an increase in the demand for the domestic currency on foreign exchange market. This means the left side of Equation 9.7 is greater than the right side, or money demand exceeds money supply. The benefit of the devaluation is that the balance of payments moves into surplus as exports exceed imports. To prevent the domestic currency appreciating, the authorities have to purchase foreign currency with domestic currency. The increase in reserves leads to an expansion of the domestic money supply which in turn raises aggregate demand for domestically produced goods. This pushes up domestic prices. Once the domestic price level is restored to PPP level and the money supply has increased until the right side of Equation 9.7 equals to the left side, the competitive advantage of the devaluation has been offset. The balance of payments will be back in equilibrium as money supply is once again equal to money demand. So the monetarists think the surplus resulting from a devaluation is merely a transitory phenomenon.

Now consider what happens if the central bank purchases treasury bonds to raise domestic credit (D) under fixed exchange rate system. The immediate effect of an expansionary open market operation is that domestic residents have excess real money balances, that is, the money supply exceeds money demand. To reduce their excess real balances residents increase aggregate demand for goods and services, this puts upward pressure on domestic goods prices. Since the domestic prices increase, exports decrease, and the balance of payments moves into deficit. That is:

$$k \times S^{d/f}P^f \times y < m \times (D\uparrow + R) \text{ (BOP deficit)}$$

To prevent a devaluation of the domestic currency, the authorities have to intervene to sell foreign exchange reserves so that (R) is down. The purchase back of the domestic money on foreign exchange market starts to reduce the excess money supply and at the same time reduce the aggregate demand for domestic goods. The money supply and domestic price level will fall back to its original level and the economy is restored to equilibrium as shown by the following:

$$k \times S^{d/f}P^f \times y = m \times (D\uparrow + R\downarrow)$$

In the long run, the price level, output level and money stock return to their initial levels. Thus, an increase in the monetary base will, because of the foreign exchange intervention it necessitates to maintain a fixed exchange rate, lead to an equivalent fall in the foreign exchange reserves. And the fall in reserves leads to a return of the money stock to its original level. In other words, the increased credits are offset by the reduced foreign exchange reserves. The central bank will continue to sell foreign exchange reserves until $M^s = M^d$.

Monetary approach regards the balance of payments deficits resulting from the expansion in the money stock to be merely a temporary and self-correcting phenomenon. An expansion of the money supply causes a temporary excess of money and a current and capital account deficit which to maintain the fixed exchange rate necessitates intervention in the foreign exchange market that eventually eliminates the excess supply of money.

We might mention at this point that if the central bank uses the sterilized foreign exchange intervention, the reduction of monetary base will be offset by the further open market purchase of bonds from the public. However, such an open market operation causes a balance of payments deficits requiring a further foreign exchange intervention. Hence, the sterilized intervention means a prolonged balance of payments deficits. The country's foreign exchange reserves will be finally exhausted.

Now let's consider the impact of changes in money demand on BOP. Suppose that instead of a change in domestic credit there is an increase in either the foreign price level or real income which causes an increase in the quantity of money demanded. We will first examine the effects of an increase in income.

The increase in real domestic income increases the demand to hold money so that money demand exceeds money supply. The result is reduced expenditures on both domestic and foreign goods and services and this leads to a fall in the domestic price level. The lower prices of goods and services attract foreigners to purchase more and the balance of payments moves into surplus. To prevent an appreciation of the domestic currency the central bank has to buy foreign exchange with newly created monetary base. The intervention results in a rise in the reserves and in the domestic money supply. The increased money supply leads to a rise in the domestic price level back towards its PPP value. Once the money stock has risen to the point at which money supply equals to money demand, the excess money balances are eliminated. That is:

$$k \times S^{d/f} P^f \times y \uparrow = m \times (D \uparrow + R)$$

Now we examine the effects of a rise in the foreign price level under fixed exchange rate. A rise in the foreign price level implies that the domestic goods are more competitive as compared with foreign goods. This results in reduced consumption of foreign goods creating a balance of payments surplus and an increase in the demand for the domestic currency. To prevent an appreciation of the domestic currency the central bank has to purchase foreign currency with newly created domestic money base. The increased money supply pushes the domestic prices up. That is:

$$k \times S^{d/f}P^{f}\uparrow \times y = m \times (D + R\uparrow)$$

Once, PPP is restored the balance of payments surplus ceases.

The monetary approach has an important implication. The assumption of purchasing power parity implies that the central bank must make a policy choice between an exchange rate or a domestic price level. Fixed exchange rates mean exchange rates are not allowed to change. Maintaining exchange rates implies the domestic price level will correspond to that of other countries. This is the case in which people discuss imported inflation. If the foreign price level is up, then domestic price must follow to maintain the fixed exchange rate. If foreign inflation is determined by changes in foreign money supply, the monetary approach suggests that a country that opts to fix its exchange rate must change its money supply in line with changes in the foreign money supply. Hence, countries that choose to fix their exchange rates give up their monetary autonomy.

Monetary Approach under Floating Exchange Rate System

Under a flexible exchange rate system, a country does not have the obligation to maintain the exchange rate. The R component of the monetary base, therefore, does not change. Equation 9.5 turns out to be CA + KA = 0. This means that any current account deficit or surplus has to be offset by a net capital inflow or outflow of a like amount. There are no changes in official reserves, so there is no balance of payments surplus or deficit.

When the central bank increases money base and creates excess money balance, the demand for both domestic and foreign goods increases. This will lead to a depreciation of the domestic currency. That is: the spot exchange rate, $S^{d/f}$, will adjust to eliminate any monetary disequilibrium. As a result of the excess demand for goods the domestic price level begins to rise and this leads to an increase in money demand. As the domestic price level rises this increases the demand for money leading to a contraction of aggregate demand until equilibrium price level is reached. That is:

$$k \times S^{d/f}\uparrow P^{f} \times y = m \times (D\uparrow + R)$$

For the money demand side, an increase in income under floating rates leads to an increase in real money balances because the increase in real domestic income raises the demand for transaction balances, so that the increased real money balances are willingly held. An increase in foreign price level has the same effects. In both cases, the money demand increases. With constant domestic credit, we have an excess demand for money. As people try to increase their money balances, an appreciation of the domestic currency and fall in domestic price level (to maintain PPP) offset the excess demand for money.

We may conclude that under floating exchange rate system the changes in domestic credit or foreign price level or domestic real income lead to changes in exchange rates. First, under fixed exchange rates the central bank can no longer retain independent control of the money supply. Whereas under floating exchange rates money market equilibrium is restored by changes in money demand brought about by changes in the domestic price level and exchange rate. Second, under fixed exchange rates with an increase in domestic income, final equilibrium is reached via an increase in the domestic money supply and reserves so as to satisfy the increased money demand, while under floating exchange rates equilibrium is obtained by an appreciation of the domestic currency and fall in the domestic price level with the domestic money supply unchanged. Finally, under fixed exchange rates the need to maintain exchange rates means that a country has to accept an inflation determined by the foreign money supply, and monetary independence is lost. Under floating rates, a country has the ability to avoid imported inflation/deflation. The independence of monetary policy depends crucially on the exchange rate adjusting in line with PPP.

Monetary Approach in a Two-Country Model

The monetary approach can be used to predict the exchange rate in a two-country setting. The quantity theory equation says that in any country the money supply is equal to the money demand, which is directly proportional to the money value of gross domestic product. In separate equations for the home country and the rest of the world, the quantity theory equation becomes a pair:

$$M_d^s = k_d \times P_d \times Y_d \text{ (domestic country)} \tag{9.8}$$

and

$$M_f^s = k_f \times P_f \times Y_f \text{ (foreign country)} \tag{9.9}$$

Where M_d^s and M_f^s represent domestic money supply and foreign money supply (measured in domestic currency and foreign currency respectively); k_d and k_f are domestic and foreign money parameter which represents people's behavior. If the volume of transactions increase, k indicates the amount of extra money that people want to hold to facilitate this higher level of economic activity. P_d and P_f are the domestic and foreign price levels; Y_d and Y_f are the domestic and foreign real (constant price) outputs.

Dividing **Equation 9.8** by **Equation 9.9**, we get:

$$(M_d^s / M_f^s) = (k_f/k_d)(P_d/P_f) = (Y_f/Y_d) \tag{9.10}$$

If purchasing power parity holds, which is $S^{d/f} = P^d/P^f$, we can predict the exchange rate based on domestic and foreign money supplies and national outputs. Here we assume the ks are constant numbers both in domestic and foreign countries. Rearranging the Equation 9.9 yields:

$$(P_d/P_f) = (M_d^s / M_f^s)(k_f/k_d)(Y_f/Y_d) \tag{9.11}$$

Equation 9.11 predicts that the exchange rate is determined by several variables. Other things being equal, the faster domestic money supply (M_d^s / M_f^s up), slower growth in domestic real output (Y_f/Y_d up), or a rise in the ratio (k_f/k_d) leads to depreciation of the domestic currency ($S^{d/f}$ up). Conversely, a nation with fast money growth and a stagnant real economy is likely to have a depreciating currency.

For example, if domestic money supply rises by 5%, ceteris paribus, the exchange rate $S^{d/f}$ is likely to rise by 5%. That is, the foreign currency will appreciate relative to domestic currency by 5%. The same is true if foreign real GDP rises by 5% compared to the domestic real GDP growth rate.

An exchange rate will be unaffected by balanced growth. If money supplies grow at the same rate in all countries, leaving M_d^s/M_f^s unchanged, and if domestic products grow at the same rate, leaving Y_f/Y_d unchanged, there should be no change in the exchange rate.

The monetary approach is usually proved to be correct in the long-run trends of the exchange rates. Because over long periods, exchange rates tend to move toward values consistent with such economic fundamentals as relative money supplies and real incomes. For example, Japanese yen has experienced appreciation in the early 1970s. The main reason were Japan's stronger real economic growth, slower money supply and lower domestic inflation rate during that period.

Sterilized and Non-Sterilized Intervention in the Foreign Exchange Market

Suppose domestic currency appreciates in the foreign exchange market. If the central bank buys foreign currency in order to push down the value of domestic currency, the central bank increases the supply of the domestic currency at the same time. This intervention is called a **non-sterilized intervention** which will change the domestic monetary base. Sometimes, central banks use the sterilized intervention to alter the exchange rate without changing the stock of domestic money. The **sterilized intervention** is a situation in which the central bank first buys (or sells) foreign exchanges on the foreign exchange market then offsets the increase (or decrease) in the domestic monetary base by selling (or buying) domestic bonds. The sterilized intervention leaves the domestic monetary base unchanged. Many developed countries, such as the United States and Japan, fully sterilize their foreign exchange market interventions as a matter of routine.

The monetary approach we discussed before suggests that the complete sterilized intervention in the foreign exchange market is ineffective, because it leaves the exchange rate unchanged. For example, if the PBOC (China's central bank) adopts expansionary monetary policy so that domestic money stock increases by ¥100 million, the value of domestic currency will go down because of the excess supply of the RMB. To maintain the exchange value of the RMB on the foreign exchange market, the central bank has to sell the foreign exchanges for domestic currency. Suppose the PBOC needs to sell $15 million to maintain the current exchange rate of ¥6.5/$. The PBOC will receive ¥97.5 million when it sells the U.S. dollar reserves. If it is a fully sterilized intervention which entails an open market purchase of domestic securities, the PBOC will buy domestic securities by the equivalent amount which is ¥97.5 million. Thus the domestic monetary base is approximately the same as before. The value of the RMB still faces down pressure in the foreign exchange market.

However, the portfolio balance approach (We will discuss it in the next section) believes that the fully sterilized intervention is effective. For example, if the central bank buys foreign currency to maintain the exchange rate, it actually purchases foreign-currency-denominated financial instruments such as bonds. The increase in the quantity of foreign bonds demanded causes the depreciation of the domestic currency because of the excess supply of the domestic money. The central bank then sterilizes the intervention through an open-market sale of domestic bonds, reducing domestic credit, and leaving the domestic monetary base unchanged. The increase in the supply of domestic bonds and the increase in the demand for foreign bonds lowers the domestic interest rate and raises the exchange rate. Therefore, fully sterilized intervention is an effective way to influence the exchange rate.

Some economists believe that intervention in the foreign exchange market, whether sterilized or non-sterilized, will have immediate effect on exchange rate. This is because the intervention itself delivers an important signal to the market that the current exchange rate is not what the monetary authority wants to be. This is **announcement effect** or sometimes called "signaling effect" of the intervention. For example, if the central bank sells foreign exchanges on the foreign exchange market, the currency traders have reasons to anticipate appreciation of the domestic currency. They will reduce their holdings of the foreign currencies. If most people believe it is true, they will sell the foreign currencies and cause an actual appreciation of the domestic currency. Several empirical studies conducted by some economists found evidence that the announcement effect does affect the exchange rates. The sizable interventions like those in the 1980s have larger effects on exchange rates than the actual magnitudes of the interventions themselves, especially in the short-run.

The Portfolio Balance Approach

The monetary approach focuses on the equilibrium in the money market. The theory postulates that a country's BOP and the exchange rate are determined by the quantity of money demanded and the quantity of money supplied in the money market. In other words, the monetary approach assumes that domestic and foreign financial securities are perfect substitutes. It implies that the expected yields on domestic and foreign securities are equalized via the uncovered interest rate parity condition. The portfolio balance approach expands the monetary approach by adding money, domestic financial instruments and foreign financial instruments in its model. The portfolio balance approach distinguishes itself from the monetary approach because it allows for the possibility that international investors may regard domestic and foreign securities as having different characteristics other than their currency of denomination, in particular, they might for various reasons regard one of the bonds as being more risky than the other. Therefore, the exchange rate is determined not only by the quantity demanded and supplied of the money, but also by the quantity demanded and supplied of the domestic and foreign securities. The portfolio approach focuses its analysis on the accumulation or decumulation of foreign assets resulting from imbalances in the current account following an operation to influence the exchange rate. A current account surplus means that a country is accumulating foreign assets, while a deficit in the current account corresponds to a decline in foreign assets. The accumulation or decumulation of foreign assets leads to further changes in assets-holders' portfolios with implications for the exchange rate and domestic interest rate, and so on until the model is restored to long-run equilibrium.

Wealth Identity

The portfolio balance approach suggests that the exchange value is determined by the demand and supply of domestic money, the demand and supply of domestic and foreign financial securities (bonds). According to the theory, people hold domestic money for transaction purposes. People are not willing to hold foreign money because the foreign money will not bring any interest income. If people do need foreign money they can obtain it through the foreign exchange market. A country's wealth is assumed to be composed of domestic money, domestic bonds and foreign bonds. The domestic bonds and the foreign bonds have different characteristics other than their currency of denomination. Maybe domestic bonds are more safe than foreign bonds or vice versa. In that case, people may require a higher expected return on the bond that is considered more risky to compensate for the additional risk it entails. To balance the risk and yields on different financial instruments, people desire to distribute their wealth over the domestic money, domestic bonds and foreign bonds. Thus we can express the **wealth identity** as follows:

$$W \equiv M + B^d + S^{d/f}B^f \tag{9.12}$$

Where W represents the people's wealth, M denotes the domestic money (or cash), B^d refers to the domestic bonds which will bring the interest income, $S^{d/f}$ is the spot exchange rate defined as the value of one unit foreign currency expressed as units of domestic currency, and B^f is the foreign bonds which also bring interest earnings. The product of $S^{d/f}B^f$ is the domestic currency value of foreign bonds. It means that the total wealth will increase if domestic currency depreciates against foreign currency, because the depreciation of domestic currency raises the domestic currency value of foreign bond holdings.

The Asset Demand Function

Since people will distribute their wealth over all three types of financial instruments, any change in the components of the wealth has impacts on the exchange rate or the interest rate. We now proceed to analyze the effects of monetary authority's actions on the exchange rate and domestic interest rate.

The demand to hold money is the function of several variables. It is positively related to domestic wealth and income. The demand to hold money is negatively related to the domestic interest rate and negatively related to the expected rate of return on foreign bonds. We can depict money market schedule in the exchange rate-interest rate plane. The money market curve (MM curve) depicted in **Figure 9.1** shows various combinations of the domestic interest rate for which money supply is equal to money demand. It is upward-sloping from left to right. The reason is that a rise in exchange rate (depreciation of the domestic currency) leads an increase in people's wealth as it raises the domestic currency value of foreign bonds people hold. This being the case, people will wish to hold more domestic money, but given the existing money stock the increased money demand can only be offset by a rise in domestic interest rate. An increase in the money supply for a given exchange rate requires a fall in domestic interest rate to be willingly held, implying a rightward shift of the MM curve.

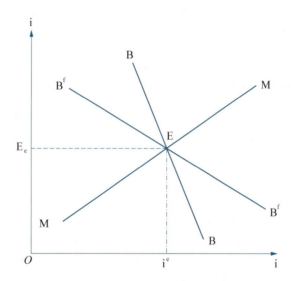

Figure 9.1 The Equilibrium in the Asset Market

The BB curve is the various combinations of the domestic interest rate for which the demand for and supply of domestic bonds are equal. The demand for domestic bonds is positively related to the domestic interest rate and wealth, negatively related to the expected rate of return on foreign assets. The BB curve is downward-sloping from left to right. The reason is that depreciation of domestic currency leads to increase of total wealth and thus increase of holding domestic bonds which, given the existing stock of domestic bonds, can only be offset by a fall in the domestic interest rate which will reduce their attractiveness to investors. An increase in the supply of domestic bond supply for a given exchange rate requires a rise in the domestic interest rate for the bonds to be willingly held, implying a rightward shift of the BB curve.

Also in Figure 9.1, the B^fB^f curve is downward-sloping. The demand for foreign bonds is positively related to the wealth and the expected rate of return from holding foreign bonds, negatively related to the domestic interest rate. If domestic interest rate is high, people prefer domestic bonds to foreign bonds. As more people sell foreign bonds for domestic bonds, domestic currency will appreciate in the foreign exchange market. An increase in the supply of foreign bonds, given the fixed foreign interest rate and a given exchange rate, requires a fall in the domestic interest rate for the foreign bonds to be willingly held, implying a leftward shift of the B^fB^f curve. Notice that the B^fB^f curve is steeper than the BB curve because the two assets are different. Another reason is that changes in the domestic interest rate affect the demand for domestic bonds more than they do on the foreign bonds.

The asset market is in equilibrium when three curves meet at the point E. At point E, the equilibrium exchange rate is S^e, and the equilibrium interest rate is i^e. The actions of the central bank on the money market and bond market will affect the foreign exchange rate.

We now analyze the short-run effects of the operations by the central bank. It should be noted that the purpose of central bank's operations is to depreciate the value of domestic currency in an attempt to improve the international competitiveness of the country.

The Effects of an Operation of Purchasing Foreign Bonds

The central bank first purchases foreign exchanges on the foreign exchange market and then uses them to buy foreign bonds from the private sector. The newly created monetary base increases public's holdings of money and decreases their holdings of foreign bonds. The short-run effects of this operation are depicted in **Figure 9.2**.

The purchase of foreign exchanges on the foreign exchange market leads to an increase in domestic money supply, the MM curve shifts rightward to the M'M' curve. The immediate effect of this operation on the exchange rate is the depreciation of the domestic currency, or, equivalently, the rise of the exchange rate, from S_0 to S_1. The purchase of foreign bonds also pushes the B^fB^f curve move rightward to the $B^{f1}B^{f1}$ curve. This operation has no effect on the holdings of domestic bonds so the BB curve is unchanged. At the new equilibrium point E' we find lower interest rate and higher exchange rate compared to the equilibrium point E. The lower interest rate is necessary to encourage public to hold more money because of the increased money supply. The depreciation of the domestic currency raises the domestic currency value of public's remaining holdings of foreign bonds which can compensate them with the reduction of their original holdings.

The Effects of an Operation of Purchasing Domestic Bonds

The central bank purchases domestic bonds in an attempt to increase domestic monetary base. This time, the public's money holdings increase and bond holdings decrease. The effects of the open market operation are depicted in **Figure 9.3**.

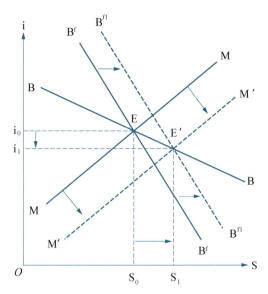

Figure 9.2　The Effects of Purchasing Foreign Bonds

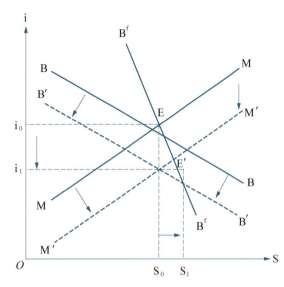

Figure 9.3　The Effects of Purchasing Domestic Bonds

This operation has no effect on the B^fB^f curve so the B^fB^f curve will not change. The MM curve shifts to the right as the money supply increased. The BB curve shifts leftward because an increased demand for domestic bonds which given the existing stock of domestic bonds can only be offset by a fall in the domestic interest rate. The lower interest rate will reduce their attractiveness to investors. As Figure 9.3 indicates, the new equilibrium point E' is reached at the higher exchange rate and lower interest rate compared to the original equilibrium point E. The depreciation of the domestic currency raises the value of foreign bond holdings.

The Effects of a Sterilized Foreign Exchange Operation

If the central bank combines the above two operations by which it sells domestic bonds and simultaneously buys foreign bonds, it is a typical sterilized foreign exchange operation. The result of this operation is the rise in domestic interest rate and the depreciation of the domestic currency, while the monetary base keeps the same as before. The effects of this operation are illustrated in **Figure 9.4**.

The BB curve shifts rightward because of the increased domestic bond supply. The B^fB^f curve shifts to the $B^{f1}B^{f1}$ curve because the public's holdings of foreign bonds reduced. The monetary base is left unchanged because the money used to purchase the foreign bonds is equivalent to the money received from selling the domestic bonds. Therefore, the MM curve remains unchanged. The net effect of the sterilized foreign exchange operation is a depreciation of the domestic currency and a rise in domestic interest rate. The depreciation of domestic currency is required because purchasing foreign bonds causes a shortage of foreign bonds in their portfolios. In order to encourage the public to keep the remaining

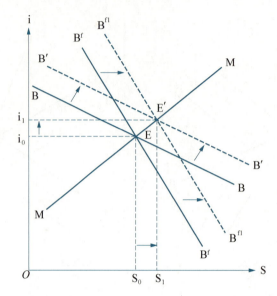

Figure 9.4 The Effects of a Sterilized Foreign Exchange Intervention

holdings, their domestic value of foreign bonds should be raised. The interest rate rises because the excess supply of domestic bonds in public's portfolios depresses the domestic bond prices.

The implications of the portfolio balance approach differ from those of monetary approach if we examine the diagrammatic framework in Figure 9.3 again. The monetary approach assumes domestic and foreign bonds are perfect substitutes, so a swap of domestic for foreign bonds by the central bank is an exchange of identical assets as far as the public are concerned. If the central bank expands money supply through purchasing bonds from the public, the supply of bonds available to the public is reduced. The monetary approach predicts, ceteris paribus, that an increase in money supply will cause a depreciation of the domestic currency by the same percentage as money supply increases. The portfolio balance approach recognizes that in addition to the direct effect of the money supply, there is also an effect of the excess demand for both domestic and foreign bonds. The excess demand for domestic and foreign bonds can be prevented if interest rate is lower or if exchange rate is lower. A lower domestic interest rate reduces the quantity of domestic bonds demanded, helping match the reduced bond supply. Similarly, less of domestic public's wealth in foreign bonds caused by a lower exchange rate helps achieve the preferred relative increase in domestic versus foreign bond holdings. In other words, an increase in money supply causes less of a depreciation of the domestic currency when the domestic bond supply is reduced, as it is with open market operation, than when the money supply is increased but the bond supply is not reduced. That is, unlike the monetary approach, the portfolio balance approach predicts that the effect of changes in money supplies on exchange rates depends on how money supplies are changes. Also, we no longer have a depreciation in the same proportion as the relative growth in the money supply as indicated by the monetary approach in Equation 9.11.

The above analysis focuses on short-run equilibrium. In the long run we should consider the factor of current account balance. The portfolio balance approach is much better than the monetary approach in terms of explaining the exchange rate changes. However, the empirical evidence is not at all clear on this matter.

Summary

1. Monetary approach postulates that the balance of payments disequilibrium is based on a monetary disequilibrium — that is, the amount of money people wish to hold does not match the amount supplied by the monetary authority.
2. The Cambridge Equation shows people hold a fraction of their nominal incomes as money balances. It also indicates that the money demand depends on price level and real income.
3. A country's money supply is composed of domestic credits and foreign exchange reserves under fixed exchange rate system.
4. When the money demand is greater than money supply, the BOP has surplus; if the money demand is less than money supply, the BOP runs deficit.
5. Monetarists believe that the balance of payments consists of the current account balance, financial and capital account balance and changes in the authorities' reserves. The BOP disequilibrium results from decrease or increase of the authorities' reserves. It is completely reverse of the Keynesian Model.
6. Under fixed exchange rate system, expansionary monetary policy leads to the BOP deficit; the depreciation of the domestic currency requires the central bank to defend the exchange rate. The extra money supply is offset by the foreign exchange market intervention. The BOP thus restores equilibrium.
7. Under fixed exchange rate, the increase in real domestic income or increase in foreign price level increases the demand to hold money so that money demand exceeds money supply. The BOP disequilibrium is corrected by the increase in domestic monetary base: the domestic credits or foreign exchange reserves.
8. Under the floating exchange rate system, the BOP disequilibrium is corrected by the changes in exchange rate. When money demand does not equal to money supply, the exchange rate will change until money demand equals to money supply.
9. The monetary approach in a two-country model shows that the exchange rate is determined by the related countries' money supply, economic growth rate and the ratio of desired money balance to income.
10. A sterilized foreign exchange market intervention involves a combination of two

transactions. First there is the purchase or sale of foreign currency reserves, which by itself changes the monetary base. But this is immediately followed by an open market operation of exactly the same size, designed to offset the impact of the first transaction on the monetary base.

11. A non-sterilized intervention, on the other hand, will change the monetary base. If the monetary authority purchases foreign exchanges, the monetary base increases. If it sales reserves, the monetary base decreases.
12. The portfolio balance approach extends the monetary approach by adding domestic money, domestic bonds and foreign bonds in its model. The portfolio approach thinks that the domestic securities and foreign securities are not perfect substitutes. In the short-run, the exchange rate is determined by the changes in domestic money supply, domestic financial instruments and foreign financial instruments.
13. The demand for holding money is positively related to the income and wealth, negatively related to the domestic interest rate and negatively related to the expected rate of return on foreign bonds. The money market schedule (MM curve) is upward-sloping from left to right in the exchange rate-interest rate plane.
14. The demand for domestic bonds is positively related to the domestic interest rate and wealth, negatively related to the expected rate of return on foreign bonds. The BB schedule is downward-sloping from left to right.
15. The demand for foreign bonds is positively related to the expected rate of return on foreign bonds and wealth, negatively related to the domestic interest rate. The B^fB^f schedule is also downward-sloping, but it is flatter than the BB schedule. It shows that changes in the domestic interest rate affect the demand for domestic bonds more than they do on the foreign bonds.
16. Changes in the demand or supply of money, domestic and foreign bonds will shift the relative curves either to the left or right, resulting in the adjustment in the asset market.
17. The implications of the portfolio balance approach differ from those of monetary approach. The portfolio balance approach recognizes that when the monetary authority purchases or sales foreign exchange reserves, the action will have the direct effect on the money supply. There is also an effect of the excess demand for both domestic and foreign bonds. In terms of the portfolio balance approach, sterilized intervention makes more sense.

Key Concepts and Terms

1. Announcement effect   宣告效应，公示效应

Chapter 9 EQUILIBRIUM IN BALANCE OF PAYMENTS AND EXCHANGE RATE

2. Cambridge Equation — 剑桥方程式
3. Monetary approach — 货币论
4. Monetary base — 货币基数
5. Monetary multiplier — 货币乘数
6. Money demand — 货币需求
7. Money supply — 货币供应
8. Non-sterilized intervention — 非冲销式干预
9. Portfolio balance approach — 组合资产平衡论
10. Quantity theory of money — 货币数量论
11. Sterilized intervention — 冲销式干预
12. Wealth identity — 财富恒等式

Questions

1. What is Cambridge Equation?
2. What are the assumptions underlying the monetary approach to the balance of payments? Why?
3. What is the monetarist concept of a balance of payments disequilibrium?
4. "Monetary disequilibrium leads to the balance of payments disequilibrium under fixed exchange rates, and a currency problem under floating exchange rates." Discuss this statement with reference to the monetary approach.
5. How does the central bank control the money supply?
6. What does the monetary approach of exchange rates imply for
   a. Relatively rapid growth in a country's money supply?
   b. Relatively rapid growth in a country's national income?
   c. An increase in a country's interest rates versus interest rates in another country?
7. What is the relationship between the money supply and the BOP?
8. How is the BOP disequilibrium corrected under the fixed exchange rate system?
9. Explain the sterilized intervention. Does sterilized intervention affect exchange rate according to the portfolio approach?
10. What is announcement effect of the foreign exchange market intervention?
11. Why might a sterilized intervention have a greater impact on the exchange rate in times of financial stress than in times of normal market conditions?
12. What does the portfolio balance approach assume? why?
13. Describe the wealth identity.
14. Why does the money market curve (MM curve) slope upward?
15. Why is the domestic bond market curve (BB curve) flatter than the foreign bond market

curve (B^fB^f curve)?

16. Suppose that a central bank buys bonds on the open market and uses money to pay for them, thereby increasing the supply of money and decreasing the supply of bonds. Use the portfolio balance approach to explain what would happen to (1) domestic interest rate, (2) demand for foreign bonds, (3) foreign interest rate, and (4) the spot exchange rate.
17. What are the effects of sterilized intervention according to the portfolio balance approach?
18. Illustrate the RMB exchange rate using the supply and demand framework. Explain the effect of the PBOC open sales of government bonds on the exchange value of RMB.
19. Discuss the following statement: "The foreign exchange policy of the United States is the responsibility of the secretary of the Treasury; I have no comment." The person who made this statement was the chairman of the Federal Reserve Board of the United States.
20. Compare the monetary approach and the portfolio balance approach.

Chapter 10

MACROECONOMICS IN AN OPEN ECONOMY

LEARNING OBJECTIVES

- Review the basics of macroeconomics such as the consumption function, the marginal propensity to consume, the marginal propensity to save and the marginal propensity to import.
- Introduce the IS, LM and BP curves in an open economy.
- Examine the impacts of fiscal and monetary policies on aggregate output or aggregate income.
- Establish the IS–LM–BP model.

The objectives of macroeconomic policy are different for a closed economy and an open economy. A nation that has a **closed economy** (one that is not exposed to international trade and financial flows) is interested in **internal balance** which is a steady growth of the domestic economy with high employed workforce and low inflation. An economy open to international transactions will face different problems than an economy closed to the rest of the world. With an **open economy**, the nation must also consider the external balance. The **external balance** means a nation realizes neither deficits or surpluses in its balance of payments. A nation realizes overall balance when it attains internal and external balance.

Now we are going to survey macroeconomics in an open economy. In a closed economy, only the goods market and funds market should be equilibrium. In an open economy, the foreign exchange market should also be in equilibrium. As we discussed in Chapter 2, a country's balance of payments is linked to domestic saving, investment and output. In this chapter, we will discuss a general framework for analyzing the performance of an economy that is open to the rest of the world. We will also examine the conditions that all the three markets reach equilibrium together.

We first review and outline some basic concepts of macroeconomics. We will derive the IS curve, the LM curve, and the BP curve in an open economy. We then use them to see how changes in government purchases (G) (the part of fiscal policy) and the money supply (M) (the part of monetary policy) affect the equilibrium values of aggregate output (income) and interest rate. Finally, we will establish the IS–LM–BP model.

The Aggregate Demand for the Aggregate Output

An open economy is consists of four groups: (1) households, (2) firms, (3) government and (4) the exporting and importing units. The households and firms together comprise the private sector. The government is the public sector and the exporting and importing units are international sector. These four groups interact in three markets: goods market, funds (financial) market, and foreign exchange market. A healthy economy needs all markets to get equilibrium, that is to say, the supply should be equal to demand in all markets. If the markets are in disequilibrium, the economy will have a lot of problems such as inflation, unemployment and recession, etc. In the case of open economy, it also needs to address the problem of external balance. How does an economy achieve equilibrium in all three markets? What are the equilibrium conditions for all those markets? Before answering these questions, we have to expand our discussion of the closed economy in the macroeconomics to take into account the exports and imports sector.

The Consumption Function

A nation's aggregate output is called the **gross domestic product**, or **GDP**. The GDP can be regarded as the total demand for goods and services by the four groups of an economy. If Y denotes the aggregate output, we can write Y as:

$$Y \equiv C + I + G + X - M \tag{10.1}$$

This identity defines Y as the sum of consumption, investment, government spending and the difference of exports and imports. The right side of this identity represents **aggregate demand** for aggregate output. The first three terms, consumption (C), investment (I) and government spending (G) constitute the domestic demand for goods and services. In an open economy, we need to add exports and subtract imports (X − M).

Now let's review the determinants of the consumption (C) which is the largest part of aggregate demand. It refers to personal consumption expenditures. Consumption decisions mainly depend on income. The income is actually the **disposable income** which is the after-tax income. There is a positive relationship between the consumption and disposable income. Let Y_d denote disposable income, we can then write:

$$C = C(Y_d) \tag{10.2}$$

This is the consumption function. It indicates when disposable income goes up, so do consumption expenditures. Since this equation captures behavior of consumers, it is also called **behavioral equation** by some economists.

For simplicity, assume that points of total consumption, when plotted against total disposable income, lie along a straight line, as **Figure 10.1** depicts. Because the consumption function is a straight line, we can write the following equation to describe it:

$$C = c_0 + c_1 Y_d \tag{10.3}$$

Y_d is the disposable income, C is the total consumption, and c_0 is a point at which the consumption function intersects the vertical axis. The constant c_0 means people would consume even if they don't have disposable income in the current year. c_0 is also called **autonomous consumption**. c_1 is the slope of the function. It is called **marginal propensity to consume (MPC)** which measures the increased consumption due to the increased disposable income. For example, an MPC of 0.85 means an increase in income of ¥100 would increase consumption by ¥85.

The Saving Function

In a closed economy, people have their disposable income either to be spent or saved. If marginal propensity to consume is 85%, it implies that people will save 15% of their additional disposable income. The **marginal propensity to save (MPS)** is the fraction of a change in income that is saved. It is defined as $\Delta S / \Delta Y_d$. The saving function is pictured in **Figure 10.2**. Saving is also positively related to the income. In the figure, s_0 is a point at which the saving function intersects the vertical axis. When people don't have income in

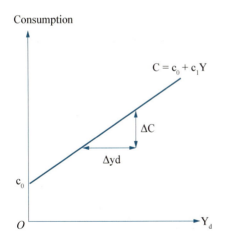

Figure 10.1 **Consumption and Disposable Income**

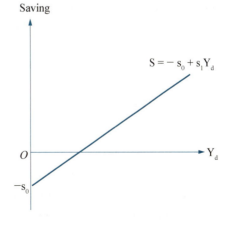

Figure 10.2 **Saving and Disposable Income**

the current period, they have to borrow or withdraw their savings to spend. So s_0 is called dissaving. In this case, they don't have savings, their savings are negative. s_1 is the MPS.

The Investment and Government Spending, Export and Import Function

The determinants of investment (I) and government spending (G) are related to the aggregate output or income. As we know, the investment is also a function of interest rate. The government spending may not depend only on aggregate output, because governments do not behave with the same regularity as consumers or firms. Here we take investment and government spending as given to keep our model simple. Now let us consider export and import in an open economy.

The export represents the demand for domestic products not by domestic households and firms and the government but by the rest of the world. Changes in domestic aggregate output or income have no direct impacts on export. We also take export as given. The import is not a part of domestic output. When we calculate total private sector's consumption spending, investment spending, and government spending, imports are included. Therefore, to calculate aggregate output correctly, we must subtract the parts of consumption, investment, and government spending that constitute imports.

The same factors that affect people's consumption and investment behavior are likely to affect the demand for import. Therefore, the demand for import is basically the function of income. Higher domestic income leads to a higher domestic demand for all goods, both domestic and foreign. Imports are often used as inputs into the production of goods and services that constitute the domestic product. So, a higher domestic income leads to higher import. The **marginal propensity to import** (**MPM**) is the increase in import for the increase in income. The marginal propensity to import is closely related to the marginal propensity to save. MPS tells us what fraction of an additional unit of income is not spent but leaks into saving. So it tells us how much of additional output and income leaks into import. Keep in mind that the sum of three marginal propensities MPC, MPS, and MPM equals to 1. That is,

$$MPC + MPS + MPM = 1 \tag{10.4}$$

The Total Spending Line

Now if we put together all the components of the demand for aggregate output, we derive the total spending line in **Figure 10.3** — the line plots the various components of demand against output. Assuming for simplicity that investment spending, government spending and export are all constant and do not depend on income, we just add the fixed amount of I, G, and X to consumption at every level of income. Hence, we assume that (I + G + X) equals 100. The slope of this line is determined by MPC. An increase in output results in an increase in spending but less than one for one.

Chapter 10 MACROECONOMICS IN AN OPEN ECONOMY

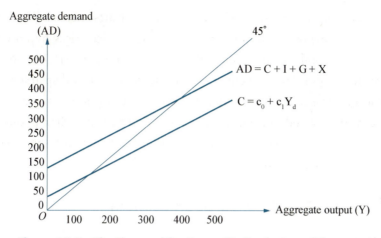

Figure 10.3 The Demand for Domestic Products and Import

However, the line (C + I + G + X) includes spending on imports, which are not part of domestic production. To get spending on domestically produced goods and services, we must subtract the amount that is imported at each level of income. **Figure 10.4** plots the spending line in an open economy (AD = C + I + G + X − M). We assume the marginal propensity to import equals 0.15, which is the assumption that 15 percent of total income is spent on goods and services produced in foreign countries. Imports under this assumption are a constant fraction of total income; therefore, at higher levels of income a larger amount is spent on foreign goods and services. For example, at Y = 300, M = 0.15Y, the amount spent on imports is 45. Similarly, at Y = 400, M = 0.15Y, the amount spent on imports is 60. The slope of spending line (C + I + G + X − M) is less than the slope of the domestic demand line (C + I + G + X). As GDP and total incomes rise, spending on consumption rises by the change in income times the MPC. At the same time, spending on imports also rises. Suppose aggregate output increases by $300 and MPC equals 0.80. Spending on

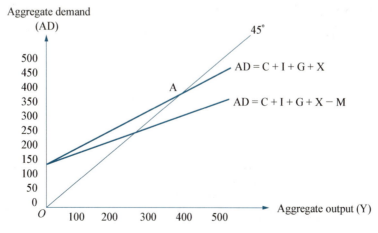

Figure 10.4 The Spending Line in an Open Economy

283

consumption increases by a total of $240, of which imports increase by $45 because the MPM is 0.15. Hence spending on domestic goods and services rises by only $195 ($240 − $45), and the slope of total spending line falls from 0.80 to 0.65 ($195/$300).

When aggregate output (income) equals aggregate demand (total spending), the economy reaches equilibrium. The figure shows that the equilibrium point is point A. If Y is below $300, spending would exceed output, inventories would be lower than planned, and output would rise. At levels above $300, output would exceed planned spending, inventories would be larger than planned, and output would fall.

The IS, LM and BP Curves in an Open Economy

The IS Curve

We assumed the investment as given in the previous model. We now relax this assumption and introduce a more realistic treatment of investment. Investment is actually a function of interest rate. There is a negative relationship between the investment and interest rate. A fall in interest rate is likely to raise investment spending and a rise in interest rate may cut investment expenditure. **Figure 10.5** depicts the investment spending line. The investment spending line is downward sloping from left to right. If interest rate falls from 4% to 3%, investment spending rises from $200 to $300. We can derive the IS curve from the relationship between investment and interest rate.

Increased investment spending means more outputs. Thus there is also a negative relationship between aggregate output and interest rate. This is shown by the **IS curve** (IS stands for investment — saving) in **Figure 10.6**. In domestic goods market, there is an equilibrium level of aggregate output (Y) for each value of the interest rate (r). For a given value of r, we can determine the equilibrium value of Y. Therefore, each point on the IS curve represents the equilibrium point in the goods market for the given interest rate. Changes in any components of the aggregate demand shift the IS curve either to the left or the right. For example, increase in government spending which is the part of the fiscal policy leads to the right shift of the IS curve. This is because when government purchases

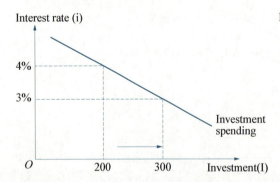

Figure 10.5 The Investment Spending Curve

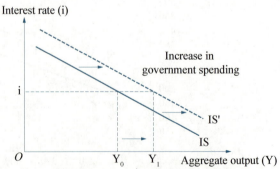

Figure 10.6 The IS Curve Shift

increase with a constant interest rate, the equilibrium value of Y increases. With the same value of r and a higher value of G, the equilibrium value of Y is larger; when G decreases, the IS curve shifts to the left. In the figure, with a given interest rate r, the increase in government spending shifts the IS curve to the IS' curve, the equilibrium value of Y increases from Y_0 to Y_1. An increase in income with a constant interest rate will also make the IS curve shift to the right. A rise in the domestic price level would cause the IS curve to shift left.

The LM Curve

Let's now turn to the money market. The interest rate which is the price of money is determined by the supply of and the demand for money. Money demand is a decreasing function of the interest rate (r). An increase in interest rate decreases the demand for money, as people put more of their wealth into savings. On the other hand, the lower the interest rate, the higher the amount of money people want to hold. The relationship between the demand for money and interest rate is shown in **Figure 10.7**. The vertical axis measures the interest rate, i. The horizontal axis measurers the quantity demanded for the money, M.

For a given interest rate, an increase in income (Y) increases the demand for money. The reason for this is that when Y increases, the demand for money increases because more money is demanded for the increased volume of transaction in the economy. In other words, an increase in income shifts the demand for money curve to the right. In Figure 10.7, for example, at interest rate i, an increase in income results in an increase in the demand for money from M_0 to M_1.

The positive relationship between the interest rate and income is depicted in **Figure 10.8**. This curve is called the **LM curve**. Each point on the LM curve represents equilibrium in the money market for the given value of aggregate output (income).

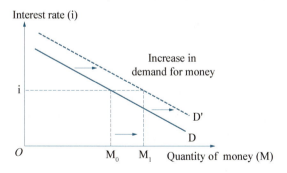

Figure 10.7 The Demand for Money

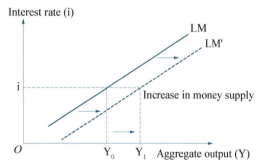

Figure 10.8 The LM Curve Shift

The LM curve is drawn for a specific money supply. If the supply of money increases, then money demand will have to increase to restore equilibrium. This requires a higher Y or lower i, or both, so the LM curve will shift right as Figure 10.8 illustrates. Similarly, a decrease in the money supply will tend to raise i and lower Y, and the LM curve will shift to the left.

The IS-LM Diagram

We now have the elements we need to understand the movements of output and the interest rate. We put together the IS curve and the LM curve in **Figure 10.9**. Since the IS curve represents the equilibrium in goods market and the LM curve represent the equilibrium in money market, the intersection of the two curves shows both the goods market and money market reach equilibrium which is point E. At point E, equilibrium aggregate output (income) is attained simultaneously with interest rate that maintains equilibrium in the money market. Expansionary monetary policy leads to decrease in interest rate and increase in output. The LM curve shifts to the right to LM'. New equilibrium point will be E'. If government decides to raise the tax rates, the impact of this fiscal policy on the economy is the lower income and the lower interest rate. The IS curve thus shifts left to IS'. Therefore, the result of the policy mix is to shift the LM curve rightward and the IS curve leftward. The economy is at new equilibrium point E" with lower interest rate (i_2) and higher output level (Y_1) compared to the original equilibrium point E.

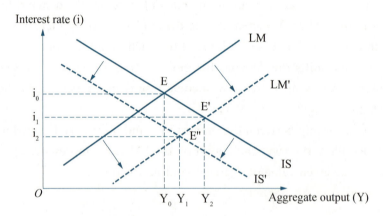

Figure 10.9 The IS-LM Curve

The BP Curve

Besides the goods market and money market, there is another market called foreign exchange market in an open economy. The equilibrium of the foreign exchange market means a balanced balance of payments. In Chapter 2 we define the balance of payments (BP) as follows:

$$BP = CA + KA = 0 \tag{10.5}$$

Where CA is the current account balance and KA is the capital and financial account balance. Since trade balance dominates the current account, the net export (X − M) is approximately equal to current account balance. The balance of payments depends on net export and net capital flows. Take a look at **Figure 10.10** to see the balance of payments

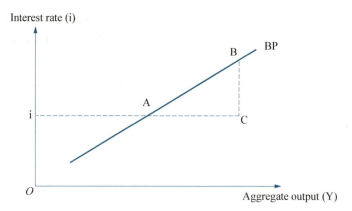

Figure 10.10 The BP Curve

(BP) curve which shows the net set of aggregate output (Y) — interest rate combinations that maintains a balance of payments equilibrium.

The BP curve is drawn for a given domestic price level, a given exchange rate, and a given net foreign debt. Equilibrium occurs when the current account surplus is equal to the capital and financial account deficit. The BP curve is upward-sloping. The reason is that higher level of income causes a deterioration in the current account, which necessitates a reduced capital outflow or higher capital inflow requiring a higher interest rate. Any point below the BP curve represents minus net export such as point C in the figure. In order to restore the BOP equilibrium, interest rate must rise. The higher interest rate attracts a greater inflow of capital, thereby improving capital and financial account balance. The point B is above and to the right of point A, and represents another income-interest rate combination consistent with a BOP equilibrium. Here we assume that the exchange rate is fixed. If the exchange rate is allowed to float, the position of the BP curve will be altered.

Both the BP curve and the LM curve slope upward. Is the slope of the BP curve steeper or flatter than that of the LM curve? It depends on how responsive money demand and the BOP are to changes in the interest rate and aggregate output. If capital flows are very sensitive to interest rates, then the BP curve is relatively flat, flatter than the LM curve. This is because if the BOP runs deficit, the interest rate needs to be raised a little to draw in enough capital to offset the deficit. On the other hand, if the BOP runs surplus, only a small decrease in the interest rate is needed to flow out enough capital to erase the surplus. The BP curve, just like the IS curve and the LM curve will shift either to the left or right. For instance, an increase in foreign income results in a rise of demand for our export. The BP curve thus shifts to the right. A higher foreign interest rate causes a capital outflow from the domestic country, deteriorating the capital and financial account balance, and shifting the BP curve to the left.

Three Markets Together: The IS–LM–BP Model

Now we put together the three curves in the interest rate — aggregate output plane.

If domestic goods market and money market reach equilibrium at the same time, we can judge the BOP status according to the position of the BP line. This is shown in **Figure 10.11**.

In Figure 10.11 (a), the BP curve passes through point A which is the intersection of the IS curve and the LM curve. The three markets reach simultaneous equilibrium at this point. This is because point A on the IS curve and the LM curve is also on the BP curve. The BP curve is steeper than the LM curve, but this need not always be the case. It may be flatter than the LM curve, depending on the degree of capital mobility internationally; the higher the degree of capital mobility, the flatter the BP curve.

If the BP curve is above or on the left side of the equilibrium point A, BOP is in deficit. This is shown in Figure 10.11 (b). It means the aggregate output level Y is too high or the interest rate i is to low, inducing an overall balance of payments deficit.

If the BP curve is below or on the right side of the equilibrium point A like Figure 10.11 (c) shows, BOP is in surplus. This surplus comes about because the level of aggregate output is too low and/or the rate of interest is too high to be compatible with overall equilibrium. The IS–LM–BP model is a useful tool for examining the determination of the equilibrium interest rate and equilibrium aggregate output level and the state of the balance of payments.

In the next chapter we well analyze the economic policies for tackling the problem in Figure 10.11(b) and (c). The government can use the fiscal and monetary policies to adjust the interest rate level or income level to make the three markets in equilibrium. However, the policies for achieving the overall equilibrium in different exchange rate systems are different.

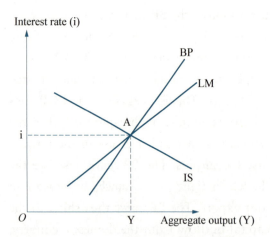

Figure 10.11(a) Three Markets Reach Equilibrium

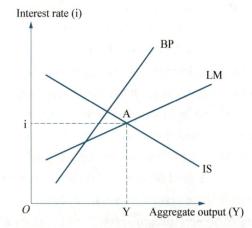

Figure 10.11(b) BOP Runs Deficit while the Domestic Market Reaches Equilibrium

Chapter 10 MACROECONOMICS IN AN OPEN ECONOMY

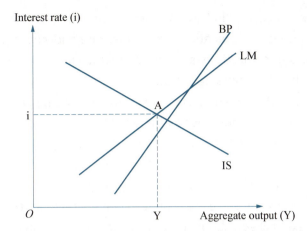

Figure 10.11(c)   The BOP Runs Surplus while Domestic Market Reaches Equilibrium

Summary

1. The desired economic outcome in an open economy is to achieve both internal balance and external balance at the same time.
2. Internal balance refers to a domestic equilibrium condition such that goods market and money market are in equilibrium and unemployment is at its natural level.
3. External balance requires the balance of payments to be in equilibrium. The condition implies zero balance on the official reserves account — the current account surplus must be equal to the capital and financial account deficit.
4. Households, firms, governments and the rest of the world interact in the three markets: goods market, funds market and foreign exchange market. All the markets are required to reach equilibrium in an open economy.
5. Consumption is an increasing function of the disposable income. The slope of the consumption function is determined by the marginal propensity to consume (MPC) which is defined as the ratio of increased consumption divided by the increased income.
6. The marginal propensity to save (MPS) is the slope of the saving function. It measures the increased saving due to the increased disposable income.
7. The marginal propensity to import (MPM) tells you the extra money spent on import when you have extra income.
8. The IS curve shows all combinations of interest rate and aggregate output (income) that are equilibrium in the domestic goods market (i.e., leakages equals to injections). The IS curve slopes downward.
9. The factors that shift the IS curve are a change in domestic price level, a change in

exchange rate, and a change in fiscal policy variable.

10. The LM curve shows all combinations of interest rate and aggregate output (income) that are equilibrium in the domestic money market (i.e., money demand equals to money supply). The LM curve slopes upward.
11. The factor that shifts the LM curve is a change in money supply.
12. The BP curve shows all combinations of interest rate and aggregate output (income) that result in a balanced BOP. It is also upward-sloping (i.e., current account surplus equals to capital and financial account deficit). The slope of this curve depends on the responsiveness of the BOP to the changes in interest rate.
13. The factor that shifts the BP curve is a change in perception of asset substitutability.
14. The internal and external equilibrium occur when three curves intersect at one point.
15. The intersection of the IS curve and the LM curve is the equilibrium point at which domestic goods market and money market are in simultaneous equilibrium. If the BP curve is not on the intersection of the IS curve and the LM curve, the country's BOP is either in deficit or surplus. If the BP curve is left to the equilibrium point of the domestic goods and money market, the BOP runs deficit; if the BP curve is right to the equilibrium point of the domestic goods and money market, the BOP is in surplus.

Key Concepts and Terms

1. Aggregate demand — 总需求
2. Aggregate output — 总产出
3. Autonomous consumption — 自主性消费
4. Behavioral equation — 行为方程式
5. BP curve — 国际收支线
6. Closed economy — 封闭经济体
7. Disposable income — 可支配收入，税后收入
8. Dissaving — 负储蓄
9. Fiscal policy — 财政政策
10. Gross Domestic Product (GDP) — 国民生产总值
11. IS curve — 投资-储蓄线
12. LM curve — 货币需求-供应线
13. Marginal propensity to consume (MPC) — 边际消费倾向
14. Marginal propensity to save (MPS) — 边际储蓄倾向
15. Marginal propensity to import (MPM) — 边际进口倾向
16. Monetary policy — 货币政策
17. Open economy — 开放经济体

Questions

1. What is the difference between a closed economy and an open economy?
2. What is the overall balance for an open economy?
3. Define the marginal propensity to consumption.
4. What is dissaving?
5. Suppose that an economy is characterized by the following behavioral equations:

    C = 110 + 0.6 Y_d

    I = 120

    G = 125

    T = 125

    X = 50

    M = 30

    Solve for

    a. Equilibrium GDP (Y).

    b. Disposable income (Y_d).

    c. Consumption spending.

6. Define the IS curve, the LM curve, and the BP curve.
7. How does the intersection of the IS curve and the LM curve relate to the concept of domestic market balance?
8. Explain the effect of each of the following on the IS curve:

    a. Government adopts expansionary fiscal policy.

    b. Foreign demand for the country's export increases.

    c. The country's central bank carries out contractionary monetary policy.

9. Explain the effect of each of the following on the LM curve:

    a. The country's central bank increases the money supply.

    b. The country's interest rate decreases.

10. Explain the effect of each of the following on the BP curve:

    a. Foreign taste for the domestic export change unfavorably.

    b. Foreign country expands its money supply.

    c. Domestic interest rates fall.

11. Why might investment not respond positively to low interest rates during a recession? Why might investment not respond negatively to high interest rates during a boom?
12. What is the impact on the IS–LM curve if the Congress decides to cut government spending while the central bank expands money supply?
13. Illustrate with the IS–LM curve if government increases its spending while the central bank changes money supply by enough to keep interest rates constant.
14. "Along the consumption function, income changes more than consumption." What

does this imply for the MPC and MPS?
15. Is the following statement true or false? "A budget deficit is bad because it leads to rapid monetary growth." Why?
16. What determines the slope of the BP curve? List several causes that will shift the BP curve.
17. How can you tell that a country is in the BOP surplus or deficit according to the position of the BP curve?
18. What are the impacts of the increase in domestic product and income on the country's export and import?
19. What are the impacts of the decrease in foreign product and income on domestic country's export and import?
20. If a country has a surplus balance of payments, what will be the appropriate government policy to restore the balance of payments back to equilibrium? What effects might this have on the economy's income?

Chapter 11
ECONOMIC POLICY UNDER FIXED AND FLOATING EXCHANGE RATE SYSTEM

LEARNING OBJECTIVES

- Explain the macroeconomic goals in an open economy.
- Review the monetary policy, fiscal policy and capital controls the government can use to influence the economy.
- Examine the monetary and fiscal policies on the economy under the fixed exchange rate system with imperfect or perfect capital mobility.
- Consider a two-country model with perfect capital mobility under the fixed rate system.
- Know the characteristics of the BP curve under the floating exchange rate system.
- Explore how the internal and external goals are achieved under the floating exchange rate system with imperfect or perfect capital mobility.
- Study a case of two-country with perfect capital mobility under the floating rate system.

We have already studied several basic international finance theories in previous chapters. In chapter 5, we learned some influential exchange rate theories, and in chapters 8 and 9 we examined two of the classical and modern theories relating balance of payments and exchange rate determination. Economic theories help us understand how the world works, but the formulation of economic policy requires a second step. We must have objectives. What do we want to change and why? Do we need a high economic growth with a low inflation and a high employment? Or do we need balanced balance of payments? If we need all of those, what can the government do? In other words, what kind of economic policies should the government make to achieve these goals? The striking change over the 20th century was the discovery and application of macroeconomics, along with a good appreciation of the role and limitations of monetary and fiscal policy. Based on the macroeconomic framework we presented in chapter 10, we shall address the issue of how both exchange rate changes and microeconomic policies have impacts on an open economy. The main difference between an open economy and a closed economy is that over time a country has to ensure that there is an approximate balance in its current account. Over the long-run, no country can run persistent BOP deficit. Conversely, it does not make sense for a country to run continuous BOP surplus. Therefore, the ultimate goal of the government is to achieve both internal and external balance.

In this chapter, we first explain the macroeconomic goals an economy tries to achieve. Then we examine the monetary policy, fiscal policy and policy of capital mobility the government uses to influence the economy. Next we analyze how the appropriate policy mix can be used under the fixed exchange rate system to achieve the desired economic goals. The defense of a fixed exchange rate through foreign exchange market intervention dramatically affects the country's monetary policy. Finally, we examine the function of policy mix under the floating exchange rate system.

Macroeconomic Goals in an Open Economy

Four of the major goals of macro economy are low inflation, low unemployment, sustainable economic growth and balanced balance of payments.

Inflation is an increase in the overall price level. The price level is a weighted average of the prices of the different goods and services in an economy. The most widely used measure of inflation is the **consumer price index (CPI)** which is a weighted average of the prices of a basket of goods and services consumed in a country. Inflation affects income distribution. Retirement pensions in some countries do not keep up with the price level. During high inflation period, retirees lose in relation to other groups. Inflation also leads to distortions and uncertainty in the economy. Price variations lead to more uncertainty, making it harder for firms to make decisions about the future, such as investment decisions. A decrease in the overall price level is called **deflation**. High deflation creates many of the problems as high inflation. Deflation can limit the ability of monetary policy to affect output. The goal of policy makers is avoid prolonged periods of deflation as well as inflation in order to pursue the macroeconomic goal of stability. Keeping inflation low has long been a goal of government policy. Especially problematic is **hyperinflation,** or periods of very rapid increases in the overall price levels.

Unemployment is the proportion of workers who are not employed or are looking for jobs. Unemployment rate is the ratio of the number of people who are unemployed to the number of people in the labor force. The unemployment has direct effects on the welfare of the unemployed. High unemployment rate signals that the economy may not be using some of resources efficiently. If unemployment rate is very high, and many people who want to work cannot find jobs, this suggests there is something wrong with the way the economy operates.

Economic growth refers to the growth in the productive potential of an economy. The productive potential is the crucial factor in determining the growth in employees' real wages and living standards. If output grows faster than the population growth, output per capita rises and living standards increases. Some government policies discourage economic growth and others encourage it. One of examples is the tax laws which can be designed to encourage the development and application of new production techniques. In some countries, research and development are subsidized by the government. In developing countries, government may encourage the construction of public facilities such as roads, highways, bridges and transportation systems because it may speed up the process of economic growth.

Those three major goals in an open economy are categorized as the goal of achieving internal balance, which is overall balance in domestic markets.

Balance of payments equilibrium is a country's external balance, which is usually defined as the achievement of a reasonable and sustainable balance of payments with the rest of the world. The goal toward BOP equilibrium under the different exchange rate system may be different.

All economies face inevitable tradeoffs among these goals. Government plays a role in influencing the economy mainly through the fiscal policy, monetary policy, the policy of capital controls and all other polices.

Monetary Policy, Fiscal Policy and Capital Mobility

Monetary Policy

The **monetary policy** is used by the government or central bank to control the money supply or to influence the economic development. The target of monetary policy includes the achievement of a desired level of economic growth, the domestic price level, the exchange rate, or the balance of payments. Three methods of monetary policy are widely used by a central bank to control the money supply. The central bank can buy and sell securities through **open market operation** to adjust the money supply. The **required reserve ratio** effectively determines how much money a bank has available to lend because required reserve ratio establish a link between the reserves of the commercial banks and the loans that commercial banks are allowed to creates. The **discount rate** is the interest rate that commercial banks have to pay when they borrow from the central bank. When the central bank lowers the discount rate, it encourages the commercial banks to borrow from it. If the central bank wants to curtail the growth of money supply, it raises the discount rate.

The central bank carries out either expansionary or contractionary monetary policy in the different stages of the economic development. If the economy is in recession, an

expansionary monetary policy will be conducted. The central bank purchases securities from the public through open market operation, which pushes up the prices of securities, expands the money supply and leads to a fall in interest rates. The central bank can also reduce the reserve requirement to the commercial banks, which increases commercial banks' loanable funds, allows them to create more deposits. The lower interest rates and increased money supply stimulate the investment and thus increase the aggregate output (income). As far as the balance of payments is concerned, the increased income increases consumption including import and thus deteriorates the current account. On the other hand, the lower interest rates speed up the capital outflows. On the whole, the expansionary monetary policy leads to the BOP deficit.

If the economic development grows too fast, the central bank can use **contractionary monetary policy** to cool down the overheating economy. The central bank sells securities in the market, which pushes down the prices of securities, reduces money supply and thus increases the interest rates. The central bank may raise the reserve requirement ratio, so that the commercial banks do not have enough funds to lend. The central bank can also raise the discount rate to discourage the commercial banks borrowing from it. The results of the contractionary monetary policy are the decreased money supply and the higher interest rates. It leads to less investment and a fall in aggregate output (income). The country's balance of payments will improve because of the fall in import and rise in capital inflows.

Fiscal policy

The **fiscal policy** refers to the use of taxation and government spending to influence the economy. The government can change tax rates or set the rules about liability to tax to affect economic activities. It can also change its spending on goods and services or transfer payments to influence the total output. Like the monetary policy, the fiscal policy can also be categorized as expansionary and contractionary. **Expansionary fiscal policy** aims at stimulating aggregate output (income). It refers to an increase in government spending or a reduction in tax rates. When the economy is depressed or the investment and employment are below normal, this policy is likely to be advocated. This policy may have consequences in the future. A reduction in tax revenue and an increase in government spending expand the government debts which store up the trouble for its successors. As far as the balance of payments is concerned, the expansion of the aggregate output will worsen the current account, but the higher interest rate attracts capital inflows and thus improves the capital and financial account. The results are ambiguous.

Contractionary fiscal policy aims at reducing aggregate output (income). The government cuts its spending or raises the tax rate to slow the economy growth. The effects of this policy are the opposite of the effects of an expansionary fiscal policy. A decrease in government spending or an increase in tax rate leads to a fall in aggregate output, a fall in the demand for money and a fall in the interest rate. However, the decrease in income is somewhat offset by the additional investment resulting from the lower interest rate. The contractionary policy is one of the important tools the government uses to fight inflation.

The Capital Mobility and The BP Curve

The **capital mobility** is the extent to which capital can be shifted between different countries. International capital mobility is frequently limited by government controls in both capital-importing and capital-exporting countries. The capital mobility determines the slope of the BP curve and The slope of the IS curve, in turn, determines how monetary policy and fiscal policy ultimately influence a country's economic performance.

The slope of the BP curve is relative steep if the degree to which capital is allowed to flow across a nation's border is low. The low capital mobility arises because of capital controls or other impediments to flows of funds and assets. This is depicted in **Figure 11.1**. When the aggregate output expands from Y_0 to Y_1, the nation reaches point A. At point A, the nation runs BOP deficit which results from high income. In order to attract enough foreign capital inward flows, the nation must increase interest rate by a sizable amount, from i_0 to i_1 to restore BOP equilibrium.

Compare to Figure 11.1, **Figure 11.2** shows the BP curve is flatter. In this case, the degree to which capital is allowed to flow between nations is high. In other words, there are fewer restrictions on the capital movements between the nations. A nation with high capital mobility is much easier to retore its BOP disequilibrium because a little higher interest rate will cause foreign capital inflows. The spread between i_1 and i_0 in this case is much smaller than the spread of $(i_1 - i_0)$ shown in Figure 11.1.

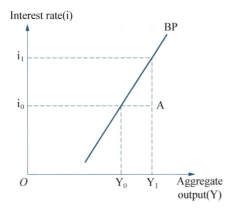
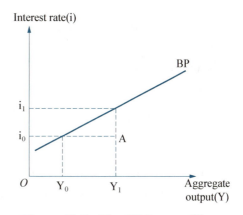

Figure 11.1 The BP Curve with Low Capital Mobility

Figure 11.2 The BP Curve with High Capital Mobility

The perfect capital mobility refers to a situation when capital is perfectly free to move between countries. For a small nation (one that is too small to influence global markets by itself), perfect capital mobility implies that the uncovered interest parity must hold if the exchange rate is fixed. Otherwise, uncovered interest arbitrage will occur because any attempt to raise or lower the domestic interest rate leads to a massive capital inflow or outflow until the interest rate returns to the world interest rate level. Therefore, for a small country the perfect capital mobility means that domestic interest rate should be the same as the foreign interest rate and its BP curve is horizontal. The small nation lowers the interest rate (from i_0^d to i_1^d) in an attempt to boost investment expenditure and raise total output (from Y_0 to Y_1). This is shown in **Figure 11.3**. At point A, the country runs the BOP deficit resulting from the increased aggregate output (income) or the low interest rate. The interest rate now is lower than the world interest rate. In order to restore the BOP back to equilibrium, the central bank should increase domestic interest rate to prevent capitals from flowing out of the country. Therefore, the interest rate restores back to the initial level i_0^d, and the output level is back to Y_0.

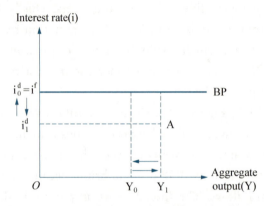

Figure 11.3 The BP Curve with Perfect Capital Mobility

Economic Policy under Fixed Exchange Rate System

The choice of exchange rate system reflects a country's priorities about the four economic goals we discussed in the first section of this chapter. The choice between the fixed and floating rates may change over time as priorities change. From 1944 to 1973, the international monetary system was characterized by the fixed exchange rate regime. Even today, a lot of countries or regions still peg their currencies to some hard currencies like the U.S. dollar, euro and the British pound, etc. A number of countries have floating rates in name, but the exchange rates are so heavily managed by the governments that they are closer to being fixed rates in many respects. Therefore, it is still worth studying how a fixed exchange rate affects both a country's economy and the use of government policies to affect the economy's performance.

The Effect of Policy Mix under The Fixed Exchange Rate and Imperfect Capital Mobility

We have learned so far monetary policy and fiscal policy in isolating. In reality, the two are often used together. Policy mix refers to the combination of monetary and fiscal policies. The two policies can be used in the same direction or opposite direction. Look at the **Figure 11.4**. Suppose a country adopts fixed exchange rate system and controls capital account transactions. The government now uses the expansionary fiscal policy in attempt to stimulate the consumption. the economy was originally in equilibrium at point A. The expansionary fiscal policy increases domestic interest rates and aggregate output level and the IS curve thus shifts right to the new IS' curve. The economy achieves internal equilibrium since the LM curve and the IS' curve intersect at point B. Higher income leads to higher consumption including the imports spending. Even though the interest rate is up (from i_0 to i_1), the country is in BOP deficit and its currency has the pressure to depreciate in the foreign exchange market. Fixed exchange rate requires the government do defend the exchange rate so the central bank contracts the money supply which leads to the LM curve shifting left to LM'. The contractionary monetary policy increases the interest rate again from i_1 to i_2. Higher interest rate cuts part of the investment spending and aggregate output (from Y_2 to Y_1). Higher interest rate also attracts foreign capital inflow. Thus the BOP improves. The economy restores back to the equilibrium at point C.

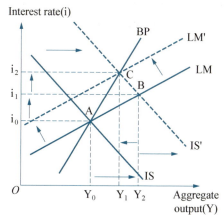

Figure 11.4 The Effect of Expansionary Fiscal Policy and Contractionary Monetary Policy under The Fixed Rate and Imperfect Capital Mobility

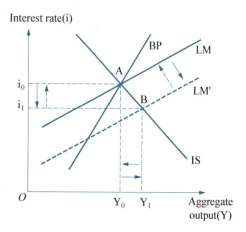

Figure 11.5 The Effect of Expansionary Monetary Policy under The Fixed Rate and Imperfect Capital Mobility

The expansionary monetary policy will have little effect on the economy if the country adopts fixed exchange rate system. **Figure 11.5** depicts such situation. Suppose the economy originally achieved both internal and external balance at point A. The central bank uses the expansionary policy so that interest rate is down and aggregate output is up. The LM curve shifts to right and the BOP deteriorates. The central bank is forced to sell foreign exchange reserves in the foreign exchange market in order to defend the fixed parity. The central bank then buys back the domestic currency so that the LM' curve shifts back to LM. Hence, using only a single policy instrument, in this case the monetary policy is proved to be nullified. The economy's equilibrium point is again back to point A. the central bank can of course pursue a sterilization intervention so that the LM' curve remains at LM', but that is not likely to last for long since finally the foreign exchange reserves will be depleted.

The conclusion is that the monetary policy which aims to influence the economic activities is ineffective if exchange rates are fixed. Fiscal policy is more powerful than monetary policy in terms of affecting the aggregate output and balance of payments status. The following small country's case also proves that fiscal policy exerts its largest feasible effects on equilibrium aggregate output (income) if the small country adopts fixed rate system and allow free capital movement.

A Small Country with Perfect Capital Mobility

In the early 1960s, Mundell and Fleming examined the implications of high capital mobility for a small country. For a small country changes in its interest rate and aggregate output have negligible repercussions for other countries. Therefore, for a small country, the choice of exchange rate system would have radical implications concerning the effectiveness of monetary and fiscal policy in influencing the level of economic activity.

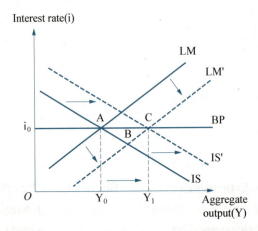

Figure 11.6 Fixed Exchange Rate and Perfect Capital Mobility in a Small Country

Figure 11.6 depicts the effects of monetary policy and fiscal expansion in a small open country that adopts fixed exchange rate system and has no restrictions on the capital mobility. The BP curve is horizontal because the domestic interest rate equals to the foreign interest rate. The economy is at initial equilibrium point A. The central bank increases its money supply which leads the LM curve to shift to the right. At point B, domestic interest rate is lower than foreign interest rate. This induces significant flow of capital out of the small open economy, which results in a balance of payments deficit. If the central bank intervenes in the foreign exchange market to prevent domestic currency from depreciation, the resulting decline in foreign exchange reserves ultimately causes the country's money stock to fall back to its original level. However, an expansionary fiscal policy is a good solution for this small open economy. The increased government spending shifts the IS curve rightward. Thus, the interest rate rises back to i_0 which improves its BOP status. The monetary policy alone is ineffective because the exchange rate is not allowed to change. However, the combination of expansionary monetary and fiscal policy increases the aggregate output (income) from Y_0 to Y_1.

The Effects of Foreign Economic Policy on the Domestic Economy: A Two-Country Model

The economic powers such as the United States and Japan play the role of locomotive in the world economy, which means the performance of their economy deeply affects the economic activities of the rest of the world. The following example indicates how the economic policy in the United States affects another country. **Figure 11.7 (a)** represents the domestic economy (Canada) and **Figure 11.7 (b)** represents the foreign economy (U.S.).

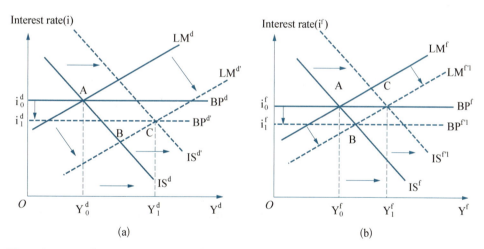

Figure 11.7 The Locomotive Effect of the Foreign Expansionary Monetary Policy

Suppose the U.S. Fed expands the money stock under the fixed exchange rate system. The increased money stock shifts LM^f curve rightward to LM^{f1} and causes the U.S. interest rat to fall. With the lower interest rate and high income at point B in panel (b), the U.S. runs the BOP deficit. Canada is the major trading partner of the United States. When the U.S. runs the trade deficit, Canada possibly has the BOP surplus. Because the exchange rate is fixed, the Canadian central bank must intervene in the foreign exchange market to buy the U.S. dollar. The Canadian central bank is thus forced to expand the supply of Canadian dollar. The LM^d curve shifts to the right which is shown in Figure 11.7 (a). At the point B, the domestic market is not at equilibrium and the interest rate is lower than that in U.S. The

Canadian government adopts expansionary fiscal policy to cooperate with the expansion of the money supply. The IS^d curve thus shifts to the right. In U.S. increased income spurs aggregate spending, IS^f curve thus shifts rightward correspondingly. The economy reaches new equilibrium point, which is point C in Figure 11.7 (b). The Canadian interest rate now is consistent with the U.S. interest rate and its economy restores back to equilibrium.

This example shows that foreign monetary expansion (the U.S. in this case) leads to a rise in both the foreign and domestic (Canada in this case) aggregate output (income) level. This is the so called "**locomotive effect**" which refers to the situation that income growth in one country leads to the income growth in another country.

The fiscal policy of the foreign country also has the impacts on the domestic economy. Unlike the monetary policy, the foreign expansionary fiscal policy increases foreign income at the expense of income decline in domestic country. This is called **beggar-thy-neighbor effect**. In this case the foreign country plays the role of beggar-thy-neighbor. **Figure 11.8** depicts how the beggar-thy-neighbor works.

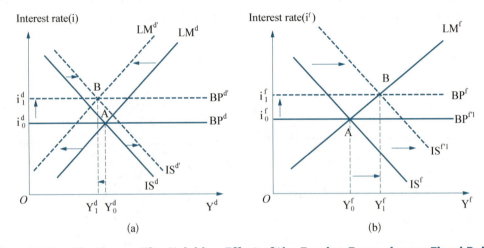

Figure 11.8 The Beggar-Thy-Neighbor Effect of the Foreign Expansionary Fiscal Policy

Again Figure 11.8 (b) represents the foreign economy (U.S.) and Figure 11.8 (a) denotes the domestic economy (Canada). The expansionary fiscal policy in U.S. increases both the U.S. aggregate output (income) and interest rate. The higher interest rate in the U.S. economy attracts the flow of financial resources from Canada to U.S. Canada now probably runs the BOP deficit. In order to maintain the fixed exchange rate, Canadian central bank has to sell U.S. dollar for Canadian dollar, causing the domestic money stock to shrink. The domestic LM^d curve thus shifts left to $LM^{d'}$. We find in Figure 11.8 (a) the domestic aggregate (income) declines from Y_0^d to Y_1^d. Since the Canadian interest rate is still lower than that in U.S., the Canadian government may increase its spending expenditure to stimulate the domestic consumption. The IS curve then shifts to the right. At the equilibrium point B, the domestic interest rate is the same as the U.S. interest rate. In this example, the U.S. expansionary fiscal policy is a beggar-thy-neighbor policy. The rise in U.S. aggregate output (income) is at the expense of income decline in Canada.

Economic Policy under Floating Exchange Rate System

After the collapse of the Bretton Woods System in the beginning of 1970s, the major currencies began to float against each other. Today many industrialized countries let their currencies float. The floating exchange rate system means the government has no obligation to defend the exchange rate. When a country has the BOP deficit, the country's currency depreciates in the foreign exchange market. If a country runs the BOP surplus, its currency appreciates. The BP curve, therefore, shifts rightward in case of the deficit and leftward in case of the surplus.

The Effects of Monetary Policy and Fiscal Policy under Floating Exchange Rate system

Figure 11.9 describes the situation that the central bank uses expansionary monetary policy under the floating rate system. The economy reaches initial equilibrium point A. The expansionary monetary policy leads the LM curve to shift to the right. With the lower interest rate and higher aggregate output, borrowing and spending rise which results in the shift of the IS curve to IS'. Two possible causes lead the country's BOP to deteriorate. First, the drop in interest rate tends to worsen the capital and financial account as capital flows out of the country. Second, the rise in income tends to worsen the current account as imports rise. The exchange rate of the domestic currency depreciates in the foreign exchange market. Then the BP curve shifts to the right. At the point B, the balance of payments equilibrium is achieved. Therefore, under floating exchange rate system, monetary policy exerts a strong influence over domestic aggregate output (income).

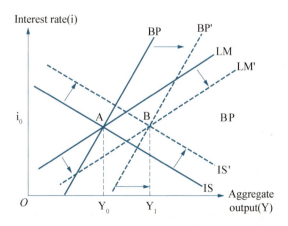

Figure 11.9 The Effects of Expansionary Monetary Policy under Floating Exchange Rate System

The effects of fiscal policy alone on the economy are a little more complicated if the exchange rate is allowed to change. The rise in income and value of its currency depend largely on the country's capital mobility. The extent of the rise in income declines as the degree of capital mobility rises. **Figure 11.10** indicates the effects of the fiscal policy on the economy.

In figure 11.10 (a), the BP curve is steeper than the LM curve, which means the capital mobility is low. The expansionary fiscal policy shifts the IS curve right to IS'. At point B, interest rate is high and output increases. Since the capital mobility is low, high interest rate does not attract capital inflows. On the other hand, high income induces more spending including imports; the current account deteriorates and the BOP moves into deficit. In turn, the deficit leads to a depreciation of the domestic currency in the foreign exchange market. The depreciation of the domestic currency induces net export expenditures to increase resulting in the IS' curve shifting rightward once more. At the same time the BP curve also shifts to the right. the final equilibrium with a balanced BOP reaches at point C. The impacts of the expansionary fiscal policy are the increased aggregate output (income) (from Y_0 to Y_1 to Y_2), increased interest rate (from i_0 to i_1 to i_2), and the decreased value of the domestic currency in the foreign exchange market.

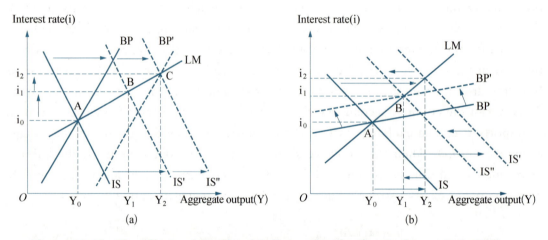

Figure 11.10 The Effects of the Fiscal Policy under Floating Exchange Rate System

In figure 11.10 (b), because of high capital mobility the BP curve is flatter than the LM curve. Initially, the expansionary fiscal policy leads to higher interest rate and high aggregate output (income). This time higher interest rate attracts foreign capital inflows. Point B which is the internal equilibrium point falls above the BP curve. With capital inflows, the country's capital account improves. The demand for domestic currency in the foreign exchange market rises, causing the appreciation of the domestic currency. The appreciation of the domestic currency results in reduction of exports. Therefore, the IS' curve shifts leftward to IS", the BP curve also shifts to the left. The net impacts of the expansionary fiscal policy are higher interest rate and higher aggregate output (income), but the income level is lower than that in panel (a) because of the high capital mobility.

A Small Country with Floating Rate and Perfect Capital Mobility

Now let's examine the effects of economic policy on a small country with floating exchange rate and perfect capital mobility. In the case of perfect capital mobility, any attempt to raise the domestic interest rate in a small country leads to a massive capital inflow to purchase domestic securities pushing up the prices of securities until the interest rate keeps the same as the world interest rate. When the domestic interest rate is lower than the world interest rate, there is a massive capital outflow to sell domestic securities for foreign securities until the interest rate goes up.

Figure 11.11 (a) shows the impacts of expansionary monetary policy and (b) describes the expansionary fiscal policy. Just like the case of the floating rate with imperfect capital mobility, expansionary monetary policy exerts a strong effect on the economy. Panel (a) shows that both the LM curve and the IS curves shift to the right, and the BP curve keeps as the same before. Aggregate output (income) increases as fully as possible, from Y_0 to Y_2.

In Figure 11.11 (b), the expansionary fiscal policy is nullified if the capital mobility is free. The domestic interest rate is higher than the world interest rate. Capital inflows cause the BOP surplus and appreciation of the domestic currency on the foreign exchange market. Consequently, export industry shrinks and the IS curve shifts back to its initial level. On net, the expansionary fiscal policy has no effect on the aggregate output (income).

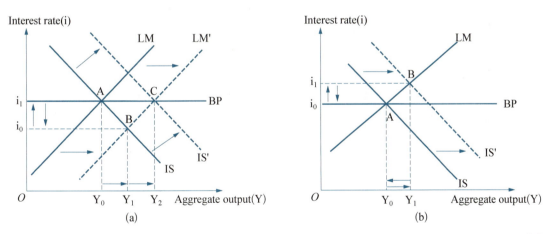

Figure 11.11 The Effects of Economic Policy under Floating Exchange Rate System with Perfect Capital Mobility

The Effects of Domestic Economic Policy on the Foreign Economy: A Two-Country Model

We have examined the policy implications of one nation for the economy of another nation under the fixed exchange rate system. Now we apply the two-country model to a setting with floating exchange rate system in **Figure 11.12**.

Figure 11.12 (a) depicts a situation that domestic central bank expands the money stock. The LM^d curve shifts to the right and equilibrium point moves from A to B. The lower interest rate induces the domestic financial resources outflows. The value of domestic currency declines on the foreign exchange market. The depreciation of the domestic currency plus the higher income spurs the expansion of the domestic expenditures on domestic output, so the IS^d curve shifts rightward to $IS^{d'}$. The impacts of the domestic expansionary monetary policy on the foreign economy are shown in Figure 11.12 (b). A depreciation of the domestic currency implies an appreciation of the foreign currency. The appreciation of the foreign currency causes the foreign IS^f curve shift leftward to IS^{f1}. Foreign aggregate output (income) thus falls which directly affects domestic export. When domestic export decline, domestic $IS^{d'}$ curve shifts back a little bit to $IS^{d''}$. On the other hand, higher domestic income increases domestic expenditures on foreign import, resulting in the rise of export of the foreign country. Therefore, the foreign IS^{f1} curve shifts to IS^{f2}. The equilibrium domestic interest rate converges to the foreign equilibrium interest rate. Both domestic and foreign BP curves shift downward. Clearly, this case shows the domestic expansionary monetary policy has a beggar-thy-neighbor effect on the foreign country. In other words, the increase in domestic income is at the expense of reduction in foreign income.

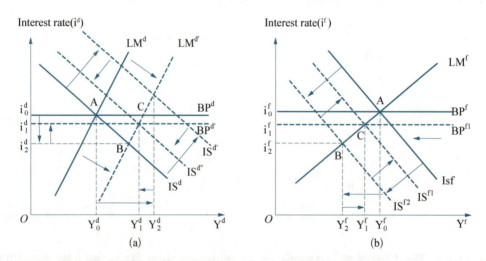

Figure 11.12 The Effects of the Domestic Expansionary Monetary Policy on the Foreign Economy

Finally, let's examine the impacts of domestic expansionary fiscal policy on the foreign economy.

The domestic country increases government spending as shown in **Figure 11.13 (a)**. Fiscal expansion lifts the domestic interest rates, which causes inflow of financial resources from the foreign country. The domestic currency appreciates against the

Chapter 11 ECONOMIC POLICY UNDER FIXED AND FLOATING EXCHANGE RATE SYSTEM

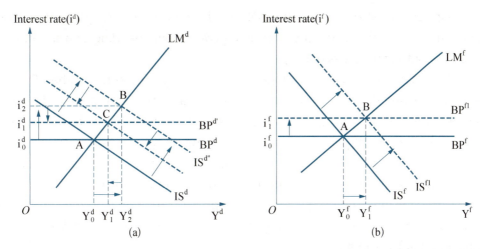

Figure 11.13 The Effects of the Domestic Expansionary Fiscal Policy on the Foreign Economy

foreign currency. The appreciation of the domestic currency promotes the export from the foreign country. In figure 11.13 (b), the foreign IS^f curve shifts to the right because of the increased expenditure on aggregate output. On the other hand, the domestic $IS^{d'}$ curve shifts left to $IS^{d''}$ because of the reduction in export expenditures. The net effect of the domestic expansionary fiscal policy is to increase both countries' aggregate output (income). The domestic fiscal policy is thus said to have locomotive effect on the foreign economy.

Summary

1. All economies face inevitable tradeoffs among the economic goals such as low unemployment, low inflation sustainable economic growth and balanced balance of payments.
2. The overall balance in domestic markets is a country's internal balance while the BOP equilibrium is a country's external balance.
3. Three methods of the monetary policy are purchases and sales of securities in the money market, changes in the required reserve ratio and changes in the discount rate. An expansionary monetary policy leads to increase in money supply and a decrease in interest rate, thus stimulates investment and results in a rise in output. The BOP position may deteriorate. Conversely, a contractionary monetary policy contracts money supply and raises the interest rate. Investments shrink and output reduces. The BOP will improve.
4. An expansionary fiscal policy is a decrease in government spending or a reduction in tax rate aimed at increasing aggregate output (income). The effects of the

expansionary fiscal policy on the BOP are indeterminate. On the other hand, a contractionary fiscal policy is a decrease in government spending or a rise in tax rate aimed at contracting the economy.

5. Capital mobility determines the slope of the BP curve. The slope of the BP curve, in turn, determines the effectiveness of the monetary and fiscal policy. The slope of the BP curve with the low capital mobility is steeper than that with the high capital mobility. In the case of perfect capital mobility, the BP curve is horizontal.
6. The expansionary monetary policy has little effect on the economy if the exchange rate is not allowed to change. On the contrary, the expansionary fiscal policy is proved to be useful. The expansionary fiscal policy combined with the contractionary monetary policy can increase aggregate output (income) and keep the BOP equilibrium at the same time.
7. If a small country chooses fixed exchange rate system and puts no limitation on the capital movement, the country's interest rate must equal the foreign interest rate. The combination of both expansionary monetary and fiscal policy promotes the economic growth in the small country.
8. The locomotive effect means income growth in one country (usually the economic power) leads to income growth in another country. The beggar-thy-neighbor effect, on the contrary, is the situation that one country's income growth is at the expense of income decline in another country.
9. Under the floating exchange rate system, the monetary policy exerts strong influence on the economy while impacts of the fiscal policy on the economy depend on the capital mobility. The lower the capital mobility of the nation, the more the aggregate output (income).
10. If a country does not control capital account transactions, the monetary policy is more powerful than the fiscal policy when the exchange rate is allowed to move freely. The fiscal policy alone is ineffective under the floating exchange rate system.
11. In a two-country model, if the exchange rate is allowed to float, domestic expansionary policy has the beggar-thy-neighbor effect on its trading partner and domestic expansionary fiscal policy has the locomotive effect on its trading partner.

Key Concepts and Terms

1. Deflation 通货紧缩
2. Balance of payments equilibrium 国际收支均衡
3. Beggar-thy-neighbor effect 以邻为壑效应
4. Capital mobility 资本流动性

5. Consumer price index (CPI)	消费物价指数
6. Contractionary fiscal policy	紧缩性财政政策
7. Contractionary monetary policy	紧缩性货币政策
8. Discount rate	贴现率，商业银行在中央银行贴现票据时支付的利率
9. Economic growth	经济增长
10. Expansionary fiscal policy	扩张性财政政策
11. Expansionary monetary policy	扩张性货币政策
12. External balance	外部平衡
13. Hyperinflation	恶性通胀
14. Imperfect capital mobility	非完全资本流动性
15. Inflation	通货膨胀
16. Internal balance	内部平衡
17. Locomotive effect	火车头效应
18. Open market operation	公开市场操作
19. Perfect capital mobility	完全资本流动性
20. Policy mix	政策组合
21. Required reserve ratio	法定存款准备金
22. Unemployment	失业

Questions

1. What is widely used to measure a country's inflation? What are the consequences of high inflation?
2. Consider the following statements:
   a. "More people are employed in our country now than at any time in the past years."
   b. "The unemployment rate in our country is higher now than it has been in 30 years."

   Can both of these statements be true at the same time? Why?
3. Assume a government increases its spending in attempt to reduce its high unemployment rate. The country currently adopts floating exchange rate system. What is the impact of this policy on the country's currency value? The change in the country's currency value in turn has impacts on the fiscal expansion. Discuss this fiscal policy.
4. What methods does a central bank usually use for the expansionary monetary policy? In which way does a government adopt expansionary fiscal policy?
5. If a country's overall price level is rising, the value of its currency drops in the foreign exchange market. What are the impacts of the depreciation on the country's internal

balance?

6. What does it mean if a country's BP curve is vertical? Explain the impacts of an expansionary monetary policy on the equilibrium interest rate and aggregate output (income) under the fixed exchange rate system.
7. What is the difference in the regard of the BP curve between a fixed exchange rate system and a floating exchange rate system?
8. Explain the locomotive effect and the beggar-thy-neighbor effect.
9. In the early 1990s the United States experienced economic recessions. The U.S. government asked the Japanese government to expand fiscal expenditures and cut the taxes. Both U.S. and Japan had nearly perfect capital mobility and both countries adopted floating rate system at that time. Would U.S. request appear to have been consistent with U.S. interest rates? Why?
10. Use the IS–LM–BP diagram to show the effect of a decrease in the foreign interest rate, i^f, on domestic output, Y^d, for an open economy with fixed exchange rate system. Explain in words.
11. Given the discussion of the effects of fiscal policy in this chapter, show the effect of a foreign fiscal contraction on foreign output, Y^f, and the foreign interest rate, i^f on the IS–LM–BP diagram.
12. Given the discussion of the effects of monetary policy in this chapter, use the IS–LM–BP diagram to show the effect of a foreign monetary expansion on the domestic country.
13. During the early 1980s, the United States adopted a very expansionary fiscal policy and very restrictive monetary policy in an attempt to rid the economy of inflation. Unfortunately, this policy mix had failed. The U.S. economy went into a deep recession. The interest rate went to record levels as high as 21%. Use the IS–LM–BP diagram to show this policy mix.
14. Referring back to the situation described in question 13, what would happen to the value of the dollar?
15. What effect will each of the following events have on the current account balance and the exchange rate if the exchange rate is fixed?
    a. The price level in China is rising and the inflation in China is much higher than France.
    b. Chinese government uses expansionary fiscal policy to stimulate domestic consumption.
    c. China's central bank PBOC decreases its money stock.
16. A country has a floating exchange rate. Government spending now increases in an effort to reduce unemployment. What is the effect of this policy change on the exchange rate value of the country's currency? Under what circumstances does the exchange rate change reduce the expansionary effect of the fiscal change?
17. A country has a rising inflation rate and a tendency for its overall payments to go into

deficit. Will the resulting exchange rate change move the country closer to or further from internal balance?

18. If a country has a surplus balance of payments, what will be the appropriate government policy to restore the balance of payments back to equilibrium? What effects might this have on the country's income?

19. Assume a country initially has achieved both external balance and internal balance. The capital mobility is pretty high. BP schedule slopes upward and is flatter than the LM schedule. Also assume the country adopts fixed exchange rate system and will use non-sterilized intervention if the fixed exchange rate changes. The foreign investors become bullish on the country because of its strong economic growth. International financial capital inflows increase dramatically and remain higher for a number of years.
    a. What shift occurs in the BP schedule because of the increased capital inflow?
    b. What intervention is necessary to defend the fixed exchange rate? why?
    c. As a result of the intervention, how does the country adjust back to external balance? Illustrate this using the IS–LM–BP model. What is the effect of all of this on the country's internal balance?

20. Assume a country initially achieves both internal and external equilibrium. There is no restrictions on the capital movement. The country now decides to reduce its money supply.
    a. What are the initial effects of this monetary policy on the goods market, the money market, the foreign exchange market, and the balance of payments of the domestic economy? Which curve(s) will shift? Use the IS–LM–BP model to illustrate and explain your answer.
    b. What is the adjustment mechanism under a fixed exchange rate system? Illustrate and explain which curve(s) will shift during the adjustment, and then compare the new equilibrium with initial equilibrium.
    c. What is the adjustment mechanism under a flexible exchange rate system? Illustrate and explain which curve(s) will shift during the adjustment, and then compare the new equilibrium with the initial equilibrium.

图书在版编目(CIP)数据

国际金融:双语/姚迪克编著. —上海:复旦大学出版社,2021.8(2023.12重印)
(创优.经管核心课程系列)
ISBN 978-7-309-15683-6

Ⅰ.①国… Ⅱ.①姚… Ⅲ.①国际金融-高等学校-教材-汉、英 Ⅳ.①F831

中国版本图书馆 CIP 数据核字(2021)第 089189 号

国际金融(双语)
GUOJI JINRONG (SHUANGYU)
姚迪克　编著
责任编辑/鲍雯妍

复旦大学出版社有限公司出版发行
上海市国权路 579 号　邮编:200433
网址: fupnet@ fudanpress.com　http://www.fudanpress.com
门市零售: 86-21-65102580　团体订购: 86-21-65104505
出版部电话: 86-21-65642845
上海新艺印刷有限公司

开本 787 毫米×1092 毫米　1/16　印张 20　字数 487 千字
2023 年 12 月第 1 版第 3 次印刷

ISBN 978-7-309-15683-6/F·2800
定价: 49.00 元

如有印装质量问题,请向复旦大学出版社有限公司出版部调换。
版权所有　侵权必究